LEADERSHIP
IN ORGANIZATIONS

LEADERSHIP
IN ORGANIZATIONS

Second Edition

Gary A. Yukl

State University of New York at Albany

PRENTICE HALL

Englewood Cliffs, New Jersey 07632

Library of Congress Cataloging-in-Publication Data

Yukl, Gary A. (date)
    Leadership in organizations / Gary A. Yukl. -- 2nd ed.
        p.   cm.
    Bibliography: p. 289
    Includes indexes.
    ISBN 0-13-527169-X
    1. Leadership.   2. Decision-making.   3. Organization.   I. Title.
HD57.7Y85 1989   88-25049
303.3'4–dc19   CIP

Editorial/production supervision and
  interior design: Millicent Lambert, Eleanor Walter
Cover design: George Cornell
Manufacturing buyer: Ed O'Dougherty

 © 1989, 1981 by Prentice-Hall, Inc.
A Division of Simon & Schuster
Englewood Cliffs, New Jersey 07632

Printed in the United States of America
10 9 8 7 6 5 4 3

ISBN 0-13-527169-X

Prentice-Hall International (UK) Limited, London
Prentice-Hall of Australia Pty. Limited, Sydney
Prentice-Hall Canada Inc., Toronto
Prentice-Hall Hispanoamericana, S.A., Mexico
Prentice-Hall of India Private Limited, New Delhi
Prentice-Hall of Japan, Inc., Tokyo
Simon & Schuster Asia Pte. Ltd., Singapore
Editora Prentice-Hall do Brasil, Ltda., Rio de Janeiro

CONTENTS

APPENDICES   318

AUTHOR INDEX   330

SUBJECT INDEX   335

PREFACE

This book is about leadership in organizations. The primary focus is on managerial leadership as opposed to parliamentary leadership, leadership of social movements, or informal leadership in peer groups. The book presents a broad survey of theory and research on leadership in formal organizations. The topic of leadership effectiveness is of special interest. Again and again the discussion returns to the question of what makes a person an effective leader. With its focus on effective leadership in organizations, this book is especially relevant for people who are currently managers and administrators, or who expect to assume such a position in the near future.

The content of the book reflects a dual concern for theory and practice. Theories are explained and critiqued, and the findings of empirical research on leadership are reviewed. References are provided to enable scholars to follow up with additional reading for topics of special interest to them. The book also has recommendations and guidelines for improving managerial effectiveness. The guidelines are intended for people who are currently managers or who expect to enter a position of leadership after completing their college education. However, this book is not a "practitioner's manual" of simple techniques and general panaceas. If anything, the book shows that managers and administrators need to recognize the difficulty of their jobs and should not expect to find a few secret recipes that will guarantee instant success.

The field of leadership is in a state of ferment, with many continuing controversies about conceptual and methodological issues. The book addresses these issues whenever feasible, rather than merely summarizing findings and recommending practices without concern for the quality of research that lies behind them. However, the literature review is intended to be incisive rather than comprehensive. This is not another "handbook." Rather than detailing an endless series of individual studies, the book focuses on the twenty percent of the literature that is most relevant and informative. The book seeks to review what we know about leadership effectiveness, and the conclusion is that we know more than is commonly believed, although much less than we need to know. This second edition of the book reflects significant progress in our understanding of leadership since the first edition was published in 1981.

The book is appropriate for use as the primary text in an undergraduate or graduate course in leadership or managerial effectiveness. Such courses are found in business schools, psychology departments, sociology departments, departments of educational administration, and schools of public administration. The book can be used in combination with other texts for courses in management, supervision, organizational administration, health care management, organizational behavior, and group dynamics. Moreover, the book is also suitable for use by managers in some types of management development courses. No prior coursework in management is required to understand the concepts and theories presented in the book. A test bank is available to facilitate assessment of student comprehension of the material.

In conclusion, I want to express my appreciation to David D. Van Fleet of Texas A&M University, Edwin Locke of the University of Maryland in College Park, Stephen G. Green of Purdue University, and Judith Gordon of Boston College for their thoughtful comments and suggestions in their reviews of the book in its manuscript form. I would also like to thank Maureen Yukl for her encouragement and assistance in preparing the manuscript, Millicent Lambert and Linda Thompson for their careful and competent production and copyediting, and Alison Reeves for her help in facilitating the revision process.

GARY YUKL
ALBANY, NEW YORK

1

INTRODUCTION: THE NATURE OF LEADERSHIP

Leadership is a subject that has long excited interest among scholars and laypersons alike. The term connotes images of powerful, dynamic persons who command victorious armies, direct corporate empires from atop gleaming skyscrapers, or shape the course of nations. Much of our description of history is the story of military, political, religious, and social leaders. The exploits of brave and clever leaders are the essence of many legends and myths. The widespread fascination with leadership may be because it is such a mysterious process, as well as one that touches everyone's life. Why do certain leaders (Gandhi, Mohammed, Mao Tse-tung) inspire such intense fervor and dedication? How did certain leaders (Julius Caesar, Charlemagne, Alexander the Great) build great empires? Why were certain leaders (Winston Churchill, Indira Gandhi, the Shah of Iran) suddenly deposed, despite their apparent power and record of successful accomplishments? How did certain rather undistinguished persons (Adolf Hitler, Claudius Caesar) rise to positions of great power? Why do some leaders have loyal followers who are willing to sacrifice their lives for their leader, and why are some other leaders so despised that their followers conspire to murder them (e.g., as occurred with the "fragging" of some military officers by enlisted men in Vietnam)?

Questions about leadership have long been a subject of speculation, but scientific research on leadership did not begin until the twentieth century. The focus of much of the research has been on the determinants of leadership effectiveness. Behavioral scientists have attempted to discover what traits, abilities, behaviors, sources of power, or aspects of the situation determine how well a leader is able to influence followers and accomplish group objectives. The reasons why some people emerge as leaders and the determinants of the way a leader acts are other important questions that have been investigated, but the predominant concern has been leadership effectiveness.

Some progress has been made in probing the mysteries surrounding leadership, but many questions remain unanswered. In this book, major theories and research findings on leadership effectiveness will be reviewed, with particular emphasis on "managerial leadership" in formal organizations such as business corporations, government agencies, hospitals, universities, and so forth. This first chapter introduces the subject by considering two questions: What is leadership? How is leader effectiveness measured?

DEFINITIONS OF LEADERSHIP

The term *leadership* means different things to different people. It is a word taken from the common vocabulary and incorporated into the technical vocabulary of a scientific discipline without being precisely redefined. As a consequence, it still carries extraneous connotations that create ambiguity of meaning (Janda, 1960). Further confusion is caused by the use of other imprecise terms such as power, authority, management, administration, control, and supervision to describe the same phenomena. Bennis (1959, p. 259) surveyed the leadership literature and concluded:

> Always, it seems, the concept of leadership eludes us or turns up in another form to taunt us again with its slipperiness and complexity. So we have invented an endless proliferation of terms to deal with it . . . and still the concept is not sufficiently defined.

Researchers usually define leadership according to their individual perspective and the aspect of the phenomenon of most interest to them. After a comprehensive review of the leadership literature, Stogdill (1974, p. 259) concluded that "there are almost as many definitions of leadership as there are persons who have attempted to define the concept." Leadership has been defined in terms of individual traits, behavior, influence over other people, interaction patterns, role relationships, occupation of an administrative position, and perception by others regarding legitimacy of influence. Some representative definitions over a quarter century are as follows:

1. Leadership is "the behavior of an individual when he is directing the activities of a group toward a shared goal." (Hemphill & Coons, 1957, p. 7)

2. Leadership is "a particular type of power relationship characterized by a group member's perception that another group member has the right to prescribe behavior patterns for the former regarding his activity as a group member." (Janda, 1960, p. 358)

3. Leadership is "interpersonal influence, exercised in a situation, and directed, through the communication process, toward the attainment of a specified goal or goals." (Tannenbaum, Weschler, & Massarik, 1961, p. 24)

4. Leadership is "an interaction between persons in which one presents information of a sort and in such a manner that the other becomes convinced that his outcomes . . . will be improved if he behaves in the manner suggested or desired." (Jacobs, 1970, p. 232)

5. Leadership is "the initiation and maintenance of structure in expectation and interaction." (Stogdill, 1974, p. 411)

6. Leadership is "the influential increment over and above mechanical compliance with the routine directives of the organization." (Katz & Kahn, 1978, p. 528)

7. Leadership is "the process of influencing the activities of an organized group toward goal achievement." (Rauch & Behling, 1984, p. 46)

The term *leadership* is a relatively recent addition to the English language. It has been in use only for about two hundred years, although the term *leader*, from which it was derived, appeared as early as A.D. 1300 (Stogdill, 1974). Most conceptions of leadership imply that at various times one or more group members can be identified as a leader according to some observable difference between the person(s) and other members, who are referred to as "followers" or "subordinates." Definitions of leadership usually have as a common denominator the assumption that it is a group phenomenon involving the interaction between two or more persons (Janda, 1960). In addition, most definitions of leadership reflect the assumption that it involves an influence process whereby intentional influence is exerted by the leader over followers. The numerous definitions of leadership that have been proposed appear to have little else in common. The definitions differ in many respects, including important differences in who exerts influence, the purpose of influence attempts, and the manner in which influence is exerted. Key points of divergence in conceptions about who should be regarded as a leader are summarized in Table 1-1 on the following page. The differences are not just a case of scholarly nit-picking. They reflect deep disagreement about identification of leaders and leadership processes. Differences between researchers in their conception of leadership lead to differences in the choice of phenomena to investigate and to differences in interpretation of the results.

One major controversy involves the issue of leadership as a distinct phenomenon. Some theorists believe that leadership is no different from the social influence processes occurring among all members of a group, and leadership is viewed as a collective process shared among the members. The opposing view is that all groups have role specialization that includes a specialized leadership role. According to these theorists, it is only meaningful to view "leadership" as distinct from "followership." The person who has the most influence in the group and who carries out most of the leadership functions is designated the leader. Other members are followers, even though some may be leaders of subgroups, or may assist the primary leader in carrying out leadership functions.

TABLE 1–1   Different Conceptions of a Leader

BROADER CONCEPTION	MORE RESTRICTIVE CONCEPTION
1. A person who influences group members ("distributed leadership").	1. A person who exerts the most influence on other group members ("focused leadership").
2. A person who influences group members in any manner.	2. A person who systematically influences member behavior toward attainment of group goals.
3. A person who influences group members to comply with his or her requests willingly or unwillingly.	3. A person who obtains the enthusiastic commitment of group members in carrying out his or her requests.

Related to this controversy is the issue of which influence attempts are part of leadership. Some theorists hold that leadership includes only influence processes related to the task and objectives of the group. According to this view, influence attempts that are extraneous or detrimental to the group's mission and are intended only to benefit the leader are not regarded as "acts of leadership." This limitation seems more appropriate to formal task groups in organizations than to social groups with no explicit task objectives.

Some theorists would go even further in limiting the definition of leadership to exercise of influence resulting in enthusiastic commitment by followers, as opposed to indifferent compliance or reluctant obedience. Proponents of this view argue that a person who uses authority and control over rewards and punishments to manipulate or coerce followers is not really "leading" them. The opposing view is that this definition is too restrictive, because it excludes influence processes that are important for understanding why a manager is effective or ineffective in a given situation. These theorists argue that the initial definition of leadership should not predetermine the answer to the research question of what makes a leader effective.

A similar controversy continues over the differences between leadership and management. It is obvious that a person can be a leader without being a manager, and a person can be a manager without leading. Indeed, some managers do not even have subordinates (e.g., a manager of financial accounts). Nobody has proposed that managing and leading are equivalent, but the degree of overlap is the point of disagreement. Some writers contend that the two are qualitatively different, even mutually exclusive. For example, Bennis and Nanus (1985, p. 21) propose that "managers are people who do things right and leaders are people who do the right thing." Zaleznik (1977) proposed that managers are concerned about how things get done, and leaders are concerned with what the things mean to people. The essential distinction appears to be that leaders influence commitment, whereas managers merely carry out position responsibilities and exercise authority. A contrary view is taken by other writers, who see considerable overlap between leadership and management, and find no good purpose served by assuming it is impossible to be both a manager and leader at the same time.

It is neither feasible nor desirable at this point in the development of the discipline to attempt to resolve the controversy over the appropriate definition of leadership. For the time being, it is better to use the various conceptions of leadership as a source of different perspectives on a complex, multifaceted phenomenon. In research, the operational definition of leadership will depend to a great extent on the purpose of the researcher (Campbell, 1977; Karmel, 1978). The purpose may be to identify leaders, to train them, to discover what they do, to determine how they are selected, or to discover why they are effective. As Karmel (1978, p. 476) notes, "It is consequently very difficult to settle on a single definition of leadership that is general enough to accommodate these many meanings and specific enough to serve as an operationalization of the variable." Whenever feasible, leadership research should be designed to provide information relevant to the entire range of definitions, so that over time it will be possible to compare the utility of different conceptualizations and arrive at some consensus on the matter. Thus, leadership is defined broadly to include influence processes involving determination of the group's or organization's objectives, motivating task behavior in pursuit of these objectives, and influencing group maintenance and culture. The terms leader and manager are used interchangeably in this book.

LEADERSHIP EFFECTIVENESS

Like definitions of leadership, conceptions of leader effectiveness differ from writer to writer. One major distinction between definitions of leadership effectiveness is the type of consequence or outcome selected as the effectiveness criterion. The outcomes include such diverse things as group performance, attainment of group goals, group survival, group growth, group preparedness, group capacity to deal with crises, subordinate satisfaction with the leader, subordinate commitment to group goals, the psychological well-being and development of group members, and the leader's retention of status in the group.

The most commonly used measure of leader effectiveness is the extent to which the leader's group or organization performs its task successfully and attains its goals. In some cases, objective measures of performance or goal attainment are available, such as profit growth, profit margin, sales increase, market share, sales relative to targeted sales, return on investment, productivity, cost per unit of output, costs in relation to budgeted expenditures, and so on. In other cases, subjective ratings of leader effectiveness are obtained from the leader's superiors, peers, or subordinates.

The attitude of followers toward the leader is another common indicator of leader effectiveness. How well does the leader satisfy their needs and expectations? Do followers like, respect, admire the leader? Are followers strongly committed to carrying out the leader's requests, or will they resist, ignore, or subvert them? Follower attitudes are usually measured with questionnaires or interviews. Various objective measures of behavior such as absenteeism, voluntary turnover, grievances, complaints to higher management, requests for transfer, slowdowns, wildcat strikes, and deliberate sabotage of equipment and facilities serve as indirect indicators of follower dissatisfaction and hostility toward the leader.

Leader effectiveness is occasionally measured in terms of the leader's contribution to the quality of group processes, as perceived by followers or by outside observers. Does the leader enhance group cohesiveness, member cooperation, member motivation, problem solving, decision making, and resolution of conflict among members? Does the leader contribute to the efficiency of role specialization, the organization of activities, the accumulation of resources, and the readiness of the group to deal with change and crisis? Does the leader improve the quality of work life, build the self-confidence of followers, increase their skills, and contribute to their psychological growth and development?

The selection of appropriate criteria of leader effectiveness depends on the objectives and values of the person making the evaluation. A leader's superiors are likely to prefer different criteria than the leader's subordinates. When there are many alternative measures of effectiveness, it is usually an arbitrary decision as to which is most relevant. The different criteria are often uncorrelated and may even be negatively correlated. For example, growth in sales or output is sometimes achieved at the cost of reduced efficiency and lower profits. Tradeoffs can occur even within the same criterion at different points of time. For example, profits may be increased in the short run by neglecting activities that have a delayed effect on profits, such as maintenance of equipment, and research and development, investment in new technology, and development of employee skills. In the long run, the net effect of cutting these essential activities is likely to be lower profits. To cope with the problems of partially incompatible criteria in research on leadership effectiveness, it is usually best to include a variety of different criteria and to examine the separate impact of the leader on each one over an extended period of time. Multiple conceptions of effectiveness, like multiple conceptions of leadership, serve to broaden our perspective and enlarge the scope of inquiry.

OVERVIEW OF MAJOR
RESEARCH APPROACHES

Leadership has been studied in different ways, depending on the researcher's conception of leadership and his or her methodological preferences. Most researchers deal with only one narrow aspect of leadership, and most of the studies naturally divide into distinct lines of research. Nearly all leadership research can be classified into one of the following four approaches: (1) power-influence approach, (2) behavior approach, (3) trait approach, (4) situational approach. The implicit assumptions about causal relationships among variables differ for each approach. These assumptions are depicted in Figure 1-1.

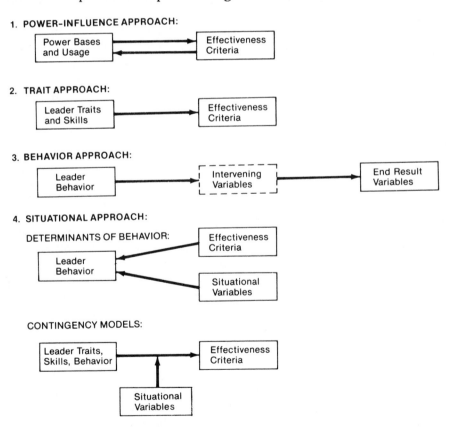

FIGURE 1-1   General Approaches in Research on Leader Effectiveness

Power-Influence Approach

Much of the research coming under the power-influence approach attempts to explain leadership effectiveness in terms of the amount of power possessed by a leader, the types of power, and how power is exercised. Power is important not only for influencing subordinates, but also for influencing peers, superiors, and people outside of the organization, such as clients and suppliers. One major question addressed by research and theory is the source of power for individuals, and the way characteristics of the individual and the situation interact in determining how much power a person will have. Another question is the way power is gained or lost through reciprocal influence processes. Parallel to the microlevel analysis of power for individuals is a macrolevel analysis of power for organizational subunits and coalitions. At this level, leadership effectiveness is often evaluated in terms of the organization's adaptation to a changing environment. Finally, a new bridge between the power and behavior approaches is research on the influence tactics used by managers. The power-influence approach is covered in Chapters 2 and 3.

A person's power depends to a considerable extent on how the person is perceived by others. Some critics have questioned whether leadership is mostly attributions made by people to explain events, rather than an objectively verifiable phenomenon. This attributional critique is considered in the final chapter (Chapter 12) as part of the larger issue of leadership importance.

Behavior Approach

The behavior approach emphasizes what leaders and managers actually do on the job. This research falls into two general subcategories. Research on the nature of managerial work relies mostly on descriptive methods such as direct observation, diaries, and anecdotes obtained from interviews. The earlier research focused on activity patterns and how managers spend their time, but research in recent years has examined the content of managerial activities, using content categories referred to as managerial roles, functions, and practices. A different perspective on managerial work is provided by research on the behavioral duties and responsibilities required in different managerial positions, and perceptions about the relative importance of the various job requirements. The behavior observation research and the job description research are covered in Chapter 4.

Another line of behavior research has sought to identify differences in behavior patterns between effective and ineffective leaders. Hundreds of studies over the last three decades have examined the correlation between questionnaire measures of leadership behavior and measures of subordinate satisfaction and performance. A much smaller number of studies have used field and laboratory experiments to investigate how leader behavior influences subordinate satisfaction and performance. This research is reviewed in Chapter 5, as well as some research using critical incidents to study effective and ineffective managerial behavior. A major question raised in this chapter is how to classify behavior in a way that facilitates research and theory on managerial effectiveness. This issue is taken up again in Chapter 7, which presents an integrating taxonomy of managerial behavior based on the category systems reviewed in Chapters 4 and 5. Leader behavior in the context of decision groups is covered in Chapter 11. Behavior of charismatic and transformational leaders is considered in Chapter 10.

Trait Approach

The trait approach emphasizes the personal attributes of leaders. Early leadership theories attributed leader success to possession of extraordinary abilities such as tireless energy, penetrating intuition, uncanny foresight, and irresistible persuasive powers. Hundreds of trait studies were conducted during the 1930s and 1940s to discover these elusive qualities, but this massive research effort failed to find any traits that would guarantee leadership success. Nevertheless, as the evidence accumulates from better designed research and new research methods, the trait research is slowly discovering how leader attributes relate to leadership behavior and effectiveness. The focus of much of the recent trait research has been on managerial motivation and specific skills, whereas earlier research focused more on personality traits or general intelligence. Some researchers now attempt to relate traits to specific role requirements for different types of managerial positions. The trait research is covered in Chapter 9. Traits associated with charismatic and transformational leadership are discussed in Chapter 10.

Situational Approach

The situational approach emphasizes the importance of situational factors such as the leader's authority and discretion, the nature of the work performed by the leader's unit, subordinate ability and motivation, the nature of the external environment, and the role requirements imposed on a manager by subordinates, peers, superiors, and outsiders. This research and theory falls into two major subcategories. One line of research treats leader behavior as a dependent variable, and researchers seek to discover how the situation influences behavior. Role theory is used to describe the process, and supplementary theories have identified key aspects of the situation that create demands and constraints on a manager. A major question is the extent to which managerial work is the same or unique across different types of organizations and levels of management. The research and theory are primarily concerned with this issue rather than with managerial effectiveness. However, much of the research is relevant for understanding managerial effectiveness, since effectiveness depends on how well a manager resolves role conflicts, copes with demands, recognizes opportunities, and overcomes constraints. This approach is described in Chapter 8.

The other subcategory of situational research attempts to identify aspects of the situation that "moderate" the relationship of leader traits or behavior to leadership effectiveness. The assumption is that different behavior patterns (or trait patterns) will be effective in different situations, and that the same behavior pattern is not optimal in all situations. This approach is sometimes called the "contingency" approach, because the effects of leader behavior are contingent on the situation. Contingency theories of effective leadership behavior are described in Chapters 6 and 7, and contingency theories involving leader traits are described in Chapter 9.

Integrating the Approaches

Leadership research has been characterized by narrowly focused studies with little integration of findings from the different approaches. The research on leader power has not examined leadership behavior except for explicit influence attempts, and there has been little concern for traits except ones that are a source of leader influence. The trait research has shown little concern for direct measurement of leadership behavior or influence, even though it is evident that the effects of leader traits are mediated by leadership behavior and influence. The behavior research has seldom included leader traits or power, even though they influence a leader's behavior. Finally, situational theories examine how the situation enhances or nullifies the effects of selected leader behaviors or traits, rather than taking a broader view of the way traits, power, behavior, and situation interact to determine leadership effectiveness.

Despite the prevailing pattern of segmentation in research on leadership over the past 40 years, the number of studies that straddle more than one approach is slowly increasing, and the different lines of research are gradually converging. Chapter 12 identifies points of correspondence between the findings from different approaches. The chapter presents an integrating conceptual framework that includes traits, behavior, power, and situation. Implications for improving leadership in organizations are discussed.

Nearly ten thousand articles and books have been published on the subject of leadership. Obviously, somebody believes that leadership is an important subject. Nevertheless, a controversy continues about the importance of any individual leader for an organization or nation. This issue is addressed in the final chapter, after the reader has seen what was learned from the multitude of research studies on leadership effectiveness.

REVIEW AND DISCUSSION QUESTIONS

1. What features are shared in common by most definitions of leadership?
2. What are some major differences in the way leadership has been defined?
3. Are "leaders" different from "managers"?
4. Does it really matter how you define leadership? Why or why not?
5. How is leadership effectiveness determined?
6. Why is it important to use multiple criteria of leadership effectiveness?
7. What is the difference between the power-influence, behavior, trait, and situational approaches for describing leadership?

2

SOURCES

OF

POWER AND INFLUENCE

The essence of leadership is influence over followers. However, the influence process between a leader and followers is not unidirectional. Leaders influence followers, but followers also have some influence over leaders. Moreover, in large organizations, the effectiveness of middle and lower-level managers depends on their influence over superiors and peers as well as their influence over subordinates. To understand what makes managers effective requires an analysis of the complex web of power relationships and influence processes found in all organizations. In this chapter we examine the different sources of power, and the nature of reciprocal influence processes as they relate to the gain and loss of power.

CONCEPTIONS OF INFLUENCE
AND POWER

There is more conceptual confusion about influence processes than about any other facet of leadership. Terms such as influence, power, and authority have been used in different ways by different writers. Often the terms are used without providing any explicit definition. It is worthwhile to examine some of the different interpretations of key terms and to consider how the success of an influence attempt may be evaluated.

Influence

Influence is a word that everybody seems to understand intuitively. In general terms, influence is merely the effect of one party (the "agent") on another (the "target"). However, closer examination reveals ambiguities and complexities even in this relatively simple concept. The process by which the agent affects the target can take many different forms. The influence may be over people, things, or events. In the case of people, the influence may be over attitudes, perceptions, behavior, or some combination of these outcomes. The consequence of the agent's influence may be what was intended by the agent, or the influence may be in the form of an unintended outcome. The magnitude of the change in the target may be what the agent intended, or it may fall short of the agent's objectives. The agent's influence may be strong enough to ensure "control" over the target person's behavior, or so weak that the target person feels "pressure" but is not induced to do anything different.

Outcomes of Influence Attempts

Success of an influence attempt is clearly a matter of degree. However, it is useful to differentiate among three qualitatively distinct outcomes of influence attempts: commitment, compliance, and resistance. The most successful outcome is commitment. It means that the target person internally agrees with a decision or request from the agent and makes a great effort to carry out the request or implement the decision effectively.

Compliance means that the target is willing to do what the agent asks but is apathetic rather than enthusiastic about it and will make only a minimal effort. The agent has influenced the target person's behavior but not the person's attitudes. The target person is not convinced that the decision or action is the best thing to do, or even that it will be effective for accomplishing its purpose. For a complex, difficult task, compliance is clearly a less successful outcome than commitment. However, for a simple, routine request, compliance may be all that is necessary for the agent to accomplish task objectives.

Resistance is the least successful outcome. Resistance means that the target person is opposed to the proposal or request, rather than merely indifferent about it, and actively tries to avoid carrying it out. The target person will respond in one or more of the following ways: (1) make excuses about why the request cannot be carried out, (2) try to persuade the agent to withdraw the request, (3) ask higher authorities to overrule the agent's request, (4) delay acting in the hope that the agent will forget about the request, (5) make a pretense of complying but try to sabotage the task, or (6) refuse to carry out the request.

Power

Power generally refers to an agent's capacity to influence a target person, but the term has been used in different ways by different theorists (Dahl, 1957; Grimes, 1978; House, 1988; Jacobs, 1970; Kotter, 1985; Mintzberg, 1983; Pfeffer, 1981). Sometimes power means the agent's capacity to influence a target person's behavior, whereas other times, it means influence over the target person's attitudes as well as behavior. Sometimes power is defined in relative rather than absolute terms as the extent to which the agent has more influence over the target than the target has over the agent ("net power"). A variation of this definition is the target's capacity to influence the agent without fear of retaliation ("usable power"). Sometimes, power refers to the agent's influence over a single target person, and sometimes power is measured in relation to multiple target persons. Sometimes, power is used to mean potential influence over things as well as people. Finally, recognizing the difficulty of measuring potential influence, some people define power as the amount of influence actually exercised by the agent ("enacted power"). None of these definitions is inherently superior for all purposes, but for clarity of communication it is necessary to settle on one definition.

In this book, power will be defined as an agent's potential influence over the attitudes and behavior of one or more designated target persons. The focus of the definition is on influence over people, but control over things will be treated as one source of power. The agent is usually an individual, but occasionally it will be an organizational subunit.

SOURCES OF POWER

There are many different sources of power in organizations (see Table 2-1). Power is derived in part from the opportunities inherent in a person's position in the organization; this "position power" includes legitimate

TABLE 2–1   Sources of Power in Organizations

Position Power	• Formal authority
	• Control over resources and rewards
	• Control over punishments
	• Control over information
	• Ecological control
Personal Power	• Expertise
	• Friendship/loyalty
	• Charisma
Political Power	• Control over decision processes
	• Coalitions
	• Co-optation
	• Institutionalization

authority, control over resources, control over information, control over punishments, and ecological control. Power also depends on attributes of the interpersonal relationship between agent and target person; this "personal power" includes relative task expertise, friendship and loyalty, and a leader's charismatic qualities. Finally, power depends upon some political processes ("political power") such as controlling key decisions, forming coalitions, and co-opting opponents. Individual, situational, and political determinants of power interact in complex ways, and sometimes it is difficult to distinguish among them.

In order to understand the effectiveness of a leader, it is necessary to consider several types of power relationships: the downward power of the leader over subordinates, the upward power of subordinates over the leader, the upward power of the leader over superiors, and the lateral power of the leader over other people in the organization. There are similar sources of power for these four types of relationships, but there are also differences in the relative importance of the various sources depending upon the type of relationship. In the next section of the chapter, position, personal, and political sources of power are reviewed in relation to downward, upward, and lateral influence processes.

POSITION AS A SOURCE OF POWER

Formal Authority

Power stemming from formal authority is sometimes called *legitimate power* (French & Raven, 1959). Authority is based on perceptions about the prerogatives, obligations, and responsibilities associated with particular positions in an organization or social system. Authority includes the perceived right of one position occupant to influence specified aspects of the behavior of other position occupants. The agent has the right to make particular types of requests, and the target person has the duty to obey. For example, a manager may have the legitimate right to establish work rules, give work assignments, and direct the task behavior of subordinates. The subordinates in turn may have the legitimate right to request information and assistance from the manager or from persons in a lateral relationship. Authority also involves the right of a person to exercise control over things, such as money, resources, equipment, and materials, and this control is another source of power.

The motivation for compliance with legitimate rules and requests may be an internalized value, such as obedience to authority figures, loyalty to the organization, respect for law, reverence for tradition, or merely the recognition that submission to authority is a necessary condition for membership in the organization. Members agree to comply with rules and directions from leaders in return for the benefits of membership (March &

Simon, 1958). The conditions for membership in an organization may be set forth in a formal, legal contract, but the agreement to submit to legitimate authority is usually an implicit mutual understanding. This "implicit social contract" is the ultimate basis for authority. Although some theorists have emphasized the downward flow of authority from owners and top management, the potential influence derived from authority depends as much on the consent of the governed as on the ownership and control of property (Jacobs, 1970).

Authority is necessary for large organizations to function smoothly and effectively. The complex pattern of role specialization and role interdependence in large organizations make it essential for each person to fulfill role expectations in a reliable manner, including unpleasant duties and unpopular rules (Katz & Kahn, 1978). Since people come and go in organizations, it is not feasible to rely solely upon sources of influence such as shared values or expertise to obtain necessary compliance (Hamner & Organ, 1978). Authority is more acceptable and less difficult to use than most forms of power as the basis of day-to-day influence. Influence based on authority can be used to accomplish routine activities without incurring costs associated with other types of power, such as the expenditure of resources or the obligation to repay favors.

One prerequisite for acceptance of a person's authority is the perceived legitimacy of the person as an occupant of a leadership position in the organization. This aspect of legitimacy depends to a large extent on how the leader was selected. In earlier times, leaders were usually selected on the basis of blood lines and rules of succession; for example, the eldest male child was first in line to succeed a ruler or inherit the family business. Now in most large organizations, leaders are usually appointed by superiors or elected by the membership. For example, the chief executive officer (CEO) of a corporation is appointed by the board of directors, and the president of a labor union is elected by the membership. The specific procedures for selecting a leader are usually based on tradition and the provisions of a legal charter or constitution. If a leader is selected in a way that deviates from the process considered legitimate by members, the authority of the leader is likely to be weakened. The importance of legitimate selection is evident in the concerted effort of most leaders to establish a recognized basis for their authority. Elected leaders are concerned about being able to claim a "mandate" by voters, and elaborate inauguration ceremonies are held by many kinds of leaders to formalize the transfer of power and enhance the legitimacy of their selection.

A person's scope of authority is the range of requests that can properly be made and the range of actions that can properly be taken. Scope of authority depends in large part on the influence needed to accomplish recognized role requirements and organizational objectives (Barnard, 1952). However, even when a leader's scope of authority is delineated by documents such as an organization charter, a written job description, or an employment contract, there usually remains considerable ambiguity (Davis, 1968). Reitz (1977, p. 468) provides some examples of the kinds of questions that may be raised about a leader's scope of authority:

> An executive can rightfully expect a supervisor to work hard and diligently; may he also influence the supervisor to spy on rivals, spend weekends away from home, join an encounter group? A coach can rightfully expect his players to execute specific plays; may he also direct their life styles outside the sport? A combat officer can rightfully expect his men to attack on order; may he also direct them to execute civilians whom he claims are spies? A doctor can rightfully order a nurse to attend a patient or observe an autopsy; may he order her to assist in an abortion against her will?

Questions about scope of authority are especially difficult in lateral relations. Even though a person has no direct authority over someone in a position outside of the chain of command, the person often has the legitimate right to make requests necessary to carry out job responsibilities, such as requests for information, supplies, support services, technical advice, and assistance in carrying out joint tasks.

Control Over Resources and Rewards

Another source of power in organizations is control over resources and rewards. This control stems in part from formal authority. The higher a person's position in the authority hierarchy of the organization, the more control over scarce resources the person is likely to have. Executives have more control than middle managers, who in turn have more control than first-line managers. Executives have authority to make decisions about the allocation of resources to various subunits and activities, and in addition, they have the right to review and modify resource allocation decisions made at lower levels.

Potential influence based on control over rewards is sometimes called *reward power* (French & Raven, 1959). Reward power depends not only on control over resources, but also on the perceptions of the target person that a request or assignment is feasible and, if carried out, will actually result in the promised reward. An attempt to use reward power will be unsuccessful if the agent lacks credibility or the requirements for obtaining the reward appear impossible.

One form of reward power is influence over compensation and career progress. Most managers are authorized to give pay increases, bonuses, or other economic incentives to deserving subordinates. Reward power is derived also from control over tangible benefits such as a promotion, a better job, a better work schedule, a larger operating budget, a larger expense account, more authority and responsibility, formal recognition of accomplishments (e.g., awards, commendations), and status symbols such as a larger office or a reserved parking space. The extent of a manager's authority and discretion to allocate rewards to subordinates varies greatly from one organization to another, as well as across levels of authority. Some managers have the opportunity to use all of these rewards, whereas other managers are severely limited in their authority over rewards.

Reward power is also a source of influence over peers. Some organizations, especially those with a matrix structure (e.g., product managers, project managers) utilize the formal evaluations by a manager's peers in making decisions about pay increases or promotions. Another source of reward power in lateral relations is dependence on a peer for resources, information, assistance, or support that is not prescribed by the formal authority system. Trading of favors needed to accomplish task objectives is a common form of influence among peers in organizations, and research indicates that it is important for the success of middle managers (Kotter, 1982; Kaplan, 1984; Strauss, 1962).

Subordinates also have sources of reward power. Although few organizations provide a formal mechanism for subordinates to evaluate leaders, subordinates usually have some indirect influence over the leader's reputation and prospects for a pay increase or promotion. If subordinates perform well, they can enhance the reputation of their manager. Some subordinates have reward power based on the ability to acquire resources outside of the formal authority system of the organization. For example, a department chairperson in a state university was able to obtain discretionary funds from grants and contracts, and these funds were used as a basis for influencing the decisions made by the college dean, whose own discretionary funds were very limited.

Control Over Punishments

Another source of power is control over punishments and the capacity to prevent someone from obtaining desired rewards. This form of power is sometimes called *coercive power* (French & Raven, 1959). The formal authority system of an organization and its traditions deal with the use of punishment as well as use of rewards. A leader's authority over punishments varies greatly across different types of organizations. The coercive power of military and political leaders is usually greater than that of corporate managers. Over the last two centuries, there has been a general decline in use of legitimate coercion by all types of leaders (Katz & Kahn, 1978). For example, managers once had the right to dismiss employees for any reason they thought was justified. The captain of a ship could flog sailors who were disobedient or who failed to perform their duties diligently. Military officers could execute a soldier for desertion or failure to obey an order during combat. Nowadays, these forms of coercive power are prohibited or sharply restricted in most nations.

Even though coercion has been one of the most common forms of leader influence throughout history, its frequent use may be due more to ignorance or to the psychological needs of some leaders than to demonstrated effectiveness. Even under extreme conditions where leaders have the power to torture and murder workers, coercion is often ineffective. Webber (1975) relates an example of the disastrous consequences resulting from reliance on coercion in a Nazi bomb factory using slave labor during World War II. The workers hindered production by persistently requesting detailed instructions and doing nothing constructive on their own initiative. They sabotaged production by improperly fitting the bomb fuses, and it was impossible for the guards to detect the sabotage and ensure minimal performance unless they watched each worker closely, which required nearly as many guards as slaves.

There are some situations where coercion is appropriate, and historical accounts provide evidence of its effective use by political and military leaders in maintaining discipline and dealing with rebels and criminals. Nevertheless, coercion is effective only when applied to a small percentage of followers under conditions considered legitimate by a majority of them. When leaders are tempted to use coercion on a large scale against followers, it undermines their authority and creates a hostile opposition seeking to restrict their power or remove them from office (Blau, 1956).

The extent of coercive counterpower available to subordinates varies greatly from one kind of organization to another. As noted earlier, subordinates in most organizations have the capacity to influence indirectly the performance evaluation of their leader. If subordinates restrict production, sabotage operations, initiate grievances, hold demonstrations, or make complaints to higher management, they can damage the reputation of the boss. In some types of organizations, such as those with elected leaders, subordinates have sufficient counterpower even to remove a leader from office. Occasionally, the coercive power of subordinates involves more extreme methods of removing leaders from office. In the Vietnam War, there were known cases of subordinates who "fragged" a despised leader during a firefight where the cause of death could not be determined. In the case of political leaders, the ultimate form of coercive power for subordinates is a violent revolution that results in the imprisonment, death, or exile of the leader.

In lateral relations, opportunities for coercion are limited. A manager may threaten to complain to the superior of a peer who refuses to carry out legitimate requests. If the peer is dependent upon the manager for assistance in performing important tasks, the manager may threaten to withhold cooperation if the peer fails to carry out a request. Sometimes it is possible to use political tactics to magnify one's lateral coercive power, such as gaining the authority to reject the products or plans of another subunit or forming a coalition with other managers to put more pressure on a manager to support a proposal. However, since mutual dependencies usually exist between managers of different subunits, coercion is likely to elicit retaliation and escalate into a conflict that benefits neither party.

Control Over Information

Another important source of power is control over information. This control involves a person's access to vital information and control over the distribution of information to others (Pettigrew, 1972). Some access to information results from a person's position in the organization's communication network. Managerial positions often provide opportunities to obtain information that is not directly available to subordinates or peers (Mintzberg, 1973, 1983). Boundary role positions provide access to important information about events in the external environment of an organization. However, it is not a matter merely of occupying a particular position and having information appear as if by magic; a person must be actively involved in cultivating a network of information sources and gathering information from them (Kotter, 1982).

A middle manager who is the only channel for downward communication of decisions made by superiors is in a position to interpret them selectively for subordinates and peers. In a similar manner, a leader who controls the flow of vital information about outside events has an opportunity to interpret these events for subordinates and influence their perception and attitudes (Kuhn, 1963). A leader may use deliberate distortion of information to persuade subordinates that a particular course of action is desirable. Examples of information distortion include selective editing of reports and documents, biased interpretation of data, and presentation of false information. Some leaders attempt to increase subordinate dependence upon them by hoarding information necessary to solve task problems, plan operations, and make strategic decisions. In effect, control over information is used to enhance the leader's expertise and give the leader more expert power than subordinates. If the leader is the only one who "knows what is going on," subordinates will lack evidence to dispute leader claims that an unpopular decision is justified by circumstances. Moreover, control of information makes it easier for a leader to cover up failures and mistakes that would otherwise undermine a carefully cultivated image of expertise (Pfeffer, 1977a). Another tactic used by some political leaders to protect their reputations is to blame external scapegoats for internal problems; followers are fed a steady flow of unfavorable propaganda that arouses fears, creates distrust, and supports unfavorable stereotypes of outsiders.

Control over information is a source of upward influence as well as downward and lateral influence. When subordinates have exclusive access to information needed by superiors to make decisions, this advantage can be used as a source of influence over the superior's decisions. Some subordinates actively seek this type of influence by gradually assuming more and more responsibility for collecting, storing, analyzing, and reporting operating information. If a leader is completely dependent on a subordinate to interpret complex analyses of operating information, the subordinate may be invited to participate directly in making decisions based on these analyses (Korda, 1975). However, even without direct participation, a subordinate with information control will be able to influence a superior's decisions. For example, in a study by Pettigrew (1972), a manager was able to influence the selection of a new computer by providing the board of directors with information that favored one option and discredited others. Control over the flow of operating information also enables subordinates to magnify their accomplishments, cover up mistakes, and exaggerate the amount of expertise and resources needed to their work.

Ecological Control

An important source of leader influence over the behavior of subordinates is control over the physical environment, technology, and organization of the work. Manipulation of these physical and social conditions allows one to influence indirectly the behavior of others. This form of influence is sometimes called *situational engineering*.

One form of situational engineering is job design. Leaders with the authority to modify the design of jobs have potential influence over the motivation of subordinates (Oldham, 1976). Intrinsic motivation is usually greater for jobs in which people use a variety of skills, have considerable autonomy in how the work is done, experience a sense of completing a meaningful task, and obtain direct feedback about task performance (Aldag & Brief, 1979; Hackman and Oldham, 1976). Research on job enrichment suggests that significant improvements in work quality and job satisfaction are sometimes possible (Hackman & Oldham, 1980).

Another form of situational engineering is control over the physical work environment. Since a person's behavior is determined in part by perception of situational opportunities and constraints, behavior can be altered in subtle ways by rearranging the situation (Cartwright, 1965). For example, special lights or auditory signals on equipment can be used to inform the operator that it is time for necessary maintenance or to warn the operator not to continue doing something that will cause an accident or breakdown. Equipment can be designed to reduce the chance that an operator can be injured by careless actions. Machine-paced assembly lines set the speed at which employees work. The workflow design and layout of physical facilities determine which employees interact with each other and who initiates action for whom.

For the top executives of an organization, another form of situational engineering is the design of the formal organization structure, including the authority system, formal appraisal and reward systems, and the information systems. Executives are able to influence the behavior of other employees by a variety of organizing decisions that influence employee goal orientation and time orientation, such as the decision to establish product divisions rather than functional divisions, or the decision to establish competing divisions with the same function (Lawrence & Lorsch, 1967; Mintzberg, 1983). Behavior of lower-level employees is also influenced by delegating authority, setting limits of discretion, and establishing formal work rules and procedures. Instead of relying only on personal promises of rewards, as in reward power, a formal reward system may be established to distribute rewards impersonally on the basis of predetermined criteria. Thus, for example, top management may decide to make pay increases contingent on quality indicators in addition to productivity, or contingent upon group rather than individual performance, or on long-term performance in addition to short-term performance.

PERSONAL ATTRIBUTES
AS A SOURCE OF POWER

Expertise

A major source of personal power in organizations is expertise in solving problems and performing important tasks. This form of power is sometimes called *expert power* (French & Raven, 1959). Expertise is a source of power for a person only if others are dependent upon the person for the advice or assistance they need. The more important a problem or task is to the target person, the greater is the power derived from possessing the necessary expertise. Dependency is greatest if the target person lacks relevant expertise and cannot easily find another qualified person besides the agent (Patchen, 1974; Hickson, Hinings, Lee, Schneck, & Pennings, 1971).

It is not enough for the agent to possess expertise; the target person must recognize this expertise and perceive the leader to be a reliable source of information and advice. Sometimes the target person's faith in the agent's expertise is sufficiently strong to evoke compliance without any explanation for the recommended behavior. A good example is the patient who takes medicine prescribed by a doctor without knowing what the medicine is or what effects it will have. However, in most cases, mere perception of leader expertise is not sufficient to exercise expert power, and the agent must support a proposal or plan by making logical arguments and presenting evidence that appears credible.

In the short run, perceived expertise is more important than real expertise, and an agent may be able to "fake it" for a time by acting confident and pretending to be an expert. However, over time, as the agent's knowledge is put to the test, perceptions will become more accurate. Thus, it is essential for leaders to build and maintain a reputation for technical expertise. Reputation depends in part on actual expertise and in part on impression management. Actual expertise is maintained through a continual process of education and practical experience. For example, in many professions it is important to keep informed about new developments by reading technical publications and attending workshops and seminars. Evidence of expertise can be displayed in the forms of diplomas, licenses, and awards. At an opportune time, a person can refer casually to prior accomplishments or positions of importance. However, the most convincing approach is to demonstrate expertise by solving important problems, making good decisions, providing sound advice, and successfully completing challenging but highly visible projects. An extreme tactic is to intentionally but covertly precipitate crises just to demonstrate the ability to deal with them (Goldner, 1970; Pfeffer, 1977a).

Specialized knowledge and technical skill will remain a source of power only as long as there is continued dependence on the the person who possesses them. If a problem is permanently solved or others learn how to solve it by themselves, the agent's expertise is no longer valuable. Thus, people sometimes try to protect their expert power by keeping procedures and techniques shrouded in secrecy, by using technical jargon to make the task seem more complex and mysterious, and by destroying alternate sources of information about task procedures such as written manuals, diagrams, blueprints, and computer programs (Hickson et al., 1971).

Special expertise in dealing with critical problems is just as much a source of upward and lateral power as it is of downward power. A person's ability to perform a vital function that superiors or peers cannot do increases their dependence on him or her (Mechanic, 1962). Expert power is greatest for someone with rare skills who has high job mobility and cannot be replaced easily.

In highly bureaucratic organizations, knowledge of rules and regulations is a type of expertise that may become a source of counterpower for subordinates. A new leader is usually dependent for a time upon subordinates to advise him or her about standard procedures, and sometimes rules and regulations provide subordinates with an excuse for not doing something requested by the leader (Jacobs, 1970). A complex system of rules and procedures usually includes some obsolete or contradictory requirements, and it seldom specifies all behaviors necessary to do the task effectively. Subordinates with a detailed knowledge of work rules can cause slowdowns in operations merely by following the rules exactly, with little risk of being dismissed or disciplined for using this coercive tactic (Mechanic, 1962).

Friendship and Loyalty

Another important source of power is the desire of others to please a person toward whom they feel strong affection. This form of power is sometimes called *referent power* (French & Raven, 1959). People who feel a deep friendship or loyalty toward someone are usually willing to do special favors for the person. Moreover, people tend to imitate the behavior of someone whom they greatly admire, and they tend to develop attitudes similar to those expressed by a person with whom they identify.

The referent power of a leader over subordinates depends upon feelings of friendship and loyalty developed slowly over a long period of time. The referent power of a leader is increased by the leader's acting friendly and considerate, showing concern for the needs and feelings of others, demonstrating trust and respect, and treating people fairly. Referent power is diminished by acting in a hostile, rejecting, or arrogant manner. Over time, actions speak louder than words, and a leader who tries to appear friendly but manipulates and exploits people will lose referent power.

Subordinates are aware that a powerful boss has the potential to cause them great inconvenience or harm, and even the subordinates of a benevolent leader tend to be very sensitive to subtle indications of approval and disapproval. Dependence on the whims of a powerful authority figure is especially disturbing for subordinates who have a strong need for independence. The potentially disturbing aspects of the status differential between leader and subordinate increase the importance of symbolic acts that de-emphasize the differential. Whyte (1969) describes an effective production foreman, who spent his time on the shop floor, wore the same kind of work clothes as subordinates, and was willing to pitch in and help subordinates when there was an equipment breakdown, even though it occasionally meant getting dirty. Whyte concludes that symbolic actions of this type demonstrate acceptance and respect for subordinates and build loyalty for a small expenditure in time and effort.

Another approach for increasing a leader's referent power is to select as subordinates people who are likely to identify with the leader. For example, the marketing vice president of a manufacturing company recruited other immigrants from his homeland for several years before he became vice president, and their loyalty and identification was so strong that he could get them to implement new marketing programs faster than any of the company's competitors. This strategy can be extended beyond a leader's immediate work unit by using political influence to select friends for sensitive positions in other parts of an organization.

Referent power is a major source of lateral influence over peers, and it is especially important for middle managers who depend on peers to provide necessary information, assistance, and resources (Kanter, 1982; Kotter, 1982; Kaplan, 1984). Lateral referent power is established by offers of assistance to peers, by providing special favors when asked, by providing political support, by praising special accomplishments by peers, by showing appreciation for their assistance and support, and in general, by acting friendly and considerate (Kaplan, 1984). Success in developing and maintaining referent power depends upon interpersonal skills such as charm, tact, diplomacy, empathy, and humor.

Referent power is an important source of upward power as well as downward and lateral power in organizations. Flattery and praise may be used by people with lower status to ingratiate themselves with higher-status persons. Of course, flattery and praise are effective only if they appear sincere rather than manipulative. In the same way, demonstration of approval and loyalty to one's boss is a source of referent power for a subordinate. For example, loyalty can be demonstrated by defending one's boss when he or she is being criticized by others (Dubin, 1978).

Charisma

It is not clear yet whether personal charisma is best viewed as a variation of referent power or as a distinct form of power. Followers identify with a charismatic leader and experience an intense emotional attraction to the leader. The process of identification is usually faster and more intense than for a friendly but noncharismatic leader. The attributes of charismatic leaders are not well understood, but they appear to include qualities such as personal magnetism, a dramatic, persuasive manner of speaking, strong enthusiasm, and strong convictions (Berlew, 1974; House, 1977). Together, these qualities make the charismatic leader appear somewhat mysterious and larger than life, a person who can be trusted to lead followers to "victory," "success," or a "better world." Charismatic leaders have insight into the needs, hopes, and values of followers and are able to create a vision that motivates commitment to the leader's policies and strategies. The vision is communicated by the use of symbols, myths, rituals, and staged events. Charismatic leadership has been recognized for a long time, but only in recent years has there been systematic research on it. Charismatic leadership is dealt with in more detail in Chapter 10.

POLITICAL PROCESSES
FOR GAINING INFLUENCE

Political action is a pervasive process in organizations that involves efforts by members of an organization to increase their power or to protect existing power sources. Political actions may be carried out by organizational subunits or coalitions as well as by individual managers. Although the ultimate source of political power is usually authority, control over resources, or control over information, political power involves influence processes that transform and magnify the initial basis of power in unique ways (Pfeffer, 1981). A political process called institutionalization will be discussed later in this chapter. Other forms of political power include gaining control over decision processes, forming coalitions, and co-opting critics and opponents.

Control Over Decision Processes

Many political actions are designed to gain influence over important decisions, such as the allocation of scarce resources or the development of plans and policies. One way for an organizational subunit to influence important decisions is to get its representatives into important positions of authority in the organization, such as top administrative positions or decision bodies that make key decisions. In some cases, it may be possible to create new positions or committees that will be controlled by one's subunit or coalition.

If it is not possible to control important decisions directly, it may be possible to influence them indirectly by establishing formal decision procedures or decision criteria that appear to be rational and objective but actually favor one party over others. For example, in a study of university budgeting, Pfeffer and Salancik (1974) found that departments with many students wanted the number of students to be the primary criterion for decisions on allocation of resources among departments, whereas departments with considerable grant activity preferred to de-emphasize student ratios in favor of research activity as the primary criterion. The party that was able to get their criterion accepted by the university administration would get a larger share of the resources, such as faculty positions and expense funds.

Coalitions

In many cases, it is not possible for one party acting alone to get what it wants. A common form of political action in organizations is the formation of coalitions or alliances to oppose or support a particular policy, program, or change (Stevenson, Pearce, & Porter, 1985). In a coalition, each party helps the others in getting what they want. For example, a marketing vice president joined forces with the vice president of research and development to influence the president to give them both more authority over product design. The counterpower of subordinates over leaders is more effectively displayed and exerted when subordinates organize a coalition to take collective action (Lee, 1977). Even the threat of forming a union or employee association will usually serve as a restraint on the actions of a manager.

Coalitions are not limited to parties within an organization, sometimes they are formed with outside parties. It is quite common for a boundary-spanning unit, such as a marketing or purchasing department, to form an alliance with a client or supplier. For example, the purchasing department of one company asked some of its vendors to lobby with top management to preserve existing procurement procedures and prevent the production department from gaining authority over procurement decisions. The vendors supported the purchasing department because they were afraid of losing orders if control shifted to the production department (Pfeffer, 1981).

Co-optation

When someone is allowed to participate in making a decision, the person gains more influence over the decision but is also likely to become more committed to carry out the decision. Participation increases the total influence in the relationship rather than merely transferring some influence from the agent to the target person. The process illustrates the apparent paradox that you can gain more influence by giving up some influence, as long as the resulting decision is consistent with your objectives. Co-optation is a form of political action that appears to be a variation of participation. The objective of co-optation is to undermine expected opposition to a policy or project by a group or faction whose support is needed. An influential member of the group is invited to join a committee, board, or council to make decisions about the policy or project. Favorable changes in attitudes are likely to occur as a result of assuming a new role and participating in making decisions that provide a new perspective and understanding of problems. New attitudes are strengthened by rewarding the co-opted person for publicly supporting the policy or project in question. These rewards may involve increased status, a large salary, or an expense account (Pfeffer, 1981).

SOCIAL EXCHANGE THEORY

Power is not a static condition, and it changes over time. Social exchange theory attempts to explain how power is gained and lost as reciprocal influence processes occur over time between leaders and followers. The theory uses interaction processes between individuals as the basis for explaining complex social behavior in groups. The most fundamental form of social interaction is an exchange of benefits or favors, which leads to mutual attraction when repeated over time. Social exchange can include not only material benefits but also psychological benefits such as expressions of approval, respect, esteem, and affection. Individuals learn to engage in social exchanges early in their childhood, and they develop expectations about reciprocity and equity in these exchanges. Several versions of social exchange theory have been proposed (Blau, 1974; Homans, 1958; Thibaut & Kelley, 1959), but the versions by Hollander (1958; 1979) and Jacobs (1970) are most relevant because they are explicitly concerned with leadership. It is easier to begin by considering social exchange processes involving emergent leaders in small groups and then proceed to formal leaders in organizations.

Emergent Leaders in Small Groups

During the course of interaction among members of a group, some people will appear to have more competence at the task than others. By demonstrating competence and loyalty to the group, a member influences the expectations of others about the leadership role he or she should play in the group. The person gains status and influence in the group and is allowed to have more influence over group decisions. The amount of status and influence is proportionate to the group's evaluation of the person's potential contribution relative to that of other members. The contribution may involve control over scarce resources, access to vital information, or skill in dealing with critical task problems. In addition to increased status and influence, a person who has demonstrated good judgment accumulates "idiosyncrasy credits" and is allowed more latitude than other members to deviate from nonessential group norms. Group members are usually willing to suspend immediate judgment and go along with the person's innovative proposals for attaining group goals.

When an emergent leader makes an innovative proposal that proves to be successful, the group's trust in the person's expertise is confirmed, and even more status and influence may be accorded to the person. On the other hand, if the leader's proposals prove to be a failure, then the terms of the exchange relationship are likely to be reassessed by the group. The negative effects are greater if failure appears to be due to poor judgment or incompetence rather than to circumstances beyond the leader's control. A more negative evaluation will be made if the leader is perceived to have pursued selfish motives rather than loyally serving the group. Selfish motives and irresponsibility are more likely to be attributed to a leader who willingly deviates from group norms and traditions. Thus, innovation by the leader can be a double-edged sword that cuts both ways. Success resulting from innovation leads to greater credit, but failure leads to greater blame.

The extent of a leader's loss of status and influence following failure depends in part on how serious the failure is to the group. A major disaster results in greater loss of esteem than a minor setback. Loss of status also depends on amount of status the leader had prior to the failure. More is expected of a leader with high status, and such a leader will lose more status if perceived to be responsible for failure. These major propositions of exchange theory are supported by research from laboratory studies (Hollander, 1960, 1961, 1979).

Formal Leaders

The exchange process by which leaders gain influence from repeated demonstration of expertise and loyalty is probably much the same for formal leaders in large organizations as for emergent leaders in small groups. The authority and position power that comes with an administrative position makes formal leaders less dependent on subordinate evaluation of their competence, and even an incompetent leader may stay entrenched in an administrative position for a time, due to a favorable employment contract or a long term of office (if there is no recall provision). Nevertheless, an incompetent leader will lose status and expert power, and demonstrated incompetence may eventually undermine the leader's legitimate authority as well (Evan & Zelditch, 1961). According to social exchange theory, innovation is not only accepted but it is expected of leaders when necessary to deal with serious problems and obstacles. A leader who fails to show initiative and deal decisively with serious problems will lose esteem and influence, just as a leader who proposes actions that are unsuccessful.

Some differences are likely to occur for elected and appointed leaders. The process of election may create higher expectations among followers and a greater feeling of responsibility for the leader's actions. Laboratory research on small groups finds that elected leaders enjoy more initial support from followers than appointed leaders and tend to be more assertive and innovative (Hollander & Julian, 1970, 1978). However, elected leaders appear to be more vulnerable to follower rejection if the group is unsuccessful in attaining its goals.

The foregoing discussion should not imply that the only basis for evaluating leaders is their competence in helping the group to solve its problems and attain its task objectives. Leaders are expected by group members to carry out a variety of leadership functions, such as organizing the work, distributing rewards, providing psychological support, representing the group in dealings with other groups, modifying the group's goals as circumstances change, and defining reality in a way that is consistent with the underlying needs and values of members. Depending on the type of group and situation, these and other leadership functions may be considered by the group in evaluating a leader's success.

Limitations of Social Exchange Theory

Social exchange theories are descriptive rather than prescriptive. They describe how relationships develop and power is gained or lost, but they do not provide specific guidelines for leaders on how to gain power, or how to exercise it effectively. The focus of the social exchange theory is mainly on expert power and authority, and other forms of power do not receive enough attention. More attention is needed to the way reciprocal influence processes affect reward and referent power and to the use of political power and charismatic appeals by leaders. The theory has been tested with small groups in a laboratory setting, but longitudinal research is needed on social exchange processes for leaders in large organizations to verify that the process is the same.

POWER AND ORGANIZATIONAL CHANGE

The source of power for organizational subunits and coalitions, and how the power distribution affects an organization's adaptation to a changing environment is the subject of two major theories. These theories help to explain how attributes of people and attributes of positions combine to determine power, and how different parties gain or lose power over strategic decisions in organizations.

Strategic Contingencies Theory

Hickson et al. (1971) proposed a strategic contingencies theory of intraorganizational power. The theory postulates that power depends upon three characteristics of an organizational subunit: (1) skill in coping with important problems, (2) centrality of function within the workflow, and (3) extent to which the expertise is unique or substitutable.

Social exchange theory describes how individuals gain power after demonstrating effectiveness in coping with critical problems facing a group. At the level of the overall organization there is a comparable process. All organizations must cope with critical contingencies, especially problems in the technological processes used to carry out operations and problems in adapting to unpredictable events in the environment. Success in solving important problems is a source of expert power and increased authority for subunits, just as it is for individuals. The opportunity to demonstrate expertise and gain power from it depends on one's position in the organization, and it is much greater for an individual or subunit that has responsibility for dealing with critical problems. A problem is critical if it is clearly essential for the survival and prosperity of the organization. The importance of a particular type of problem is greater when there is a high degree of interdependence among subunits, and other subunits cannot perform their own functions unless this type of problem is handled effectively. An individual or subunit will gain more power if the critical function it performs cannot be done by someone else or made easier by development of standard procedures. In other words, the more unique and irreplaceable the expertise required to solve critical problems, the more power is gained by the person or subunit possessing this expertise.

Subunits with more power due to their unique expertise in solving critical problems exercise greater influence over the organization's strategic decisions. The most powerful subunit is often able to get one of its members selected as the CEO of the organization, and the representatives of this subunit have more influence in decision groups responsible for strategic planning. Thus, according to the theory, there is a process of natural selection such that the people who are most qualified to help the organization adapt successfully to the environment gain the most influence in strategic decisions, thereby facilitating successful adaptation. If major changes in the environment alter the relative importance of different functions, then the previously dominant subunit will lose power to the subunit responsible for performing the function that has now become most critical. Some support for the theory was found in several studies (Brass, 1984, 1985; Hambrick, 1981; Hinings, Hickson, Pennings, & Schneck, 1974; Hills & Mahoney, 1978; Pfeffer & Moore, 1980; Pfeffer & Salancik, 1974). A limitation of the theory is the failure to explain how a subunit sometimes retains power even after changes in the environment make its function less important and its expertise less critical. This explanation is provided in an extension of the theory by Salancik and Pfeffer (1977a).

Political Power and the Strategic Contingencies Model

Pfeffer and Salancik proposed that political power is the major explanation why some parties are able to maintain power even after their expertise is no longer critical to the organization. Parties that have gained power use it to protect and increase their power in a process called "institutionalization." Ambiguity about the nature of the environment and how it is changing provides an opportunity for top executives to interpret events in a biased manner, to magnify the importance of their expertise, and to justify their policies. Control over distribution of information about how well the organization is performing allows top executives to exaggerate the success of past decisions and cover up mistakes. The power of the dominant coalition can be used to deny others the resources and opportunity necessary to demonstrate their superior expertise, and in extreme cases, to expel potential rivals from the organization. The process of institutionalization is more successful when there is consensus within the dominant coalition about the best way to cope with the environment.

When major changes occur in the environment and power is strongly institutionalized in a dominant coalition that lacks the expertise to develop a strategy appropriate to the new challenges, the organization will become out of phase with the environment. Performance of the organization will suffer, and eventually it will become so ineffective (e.g., unprofitable) that it will fail (e.g., go bankrupt) or be taken over by outsiders who desire its assets. Of course, this process will occur much faster when the organization has strong competition for its products and services, and competitors are able to adapt more rapidly to changes in the environment. Alternatively, as it finally becomes obvious that the strategies of the dominant coalition are unsuccessful, rival factions may be able to take over the leadership of the organization. If the new coalition lacks the expertise to successfully handle the crisis, it is likely to go outside to find a new chief executive rather than selecting one of its own members for this position (Brady & Helmich, 1984; Brown, 1982; Samuelson, Galbraith, & McGuire, 1985; Schwartz & Menon, 1985). The subject of how top leaders make major changes in the objectives and strategies of an organization and build a coalition to support these changes is considered in more detail in later chapters.

SUMMARY

Power is the capacity to influence unilaterally the attitudes and behavior of people in the desired direction. Authority is the right to influence others in specified ways, and it is an important basis for influence in formal organizations. Acceptance depends in part on the perceived legitimacy of the person who occupies the position of authority, which in turn depends on how the person was selected. Scope of authority for a manager is dependent on the influence needed to accomplish role requirements, and there is usually some ambiguity about the appropriate scope. Authority includes a manager's right to reward and punish subordinates, to control vital information, to modify the work environment, and to determine how the work is organized and performed, and each of these is an additional source of position power for managers. Managers vary greatly in the amount of position power they have, and it is usually limited by organizational policies, formal reward systems, legal constraints, and union contracts.

Potential influence derived from the characteristics of the person who occupies a leadership position is called personal power. It is greater for leaders who are perceived to have expertise in doing the work and solving important problems, for leaders who are attractive and likeable, and for leaders who have charismatic qualities or abilities. Personal power is important for influencing peers and superiors as well as subordinates.

Political power processes are used by people to protect and increase their power in an organization. Political processes include forming coalitions with other parties, co-opting opponents and critics, and influencing decision processes by determining decision criteria, selecting top executives, and selecting the membership of key decision bodies.

The process by which leaders gain and lose power over time is described by the social exchange theory. Greater status and power is accorded to someone who demonstrates loyalty to the group and competence in solving task problems and making task decisions. Innovative proposals are a source of increased status and expert power when successful, but they will result in lower status and expert power if failure occurs and is attributed to poor judgment, irresponsibility, or pursuit of self interest.

The manner in which characteristics of the position and the person occupying it combine to determine the relative power of an individual or subunit is described by the strategic contingencies theory. Power depends both on the expertise to solve important problems facing the organization and on the opportunity to demonstrate this expertise by being in the right position at the right time. Power is greater when the position is central in the workflow, the problems immediately disrupt the operations of other subunits if not handled competently, and there is no substitute for the expertise of the person or subunit responsible for the critical function. Extensions of the theory explain how power may be institutionalized through political processes, preventing it from shifting to another subunit when conditions change in the environment and the dominant coalition no longer has the expertise necessary to solve critical problems. When this occurs, the organization may eventually fail, or the dominant coalition may be overthrown abruptly rather than power shifting through the gradual process proposed by the strategic contingencies theory.

REVIEW AND DISCUSSION QUESTIONS

1. What are some different ways of defining power?
2. Why is authority necessary in formal organizations?
3. What sources of power stem primarily from the leader's attributes?
4. What sources of power stem primarily from the situation and leadership position?
5. What political processes are used to maintain and increase power?
6. Briefly describe the social exchange theory.
7. What advantages are gained from examining reciprocal influence processes rather than unilateral influence?
8. What are the practical implications of the social exchange theory for leaders?
9. Explain the strategic contingencies theory of power.
10. How is power related to an organization's adaptation to a changing environment?

3

POWER, INFLUENCE TACTICS, AND LEADER EFFECTIVENESS

The last chapter discussed sources of leader power and revealed some limitations on the use of various types of power in particular situations. The present chapter reviews research on the relationship among power, influence behavior, and leadership effectiveness. The research considers whether effective leaders have more power or different sources of power than ineffective leaders, and whether they exercise power in different ways.

RESEARCH ON POWER AND EFFECTIVENESS

Most research on the consequences of using different types of power relies upon the power taxonomy proposed by French and Raven (1959). The five types of power proposed by French and Raven are defined in Table 3-1. This research literature has been reviewed by Podsakoff and Schriesheim (1985). Of the 18 field studies in their review, most were concerned only with leader power over subordinates, not with lateral or upward power. All of the studies used questionnaires administered to subordinates to measure how much a leader used each type of power. The criterion of successful power usage in most studies was some measure of subordinate satisfaction or performance. Podsakoff and Schriesheim found that expert and referent power were positively correlated with subordinate satisfaction and performance in a majority of the studies. Use of legitimate, reward, and coercive power sometimes resulted in lower satisfaction and performance, and other times did not affect these criteria. The results suggest that effective leaders rely more than ineffective leaders on expert and referent power to influence subordinates.

TABLE 3–1   French and Raven Power Taxonomy

Reward power	The target person complies in order to obtain rewards he or she believes are controlled by the agent.
Coercive power	The target person complies in order to avoid punishments he or she believes are controlled by the agent.
Legitimate power	The target person complies because he or she believes the agent has the right to make the request and the target person has the obligation to comply.
Expert power	The target person complies because he or she believes that the agent has special knowledge about the best way to do something.
Referent power	The target person complies because he or she admires or identifies with the agent and wants to gain the agent's approval.

Limitations of Power Research

Unfortunately, as noted by Podsakoff and Schriesheim, the methodological limitations of the power studies raise serious doubts about the accuracy of the findings. The most serious limitation is the lack of demonstrated validity for the measures of leader power. Responses of subordinates on power questionnaires are likely to be biased by attributions and social desirability. Most of the power studies used single-item scales and asked respondents to rank or rate the importance of different types of power as a reason for compliance with leader requests. On this type of questionnaire, subordinates who are satisfied are likely to attribute more referent power to their leader than subordinates who are dissatisfied. Subordinates with high performance are likely to attribute more expert power to their leader than subordinates with low performance.

Another limitation of the power research is failure to deal with likely confounding among different sources of power. French and Raven

(1959) proposed that different types of power are likely to be interrelated in complex ways. For example, leaders with considerable authority are likely to have more reward and coercive power, and use of these forms of power affects a leader's referent power. The power studies did not attempt to separate the effects of different types of power, nor did they examine the interactions among different types of power.

Added to the problem of objective interdependency among different forms of power is the subjective confounding due to attributions and social desirability. A leader with substantial reward and punishment power is more likely to obtain subordinate compliance with requests and orders, even when the leader makes no explicit promises or threats (Kahn et al., 1964). However, it is more acceptable for subordinates to attribute their compliance to the leader's expert or referent power than to acknowledge they have been influenced by desire for material rewards or fear of punishment. Thus, the importance of rewards and coercion would tend to be underestimated, especially for subordinates who are more satisfied and productive.

Another reason why the power studies probably underestimate the importance of legitimate, reward, and coercive power is the emphasis on satisfaction and performance as criteria of leader effectiveness rather than immediate outcomes such as changes in subordinate attitudes and behavior. An effort was made to measure the latter criteria in only two studies. Warren (1968) found expert, referent, and legitimate power were correlated positively with attitudinal commitment by subordinates, whereas reward and coercive power were correlated with behavioral compliance. In a study by Thambain and Gemmill (1974), the primary reason given for compliance was the leader's legitimate power, and reward power was also an important reason for compliance, even though neither type of power was associated with commitment. For many legitimate but routine requests or orders, compliance is a sufficient outcome, and use of legitimate power backed up by some reward and coercive power is likely to produce this outcome.

Results of other leadership research on rewards and punishments support the conclusion that the power studies are biased. In a review of this research, Podsakoff, Todor, Grover, & Huber (1984) concluded that positive reward behavior contingent upon subordinate performance leads to higher subordinate satisfaction and performance. Some leader behavior research also suggests that contingent punishment can have a positive effect on subordinate performance when used in combination with rewards (Arvey & Ivancevich, 1980; Podsakoff, Todor, & Skov, 1982).

Further research on effects of power use may confirm the finding that effective leaders emphasize expert and referent power, but the research is unlikely to find that other types of power are unimportant, or that effective leaders do not use them. A more likely conclusion is that effective leaders use a mix of different types of power (Kotter, 1982).

A Model of Power and Influence

Power alone is not sufficient to explain a leader's effectiveness in influencing people. A leader's influence behavior and skills must be considered also if we want to make progress in understanding how leaders influence people. Effective leaders have the skill to recognize when different types of influence attempts are appropriate, and the skill to carry out influence attempts in an effective manner. Leader power does not directly affect a target person's attitudes and behavior. Instead, personal and position power are moderating variables that strengthen the effects of influence attempts by the leader. A model of the joint effects of leader power, influence behavior, and skill is shown in Figure 3-1.

In the proposed model, a leader's influence behavior directly affects intervening variables such as the target person's attitudes and behavior, which can be described in terms of commitment, compliance, or resistance. The effect of the leader's influence behavior on the intervening variables is moderated by the leader's position power and personal power, both of which tend to enhance the effectiveness of an influence attempt. The intervening variables affect end-result variables such as group success or failure and subordinate satisfaction. Feedback effects of group success increase the leader's personal power, especially expert power, whereas failure decreases it. This feature of the model incorporates the dynamic aspect of power acquisition described by the social exchange theory in Chapter 2.

The leader's personal power also depends on the leader's skills. Expert power depends on technical expertise, and referent power depends on interpersonal skills. Leader skills directly affect leader influence behavior in two ways. First, skills determine whether a leader is able to diagnose the situation correctly and select an appropriate influence tactic. Second, relevant skills determine whether the influence attempt is executed in a competent or incompetent manner.

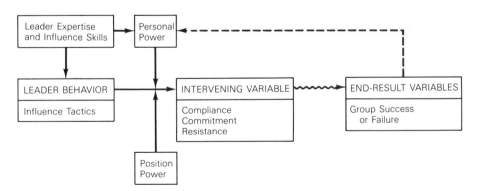

FIGURE 3–1   Effects of Leader Power and Influence Behavior

The following example illustrates how the model applies to an influence attempt involving the leader's use of rational persuasion. Perceived expertise (expert power) and exclusive access to information (position power) are important moderators of influence attempts involving appeals to reason; both types of power increase the effectiveness of a persuasive appeal. Persuasive skill and access to relevant information enable the leader to make more convincing arguments, thereby increasing the effectiveness of a logical appeal. The model allows for the possibility that logical arguments alone can sometimes influence people, even if a leader is not perceived to have superior expertise. The model also allows for the possibility that a leader perceived to be an expert can sometimes influence people even with weak arguments. Of course, success is much more likely when the leader is an acknowledged expert, and also has the skills necessary to present persuasive, logical arguments that make full use of his or her expertise and information.

RESEARCH ON INFLUENCE TACTICS

In recent years, the power research has begun to examine the specific types of behavior used to exercise influence, rather than focusing exclusively upon the source of the influence. Several studies have been conducted on this question (Kipnis, Schmidt, & Wilkinson, 1980; Mowday, 1978; Porter, Allen, & Angle, 1981; Schilit & Locke, 1982). This research takes a first step toward the eventual merging of the power and behavior approaches, a step that is long overdue.

In the study by Kipnis et al. (1980), people from different organizations were asked to describe an incident in which they succeeded in getting a superior, subordinate, or coworker to do what they wanted. These critical incidents were used to develop categories of influence behavior. In the research by Mowday (1978) and Schilit and Locke (1982), only upward influence attempts were studied. The influence categories developed in this research vary somewhat, depending on whether the focus of the research was on downward, upward, or lateral influence processes. However, five categories of interpersonal influence tactics appear to be common to all of the studies, and are relevant regardless of whether the target person is a subordinate, superior, or peer. These five influence categories correspond approximately to the five bases of power (i.e., expert, reward, legitimate, coercive, and referent) proposed by French and Raven (1959):

Rational persuasion: Use of logical arguments and factual evidence by the agent to persuade the target person that a proposal or request is viable and likely to result in the attainment of desirable task outcomes.

Exchange tactics: A request or proposal that includes an explicit or implicit promise by the agent to reward the target person.

Legitimate requests: A request that is based on the agent's authority or role requirements and is consistent with organizational rules, policies, and practices.

Pressure tactics: Persistent demands, and explicit or implicit threats by the agent that failure to comply will result in unpleasant consequences mediated by the agent for the target person.

Personal appeals: Use of ingratiation and personal friendship as the basis for a request for assistance.

The research on influence tactics also found evidence of some indirect tactics such as forming coalitions, manipulating the situation, and filtering information to bias a decision.

The descriptive research by Kipnis et al. (1980) found differences in patterns of influence behavior, depending upon the relative status of the agent and target. Some pressure tactics (assertiveness and sanctions) were used more often for influencing subordinates than for influencing superiors or peers. Another pressure tactic (appealing to someone's superior) was used more often for influencing superiors and peers than for influencing subordinates. These findings are consistent with the fact that managers usually have more coercive power over subordinates than over peers or superiors. Rational persuasion was used more often for influencing superiors than for influencing peers or subordinates. Ingratiation and exchange tactics were used more often for influencing coworkers and subordinates than for influencing superiors. The choice of influence tactics also depended on the purpose of the influence attempt, but the results were not consistent across research methods, and more research is needed on this question.

Only one study has investigated the relationship of influence behavior to outcomes. Schilit and Locke (1982) asked respondents to describe both a successful and an unsuccessful example of an upward influence attempt. In one study, subordinates described attempts to influence their superiors; in another study, superiors described influence attempts made by their own subordinates. The respondents were also asked to explain the reason why the influence attempt was successful or unsuccessful. From the perspective of subordinates, an influence attempt was more likely to be successful if the subordinate was competent (expert power), the influence attempt was made in a skillful manner, the objective of the influence attempt was acceptable to the superior, there was an absence of organizational constraints on carrying out the request (e.g., budgetary restrictions), and the superior was open-minded. From the perspective of the superior, success was more likely if there was a good interpersonal relationship (referent power), there was an absence of organizational constraints, and the superior was open-minded. The findings are generally consistent with the model of power and influence proposed earlier, although the discrepancy in results from subordinates and superiors indicates a need for additional research.

The research on influence behavior is promising, but initial efforts to identify different types of influence behavior have been too limited in scope. Some important forms of influence (e.g., consultation and inspirational appeals) are not adequately represented, either among the power categories in the French and Raven typology or the influence categories proposed by Kipnis and others. Participative tactics such as consultation and co-optation have been the subject of extensive research over the past quarter century, and this type of influence process is examined in Chapter 5. Inspirational appeals by charismatic leaders are examined in Chapter 10.

VERTICAL DYAD LINKAGE THEORY

Another line of research that has begun to bridge the gap between the power and behavior approaches is the work on role-making processes between a leader and individual subordinates. A version of social exchange theory called vertical dyad linkage theory, or leader-member exchange theory (LMX), describes how leaders use their position power to develop different exchange relationships with different subordinates (Dansereau, Graen, & Haga, 1975; Graen & Cashman, 1975). The exchange relationships developed with subordinates have implications for leadership effectiveness.

The term *vertical dyad* refers to the relationship between a leader and one individual subordinate. The basic premise of the theory is that leaders usually establish a special relationship with a small number of trusted subordinates (the *in-group*) who function as assistants, lieutenants, or advisors. The exchange relationship established with the remaining subordinates (the *out-group*) is substantially different. According to the theory, the in-group or out-group relationship is established early in the history of the dyadic interaction between leader and subordinate. Graen and Cashman (1975) suggested that selection is made on the basis of personal compatibility and subordinate competence and dependability. Over time, the dyadic exchanges with in-group subordinates follow a different developmental sequence than that for out-group subordinates.

In the exchange relationship with out-group subordinates, there is a relatively low level of mutual influence. The primary source of leader influence is legitimate authority in combination with coercive power and a limited degree of reward power. To satisfy the terms of the exchange relationship, out-group subordinates need only comply with formal role requirements (e.g., duties, rules, standard procedures) and legitimate directions from the leader. As long as such compliance is forthcoming, the subordinate receives the standard benefits—primarily compensation—for the job.

The basis for establishing a deeper exchange relationship with in-group subordinates is the leader's control over outcomes that are desirable to the subordinates. These outcomes include such things as assignment to interesting and desirable tasks, delegation of greater responsibility and authority, sharing of "inside information," participation in making some of the leader's decisions, tangible rewards such as a pay increase, special benefits (e.g., better work schedule, bigger office), personal support and approval, and facilitation of the subordinate's career (e.g., recommending a promotion, giving developmental assignments with high visibility). In return for greater status, influence, and benefits, in-group subordinates have certain obligations and costs beyond those required of out-group subordinates. In-group subordinates are expected to work harder, to be more committed to task objectives, to be loyal to the leader, and to share administrative duties. The development of in-group relationships occurs gradually over a period of time, through reciprocal reinforcement of leader and member behavior as the exchange cycle is repeated over and over again. Unless the cycle is broken, the relationship is likely to develop to a point where there is a high degree of mutual dependence, loyalty, and support.

The benefits to the leader from an in-group relationship are evident. Subordinate commitment is important when the group has tasks that require considerable initiative and effort on the part of some group members to be carried out successfully. The assistance of committed subordinates can be invaluable to a manager who lacks the time and energy to carry out all of the administrative duties for which he or she is responsible. However, the special relationship with in-group subordinates creates certain obligations and constraints for the leader. In order to maintain the relationship, the leader must continue to provide attention to in-group subordinates, remain responsive to their needs and feelings, and rely more on time-consuming influence methods such as persuasion and consultation. The leader cannot resort to coercion or heavy-handed use of authority without endangering the special relationship.

In research by Cashman, Dansereau, Graen, and Haga (1976), the vertical dyad linkage theory was extended to include a leader's upward exchange relationship as well as the downward relationships with subordinates. These researchers studied vertical dyads at two levels in the authority, in contrast to the initial research on dyads at only one level. The results indicated that a manager's capacity to develop special in-group relationships with subordinates depended in part on the manager's upward dyadic relationship. A manager who had a favorable in-group relationship with his or her boss was better able to establish in-group relationships with subordinates. A favorable upward relationship enabled a manager to obtain more benefits for subordinates and facilitate their performance by obtaining necessary resources, cutting red tape, and gaining approval of changes they desired. The effects of a manager's upward relationship were felt by subordinates regardless of their own relationship with the manager. Managers with a favorable upward relationship were described by subordinates as having more technical skill, providing more outside information, permitting more participation in decision making, allowing more subordinate autonomy, and providing more support and consideration. The results from this study point out a major situational constraint on a leader's ability to establish special exchange relationships with subordinates. If the leader has little to offer in the way of extra benefits and opportunities, then there is little reason for subordinates to incur the extra obligations of a special exchange relationship.

Vertical Dyads and Leadership Effectiveness

Vertical-dyad linkage (or LMX) theory has a number of conceptual weaknesses, and the supporting research has failed to address some important issues (Dienesh & Liden, 1986; Vecchio & Gobdel, 1984). The theory assumes leader-member relations develop through a role-making process, but there has been little research on the way this process occurs. A few studies have tried to identify factors predicting who will be selected as an in-group member (Duchon, Green, & Taber, 1986; Kim & Organ, 1982), but we still know little about how the process occurs. Selection may be influenced by several attributes of the subordinate that are not necessarily inter-correlated, such as task competence, loyalty, shared values, and friendliness. The relative importance of these subordinate characteristics for selecting in-group members probably varies from leader to leader. The selection is probably influenced by characteristics of the leader (e.g., self-confidence, needs, values, skills) as well as by subordinate characteristics. It is not clear how much influence a new subordinate has on the role-making process, but some subordinates will be proactive about developing a favorable relationship rather than passively accepting whatever the leader decides to do. Dienesh and Liden suggest that progress in the development of the theory will probably require incorporation of attributional processes that explain how leaders interpret member actions and members interpret leader actions. In their article they present a tentative extension of the theory in this direction.

The theory fails to address directly the implications of in-group formation for leader effectiveness, and the research has not investigated this question. Some studies suggest that in-group subordinates may have better performance than out-group subordinates, but the implications for overall group performance have not been evaluated. For example, it is quite plausible that leaders who develop sharply differentiated in-groups and out-groups are less effective than leaders who attempt to develop deeper relationships with all of their subordinates. Indirect support for this proposition comes from a study by Scandura and Graen (1984), in which leaders were given training in how to develop special exchange relationships with subordinates. More improvement in performance occurred for subordinates who had been in the out-group than for subordinates who already had a special exchange relationship before training.

One danger of having a differentiated in-group and out-group is the development of hostility between the two groups; this hostility is likely to undermine necessary cooperation and teamwork. Another danger is that the minimal level of compliance expected of out-group subordinates by the leader may fail to occur if out-group subordinates perceive the leader's "favorites" to be getting more benefits than deserved, resulting in feelings of alienation, apathy, and hostility.

The choice for a leader is not merely between treating all subordinates exactly the same (which no theorist advocates) and creating a sharply differentiated in-group and out-group. Rather, there are a variety of intermediate possibilities. It is important to recognize that some aspects of a special exchange relationship, such as greater delegation of responsibility and sharing of administrative duties, may occur for a few subordinates without precluding the leader from developing a relationship of trust, supportiveness, mutual respect, and mutual loyalty with other subordinates. Although not every subordinate may desire increased responsibility and advancement, it is important for each subordinate to perceive that he or she has an equal opportunity and is not arbitrarily relegated to that status of a "second-class citizen" in the work unit. It is especially important in view of the tendency for in-group subordinates to be promoted much faster and further in the organization (Wakabayashi & Graen, 1984).

GUIDELINES FOR
INFLUENCING SUBORDINATES

Most of the power research has been too superficial to provide clear and unequivocal guidelines for leaders on the best way to exercise power with subordinates. Nevertheless, by drawing upon a diverse literature in the social sciences that includes research on power, leader behavior, motivation, communication, counseling, supervision, and conflict resolution, it is possible to develop some tentative guidelines for leaders. These guidelines vary in degree of empirical support; some are fairly well supported, while others are mostly speculative. However, for managers faced with the immediate necessity of influencing others, the guidelines provide the best advice possible given the relatively primitive state of the research literature on power and influence. The guidelines are consistent with the model proposed earlier in the chapter, and they utilize terminology from French and Raven's power typology as well as the taxonomy of five influence behaviors described in the preceding section (see Table 3-2). The guidelines are usually phrased in terms of leader influence attempts with subordinates to simplify the presentation, but most of the principles underlying the guidelines apply equally well to influence attempts with peers, and many apply to influence attempts with superiors.

TABLE 3–2   Sources of Leader Influence over Subordinates and Likely Outcomes

SOURCE OF LEADER INFLUENCE	TYPE OF OUTCOME		
	COMMITMENT	COMPLIANCE	RESISTANCE
Referent Power	Likely* If request is believed to be important to leader	Possible If request is perceived to be unimportant to leader	Possible If request is for something that will bring harm to leader
Expert Power	Likely* If request is persuasive and subordinates share leader's task goals	Possible If request is persuasive but subordinates are apathetic about task goals	Possible If leader is arrogant and insulting, or subordinates oppose task goals
Legitimate Power	Possible If request is polite and very appropriate	Likely* If request or order is seen as legitimate	Possible If arrogant demands are made or request does not appear proper
Reward Power	Possible If used in a subtle, very personal way	Likely* If used in a mechanical, impersonal way	Possible If used in a manipulative, arrogant way
Coercive Power	Very Unlikely	Possible If used in a helpful, nonpunitive way	Likely* If used in a hostile or manipulative way

* Indicates most common outcome.

Legitimate Power

Authority is exercised by making a "legitimate request," either orally or in written form. A polite request ("please compute the new sales figures") is more effective than an arrogant demand ("I don't care if you like it, just do it"). A polite request does not emphasize a status gap or imply subordinate dependence on the leader. Use of a polite request is especially important for people who are likely to be sensitive about status differentials and authority relationships, such as a subordinate who is older than the leader or a peer who is part of the leader's project team but not a direct subordinate.

Making a polite request does not imply that the leader should plead or appear apologetic about the request. To do so risks the impression that the request is not worthy or legitimate, and it may give the impression that compliance is not really expected (Sayles, 1979). A legitimate request should be made in a firm, confident manner. In an emergency situation, it is more important to be assertive than polite. A direct order by a leader in the "command tone of voice" is sometimes necessary to shock subordinates into immediate action in an emergency. In this type of situation, subordinates associate confident, firm direction with expert knowledge as well as authority (Mulder, Ritsema Van Eck, & de Jong, 1970). To express doubts or appear confused risks the loss of influence over subordinates.

Compliance with a request is more likely if it is perceived to be within the leader's scope of authority. An illegitimate request is likely to be ignored or otherwise resisted, especially if the requested activity is tedious, dangerous, or unpleasant. The issue of legitimacy is likely to be raised for unusual requests and for requests made to people over whom the leader has no direct authority. If there is any doubt about the leader's right to make a request, its legitimacy should be verified by the leader. One way to verify legitimacy is to refer to documentation, such as written rules, policies, charters, contracts, plans, or job descriptions. If the authority has been delegated by higher-level management or is the result of a reorganization, the leader can refer the target person to superiors for verification that the request is proper.

Legitimate requests should be made in a clear, concise manner, using language that the target person can easily understand. If the message is complex, it is advisable to communicate it in writing as well as orally. Oral requests should be made directly rather than being communicated through an intermediary such as a coworker of the target person. If one of a leader's subordinates is told to do something unusual or unpleasant by another subordinate of equal or higher status, there may be resentment or doubt that the request really came from the leader. Use of intermediaries to convey oral requests also risks the chance of distortion in the message, and the agent gives up the opportunity to observe the target person to assess whether the message was understood and accepted.

It is important for leaders to avoid instances of outright refusal by subordinates to carry out a legitimate order or request. The authority of the leader is undermined in the eyes of other subordinates and the likelihood of future disobedience is increased. Sometimes a subordinate will delay in complying with an unusual or unpleasant request to test whether the leader is really serious about it. If the leader does not follow up the initial request to check on compliance, the subordinate is likely to conclude that the request may be ignored. The leader should insist on compliance, and if resistance continues, Sayles (1979) recommends talking with the person to discover the reasons for it. Understanding the person's concerns, fears, or objections will help the leader determine whether it is appropriate to use other forms of influence such as rational persuasion, to justify the need for the request, or joint problem solving (consultation) to seek a mutually acceptable solution dealing with the person's concerns. Coercive pressure for compliance should be used only as a last resort.

Reward Power

Reward power is most commonly used by making an explicit or implicit promise to give a person something under the leader's control for carrying out a request or performing a task. For example, the person may be promised a pay increase, promotion, better assignments, special privileges, more time off, and so on. In the case of peers, the rewards are likely to be less tangible, such as the promise of future assistance and support on something important to the person, or the promise to put in a good word with the person's boss.

Compliance is most likely if the reward is something valued by the target person, and the leader is perceived as a credible source of the reward. Thus, leaders should try to discover what rewards are valued by the people they need to influence, and credibility should not be risked by making unrealistic promises, or failing to deliver on a promise after compliance occurs.

Even when the conditions are favorable for using rewards, they are more likely to result in compliance rather than commitment. A promised reward is unlikely to motivate someone to put forth extra effort beyond what is required to complete the task. The person may be tempted to take shortcuts and neglect aspects of the task not included in the specification of performance criteria, or aspects not easily monitored by the leader.

Rewards may result in resistance rather than compliance if used in a very manipulative manner. The leader's power to give or withhold rewards may cause resentment among subordinates who dislike being dependent upon the whims of a powerful authority figure, or who believe that the leader is manipulating them to his or her own advantage. Resistance may occur also if the person is asked to do something improper or unethical, even though the reward is attractive. Many people are unwilling to be manipulated by what appears to be a bribe to do something improper.

When a leader relies frequently on incentives as a source of influence, people may come to perceive their relationship to the leader in purely economic terms. A reward is expected every time the leader asks them to do something new or unusual. It is more satisfying for both parties to view their relationship in terms of mutual loyalty and friendship.

Rather than using rewards as incentives, a leader should use rewards in a more symbolic manner to recognize accomplishments and express personal appreciation for special contributions or exceptional effort. To use rewards in this way, it is necessary to tie them to performance and accomplishments, but without using explicit, mechanical incentives. Recent research (Peters & Waterman, 1982) suggests that effective managers provide sincere, public recognition to subordinates in the form of awards, ceremonies, and special symbols. Significant rewards accompany the recognition, but the focus is on the person's contributions and achievements, not on the reward. Used in this way, reward power can be a source of increased referent power over time (French & Raven, 1959).

Expert Power

Expert power is commonly exercised in the form of rational persuasion. The leader presents logical arguments and supporting evidence for a particular proposal, plan, or request. Success depends on the leader's credibility and persuasive communication skills in addition to technical knowledge and logical or analytical ability. Proposals or requests should be made in a confident manner, and the leader should avoid making contradictory statements or vacillating between inconsistent positions.

Expert power is based on a knowledge differential between the leader and the target person, but the very existence of such a differential can cause problems if the leader is not careful about the way expert power is exercised. A leader who acts superior and flaunts superior expertise may elicit resistance, even if the target person otherwise agrees with the position advocated by the leader. In the process of presenting rational arguments, some leaders lecture in an arrogant, condescending manner and convey the impression that the listener is ignorant. In their efforts to sell proposals, some leaders fire a steady stream of arguments, rudely interrupt any attempted replies, and dismiss any objections or concerns without serious consideration. Even when the leader is acknowledged to have more expertise, the target person usually has some relevant information, ideas, and concerns that should be heard and considered by the leader.

Rational persuasion is most effective when the target person shares the leader's objectives but is not initially convinced that the leader's proposals are the best way to achieve the objectives. In this situation, the influence attempt may result in compliance or even commitment, depending on the perceived expertise of the leader and the quality of the leader's persuasive presentation. However, if the target person is opposed to the leader's objectives, or it is obvious that the leader's proposal would entail unacceptable costs to the target person, then rational persuasion alone is unlikely to result either in attitude change or behavioral compliance.

Referent Power

The most common way to exercise referent power is merely to ask the target person with whom one has a friendship to do something. Sometimes is it necessary to invoke the salience of the relationship by making a personal appeal. One variation of a personal appeal is to say you are depending on the person's support. It is useful to indicate the importance of the request because a request that is important to the leader is more likely to result in subordinate commitment. A request based solely on referent power should be commensurate with the extent of the target person's loyalty and friendship toward the leader. Some things are simply too much to ask, and when a leader asks for too great a sacrifice, the request may irritate the target person and undermine the relationship. For the same reason, personal requests should not be used too often. In terms of social exchange theory, a leader can use up credits faster than they are replenished.

Another way to exercise referent power is through *role modeling*. Since subordinates tend to imitate a leader with whom they identify, the leader should set an example of appropriate role behavior by performing duties in a responsible and dedicated manner and avoiding improper behavior.

Coercion

It is best to avoid using coercion except when absolutely necessary, because it is difficult to use and it is likely to result in undesirable side effects such as anxiety and resentment. In work organizations, the most appropriate use of coercion is to deter behavior that is very detrimental to the organization, such as illegal activities, theft, violation of safety rules, reckless behavior that endangers others, and direct disobedience of legitimate requests. Coercion is unlikely to result in commitment but when used skillfully, there is a reasonably good chance that it will result in compliance rather than resistance. Use of coercion with subordinates is usually discussed in the context of maintaining discipline. A number of writers have proposed guidelines for "positive discipline" (Arvey & Ivancevich, 1980; Haimann & Hilgert, 1977; Preston & Zimmerer, 1978; Schoen & Durand, 1979; White, 1975). A brief summary of these guidelines is as follows:

1. Explain rules and requirements, and ensure that subordinates understand the serious consequences of violations.

2. Respond to any infractions promptly and consistently without showing any favoritism to ensure that subordinates understand what is expected, and to avoid the appearance of being arbitrary and impulsive.

3. Investigate to get the facts before using reprimands or punishment, and avoid jumping to conclusions or making hasty reprimands.

4. Except for the most serious infractions, provide sufficient oral and written warnings before resorting to punishment.

5. Administer warnings and reprimands in private to avoid public embarrassment and the possibility that a subordinate will act defiant to show coworkers he or she is not intimidated by the leader.

6. Stay calm and avoid the appearance of hostility or personal rejection of the subordinate.

7. Express a sincere desire to help the subordinate comply with role expectations and thereby avoid punishment.

8. Invite the subordinate to participate in suggesting ways to deal with a performance deficiency, and seek agreement on a concrete plan to correct the problem.

9. Maintain credibility by administering punishment if noncompliance continues after threats and warnings have been made.

10. Use punishments that are legitimate, fair, and commensurate with the seriousness of the infraction.

HOW MUCH POWER
SHOULD LEADERS HAVE?

It is obvious that leaders need some power and influence to be effective, but it does not follow that more power is always better. The amount of overall power that is necessary for effective leadership and the mix of different types of power are questions that research has only begun to answer. Clearly the amount of necessary power will depend upon what the leader needs to accomplish and on the leader's skill in using what power is available. Less power is needed by a leader who has the skills to use power effectively and who recognizes the importance of concentrating on essential objectives. Bauer (1968, p. 17) explains the need for careful application of power so as to maintain a favorable relationship with subordinates, peers, and superiors:

> In any ongoing institution, the ability to get important things done is dependent upon maintaining a reservoir of goodwill. The person who fights every issue as though it were vital exhausts his resources, including, most especially, the patience and goodwill of those on whom he has to depend to get things done. Therefore, it should be considered neither surprising nor immoral that, when an issue is of low salience, the sensible individual may use it to build goodwill for the future, or pay off past obligations, by going along with some individual for whom the issue is of high salience.

Some leadership situations require more power than others for the leader to be effective. More influence is necessary in an organization where major changes in member attitudes and behavior are required than in an organization that can continue to survive and prosper by doing things the same way as before. More power is necessary if there is strong initial opposition to the leader's proposals for change. Less power is necessary if there are strong potential allies with whom a leader can form a coalition to accomplish mutual objectives. It is especially difficult for a leader who recognizes that the organization will face a major crisis in coming years, a crisis that can be overcome only if preparations are begun immediately, but the evidence of the coming crisis is not yet sufficiently strong to persuade members to act now. A similar situation is the case where a leader desires to make changes that will require short-term sacrifices and a long period of implementation before the benefits are realized, but there is opposition by factions with a short-term perspective. In difficult situations such as these, leader effectiveness will require either sufficient expert and referent power to persuade people that the leader's proposals are necessary and desirable, or sufficient position and political power to overcome the opposition and buy time to demonstrate that the changes are necessary and effective. These are situations where charismatic or transformational leadership is especially relevant, and this subject is discussed further in Chapter 10.

Questions about the optimal mix of power for leaders are complicated by the interdependence among different sources of power. The distinction between position and personal power is sometimes convenient, but it should not be overdrawn. Position power is important, not only as a source of influence but also because it can be used to enhance a leader's personal power. Control over information complements expert power based on technical skill by giving the leader an advantage in solving important problems and by enabling a leader to cover up mistakes and exaggerate accomplishments. Reward power facilitates development of a deeper exchange relationship with subordinates, and when used skillfully, it enhances a leader's referent power. The authority to make decisions and the upward influence to get them approved enables a leader to demonstrate expertise in problem solving, and it also facilitates development of deeper exchange relationships with subordinates. Some coercive power is necessary to buttress legitimate and expert power when a leader needs to influence compliance with rules and procedures that are unpopular but necessary to do the work and avoid serious accidents. Likewise, coercive power is needed by a leader to restrain or banish rebels and criminals who would otherwise disrupt operations, steal resources, harm other members, and cause the leader to appear weak and incompetent.

However, too much position power may be as detrimental as too little. Leaders with a great deal of position power may be tempted to rely on it instead of making an effort to develop and use expert and referent power. The notion that power corrupts is especially relevant for position power. It has been all too common throughout history for political leaders with strong position power to use it to dominate and exploit subordinates. An experiment by Kipnis (1972) found that leaders with greater reward power perceived subordinates as objects of manipulation, devalued the worth of subordinates, attributed subordinate efforts to their own power use, maintained more social distance from subordinates, and used rewards more often to influence subordinates. Although only a laboratory experiment with students, the research clearly points out the dangers of excessive position power. In general, it is probably desirable for a leader to have a moderate amount of position power, although the optimal amount will vary somewhat depending on the situation.

What about personal power? Are there dangers as well from having a great deal of expert and referent power? Personal power is less susceptible to misuse, since it erodes quickly when a leader acts contrary to the interests of followers. Nevertheless, the potential for corruption remains. It is quite possible that a leader with extensive expert power or charismatic appeal will be tempted to act in ways that will eventually lead to failure (Zaleznik, 1970). McClelland (1975, p. 266) describes this phenomenon:

> How much initiative he should take, how persuasive he should attempt to be, and at what point his clear enthusiasm for certain goals becomes personal authoritarian insistence that those goals are the right ones whatever the members of the group may think, are all questions calculated to frustrate the well-intentioned leader. If he takes no initiative, he is no leader. If he takes too much, he becomes a dictator—particularly if he tries to curtail the process by which members of the group participate in shaping group goals. There is a particular danger for the man who has demonstrated his competence in shaping group goals and in inspiring group members to pursue them. In time both he and they may assume that he knows best, and he may almost imperceptibly change from a democratic to an authoritarian leader.

Studies of the amount of influence exercised by people at different levels in the authority hierarchy of an organization reveal that the most effective organizations have a high degree of reciprocal influence (Bachman, Smith, & Slesinger, 1966; Smith & Tannenbaum, 1963). The results suggest that leaders in effective organizations create relationships in which they have strong influence over subordinates, but are also receptive to influence from them.

One of the best ways to ensure that leaders remain responsive to follower needs is to provide formal mechanisms to promote reciprocal influence and discourage arbitrary actions by the leader. Rules and policies can be enacted to regulate the exercise of position power, especially reward and coercive power. Grievance and appeals procedures can be enacted and independent review boards established to protect subordinates against misuse of power by leaders. Bylaws, charter provisions, and official policies can be drafted to require leaders to consult with subordinates and obtain their approval on specified types of decisions. Regular attitude surveys can be conducted to measure subordinate satisfaction with their leaders. In types of organizations where it is appropriate, periodic elections or votes of confidence can be held to determine if the leader should continue in office. Recall procedures can be established to remove incompetent leaders in an orderly manner. Finally, leaders themselves can facilitate reciprocal influence by encouraging subordinates to participate in making important decisions.

SUMMARY

Research on the use of different forms of power by leaders suggests that effective leaders rely more on personal power than on position power. Nevertheless, position power is still important, and it interacts in complex ways with personal power to determine a leader's influence on subordinates. The potential to use position power for influence attempts with peers or superiors is much more limited, and here personal power is clearly the predominant source of influence.

Descriptive research on influence behavior usually deals with influence tactics such as rational persuasion, exchange tactics, pressure tactics, legitimate requests, and personal appeals (including ingratiation). The research finds that the selection of influence tactics varies with the relative status of the target person and the purpose of the influence attempt.

The success of an influence attempt depends greatly on the manner in which power is exercised. Effective leaders are likely to use power in a subtle, careful fashion that minimizes status differentials and avoids threats to the target person's self esteem. In contrast, leaders who exercise power in an arrogant, manipulative, domineering manner are likely to engender resistance.

The vertical dyad linkage theory describes how leaders develop different exchange relationships over time with different subordinates. Some subordinates are given greater influence, autonomy, and benefits in return for greater loyalty, commitment, and assistance in performing administrative duties. A leader's upward influence is an important determinant of the potential for establishing a special exchange relationship with subordinates. The implications for leadership effectiveness are still not clear.

The amount of position power necessary for leader effectiveness depends on the nature of the organization, task, and subordinates. A leader with extensive reward and coercive power is tempted to rely on them excessively, instead of using referent and expert power. This path leads to resentment and rebellion. On the other hand, a leader lacking sufficient position power to reward competent subordinates, make necessary changes, and punish chronic troublemakers will find it difficult to develop a high-performing group.

REVIEW AND DISCUSSION QUESTIONS

1. Describe and evaluate the French and Raven power taxonomy.
2. How is downward power related to upward and lateral power?
3. Briefly explain the vertical dyad linkage (or LMX) theory.
4. What pattern of power usage is most effective?
5. What was learned from descriptive research on influence tactics?
6. What should leaders do to acquire referent power and use it effectively?
7. What should leaders do to acquire expert power and use it effectively?
8. What are some guidelines for exercising authority?
9. What are some guidelines for exercising reward power?
10. Do you agree or disagree with the proposition that leaders should never use coercion and punishment? Explain your position.
11. Does the concept of power add anything beyond what is already known from studying influence behavior?

4

THE NATURE
OF
MANAGERIAL WORK

The subject of leadership behavior was introduced in the preceding chapter with the discussion about influence tactics. The present chapter is the first of several devoted exclusively to behavioral research on managers and other leaders. This chapter reviews descriptive research on typical patterns of managerial activities. Other aspects of leader and manager behavior are discussed in Chapters 5–8.

ACTIVITY PATTERNS
IN MANAGERIAL WORK

For the past quarter century, researchers have used descriptive methods such as direct observation, diaries, and interviews to discover what managers do and how they spend their time. The amount of this descriptive research has increased in recent years, and a clear picture is beginning to emerge about the nature of managerial work for most people in formal leadership positions. Reviews of this research have been published by Mintzberg (1973), and McCall, Morrison, and Hannan (1978). Recent studies include those by Gabarro (1985), Isenberg (1984), Kanter (1983), Kaplan (1984, 1986), and Kotter (1982). This section of the chapter reviews the major findings about the nature of managerial work.

Pace of Work Is Hectic and Unrelenting

The typical manager works long hours. An executive's workweek typically lasts at least 50 hours, and many managers take work home with them. In part, this workload can be traced to the preferences of people in managerial positions. Having trained their minds to search for and analyze new information continually, most managers do this automatically and find it difficult to forget about their jobs when at home or on vacation. During the typical manager's day, there is seldom a break in the workload. Managers receive almost continuous requests for information, assistance, direction, and authorization from a large number of people, such as subordinates, peers, superiors, and people outside of the organization. Nothing could be further from the truth than the conception of managers as people who carefully plan and orchestrate events and then sit around in their office waiting for an occasional exception to normal operations that requires their attention, or for the opportunity to perform a simplistic "1-minute management" episode that will magically guarantee success.

Content of Work Is Varied and Fragmented

Managers typically engage in a large number of discrete activities each day, and the average number of activities appears to increase at lower levels of management. The activities are usually very brief in duration. Mintzberg's (1973, p. 33) observations of executives found that "half of the activities were completed in less than nine minutes, and only one-tenth took more than an hour." Research on supervisors found that most activities lasted less than 2 minutes (Guest, 1956; Ponder, 1957; Walker et al., 1956).

Managerial activities during a typical day are typically quite varied, in contrast to many nonmanagerial jobs. An example of one day in the life of an executive is provided in Appendix A. The activities of managers tend to be fragmented as well as varied. Interruptions occur frequently, conversations are disjointed, and important activities are interspersed with trivial ones, requiring rapid shifts of mood. A manager may go from a budget meeting involving decisions about millions of dollars in spending to a discussion about how to fix a broken water fountain (Sayles, 1979).

The fragmented nature of managerial activity reflects the fact that many interactions are initiated by others, and much of a manager's behavior is reactive rather than proactive in nature. Problems occur in a mostly random order, and managers choose to react to some problems as they become aware of them, while others are ignored or postponed. There are always more problems than a manager can handle at any given time, and some types of problems are more likely to get immediate attention than others. The importance of a problem is not the only consideration determining whether it will be recognized and handled. McCall, Kaplan, & Gerlach (1982, p. 9) emphasize that problems are not served up "neatly wrapped and ready for choice." It is often unclear to a manager how important a problem is. Different managers may disagree about the nature of a problem or whether a problem even exists. Managers are more likely to respond to problems if there is pressure for immediate action due to a crisis, deadline, or expectations of progress by someone important, such as the manager's boss or an external client. In the absence of such pressure, a problem is more likely to get action when it is perceived to be similar to other problems that a manager has solved successfully in the past, when the problem is perceived to be clearly within the manager's domain of responsibility, and when the manager perceives that the actions and resources necessary to solve the problem are available. Managers tend to ignore or postpone dealing with problems for which there is no external pressure for action, problems that are fuzzy and difficult to diagnose, problems for which other managers or subunits are responsible, and problems that cannot be solved without additional resources and support that would be difficult or impossible to obtain.

A common stereotype of managers is that they spend a considerable part of their time in careful analysis of business problems and development of elaborate plans to deal with them. However, the descriptive studies find that managers devote little time to reflective planning. The fragmented activities and continual heavy demands characteristic of managerial work make it difficult for managers to find the long periods of uninterrupted time necessary for this type of activity. Reflective planning and other activities that require large blocks of time, such as team building and training complex skills to subordinates, are usually preempted by "fire-fighting" activities involving immediate operational problems. What little time managers spend alone in the office is typically used to read correspondence, handle administrative paperwork, read reports from subordinates, write reports or memos, and scan journals or technical publications. Moreover, managers themselves usually gravitate toward the active aspects of their jobs, and even during oral interactions, they tend to focus on specific, immediate problems rather than general issues or long-term strategies.

Interactions Often Involve Peers and Outsiders

Although much of the leadership literature focuses on the relationship between leader and subordinates, the descriptive research has found that managers typically spend considerable time with persons other than direct subordinates or the manager's boss. Kotter (1982) found that the network of relationships for general managers often consisted of hundreds of people inside and outside of their organization. These contacts may involve subordinates of subordinates, superiors of the boss, lateral peers, subordinates of lateral peers, and superiors of lateral peers (see Figure 4–1). In addition, many managers spend considerable time with people outside of the organization, such as customers, clients, suppliers, subcontractors, people in government agencies, important people in the community, managers of other organizations in the same field, and managers in the same area of specialization (e.g., personnel managers, marketing managers). The number of external contacts is typically greater for managers at higher levels of authority than for low-level managers, although low-level managers in boundary role positions (e.g., sales, purchasing, public relations) also have considerable contact with outsiders.

The high incidence of lateral and external interactions can be explained in terms of a manager's need for information about complex and uncertain events that influence the operations of his or her organizational subunit, and the manager's dependence upon the cooperation and assistance of numerous people outside of the immediate chain of command (Kotter, 1982). These conditions occur to some extent for all managers, but the importance of lateral and external relations depends on the type of business a firm is in and the way it is organized. For example, managers in a firm that provides many customized products or services to clients are likely to have more external contacts than managers in a firm that provides a few uniform services or mass-produced products. Managers in a self-contained unit of a larger organization (e.g., regional securities office, local department store) are likely to have fewer lateral contacts with other parts of the organization than managers in a matrix organization with many different product and functional units (Kotter, 1982; Stewart, 1976).

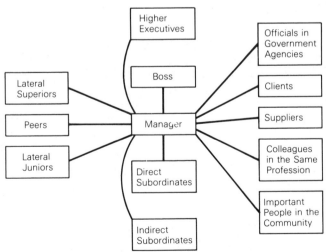

FIGURE 4–1   A Manager's Network of Contacts

Kanter (1982, 1983) found that lateral relationships were especially important when managers desired to implement innovative changes, as opposed merely to conducting routine operations. Kanter's research showed that successful entrepreneurial managers built a coalition of supporters and sponsors, beginning with peers and then adding superiors. A coalition of supporters is usually necessary to gain approval and funding for a new product or project and to guarantee it will be implemented successfully, rather than being derailed due to lack of attention, apathy, interference, or political opposition.

Interactions Typically Involve Oral Communication

Managers have five principal ways to obtain information: written messages (e.g., memos, letters, reports, work orders, contracts), telephone messages, scheduled meetings, unscheduled meetings, and observational tours. Managers show a strong preference for the use of oral communication media such as the telephone and meetings. The research on managerial activities found that lower and middle managers spent from 27 to 82 percent of their time engaged in oral communication, and the figure was 65 to 75 percent for higher-level managers. Most of the oral communication involved face-to-face interaction during scheduled or unscheduled meetings.

The content of oral communication provides some clues about the possible reasons for its prevalence. The research shows that much of the oral communication by managers involves exchange of information and attempts to influence people. Managers tend to prefer current information to old information, and current information is usually obtained from face-to-face contacts with people who have access to it, including many people outside of the manager's organizational subunit. Informal gossip and rumors contain detailed information about recent events and new developments, whereas written reports usually summarize old information. Neustadt (1960, p. 153-154) found a preference for recent, detailed information even at the level of a United States president:

> It is not information of a general sort that helps a President see personal stakes; not summaries, not surveys, not the bland amalgams. Rather . . . it is the odds and ends of tangible detail that pieced together in his mind illuminate the underside of issues put before him. To help himself, he must reach out as widely as he can for every scrap of fact, opinion, gossip, bearing on his interests and relationships as President.

It is likely that oral communication facilitates influence processes such as rational persuasion, consultation, personal appeals, and inspirational appeals. The oral media allows the effect of words to be magnified by the effect of intonation, gestures, and other nonverbal communication. Face-to-face interaction provides an opportunity to obtain immediate feedback about the effectiveness of an influence attempt, and this feedback can be used to modify and improve the manager's influence strategy and negotiating effectiveness. Finally, face-to-face interaction probably facilitates the development and maintenance of good interpersonal relationships; it is easier for managers to provide attention, support, recognition, coaching, and counseling to subordinates when interacting directly with them. The descriptive research found that a manager's oral interactions tend to include a surprising amount of kidding, joking, and discussing of subjects unrelated to the work (e.g., sports, hobbies) or of trivial importance to it. This socializing activity and small talk probably help managers to build and maintain effective relationships with the large network of people whose cooperation and support are needed.

Decision Processes Are Disorderly and Political

Much of the management literature has described decisions as discrete events made by a single manager or group in an orderly, rational manner. This picture is sharply contradicted by the descriptive research on managerial work and related research on managerial decision making (Cohen & March, 1974; McCall et al., 1982; Schweiger, Anderson, & Locke, 1985; Simon, 1987). Managers are seldom observed to make major decisions at a single point in time, and often they are unable to recall when a decision was finally reached. Some major decisions are the result of many small actions or incremental choices taken without regard to larger strategic issues.

Decision processes are likely to be characterized more by confusion, disorder, and emotionality than by rationality. Instead of careful analysis of likely outcomes in relation to predetermined objectives, information is often distorted or suppressed to serve preconceptions about the best course of action or a self-serving interest in a particular choice. The emotional shock of discovering a serious problem, and anxiety about choosing among unattractive alternatives may result in denial of negative evidence, wishful thinking, procrastination, vacillation between choices, and panic reactions by individual managers or by decision groups (Janis & Mann, 1977).

Organizational decision processes are highly political, and important decisions typically require the support and authorization of many different people at different levels of management and in different subunits of the organization. Even when decision makers agree about objectives, they often disagree about the true nature of a problem and the likely outcomes of various solutions, due to the different perspectives, assumptions, and values typical of managers from different functional specialities and backgrounds. As a result, the decision process may drag on for months or years. Delays and interruptions occur as a proposal is sidetracked by opponents, preempted by immediate crises, or is recycled back to its initiators for revisions necessary to make it suitable to managers whose support is needed (Mintzberg, Raisinghani, & Theoret, 1976). For decisions involving major changes in organizational strategies or policies, the outcome will depend to a great extent on the influence skills and persistence of the individual managers who desire to initiate change and on the relative power of the various coalitions involved in making or authorizing these decisions (Kanter, 1982; Kotter, 1982, 1985).

Not all decisions involve major changes or prolonged political processes. Although managers are seldom observed to make major decisions at a given point in time, they do in fact make many less momentous decisions in the process of solving operational problems, setting short-term goals, assigning work to subordinates, setting up work schedules, authorizing the expenditure of funds for supplies or equipment, and approving pay increases. McCall et al. (1982) differentiate between *thick* and *thin* decision cycles. The thick decisions involve important and complex problems for which there are no ready-made good solutions, there are many affected parties with conflicting interests, and there is a diffusion of power among the parties. It is precisely these qualities that lead to a prolonged and highly political decision process. In contrast, thin decision cycles involve problems for which ready-made, low-risk solutions are available, the manager has the authority to make a decision, few important people will be affected by the decision, there is little conflict about objectives or solutions, and there is pressure for a quick decision due to a deadline or a crisis. Managers usually make this type of decision either alone or after briefly consulting with a few people, and there is likely to be only a short period of problem analysis and search for solutions. Although thin decisions are not as important as thick ones, the manner in which a manager resolves them is an important determinant of the manager's effectiveness. A successful decision requires appropriate technical skill by the manager and the capacity to find a good balance between lengthy, systematic analysis and quick, decisive action. A rash analysis may result in a poor decision that fails to solve the problem or makes it worse. On the other hand, if a manager keeps delaying action to get more information about the problem, it may get worse or become visible enough to become an embarrassment.

Most Planning Is Informal and Adaptive

Planning is often described in the managerial literature as primarily a formal process of written objectives, strategies, policies, and budgets, cascading from top management down the hierarchy, with ever more detailed versions at each lower level of management. The descriptive studies find that some planning occurs, but it is usually informal and implicit. Kotter (1982) found that general managers develop agendas consisting of loosely connected goals and plans related to their job responsibilities and involving a variety of short- and long-term issues. The short-term (1–30 days) objectives and plans are usually quite specific and detailed, but the longer-term (5–20 years) agenda items are usually vague, incomplete, and only loosely connected. A new manager begins the process of developing this agenda immediately, but initially it is likely to be very rough and incomplete. Over time, as managers gather more information about their organization or subunit (e.g., operations, people, politics, markets, competitors, problems, issues, concerns, values) the agendas are refined and expanded (Gabarro, 1985; Kotter, 1982). Kotter found that the implementation of agenda items is also a gradual, continuous process. Managers use a variety of influence techniques during their daily interactions with other people to mobilize support and shape events. The agenda guides the manager in making efficient use of random encounters and brief interactions with relevent people in the manager's network of contacts.

In his study of top executives, Quinn (1980) found that most of the important strategic decisions were made outside of the formal planning process, and strategies were formulated in an incremental, flexible, and intuitive manner. In response to major unforseen events, the executives developed tentative, broad strategies that allowed them to keep their options open until they had more opportunity to learn from experience about the nature of the environment and the feasibility of their initial actions. Strategies were refined and implemented simultaneously in a cautious, incremental manner that reflected the need to develop a political coalition in support of a strategy as well as to avoid the risks of an initial, irreversible commitment to a particular course of action. Instead of a top-down, formal process, overall objectives and strategies for the firms was more likely to be the result of a "bottom-up" political process in which the objectives and strategies of powerful individuals and organizational subunits are reconciled and integrated. The formal, annual plans were merely a confirmation of strategic decisions already reached through the informal, political process.

ACTIVITY PATTERNS
AND BEHAVIOR CONTENT

The early descriptive research on managerial work was concerned primarily with providing a description of activity patterns. The research attempted to discover the answers to questions such as the following:

1. How much time is spent in activities involving different communication media, such as talking on the telephone, reading alone, scheduled meetings, and so on?

2. Who initiates the interactions?

3. How much time is spent alone, or in interactions with different people, such as subordinates, peers, superiors, and outsiders?

4. Are the activity patterns related to the nature of the managerial job, such as the level of management or type of organization and subunit?

In recent years, the focus of descriptive research has shifted to the content of managerial activities, and the research has been more concerned with the following questions:

1. What behavior categories are meaningful for classifying the content of managerial activity in terms of its purpose or distinctive process characteristics?

2. How much time do managers spend on activities involving each type of behavior, and how often do these activities occur?

3. Is the content of a manager's activities related to the nature of the managerial job, such as the level of management or type of organization and subunit?

4. Is the content of managerial activities related to other characteristics, such as the frequency and duration of the activity, where the activity occurs, who is involved, who initiates the activity, and what communication media are used?

A major difficulty in this research has been to determine what behavior categories are meaningful, distinct, and relevant for classifying the content of observed behavior and descriptions of behavior obtained from diaries and interviews. In attempting to resolve this question, different researchers have developed different taxonomies of behavior content (Komaki, 1986; Luthans & Lockwood, 1984; Mintzberg, 1973). One representative and widely known example of these taxonomies is the work of Mintzberg, which is described briefly.

Mintzberg's Managerial Roles

Mintzberg (1973) developed a taxonomy of ten managerial roles to use for coding content of the activities observed in his study of executives. The ten roles account for all of a manager's activities, and each activity can be explained in terms of at least one role, although many activities involve more than one role. Three roles deal with the interpersonal behavior of managers (leader, liaison, figurehead), three roles deal with information processing behavior (monitor, disseminator, and spokesman), and four roles deal with decision making behavior (entrepreneur, disturbance handler, resource allocator, negotiator). All of the managerial roles apply to any manager or administrator, but their relative importance may vary from one kind of manager to another. According to Mintzberg, a manager's roles are largely predetermined by the nature of the managerial position, but managers have some flexibility in the way each role is interpreted and enacted. Each role will be described briefly.

1. FIGUREHEAD ROLE

As a consequence of their formal authority as the head of an organization or one of its subunits, managers are obliged to perform certain symbolic duties of a legal and social nature. These duties include signing documents (e.g., contracts, expense authorizations), presiding at certain meetings and ceremonial events (e.g., retirement dinner for a subordinate), participating in other rituals or ceremonies, and receiving official visitors. The manager must participate in these activities, even though they are usually of marginal relevance to the job of managing.

2. LEADER ROLE

Managers are responsible for making their organizational subunit function as an integrated whole in the pursuit of its basic purpose. Consequently, the manager must provide guidance to subordinates, ensure they are motivated, and create favorable conditions for doing the work. A number of managerial activities are expressly concerned with the leader role, including hiring, training, directing, praising, criticizing, promoting, and dismissing. However, the leader role pervades all managerial activities, even those with some other basic purpose.

3. LIAISON ROLE

The liaison role includes behavior intended to establish and maintain a web of relationships with persons and groups outside of a manager's organizational unit. These relationships are vital as a source of information and favors. Development of such contacts and relationships is part of a chief executive's responsibility for linking the organization to the external environment. Horizontal relationships are essential for middle-level and lower-level managers. The essence of the liaison role is in "making new contacts," "keeping in touch," and "doing favors" that will allow the manager to ask for favors in return. Some examples of activities involving the liaison role include attending social events or professional conferences, joining outside boards, clubs, or associations, writing to congratulate a colleague, and calling another manager to provide some helpful information or offer assistance.

4. MONITOR ROLE

Managers continually seek information from a variety of sources, such as reading reports and memos, attending meetings and briefings, and conducting observational tours. Some of the information is passed on to subordinates (*disseminator role*) or to outsiders (*spokesperson role*). Most of the information is analyzed to discover problems and opportunities and to develop an understanding of outside events and internal processes within the manager's organizational subunit.

5. DISSEMINATOR ROLE

Managers have special access to sources of information not available to subordinates. Some of this information is factual in nature, and some of it concerns the stated preferences of individuals desiring to influence the manager, including persons at high levels of authority. Some of the factual information must be passed on to subordinates, either in its original form or after interpretation and editing by the manager. The information about preferences must be assimilated according to the influence of the source, and it is then expressed to subordinates either in the form of value statements (e.g., rules, goals, policies, standards) or as specific responses to subordinate's questions.

6. SPOKESMAN ROLE

Managers are also obliged to transmit information and express value statements to persons outside of their organizational subunit. Middle- and lower-level managers must report to their superiors; a chief executive must report to the board of directors or owners. Each of these managers is also expected to serve as a lobbyist and public relations representative for the organizational subunit when dealing with superiors and outsiders. As Mintzberg (1973, p. 76) points out, "To speak effectively for his organization and to gain the respect of outsiders, the manager must demonstrate an up-to-the-minute knowledge of his organization and its environment."

7. ENTREPRENEUR ROLE

The manager of an organization or one of its subunits acts as an initiator and designer of controlled change to exploit opportunities for improving the existing situation. Planned change takes place in the form of *improvement projects* such as development of a new product, purchase of new equipment, or reorganization of formal structure. Some of the improvement projects are supervised directly by the manager, and some are delegated to subordinates. Mintzberg (1973, p. 81) offers the following description of the way a manager deals with improvement projects:

> The manager as a supervisor of improvement projects may be likened to a juggler. At any one point in time he has a number of balls in the air. Periodically, one comes down, receives a short burst of energy, and goes up again. Meanwhile, new balls wait on the sidelines and, at random intervals, old balls are discarded and new ones added.

8. DISTURBANCE-HANDLER ROLE

In the disturbance handler role, a manager deals with sudden crises that cannot be ignored, as distinguished from problems that are voluntarily solved by the manager to exploit opportunities (*entrepreneur role*). The crises are caused by unforeseen events, such as conflict among subordinates, the loss of a key subordinate, a fire or accident, a strike, and so on. A manager typically gives this role priority over all of the others.

9. RESOURCE ALLOCATOR ROLE

Managers exercise their authority to allocate resources such as money, personnel, material, equipment, facilities, and services. Resource allocation is involved in managerial decisions about what is to be done, in the manager's authorization of subordinates' decisions, in the preparation of budgets, and in the scheduling of the manager's own time. By retaining the power to allocate resources, the manager maintains control over strategy formation and acts to coordinate and integrate subordinate actions in support of strategic objectives.

10. NEGOTIATOR ROLE

Any negotiations requiring a substantial commitment of resources will be facilitated by the presence of a manager having the authority to make this commitment. The manager may also aid negotiations by serving as an expert spokesperson for his or her organization subunit. Finally, the manager's participation as the figurehead for the subunit adds credibility to the negotiations. Thus, a manager's activities during negotiations are likely to involve the resource allocator, spokesman, and figurehead roles in addition to the negotiator role. A chief executive is likely to participate in several different types of negotiations, including negotiations with unions involving labor-management contracts or grievances, contract negotiations with important customers, suppliers, or consultants, employment negotiations with key personnel, and other nonroutine negotiations (e.g., acquisition of another firm, application for a large loan). Middle-level and lower-level managers also perform this role, but the negotiations are more likely to occur between different subunits of the organization and are more informal.

Job Description Research

A different approach for understanding the content of managerial work is to examine job requirements rather than the behavior of the job holder. The focus of this research is to determine what responsibilities and duties must be carried out, regardless of who holds the position. Early research on job descriptions for executives was conducted by Hemphill (1959, 1960) and Mahoney, Jerdee, and Carroll (1965). The most extensive research on the subject is an ongoing program that began at Control Data Corporation in 1974 (Tornow & Pinto, 1976; Page, 1985; Page & Tornow, 1987). The purpose of the research was to develop a questionnaire useful for describing managerial jobs and determining appropriate salary levels. The source of the items in the initial version of the questionnaire included items from Hemphill's (1960) Executive Position Description Questionnaire, concepts from the management literature, and interviews with managers. The questionnaire is administered to managers, who are asked to rate how important each activity or behavior is in doing the job, or how much time the manager spends on it. The primary approach for identifying behavior categories has been factor analysis. Over a period of 11 years, research was conducted on seven different versions of the questionnaire with more than 10,000 managers in 12 companies, including several hundred managers at facilities in 20 different countries.

The resulting questionnaire is called the Managerial Position Description Questionnaire (MPDQ). Nine factors representing distinct categories of managerial work content were found fairly consistently across the seven studies. An abbreviated definition of each factor, based on Form 2 of the MPDQ, is presented in Table 4–1.

TABLE 4–1   **Page's Taxonomy of Managerial Position Duties and Responsibilities**

Supervising. Improving the performance of subordinates by working with them to analyze their strengths and weaknesses, providing training, developing skills, scheduling their work, and setting performance goals.

Planning and Organizing. Formulating short-term plans, carrying out projects, and developing budgets, evaluating organizational structure to determine optimal allocation and utilization of resources; translating long-range plans into short-range operational goals; recommending and developing operational policies and procedures.

Decision Making. Making business decisions without hesitation in an unstructured situation; authorizing minor or major deviations from established procedures to meet new or unusual situations.

Monitoring Indicators. Monitoring internal and external forces that may affect the company, including performance indicators, corporate finances and assets, market conditions, and cultural, social, and political climate.

Controlling. Developing schedules and cost-time estimates for producing or delivering products/services, tracking productivity, assuring the quality of products or effectiveness of services, and analyzing operational effectiveness.

Representing. Answering questions and responding to complaints from outsiders; communicating with outsiders to promote company relations; negotiating with outsiders; conducting promotional activities to establish or maintain company image; and convincing others of your point of view.

Coordinating. Coordinating efforts with other individuals and groups within the company over whom the manager has no direct control in order to share information, meet previously established schedules, solve problems and achieve objectives; maintaining a smooth working relationship with peers; mediating problems and conflicts between key individuals.

Consulting. Keeping current with technical developments in one's field, introducing new techniques or technologies into the organization, and acting as expert advisor, consultant, or troubleshooter for other managers.

Administering. Performing basic administrative activities, such as locating information on company practices and procedures, analyzing routine information, maintaining detailed and accurate records and documents.

Limitations of Descriptive Research

Most of the research on the nature of managerial work was designed to describe the typical pattern and content of managerial activities, not to answer directly the question of what activity patterns or behavior patterns are necessary and effective. Discovering that many managers carry out a particular activity does not tell us whether it is essential for managerial effectiveness. A few of the descriptive studies included only managers predetermined to be effective (Kanter, 1982; Kotter, 1982; Kotter & Lawrence, 1974), or only managers in organizations designated as effective (Peters and Waterman, 1982; Peters & Austin, 1985). These researchers attempted to find patterns of behavior or common "themes" that might explain why the managers and/or organizations were effective. However, the findings of this research are still quite speculative, since there was no comparison of effective managers to ineffective managers. The best insights come from descriptive studies that (1) compare activity patterns for effective managers and ineffective managers of the same type (e.g., production supervisors, regional sales managers, elementary school principals), and (2) explicitly examine the relation of activity patterns to obvious requirements of the managerial job situation. Unfortunately, this type of research is rare. To date, only a few observational studies have compared effective and less effective managers (Komaki, 1986; Luthans, Rosenkrantz, & Hennessey, 1985; Martinko & Gardner, 1984; Ponder, 1959).

As for the problem of classifying the content of managerial activities, some convergence is evident among the various descriptive approaches, but only at the level of broad categories or processes. Taken together, the descriptive approaches suggest that most managerial activity can be described in term of four general processes: (1) developing and maintaining relationships, (2) getting and giving information, (3) making decisions, and (4) influencing people. These processes are interwoven among a manager's activities, and any specific activity may involve two or more processes. The resulting overlap among categories is depicted in Figure 4–2.

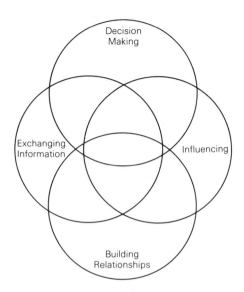

FIGURE 4–2   Four Primary Processes in Managing

APPLICATIONS: GUIDELINES
FOR EFFECTIVE ACTION

Even though most descriptive research on managerial activities was not designed for relating activity patterns to managerial effectiveness, the research provides some insights about coping more effectively with the requirements of managerial work. This section summarizes some tentative guidelines based on the descriptive research using observation, diaries, and interviews. The reader is cautioned to remember that these guidelines are patterns and "themes" inferred from exploratory descriptive research, not results from research designed to explicitly test propositions about effective leader behavior. As a consequence, the guidelines are still somewhat general and speculative.

1. Take Advantage of Reactive Activities

Courses and texts on time management stress the need to avoid time wasters and marginal activities in order to manage the heavy workload and incessant demands on a manager's time. Time is a valuable resource to be allocated like other resources, and some degree of control over the use of one's time is clearly desirable. However, it is not feasible for a manager to plan in advance exactly how the day will be spent. The unpredictable nature of the environment makes it essential to view chance encounters, interruptions, and unscheduled meetings initiated by others not just as intrusions on scheduled activities, but rather as opportunities to gain important information, discover problems, influence others, and move forward on implementation of plans and informal agendas (Kotter, 1982). Obligations that might otherwise be time wasters, such as required attendance at some meetings and ceremonial occasions, can be turned to the manager's advantage. As Mintzberg (1975, p. 61) points out, "A speech is a chance to lobby for a cause; a meeting is a chance to reorganize a weak department; a visit to an important customer is a chance to extract trade information."

2. Cultivate Large Networks of Contacts

It is important for a manager to develop a network of contacts within the organization to obtain information about current events in the organization that may affect the manager's job performance and career. Equally important is a network of contacts from which to obtain information about relevant events outside of the organization, such as economic trends, trends and shifts in customer preferences, actions of competitors, new technological developments, changes in laws and government regulations, and so forth. The size of the network will vary somewhat from manager to manager, depending upon factors such as the level of management, amount of change and uncertainty in the environment, and the degree of dependence on other members of the organization and on outsiders. Contacts can be made and maintained by talking with people before, during, and after organization meetings and social events, by calling or visiting people, and by joining community groups, boards, social clubs, and professional associations. Exchange relationships are established by actions that establish a manager's utility and attractiveness as a "trading partner" (Kaplan, 1984). Examples include the following: calling someone to give them some useful information that they would otherwise not obtain quickly, complimenting someone on an accomplishment or promotion, inviting someone to visit your facility to find out about its operations and exchange ideas for handling common problems, suggesting joint projects to undertake that will be beneficial to both parties, visiting someone (especially users and clients) to learn more about their needs with regard to your products and services, and setting up periodic meetings with people from other units to coordinate activities.

3. Identify Connections Among Problems

In the process of trying to make sense out of the streams of problems, issues, and opportunities encountered by a manager, it is important to recognize relationships among them rather than assuming they are distinct and independent. Isenberg (1984) talks about "problem management" as a process of "mapping" a network of relationships among problems. This approach offers several advantages. First, it helps a manager cope with the overload of too much information to analyze and the stress of too many problems to handle. Second, a broader view of problems provides better insights for understanding them. By relating problems to each other and to informal strategic objectives, a manager is more likely to recognize opportunities to take actions that contribute to the solution of several related problems at the same time. Finding connections among problems is facilitated if the manager is able to remain flexible and open-minded about the definition of a problem and actively considers multiple definitions for each problem. It is also helpful to consider causal connections among different activities, issues, and performance criteria. For example, a product manager may ask how product quality relates to production scheduling, capital expenditures, performance appraisal practices, and marketing strategy.

4. Learn from Surprises and Failures

Some of the information that a manager receives is inconsistent with expectations or prior beliefs. Some information is bad news: A decision made by the manager has not been successful, performance is below targeted levels, a project is behind schedule. In order to make full use of negative information, a manager must avoid the common tendency to ignore or discount it (Isenberg, 1984). In order to ensure that such information is received, a manager must avoid the practice of "killing the messenger" who brings bad news. Research shows that effective managers are more likely to acknowledge failure and learn from it and are less defensive about mistakes. Managers who fail to recognize when a project or plan is failing are likely to continue wasting resources on it long after it should have been terminated or drastically changed. Managers who make excuses and find scapegoats for failures are likely to repeat the same mistakes again. Managers who ignore inconsistent information are less likely to recognize problems and comprehend them.

5. Be Willing to Experiment

Feedback about the success of a decision or innovation is often difficult to obtain. As noted earlier, many managers prefer not to receive such information, and they seek to avoid responsibility for failure by refusing to accept responsibility for solving a problem ("buck passing"), by delaying a decision (e.g., form a committee to study the problem and write a detailed report, send an invention or new product back for more testing), by involving more people than necessary in making the decision to diffuse responsibility, or by sticking with the same old remedies for dealing with problems. In contrast, effective managers are more willing to experiment actively with innovative approaches, and they recognize that some of these are bound to fail. Whenever possible, experiments are conducted initially on a small scale to minimize the risk, and ways are found to obtain the information necessary to evaluate results. For example, a new product may be market-tested only in one region, or a new process may be tested in one plant and results compared to those for a comparable plant using the old process. Peters and Waterman (1982, p. 13) found that managers in effective companies overcame the tendency toward inertia and conformity by a bias for action characterized as: "do it, fix it, try it." One successful strategy for quickly introducing innovative products was described as follows: Instead of allowing 250 engineers and marketers to work on a new product in isolation for 15 months, they form bands of 5 to 25 and test ideas out on a customer, often with inexpensive prototypes, within a matter of weeks. In some cases, an action is taken not because the manager believe it is the best way to solve a problem but rather because taking limited action is the only way to develop an adequate understanding of the problem (Isenberg, 1984; Quinn, 1980).

6. Select Problems Judiciously

A bias for action does not imply that a manager should respond equally to all problems. It was noted in Chapter 3 that the effective use of available power requires a manager to recognize its limitations. It is important for a manager to evaluate quickly whether a problem can be solved within a reasonable time period with available resources and whether it is worthwhile to invest the time, effort, and resources on this problem rather than on others (Isenberg, 1984; McCall et al., 1982). Solving problems successfully is not only a matter of doing the job more effectively, it is important also for a manager's reputation and career. A manager with a good track record of successfully handling important problems will have more expert power and increase the likelihood of advancement. Problems that are important and solvable deserve a manager's attention, and some problems are so important that they cannot be avoided even when the initial probability of a successful solution is not high. However, in general, managers should attempt to avoid or postpone action on problems that are either trivial or intractable.

7. Learn How the Political System Works in the Organization

In order to make a judgment about the feasibility of successfully solving a problem or accomplishing a change, a manager needs to learn how the political system works (Kotter, 1982, 1985). A manager should consider the following types of questions: What sequence of sign-offs and approvals is necessary to implement a proposed solution? Who are the key players that will determine if a proposed solution will be successfully implemented? Who is likely to support the proposal? How much resistance is likely and from whom? How much power of what types would be necessary to overcome the resistance and convert or co-opt the opponents? How long will it take to get approval and implement the necessary changes? In part it is a matter of learning how to use one's network of contacts effectively both to evaluate feasibility and to build a coalition to accomplish a desired change. Scanning the network for people who can help or hinder a change is especially important when the issue is novel or the change highly innovative (Kanter, 1982; Kaplan, 1986).

8 . Make Time for Reflective Planning

Given the fragmented and demanding nature of the job, one important aspect of time management is to set aside some time for reflective analysis and planning. Some of the cognitive activities described by the preceding guidelines require the manager to step back from the job and see it in a larger, strategic perspective. As Mintzberg (1975, p. 61) notes, "Free time is made, not found, in the manager's job. . . . Hoping to leave some time open for contemplation or general planning is tantamount to hoping that the pressures of the job will go away." Some managers are able to find time for reflective thinking when commuting or while traveling by plane on long business trips, but most managers need to handle this aspect of time management in a more deliberate manner. One approach is to set aside a block of time (one or two hours) each week when the manager is not available for any calls, visits, or interruptions except in the rare case of a serious crisis (which needs to be carefully defined for gatekeepers). Time for planning and strategic thinking can be made by scheduling periodic strategy sessions with subordinates or peers. Sometimes these sessions are scheduled at a site away from the work setting, such as a conference center at a resort, to insulate the participants from interruptions and help to focus attention on strategic issues. Another approach to make time for strategic planning is to initiate a major improvement project, delegate primary responsibility to a subordinate or task force, then schedule regular meetings with the individual or group to review plans and progress.

SUMMARY

The descriptive research found that managerial work is inherently hectic, varied, fragmented, reactive, disorderly, and political. Brief oral interactions predominate, and many of these involve people outside of the manager's immediate work unit and chain of command. Decision processes are highly political, and most planning is informal and adaptive. Managers face several dilemmas, including the need to obtain recent, relevant information that exists only in the heads of people who are widely scattered within and outside of the organization, to make decisions based on information that is both overwhelming and incomplete, and to get cooperation from people over whom the manager has no formal authority.

Identifying meaningful and widely applicable categories to describe the content of managerial work has been a problem for a long time. One approach is the taxonomy of ten managerial roles proposed by Mintzberg. Another approach is provided by job description research. Determining the importance of different behavioral duties and responsibilities is not the same as classifying observations of actual managerial behavior, but both approaches provide useful insights into the content of managerial work. The two approaches and related research using interviews with managers suggest that managerial work includes four general types of processes: (1) building and maintaining relationships, (2) getting and giving information, (3) influencing people, and (4) decision making. The next chapter examines another body of research that adds further to our understanding about the behavior of effective leaders.

REVIEW AND DISCUSSION QUESTIONS

1. Briefly describe typical attributes of managerial work.
2. What does descriptive research tell us about managerial decision making and problem solving?
3. What is the difference between studying activity patterns and behavior content?
4. Do managers actually engage in reflective planning, or is it just a myth promulgated by behavioral scientists to glorify managers or make sense out of their chaotic jobs?
5. Briefly describe Mintzberg's ten managerial roles.
6. What similarities and differences are there between position description research and descriptive research using observations of managerial activities?
7. What points of convergence are there between the descriptive research on managerial work and findings from the power-influence research (Chapters 2 and 3)?
8. What are four general aspects of managerial behavior suggested by the descriptive research as likely to be related to managerial effectiveness?
9. What guidelines are suggested for managers by the descriptive research on managerial activities?

5

EFFECTIVE
LEADERSHIP BEHAVIOR

The last chapter reviewed findings from research using observations, diaries, and interviews to describe typical patterns of managerial activity, and some of the research also examined the content of managerial activities. The present chapter reviews other types of research on the behavior of leaders and managers. This research has employed methods such as questionnaires, laboratory experiments, field experiments, and critical incidents to discover how effective leaders differ in behavior from ineffective ones. We begin by examining some of the early research on leader behavior conducted by psychologists in the 1950s and 1960s. Much of the research on leadership behavior during the past three decades has followed the pattern set by pioneering research programs at the Ohio State University and the University of Michigan.

OHIO STATE
LEADERSHIP STUDIES

Questionnaire research on effective leadership behavior has been dominated by the influence of the Ohio State University Leadership Studies. A major objective of this program of research was to identify effective leadership behavior. The initial task of the researchers was to develop questionnaires for subordinates to use in describing the behavior of their leader or manager. The researchers compiled a list of about 1800 examples of leadership behavior, then reduced the list to 150 items that appeared to be good examples of important leadership functions. A preliminary questionnaire composed of these items was administered to samples of military and civilian personnel, and each person was asked to describe the behavior of his or her supervisor (Fleishman, 1953; Halpin & Winer, 1957; Hemphill & Coons, 1957). Factor analysis of the questionnaire responses indicated that subordinates perceived their supervisor's behavior primarily in terms of two dimensions or behavior content categories, which were subsequently labeled "consideration" and "initiating structure." Both were broadly defined categories containing a wide variety of specific types of behaviors.

Consideration and Initiating Structure

Consideration is the degree to which a leader acts in a friendly and supportive manner, shows concern for subordinates, and looks out for their welfare. Some examples include: doing personal favors for subordinates, finding time to listen to subordinates' problems, backing up or going to bat for a subordinate, consulting with subordinates on important matters before going ahead, being willing to accept subordinate suggestions, and treating a subordinate as an equal.

Initiating structure is the degree to which a leader defines and structures his or her own role and the roles of subordinates toward attainment of the group's formal goals. Some examples include: criticizing poor work, emphasizing the importance of meeting deadlines, assigning subordinates to tasks, maintaining definite standards of performance, asking subordinates to follow standard procedures, offering new approaches to problems, coordinating the activities of subordinates, and seeing that subordinates are working up to capacity.

Consideration and initiating structure were found to be relatively independent behavior categories. What this means is that some leaders are high on consideration and low on initiating structure; some leaders are low on consideration and high on initiating structure; some leaders are high on both; and some leaders are low on both. Of course, most leaders probably fall along a continuum between the extreme high and low scores. Based on the results of the initial studies, two revised and shortened questionnaires were constructed to measure consideration and initiating structure. These questionnaires were called the Leader Behavior Description Questionnaire (LBDQ) and the Supervisory Behavior Description (SBD or SBDQ). Although often treated as equivalent, the scope and content of the behavior categories actually differs for these two versions of the questionnaire (Schriesheim & Stogdill, 1975). A third questionnaire, called the Leader Opinion Questionnaire (LOQ), has been treated by some researchers as a measure of behavior, but it is viewed more appropriately as a measure of attitudes rather than behavior.

Eventually a fourth questionnaire (Leader Behavior Description Questionnaire, Form XII) was developed by some Ohio State University researchers who narrowed the scope of consideration and initiating structure and added ten additional scales (Stogdill, Goode, & Day, 1962). Some of the new scales in the LBDQ XII measure aspects of leadership behavior (e.g., representation, integration), but others measure traits (e.g., uncertainty tolerance) or skills (i. e., predictive accuracy, persuasiveness). The Ohio State leadership questionnaires and modified versions of them have been used in many hundreds of studies by many different researchers over the last quarter century. However, even after the LBDQ XII was developed, most researchers continued to use only the consideration and initiating structure scales.

Example of a Questionnaire-Correlational Study

A study by Fleishman and Harris (1962) provides one of the best examples of correlational field research on consideration and initiating structure. The study was conducted in a truck-manufacturing plant of the International Harvester Company. The behavior of 57 production supervisors was described by subordinates who filled out the SBDQ. The criteria of leadership effectiveness included the number of written grievances and the amount of voluntary turnover during an 11-month period. Supervisors who were very considerate had less grievances and turnover in their work units than supervisors who were low on Consideration. The relationship was in the opposite direction for Initiating Structure; foremen who used a lot of structuring behavior had more turnover and grievances. Statistical analyses confirmed the existence of a significant curvilinear relationship. As noted by Fleishman and Harris (1962, p. 53), "There appear to be certain critical levels beyond which increased Consideration or decreased Initiating Structure have no effect on turnover or grievance rate." The relationship between leader behavior and turnover is shown in Figures 5–1 and 5–2.

The researchers also examined the combined effect of consideration and initiating structure. A significant interaction was found, indicating that the effects of one behavior cannot be understood without looking at the other behavior. The results are shown in Figures 5–3 and 5–4. Structuring behavior resulted in high grievances and turnover for leaders who were inconsiderate, whereas for leaders who were very considerate, structuring behavior had little effect on grievances or turnover. The results in this study were mostly corroborated by a later study by Skinner (1969) with supervisors in a textile firm.

The results from this research are impressive, but it is necessary to consider whether they can be generalized to other types of leaders or to other effectiveness criteria such as group performance. Hundreds of studies have been conducted on the effects of consideration and initiating structure, but the results for most criteria have been inconsistent and inconclu-

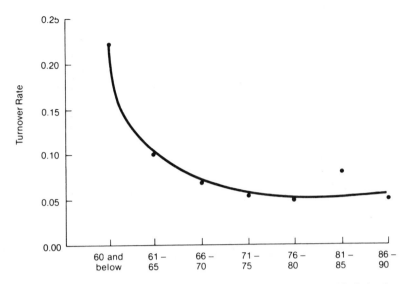

Source: From E. A. Fleishman and E. F. Harris, "Patterns of Leadership Behavior Related to Employee Grievances and Turnover." *Personnel Psychology*, 1962, 15, 43–56.

FIGURE 5–1   Relation Between Consideration and Turnover Rate

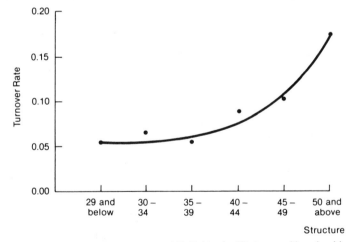

Source: From E. A. Fleishman and E. F. Harris, "Patterns of Leadership Behavior Related to Employee Grievances and Turnover." *Personnel Psychology*, 1962, 15, 43–56.

FIGURE 5–2   Relation Between Initiating Structure and Turnover Rate

sive (Bass, 1981; Kerr & Schriesheim, 1974; Yukl, 1971). In some studies subordinates were more satisfied and performed better with a structuring leader, whereas in other studies the opposite relationship or no significant relationship was found. Similar inconsistencies occur for the relationship between consideration and performance criteria. The only relationship that has been fairly consistent is the effect of consideration on satisfaction criteria. As suggested by the Fleishman and Harris study, subordinates are usually more satisfied with a leader who is at least moderately considerate. Unlike Fleishman and Harris, most researchers have neglected to test for the possibility of curvilinear relationships, or for interactions between consideration and initiating structure.

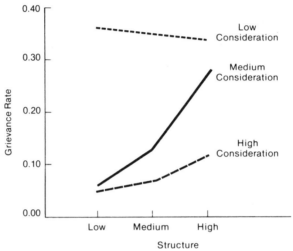

FIGURE 5–3   Combinations of Consideration and Initiating Structure Related to Grievance Rate

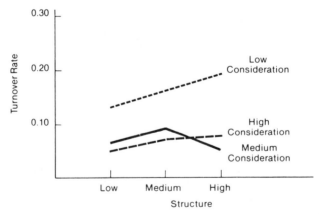

Source: From E. A. Fleishman and E. F. Harris, "Patterns of Leadership Behavior Related to Employee Grievances and Turnover." *Personnel Psychology*, 1962, 15, 43–56.

FIGURE 5–4   Combination of Consideration and Initiating Structure Related to Turnover

Limitations of Behavior Questionnaires

Leadership researchers following in the Ohio State tradition have relied too heavily on behavior description questionnaires that are susceptible to several types of bias and error (Schriesheim & Kerr, 1977; Luthans & Lockwood, 1984). One source of error is the use of ambiguous items that can be interpreted in different ways by different respondents. Most leadership questionnaires have a fixed-response format that requires respondents to think back over a period of several months or years and indicate how often or how much a leader used the behavior described in an item. An accurate judgment is difficult to make, since the respondent may not have noticed the behavior at the time it occurred or may be unable to remember how many times it occurred over the specified time period. Another source of error for fixed-response items is response bias. For example, some respondents answer each item much the same way despite real differences in the leader's behavior, because the respondent likes (or dislikes) the leader (Schriesheim, Kinicki, & Schriesheim, 1979). Responses are distorted also by stereotypes and implicit theories about what behaviors occur together (Eden & Leviatan, 1975; Gioa & Sims, 1985; Rush, Thomas, & Lord, 1977). Still another source of distortion is the tendency of some respondents to attribute desirable behavior to a leader who is perceived to be effective, even though the behavior was not actually observed (Green & Mitchell, 1979; Lord, Binning, Rush, & Thomas, 1978; Mitchell, Larson, & Green, 1977). When all of these sources of error are taken into account, it is easy to see why retrospective behavior description questionnaires are not very accurate measures of behavior.

Problems in Determining Causality

Most of the research on effects of leadership behavior has measured behavior with questionnaires filled out by subordinates, and the resulting behavior scores have been correlated with criterion measures obtained at the same point in time. When a significant correlation is found, there is no way to determine the direction of causality. For example, when a positive correlation is found between consideration and subordinate performance, there are a variety of possible interpretations. Researchers usually assume that causality is from behavior to outcomes, which favors the interpretation that considerate leaders cause the subordinates to be more motivated and productive. An equally plausible assumption is that causality is in the opposite direction, which favors the interpretation that leaders are more considerate to subordinates who perform well. Another possible interpretation is the "attribution hypothesis" mentioned earlier, namely, that subordinate descriptions of leader behavior are systematically influenced by perceptions of outcomes such as their own performance or group success. A fourth interpretation is that both consideration and performance are affected in the same way by a third variable, which may result in a significant correlation even when there is no causal relationship between leader behavior and performance. This possibility is not very likely for research in which outcome variables are measured independently of leader behavior. However, many studies obtain measures of both the leader behavior and the outcome criterion (e.g., effort, group performance) from the same respondent. In this case, it is likely that the correlation will be inflated due to some extraneous factor, such as how much the respondent likes the leader. For example, respondents who like the leader may give high ratings on both the behavior and the outcome, whereas respondents who dislike the leader may give low ratings on both.

The best way to determine causality is to conduct an experiment in which leader behavior is manipulated rather than being measured by questionnaire. Several experiments of this type have been conducted in a laboratory setting with university students (Day, 1971; Day & Hamblin, 1964; Herold, 1977; Lowin & Craig, 1968; Misumi & Shirakashi, 1966; Sims & Manz, 1984). This research demonstrated that causality operates in both directions, from behavior to outcomes, and vice versa. A few field experiments have been conducted in real or simulated organizations, using leaders who are asked to act in a predetermined way for a period of time to determine the effects of this behavior on subordinates (Gilmore, Beehr, & Richter, 1979; Lowin, Hrapchak & Kavanagh, 1969; Schachter, Willerman, Festinger, & Hyman, 1961). In other field experiments, leader behavior was manipulated by training managers to increase some types of behavior (Hand & Slocum, 1972; Wexley & Nemeroff, 1975). Most of the experimental studies found evidence that considerate leaders were more effective than inconsiderate leaders, but the results varied somewhat from study to study and were stronger for subordinate satisfaction than for performance. Results for effects of leader structuring behavior were not clear or consistent.

Indications of causality are also provided by longitudinal field studies (Greene, 1975, 1979; Misumi, 1985). Again, the research provides evidence that leader behavior may be influenced by outcomes as well as influencing them. A good example is a quasi-experimental study on Japanese bank managers (Misumi, 1985). Leader behavior and subordinate satisfaction were measured by questionnaire at different points in time, and banks that changed managers during a 15-month interval were compared to banks with no change in managers. Subordinate satisfaction usually improved when a manager was replaced by someone higher on both task and relations-oriented behavior, and satisfaction usually declined when a manager was replaced by someone lower on both behavior dimensions. A static correlational analysis of the data yielded consistent results, with leaders high on both dimensions having the most satisfied subordinates.

THE MICHIGAN LEADERSHIP STUDIES

A second major program of research on leadership behavior was carried out by researchers at the University of Michigan at approximately the same time as the Ohio State leadership studies. The focus of the Michigan research was the identification of relationships among leader behavior, group processes, and measures of group performance. The initial research was a series of field studies with a variety of leaders, including section managers in an insurance company (Katz, Maccoby, & Morse, 1950), supervisors in a large manufacturing company (Katz & Kahn, 1952), and foremen of railroad section gangs (Katz, Maccoby, Gurin, & Floor, 1951). Information about managerial behavior was collected with interviews and questionnaires. Objective measures of group productivity were used to classify managers as relatively effective or ineffective. Comparison of effective and ineffective managers revealed some interesting differences in managerial behavior. The results from these and later Michigan studies were summarized by Likert (1961, 1967). The research found that three types of leadership behavior differentiated between effective and ineffective managers.

1. *Task-oriented behavior.*   Effective managers did not spend their time and effort doing the same kind of work as their subordinates. Instead, the more effective managers concentrated on task-oriented functions such as planning and scheduling the work, coordinating subordinate activities, and providing necessary supplies, equipment, and technical assistance. Moreover, effective managers guided subordinates in setting performance goals that were high but realistic. The task-oriented behaviors found to be important in the Michigan studies appear similar to initiating structure as defined by the Ohio State researchers.

2. *Relationship-oriented behavior.*   For the effective managers, task-oriented behavior did not occur at the expense of concern for human relations. The effective managers were more considerate, supportive, and helpful with subordinates. The type of relationship-oriented behavior found to be correlated with effective leadership included showing trust and confidence, acting friendly and considerate, trying to understand subordinate problems, helping to develop subordinates and further their careers, keeping subordinates informed, showing appreciation for subordinates' ideas, and providing recognition for subordinate contributions and accomplishments. Moreover, effective managers tended to use general supervision rather than close supervision. That is, the managers established goals and general guidelines for subordinates but allowed them some autonomy in deciding how to do the work and how to pace themselves. Likert (1961) proposed that a manager should treat each subordinate in

such a way that the person will view the experience as supportive and it will build and maintain the person's sense of personal worth and importance. The relationship-oriented behaviors found to be important in the Michigan studies appear similar to consideration.

3. *Participative leadership.*   Likert proposed that managers should make extensive use of group supervision instead of supervising each subordinate separately. Group meetings facilitate subordinate participation in decision making, improve communication, promote cooperation, and facilitate conflict resolution. The role of the manager in group meetings should be primarily to guide the discussion and keep it supportive, constructive, and oriented toward problem solving. However, use of participation does not imply abdication of responsibilities, and the manager remains responsible for all decisions and their results. The emphasis on use of groups reflects the findings in several field experiments by University of Michigan researchers that subordinate participation in making decisions tends to result in higher satisfaction and performance (Coch & French, 1948; French, 1950; French, Israel, & As, 1960; Morse & Reimer, 1956; Tannenbaum & Allport, 1956). Participative leadership will be examined more closely later in this chapter.

Bowers and Seashore (1966) extended the investigation of leadership behavior by suggesting that most leadership functions can be carried out by subordinates as well as managers. Sometimes a manager asks subordinates to share in performing certain leadership functions, and sometimes subordinates do these functions on their own initiative. Since leadership functions do not need to be carried out solely by the designated leader, group effectiveness will depend more on the overall quality of leadership in a work unit than on who actually performs the functions. However, the possibility of shared leadership does not imply that it is unnecessary to have a designated leader. According to Bowers and Seashore (1966, p. 249), "There are both common sense and theoretical reasons for believing that a formally acknowledged leader through his supervisory leadership behavior sets the pattern of the mutual leadership which subordinates supply each other." Bowers and Seashore were the only researchers to develop a questionnaire to describe peer leadership as well as leadership behavior by the manager. These scales are part of a larger standardized questionnaire called the Survey of Organizations (Taylor & Bowers, 1972) that has been used extensively in organizations by researchers at the University of Michigan. The questionnaire has scales measuring two task-oriented behaviors (goal emphasis, work facilitation), and two relationship-oriented behaviors (supportive leadership, interaction facilitation). In a review of results from research on 21 organizations, Bowers (1975) found ample evidence that leadership behavior (by leaders and peers) was related to subordinate satisfaction and group processes, but the pattern of results varied, depending upon the type of industry and the authority level of the manager.

PARTICIPATIVE LEADERSHIP

After supportive and task-oriented behavior, the largest amount of behavior research has been on participative leadership, which involves the use of decision procedures intended to allow other people some influence over the leader's decisions. Other terms used to refer to this type of behavior include consultation, joint decision making, power sharing, decentralization, and democratic management. The participation process may be carried out with subordinates, peers, superiors, or outsiders. Participative leadership is a distinct category of behavior from task and relationship-oriented behavior, even though the three categories overlap to some extent (Yukl, 1971). This distinction was recognized in the Michigan leadership studies, but not in the Ohio State studies, where consultation was treated as part of consideration and autocratic decision making was treated as part of initiating structure.

Participation may be used to accomplish a variety of different objectives, including: (1) improved decision quality, (2) greater acceptance of decisions, (3) better understanding of decisions by people who must implement them, (4) development of decision making skills among subordinates, (5) enrichment of subordinate jobs by making them more interesting, and (6) facilitation of conflict resolution and team building. Managers use lateral consultation to facilitate coordination and cooperation with managers in different subunits. Managers use upward consultation to discover the reactions of their boss to their ideas and plans as well as to tap the boss's expertise. Of course, excessive upward consultation may suggest a lack of self-confidence and initiative on the part of the subordinate.

Participative leadership is a complex process that can take many forms. Before turning to the research on effects of participation, it is helpful to briefly consider variations in the way this behavior is usually described.

Varieties of Participation

Different leadership theorists have proposed different taxonomies of decision procedures, and to date, there has not been agreement about the optimal number of decision procedures or the best way to define them (Heller & Yukl, 1969; Strauss, 1977; Tannenbaum & Schmidt, 1958; Vroom & Yetton, 1973). Decision procedures can be ordered along a continuum ranging from no influence by other people to high influence (see Figure 5–5). The minimum number of distinct and meaningful categories for classifying decision procedures along a continuum of power sharing are the following four:

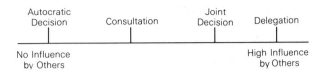

FIGURE 5-5   Continuum of Decision Procedures

1. *Autocratic Decision*: The manager makes a decision alone without asking for the opinions or suggestions of other people, and these people have no direct influence on the decision.

2 *Consultation*: The manager asks other people for their opinions and ideas, then makes the decision alone after seriously considering their suggestions and concerns.

3. *Joint Decision*: The manager meets with others to discuss the decision problem and make a decision together; the manager has no more influence over the final decision than any other participant.

4. *Delegation*: The manager gives an individual or group the authority and responsibility for making a decision; the manager usually specifies limits within which the final choice must fall, and prior approval may or may not be required before the decision can be implemented.

Some researchers differentiate between subvarieties of these basic four procedures. For example, Tannenbaum and Schmidt (1958) distinguish two varieties of autocratic decision, one where the leader merely announces an autocratic decision ("tells" style), and one where the leader uses influence tactics such as rational persuasion ("sells" style). These writers also distinguish three varieties of consultation: (1) The leader presents a decision made without prior consultation but is willing to modify it in the face of strong objections and concerns, (2) the leader presents a tentative proposal and actively encourages people to suggest ways to improve it, and (3) the leader presents a problem and asks others to participate in diagnosing it and developing solutions but then makes the decision alone. Vroom and Yetton (1973) distinguish between consulting with an individual and consulting with a group.

The typologies of decision procedures are useful, but Strauss (1977) reminds us that it is important to distinguish between overt procedures and actual influence. Sometimes what appears to be participation is only pretense. For example, a manager may solicit ideas and suggestions from others, and then ignore them when making the decision. Likewise, the manager may ask subordinates to make a decision, but do it in such a way that the subordinates are afraid to show initiative or deviate from the choices they know the boss prefers. It is also important to remember that typologies of decision procedures provide abstract descriptions of pure or ideal types; the actual behavior of managers seldom occurs in distinct ways that neatly fit these descriptions. The research discussed in Chapter 4 suggests that consultation often occurs informally during the course of repeated interactions with other people rather than at a single point of time in a formal meeting. Consultation may occur during brief contacts in the hall, after a meeting or social event, at lunch, or on the golf course. Actual behavior may involve a mix of elements from different procedures, such as consulting about problem diagnosis but not about final choice among solutions or consulting about final choice among a limited set of predetermined solutions. Participative behavior has a dynamic quality and may change over time. For example, what was initially consultation may become a joint decision as it becomes evident that subordinates agree with the leader's preferred choice. What was initially a group decision may become consultation when it becomes obvious that the group is deadlocked and the leader must make the final decision.

Example of Research on Participation

Bragg and Andrews (1973) conducted a quasi-experimental study on participation in a hospital laundry department. The foreman of the laundry department typically made decisions in an autocratic manner, and he was persuaded by the chief administrator to try a participative approach. The 32 workers in the laundry department were told that the purpose of the group meetings was to make their jobs more interesting, not to increase productivity, which was already high. The workers and union were told that the participation program would be discontinued if they found it unsatisfactory. Over the next 18 months, meetings were held whenever the workers wanted to discuss specific proposals about hours of work, working procedures, working conditions, minor equipment modifications, and safety matters. In addition to these group meetings, the foreman consulted regularly with individuals and smaller groups of workers to discuss problems and new ideas.

Worker attitudes were measured at 2-month intervals for 14 months with a questionnaire. The attitude data showed some initial doubts about the participation program, after which workers became increasingly more favorable toward it. Productivity during the first 18 months of the program increased 42% over that for the department during the prior year, whereas for similar departments in two other hospitals (the comparison group), productivity declined slightly during the same period of time. Attendance in the department, which was high initially, became even better after the participation program was introduced, whereas for other nonmedical departments in the same hospital (the comparison groups), it became worse. The results were statistically significant, and showed that the participation program was highly successful.

After the program had been in effect for 3 years, neither the workers nor the supervisor had any desire to return to the old autocratic style of management. The success of the program led to the introduction of participation in the medical records section, where it resulted in elimination of grievances and a sharp reduction in turnover. However, an attempt to introduce a participation program in the nursing group was much less successful, due primarily to lack of support by the head nurse and resistance by administrative medical personnel.

Effects of Participative Leadership

Many studies on participation have been conducted since the pioneering field experiments by Lewin, Lippitt, and White (1939) and Coch and French (1949). The research includes laboratory experiments, field experiments, and correlational field studies using questionnaires to measure participative leadership. Most of the studies involved participation by subordinates, and the criteria of leader effectiveness was usually subordinate satisfaction and performance. The results of this participation research are summarized in some recent literature reviews and meta-analyses (Miller & Monge, 1986; Schweiger & Leana, 1986; Wagner & Gooding, 1987). The various reviewers do not agree completely on their conclusions. Some discrepancies are due to the way the reviewers interpreted the results, which serves to remind us that meta-analyses involve questionable assumptions and subjective judgments about which studies to exclude. Some other discrepancies were due to differences in type of methodology used in the research itself. Studies that used questionnaire data from the same respondents (a method more susceptible to inflated results) usually found positive effects for participation, whereas experiments and other studies with independent measures of outcome variables had results that were weaker and less consistent. Overall, the research evidence was not sufficiently strong and consistent to reach any firm conclusions. After 35 years of research on participation, we are left with the conclusion that participative leadership sometimes results in higher satisfaction, decision acceptance, effort, and performance, and at other times it does not.

Limitations of Participation Research

As with the research on consideration and initiating structure, the questionnaire-correlational studies on participative leadership are limited by measurement problems and difficulty of determining direction of causality. In most correlational studies, participation has been defined as the overall amount of influence subordinates perceive themselves to have, or subordinate perception of the leader's general use of participation. No effort was made to identify the particular mix of decision procedures used by a manager or to determine if a manager used appropriate decision procedures for the types of decisions being made. In effect, these studies tested only the general hypothesis that more participation is better.

The field experiments also have limitations. Many of the experiments involved a participation program introduced by the organization rather than participative behavior by an individual manager. In some studies, participation was combined with other types of interventions, (e.g., more supportive behavior by the leader, better training of subordinates, or use of better procedures for planning and problem solving), making it difficult to determine which consequences were due to participation. The short-term nature of many field experiments raises the possibility that improved satisfaction and effort for people in the participation condition is the result of a "Hawthorne effect," namely, temporary elation from being singled out for special attention by the organization. In some studies the nonparticipation control group knew about the participation group, which could have led to resentment about not getting the "special" treatment, thereby lowering satisfaction and making the participation group appear better. Finally, most lab and field experiments only compared two decision procedures, and the definition of "high" and "low" participation varied from study to study, making it difficult to compare results across studies. For example, in some studies participation was a joint decision, whereas in others it was consultation.

The outcome criterion in most participation research was overall satisfaction and performance of subordinates, not satisfaction with the way a particular decision was handled or commitment to implement that decision effectively. Thus, researchers usually failed to measure the most relevant and immediate outcomes, preferring instead to use a relatively insensitive criterion that is influenced by many things besides participative leadership. Most researchers either ignored the situation entirely or identified limiting conditions for participation only on a post hoc basis to explain discrepant results or lack of success. Few studies incorporated situational variables in a systematic manner or investigated whether different procedures are more effective for different types of decisions. This question is the subject of a situational leadership theory by Vroom and Yetton (1973) that is described in Chapter 6.

BEHAVIOR RESEARCH
USING CRITICAL INCIDENTS

Another type of research on managerial behavior uses the critical incident approach (Flanagan, 1951). This method represents a bridge between descriptive research on what managers do and research on effective behavior. The method is based on the assumption that respondents such as subordinates, peers, and superiors can provide descriptions of effective and ineffective behavior for a particular type of manager (e.g., production supervisors, retail store managers, military officers). The behavior incidents are collected by interview or open-ended questionnaire from a large sample of respondents. Critical incidents are especially useful in exploratory research designed to examine very specific, situationally relevant aspects of managerial behavior. Examples of critical incidents from a study of production supervisors by Kay (1959, p. 26) are as follows:

> Aware that a change in set-up was scheduled for the next day, a foreman checked a machine, noted a missing part, and ordered it. (positive incident)

> A foreman failed to notify the relief shift foreman that a machine was in need of repair before it could be operated again. (negative incident)

Examples of some more detailed incidents from a study of air force officers (Van Fleet & Yukl, 1986b) are shown in Appendix B.

In most critical incident studies, incidents are grouped together on the basis of similar behavior content, either by the researchers or a panel of the respondents. The resulting behavior categories differ greatly from study to study. These differences are due in part to the large variety of leaders that have been studied, including for example, executives (Williams, 1956), production supervisors (Gellerman, 1976; Heizer, 1972), grocery store managers (Anderson & Nilsson, 1964), and department managers in retail stores (Campbell, Dunnette, Arvey, & Hellervik, 1973). The differences in behavior categories are also due to the arbitrary and subjective nature of the classification process. Even so, a close examination of the results reveals a moderate degree of communality across studies. The following types of leader behavior were represented in most of the studies:

1. Planning, coordinating, and organizing operations.
2. Supervising subordinates (directing, instructing, monitoring performance).
3. Establishing and maintaining good relations with subordinates.
4. Establishing and maintaining good relations with superiors, peers, and outsiders.
5. Assuming responsibility for observing organizational policies, carrying out required duties, and making necessary decisions.

Limitations of Critical Incident Research

The critical incident method has a number of limitations. It assumes that most respondents know what behaviors are important and relevant for leader effectiveness, and it assumes a behavior is important if it appears frequently in incidents reported by many different people. However, the respondents may be biased in their perception of what is effective, and respondents may tend to remember and report incidents that are consistent with their stereotypes or implicit theories about effective leaders. Researchers rarely follow up a critical incidents study with additional research to verify that the behaviors are able to differentiate between effective and ineffective leaders selected on the basis of an independent criterion such as group performance. This follow-up approach was used successfully in one study by Latham and Wexley (1977) on logging crew supervisors.

Many of the behavior categories found in critical incidents research are defined in terms that relate the behavior to the specific requirements of the job for the type of leader studied. Defining behavior categories at this level of specificity facilitates objectives such as developing a performance appraisal instrument or determining training needs, but it is difficult to compare the categories across studies on different types of leaders. This limitation can be overcome by coding the incidents into predetermined behavior categories that are widely applicable, as was done in the study by Yukl and Van Fleet (1982). The use of both situation-specific and more generic behavior categories makes it possible for critical incident research to serve multiple purposes.

UNIVERSAL THEORIES
OF EFFECTIVE LEADER BEHAVIOR

The extensive research on supportive, task-oriented, and participative leadership during the 1950s and 1960s gave rise to some "universal theories" of effective leader behavior. Universal theories postulate that the same style of leadership is optimal in all situations. For example, some theorists have advocated that leaders who make extensive use of participative decision procedures are more effective (McGregor, 1960; Likert, 1967; Argyris, 1964). The most prominent universal theory postulates that effective leaders are both supportive and task-oriented, the so-called "high-high" leader. Different versions of this two-factor theory have been proposed. In the management literature, Blake and Mouton (1954) developed managerial grid theory to describe managers in terms of concern for people and concern for production. In Japan, a program of behavior research paralleling the Ohio State leadership studies led to the formulation of a two-factor theory called PM leadership theory (Misumi & Peterson, 1985).

Assumptions about the way the two aspects of leadership behavior are related is an important feature of these theories. In most of the research using the Ohio State leadership questionnaires, the behaviors were viewed as separate action sequences, even though some researchers found interactions in the effects of these two behaviors. This perception was consistent with the method used to develop the questionnaire scales; after factor analysis of a large item pool, the researchers selected items loading highly on only one dimension. The net effect of this procedure was to eliminate items that involved both task- and relationship-oriented behavior simultaneously. Thus, a high-high leader was viewed as someone who used two completely separate types of behavior.

A different assumption is made by universal two-factor theorists who support an "interactive" model rather than an "additive" model (Blake and Mouton, 1982; Likert, 1967; Misumi, 1985). For example, Blake and Mouton contend that leadership behavior showing concern for both production and people is qualitatively different from leadership behavior showing a concern only for people or only for production. According to Blake and Mouton, a leader cannot simultaneously display behavior that is high production–low people and behavior that is high people–low production. A leader who alternates back and forth between the two types of behavior is not equivalent to a leader who displays behavior that is high on both dimensions simultaneously.

Some examples help to clarify this distinction. A leader who is high-high consults with subordinates about ways to improve product quality. A high-task, low-relations leader in this situation pressures subordinates to improve product quality or sets quality goals that are unrealistically high. A low-task, high-relations leader ignores quality problems or consults with subordinates about ways to make the lunch room more pleasant. A medium-medium leader may encourage better quality but settle for small improvements or drop the subject if there is any resistance. A low-low leader ignores quality problems and is indifferent to subordinates' problems. A rare high-high additive combination would be a leader who pressures a subordinate in a sarcastic manner to work faster, then in the next breath asks if the subordinate is feeling better after a sudden illness the prior day.

Evaluation of Universal Theory

Little research has been conducted to compare the additive and interactive models of task and relations behavior. Most questionnaire studies failed to test for an interaction between the two types of behavior, and the few that included such a test found mixed results (e.g., Evans, 1970; Fleishman & Harris, 1962; Larson, Hunt, & Osborn, 1976). Questionnaire studies in Japan usually find that high-high leaders are the most effective, and some find a significant interaction (Misumi, 1985). As noted earlier in the chapter, a few field experiments have manipulated both task and maintenance behavior, but they usually did not include an explicit test for interactive effects. In summary, the empirical research provides only limited support for the universal proposition that high-high leaders are more effective, and few studies have directly investigated whether the behaviors are additive or interactive.

The manner in which behavior is defined and measured lies at the heart of the controversy over additive and interactive models. Blake and Mouton (1982) emphasize qualitative aspects of behavior that differentiate high-high from other combinations, and they clearly recognize the need for leaders to select specific forms of behavior appropriate for a particular time or situation, not merely respond reflexively with the same behavior in any situation. The universal aspect of their theory is the value orientation of a high-high manager that guides the manager's actions, not some fixed behavior pattern applied automatically in all situations. Effective managers have a high concern for both task and people, but the way that concern is translated into behavior varies with the situation and from one subordinate to another.

Reflecting on the nature of managerial work (see Chapter 4), it is obvious that the essence of such work is a set of interwoven processes (e.g., influencing, information handling, network building, and decision making) that constantly involve both task and relationship issues. The two dimensions of behavior may be distinct conceptually, but in practice, any behavior incident has implications for both dimensions. At the level of specific behavior incidents, the difference between high-high leaders and other leaders is not that high-high leaders have a larger number of pure task-oriented behaviors together with a larger number of pure relationship-oriented behaviors, but rather that they have a higher percentage of incidents reflecting a concern for both task and relationships. It is an inaccurate stereotype that a high-task, low relations manager does only task behaviors (such as planning, clarifying, and monitoring), or that a high-relations, low-task manager does only relation-oriented behaviors (such as supporting and team building). Likewise, it is an incorrect assumption that a high-high manager does all possible task-oriented behaviors and all possible relation-oriented behaviors. Managers are overloaded with demands and must ration their time and select only relevant and appropriate behaviors. Effective managers act in ways that accomplish multiple objectives and solve related problems. Thus, we would expect an effective manager to be one who selects behaviors that accomplish task and relationship concerns simultaneously whenever possible. Examination of effective incidents from the critical incident research supports this interpretation. In most of the effective incidents, the leader acts in ways that simultaneously contribute to task objectives and maintenance of relationships. In contrast, ineffective behavior incidents tend to reflect concern for task objectives but disregard for relationships, or concern for relationships but disregard for task objectives, or a lack of concern for both.

Greater progress will be made in understanding managerial effectiveness when researchers examine specific aspects of managerial behavior in the context of the situational requirements and constraints faced by a manager. The extent to which specific behavior incidents reflect concern for task and concern for relationships is an important qualitative aspect of managerial behavior, but it is not sufficient merely to classify behavior as task- or relations-oriented. Researchers must also consider the more specific functional aspects of this behavior. The last section of this chapter reviews major taxonomies that use more than two broad categories to describe managerial behavior.

CATEGORIES OF LEADERSHIP AND MANAGERIAL BEHAVIOR

A major problem in research on the content of leadership behavior has been the identification of behavior categories that are relevant and meaningful. In the critical incident research, we saw that the classification of incidents in each study produced somewhat different behavior categories, making it difficult to compare and integrate the results across studies. A similar condition exists for the descriptive research reviewed in Chapter 4. Different behavior taxonomies have been used by different researchers to code the content of behavior descriptions. Likewise, in questionnaire research on leadership behavior, different aspects of leader and manager behavior are measured by different researchers. As a consequence, the past four decades have witnessed the appearance of a bewildering variety of behavior concepts pertaining to managers and leaders. Sometimes different terms have been used to refer to the same type of behavior. At other times, the same term has been defined differently by various theorists. What is treated as a general behavior category by one theorist is viewed as two or three distinct categories by another theorist. What is a key concept in one taxonomy is absent from another. Different taxonomies have emerged from different research disciplines, and it is difficult to translate from one set of concepts to another. Table 5-1 lists the major behavior taxonomies. Differences among behavior taxonomies occur primarily for three reasons: (1) purpose of the taxonomy, (2) level of abstraction of the behavior constructs, and (3) method used to derive the taxonomy.

Behavior categories are abstractions rather than tangible attributes of the real world. Behavior categories are derived from observed behavior in order to organize perceptions of the world and make them meaningful, but the categories do not exist in any objective sense. There is no absolute set of "correct" behavior categories. Thus, taxonomies that differ in purpose can be expected to have somewhat different constructs. For example, taxonomies designed to facilitate research and theory on managerial effectiveness have a somewhat different focus than taxonomies designed to describe observations of managerial activities, or taxonomies designed to catalog position responsibilities of managers and administrators.

TABLE 5–1   Overview of Behavior Taxonomies

AUTHORS AND DATES	NUMBER OF CATEGORIES	PRIMARY PURPOSE	APPROACH FOR DEVELOPING
Fleishman (1953)	2	Identify effective leader behavior	Factor analysis
Stogdill (1963)	12	Identify effective leader behavior	Theoretical-deductive
Mahoney, Jerdee, &Carrol (1963, 1965)	8	Describe position requirements	Theoretical-deductive
Bowers & Seashore (1966)	4	Identify effective leader behavior	Theoretical-deductive
Mintzberg (1973)	10	Classify observed activities	Judgmental classification
House & Mitchell (1974)	4	Identify effective leader behavior	Theoretical-deductive
Morse & Wagner (1978)	6	Identify effective manager behavior	Factor analysis
Yukl & Nemeroff (1979)	15	Identify effective manager behavior	Factor analysis
Luthans & Lockwood (1984)	12	Classify observed behavior	Judgmental classification
Page (1985)	10	Describe position requirements	Factor analysis
Yukl (1988)	14	Identify effective manager behavior	Factor analysis

Another source of diversity among taxonomies, even for those with the same purpose, is the possibility that behavior constructs can be formulated at different levels of abstraction or generality. Some taxonomies contain a small number of broadly defined behavior categories, whereas other taxonomies contain a larger number of narrowly focused behavior categories. For example, Initiating structure as defined by Fleishman (1953) is a broadly defined category, clarifying work roles is a "middle-range" category, and setting concrete goals is a concrete, narrowly focused category. All three are abstract behavior categories, but goal setting is a component of clarifying, which in turn is a component of initiating structure (see Table 5-2). The optimal level of abstraction for the behavior categories in a taxonomy depends upon the purpose of the taxonomy. Some taxonomies of leader or manager behavior contain a mix of constructs at different levels of abstraction, thereby creating additional confusion.

TABLE 5-2   Examples of Behavior Descriptions at Different Levels of Abstraction

Broad, Abstract Categories	TASK-ORIENTED BEHAVIOR	
Middle-range Categories	CLARIFYING	MONITORING
Concrete, Narrow Categories	GOAL SETTING	TOURING
Observed or Reported Incidents	The manager set a goal to increase department sales 10% by March 1.	The manager walked through the new store to see if it was ready for the opening.

A third source of diversity among behavior taxonomies is the method used to develop them. Some taxonomies are developed by examining the pattern of covariance among behavior items on a behavior description questionnaire describing actual managers (*factor analysis* method), some taxonomies are developed by having judges group behavior examples according to perceived similarity in content or purpose (*judgmental classification*), and some taxonomies are developed by deduction from theory (*theoretical-deductive approach*). Each method has its own associated biases, and the use of different methods results in somewhat different taxonomies, even when the purpose is the same.

Yukl (1987) compared the different taxonomies and found considerable convergence among them, despite the differences in purpose and development (see Table 5-3). When differences occurred, they usually involved the range of behaviors in the taxonomies and the level of abstraction of the behavior concepts. Some taxonomies (e.g., Bowers & Seashore, 1966; House & Mitchell, 1974) focus on a few behaviors, whereas other taxonomies (e.g., Luthans & Lockwood, 1984; Page, 1985; Yukl, 1987) are much more comprehensive. The large number of categories in some taxonomies is due to the specificity of the categories as well as the attempt to be comprehensive. Taking into account the differences in scope and level of abstraction, there is sufficient convergence among behaviors in the various taxonomies to suggest the possibility of an integrating taxonomy that would reduce the conceptual confusion in the literature and facilitate future research and theory development. This topic is pursued in Chapter 7.

Table 5-3   Approximate Correspondence Among Major Taxonomies

YUKL	MINTZBERG	MORSE & WAGNER	STOGDILL	BOWERS & SEASHORE	HOUSE & MITCHELL	LUTHANS & LOCKWOOD	PAGE
Supporting		*	Consideration	Leader Support	Supportive Leadership	*	*
Consulting		*	*	*	Participative Leadership		*
Delegating		*	Tolerance of Freedom	*	*		
Recognizing		*	*	*	*	Motivating & Reinforcing	
Rewarding		*	*	*	*		
Motivating	Leader Role	Motivating & Conflict Handling	Production Emphasis	Goal Emphasis	Achievement-oriented Leadershiip		Supervising
Managing Conflict & Team Building			Integration	Interaction Facilitation	*	Managing Conflict	
Developing		Providing Development	*		*	Training & Developing	
Clarifying		*	Initiating Structure		Directive Leadership		
Planning & Organizing	Resource Allocator; Entrepreneur	Organizing & Coordinating		Work Facilitation		Planning & Coordinating	Planning & Organizing; Strategic Planning
Problem Solving	Disturbance Handler	Strategic Problem Solving	Role Assumption; Demand Reconciliation		*	Problem Solving & Deciding	Decision Making
Informing	Disseminator	Information Handling	*	*	*	Exchanging Information	Consulting
Monitoring	Monitor	*	*	*	*	Monitoring/ Controlling	Monitoring Indicators, Controlling
Representing	Spokesman; Negotiator; Figurehead	*	Representing; Influencing Superiors	*	*	Interacting with Outsiders; Socializing & Politicking	Representing
Networking & Interfacing	Liaison	Managing environment & Resources	*	*	*		Coordinating

* Indicates behavior not included in the earlier taxonomy

SUMMARY

For three decades, beginning in the early 1950s, research on leader behavior was dominated by a focus on task- and relationship-oriented behavior. The large majority of leadership studies during this period used questionnaires measuring consideration and initiating structure. Other studies manipulated task and relationship behavior in lab experiments and field experiments. Results from this research have not been consistent, except for the finding that considerate leaders usually have more satisfied subordinates.

Participative leadership is the third most frequently studied aspect of leader behavior after task and relationship-oriented leadership. Once again the results are inconsistent. Participative leadership results in greater subordinate satisfaction and performance in some situations but not others. Lack of stronger, more consistent results in the research on considerate, task-oriented, and participative leadership has been attributed to inaccurate measures, problems in determining causality in questionnaire studies, design weaknesses in experimental studies, and inattention to situational moderator variables.

Universal theories involving task- and relationship-oriented behavior postulate that a high-high pattern is optimal in all situations. Research on this interactive model is not conclusive, but taking into account the extensive research in Japan as well as the United States, the pattern of results seems to suggest that effective leaders have at least a moderate level of both types of behavior. Most of the questionnaire-correlational studies fail to provide a proper test of the interactive model, because behavior is measured only in terms of the total frequency of purely task and purely relations-oriented actions. Instead, researchers must examine the extent to which the specific actions of a leader reflect a concern for both task and relationships. One type of research for which this approach is possible is the critical incident method. Comparison of effective and ineffective incidents tends to support the interactive model, but more research on this question is needed before any firm conclusions can be reached.

Several different taxonomies have been proposed for describing leader and manager behavior in less general terms than task and relationship behavior. Each taxonomy is different, and the variation among taxonomies is likely due to differences in purpose, scope, and method of development. Taxonomies developed to code behavior observations cannot be expected to correspond exactly to taxonomies developed to describe position requirements, or to taxonomies of effective leadership behavior. Nevertheless, there is enough convergence to suggest the possibility of an integrating taxonomy, and one is presented in Chapter 7.

REVIEW AND DISCUSSION QUESTIONS

1. What did we learn about leadership effectiveness from the Ohio State and Michigan leadership studies?
2. What problems have impeded questionnaire research on leadership behavior?
3. What have we learned from the research on task-oriented and relationship-oriented leadership behavior?
4. What are critical incident studies, and what do they tell us about the behavior of effective leaders?
5. To what extent can leadership functions be shared with subordinates, and can they be delegated to subordinates entirely?
6. What have we learned from research on the effects of participative leadership on subordinate satisfaction, motivation, and performance?
7. What points of convergence are there between findings in research on power-influence (Chapters 2 and 3), managerial activities (Chapter 4), and leadership behavior (Chapter 5)?
8. Why are taxonomies of behavior constructs important for research and theory on managerial effectiveness?
9. Why is there so much difference among the taxonomies proposed by different theorists?

6

SITUATIONAL THEORIES

OF

EFFECTIVE LEADER BEHAVIOR

In earlier chapters we saw that situations impose particular role requirements for effective leadership, and the relative importance of different
behaviors depends on the situation. Comparative research on different
managerial situations (see Chapter 8) provides some insights about role
requirements, but this type of research is only an indirect approach for
discovering what behavior pattern is optimal in a given situation. A more
direct approach is to determine how leader behavior influences outcomes
differently from situation to situation. Aspects of the situation that enhance or nullify the effects of a leader's traits or behavior are called *situational moderator variables*. A situational theory is more complete if it
includes intervening variables to explain why the effect of behavior on
outcomes varies across situations.

This chapter reviews four of the best known situational theories of
effective leadership behavior. Most of these theories were developed
during the 1970s, and except for the Vroom-Yetton model, they reflect the
focus on task-oriented and relationship-oriented behavior that was so
prevalent then. Each theory is described briefly, and the empirical support for it is evaluated.

THE PATH-GOAL THEORY
OF LEADERSHIP

The *path-goal theory of leadership* was developed to explain how the behavior of a leader influences the satisfaction and performance of subordinates. After an early, nonsituational version by Evans (1970), House (1971) formulated a more elaborate version of the theory that includes situational variables. The theory has since been refined and extended by various writers (Evans, 1974; Fulk & Wendler, 1982; House & Dessler, 1974; House & Mitchell, 1974; Stinson & Johnson, 1975). According to House (1971, p. 324): "The motivational function of the leader consists of increasing personal payoffs to subordinates for work-goal attainment and making the path to these payoffs easier to travel by clarifying it, reducing roadblocks and pitfalls, and increasing the opportunities for personal satisfaction en route." Leaders also affect subordinate satisfaction, particularly satisfaction with the leader. According to House and Dessler (1974, p.13): ". . . leader behavior will be viewed as acceptable to subordinates to the extent that the subordinates see such behavior as either an immediate source of satisfaction or as instrumental to future satisfaction." The effect of a leader's actions on subordinate satisfaction is not necessarily the same as the effect on subordinate effort. Depending on the situation, leader behavior may affect both the same, or both differently, or one but not the other.

The intervening variables in path-goal theory explain how a leader's behavior affects subordinate satisfaction and effort. These intervening variables were borrowed from a motivation theory called *expectancy theory* (Georgopolous, Mahoney, & Jones, 1957; Vroom, 1964). There are different versions of expectancy theory, but they all explain work motivation in terms of a rational choice process in which a person decides how much effort to devote to the job at a given point of time. In choosing between a maximal effort and a minimal (or moderate) effort, a person considers the likelihood that a given level of effort will lead to successful completion of the task and the likelihood that task completion will lead in turn to desirable outcomes (e.g., higher pay, recognition, promotion, sense of achievement, having fun) while avoiding undesirable outcomes (e.g., layoffs, accidents, reprimand, rejection by coworkers, excessive stress). Perceived probability of an outcome is called an *expectancy*, and the desirability of an outcome is called its *valence*. How all the many expectancies and valences for different outcomes and levels of effort combine to determine a person's motivation is still a matter of speculation and controversy and is beyond the scope of this book. In general, if subordinates believe that valued outcomes can be attained only by making a serious effort and they believe such an effort will succeed, then they will make the effort. The effect of a leader's behavior is primarily to modify these perceptions and beliefs.

As a situational theory, path-goal theory says that the effect of leader behavior on subordinate satisfaction and effort depends on the situation, including task characteristics and subordinate characteristics. These situational moderator variables determine both the potential for increased subordinate motivation and the manner in which the leader must act to improve motivation. Situational variables also influence subordinate preferences for a particular pattern of leadership behavior, thereby influencing the impact of the leader on subordinate satisfaction. The general causal relationships in the theory are illustrated in Figure 6-1.

The initial version of path-goal theory contained only two leader behaviors: supportive leadership (similar to consideration) and instrumental, or directive, leadership (similar to initiating structure). Two other leader behaviors were added in the version by House and Mitchell (1974). The four behaviors are defined as follows:

1. *Supportive leadership*: Giving consideration to the needs of subordinates, displaying concern for their welfare, and creating a friendly climate in the work unit.

2. *Directive leadership*: Letting subordinates know what they are expected to do, giving specific guidance, asking subordinates to follow rules and procedures, scheduling and coordinating the work.

3. *Participative leadership*: Consulting with subordinates and taking their opinions and suggestions into account.

4. *Achievement-oriented leadership*: Setting challenging goals, seeking performance improvements, emphasizing excellence in performance, and showing confidence that subordinates will attain high standards.

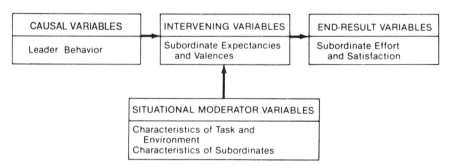

FIGURE 6-1   Causal Relationships in Path-Goal Theory of Leadership

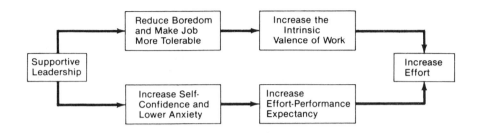

FIGURE 6-2   Causal Relationships for Effects of Supportive Leadership on Subordinate Effort

When the task is stressful, boring, tedious, or dangerous, supportive leadership leads to increased subordinate effort and satisfaction by increasing self-confidence, lowering anxiety, and minimizing unpleasant aspects of the work. In expectancy theory terminology, the leader increases both the intrinsic valence (enjoyment) of doing the task and the expectancy that it will be successfully completed. However, if a task is interesting and enjoyable, and subordinates are confident, then supportive leadership has little, if any, effect. The hypothesized causal chain for supportive leadership is depicted in Figure 6-2.

When the task is unstructured and complex, subordinates are inexperienced, and there is little formalization of rules and procedures to guide the work, then directive leadership will result in higher subordinate satisfaction and effort. The role ambiguity that exists when subordinates do not know what is expected of them or how to do the work causes them to have a low expectancy of success, even for a maximum effort. By reducing role ambiguity, the leader increases expectancies and thus effort. The theory further assumes that role ambiguity is unpleasant, and reducing it will lead to greater subordinate satisfaction. When the task is structured or subordinates are highly competent, directive leadership will have no effect on effort. Moreover, in this situation, if subordinates perceive close supervision and direction to be an unnecessary imposition of leader control, satisfaction may actually decline. The hypothesized causal chain for directive leadership is depicted in Figure 6-3. As the figure shows, there is more than one way for directive leadership to affect subordinate effort. Effort can be increased by finding new and larger performance rewards and making them more closely contingent upon subordinate performance. This option was included in the initial formulation of the theory by Evans

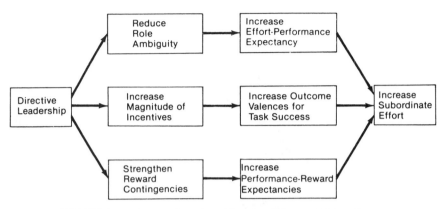

FIGURE 6-3   Causal Relationships for Effects of Directive Leadership Behavior on Subordinate Effort

(1970) and House (1971) but was neglected in most subsequent versions and in the validation research, perhaps because positive reward behavior does not fit well into the prevailing definition of directive behavior.

The propositions for participative leadership and achievement-oriented leadership are not as well developed or researched as those for supportive and directive leadership. Participative leadership is hypothesized to increase subordinate effort and satisfaction when the task is unstructured, by increasing role clarity. When the task is structured, this behavior has little or no effect. Participative Leadership may also increase the intrinsic valence of the work and thus satisfaction for subordinates with a high need for achievement and autonomy. Achievement-oriented leadership is hypothesized to increase subordinate effort and satisfaction when the task is unstructured (i.e., complex and nonrepetitive) by increasing self-confidence and the expectation of successfully accomplishing a challenging task or goal. When the task is simple and repetitive, this behavior has little or no effect.

Evaluation of Path-Goal Theory

Research conducted to test path-goal theory has yielded mixed results. Reviews of this research (Evans, 1986; Indvik, 1986) find that some studies support some aspects of the theory. The hypothesis that directive leader behavior increases subordinate satisfaction for unstructured tasks but not for structured tasks was supported in a majority of studies. However, the hypothesized moderating effect of task structure on directive behavior was not supported for other outcomes such as role clarity and subordinate performance. The hypothesis that supportive behavior increases role clarity, and performance for unstructured tasks but not structured tasks was supported, although only weakly. Consistent with other research on supportive behavior described in Chapter 5, most studies find a positive effect of supportive leadership on satisfaction, and this effect is only weakly moderated by task structure. Not enough studies have been conducted yet to test adequately the hypotheses about participative leadership and achievement-oriented leadership, but results were in the expected direction for the hypothesis that participative behavior increases satisfaction more when the task is unstructured and subordinates desire autonomy.

Methodological limitations for much of the validation research raise doubts about even the few hypotheses that have been supported. Virtually all of the studies used subordinate questionnaires to measure leader behavior, and most studies measured the variables at only one point in time. Many of the studies obtained all data from the same respondents or had criterion measures of doubtful validity. The weaknesses inherent in this type of static-correlational research with questionnaires were discussed in Chapter 5. In addition, most researchers have tested only a few aspects of the theory while ignoring other aspects. Measures of the intervening motivational processes (expectancies and valences) were not included in many of the studies. Taken together, these limitations of the research suggest that the theory has yet to be adequately tested.

Path-goal theory also has some serious conceptual deficiencies that limit its utility. Several major criticisms of the theory are the following:

1. Schriesheim and Kerr (1977) point out that the conceptual underpinnings of path-goal theory are questionable. Path-goal theory is limited by the conceptual problems of expectancy theory, upon which it relies to explain leader effects on subordinate motivation. Expectancy theory is an overly complex and seemingly unrealistic description of human motivational processes (Behling & Starke, 1973; Mitchell, 1974). Alternative decision models are currently more in favor, and one of these could be substituted for expectancy theory.

2. Questionable assumptions underlie some of the hypotheses. For example, it is assumed that role ambiguity is unpleasant to an employee, but some people seem to like a job in which duties and procedures are not specified in detail and there is ample opportunity to define their work role by themselves (Stinson & Johnson, 1975). It is also assumed that role ambiguity will cause a person to have an unrealistically low expectancy that serious effort will result in successful task performance and that leader behavior resulting in greater clarity will automatically increase expectancies. However, as House (1971) himself recognized, clarification of the subordinate's role sometimes makes it evident that successful task

performance and the attainment of specific task goals are more difficult than the subordinate initially believed.

3. The theory focuses on the motivational functions of leaders but does not explicitly consider other ways a leader can affect subordinate performance, such as training subordinates to increase their task skills, obtaining necessary resources, and organizing the work more efficiently. By doing things to influence these other intervening processes, a leader can improve performance beyond the level possible just from increasing subordinate effort.

4. Related to the preceding point, the theory focuses upon a few aspects of leader behavior and ignores other important aspects. Moreover, leader behavior is conceptualized at a very abstract level in terms of broad categories that do not relate easily to the intervening variables. For example, instead of directive/instrumental leadership, the theory should use more specific behaviors such as clarifying role expectations, recognizing accomplishments, and giving contingent rewards (Yukl & Clemence, 1984).

5. The effects of each leader behavior are considered separately, and likely interactions among leader behaviors are not addressed in the theory or in the research testing it. Path-goal theory implicitly assumes additive effects of leader behavior, whereas recent research favors an interactive model.

6. The manner in which different situational variables interact has not been specified in most cases, and it is not clear whether different aspects of the situation have a different moderating influence (Osborn, 1974).

Despite its limitations, path-goal theory has already made a contribution to the study of leadership by providing a conceptual framework to guide researchers in identifying potentially-relevant situational moderator variables. The proponents of the theory intended it to be only a tentative explanation of the motivational effects of leader behavior, and they did not attempt to include all of the variables that may be relevant.

HERSEY AND BLANCHARD'S
SITUATIONAL LEADERSHIP THEORY

Hersey and Blanchard (1969,1977, 1982), developed a leadership theory that was originally called the "life cycle theory of leadership," then was renamed "situational leadership theory." The theory attempts to explain effective leadership in terms of the moderating effect of one situational moderator variable on two broadly defined leader behaviors similar to consideration and initiating structure. Task behavior is the extent to which a leader organizes and defines the role of followers by explaining what each person must do, and when, where, and how tasks are to be accomplished. Relationship behavior is the extent to which a leader maintains personal relationships with followers by opening up channels of communication, providing socioemotional support, and giving "psychological strokes."

The situational moderator variable, called follower *maturity*, is measured only in relation to a particular task performed by a subordinate. Follower maturity includes two related components: (1) *job maturity* is a subordinate's task-relevant skills and technical knowledge, and (2) *psychological maturity* is the subordinate's self-confidence and self-respect. A high-maturity subordinate has both the ability and confidence to do a task, and this person will assume more responsibility and set high but attainable goals. A low-maturity subordinate lacks both ability and self-confidence. The causal relationships in the theory are shown in Figure 6-4.

According to situational leadership theory, the level of subordinate maturity determines the optimal level of leader behavior. As subordinate maturity increases from the minimum amount up to a moderate level, the leader should use more relations behavior and less task behavior. As subordinate maturity increases beyond a moderate level, the leader should decrease the amount of relations behavior while continuing to decrease the amount of task behavior. The prescriptions about the appropriate amount of each behavior for each level of maturity are depicted in Figure 6-5.

Four degrees of subordinate maturity are distinguished, even though they are merely segments of a continuum ranging from immature to mature. When a subordinate is very immature in relation to the task (M1), the leader should concentrate on task-oriented behavior and be very directive in defining subordinate roles and establishing objectives, standards, and procedures. When a subordinate has a moderate amount of maturity (M2 and M3), the leader should act very supportive, consult with the subordinate in making decisions, and provide praise and attention. At the same time, a moderate amount of directing and organizing is desirable, especially in the M2 quadrant. When a subordinate is very mature (M4), the

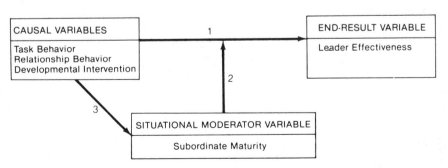

FIGURE 6-4   Causal Relationships in Hersey and Blanchard's Situational Leadership Theory

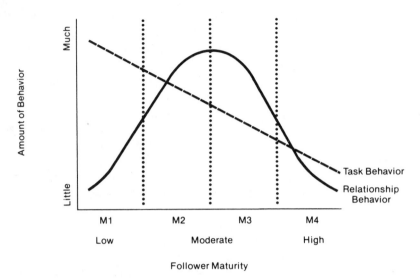

Much
Little
Amount of Behavior

M1   M2   M3   M4
Low   Moderate   High

Follower Maturity

Task Behavior
Relationship Behavior

FIGURE 6-5   Behavior Prescriptions in Hersey and Blanchard's Situational Leadership Theory

leader should delegate responsibility for deciding how the work is done and allow considerable autonomy. A mature subordinate has the ability to work without much direction from the leader and the confidence to do work without much supportive behavior by the leader.

In addition to the relationships already described between leader behavior and effectiveness (arrows 1 and 2), the leader's behavior has a delayed effect on subordinate maturity (arrow 3). According to Hersey and Blanchard, the leader can alter the maturity level of a subordinate by use of *developmental interventions.* A simple developmental intervention for an immature subordinate consists of relaxing the amount of direction and delegating more responsibility for a specific task. If the subordinate responds positively, the leader should provide praise and emotional support to reinforce the response.

A more complex developmental intervention is called *contingency contracting.* Here leader and subordinate negotiate an agreement regarding the subordinate's responsibilities and task objectives and the leader's role in helping to accomplish the objectives. How long it takes to "mature" a subordinate depends on the complexity of the task and the characteristics of the subordinate. There is no set formula, and it may take as little as a few days or as long as a few years to advance a subordinate from low to high maturity on a given task. Hersey and Blanchard recognize that subordinate maturity may regress, requiring a flexible adjustment of the leader's behavior. For example, a subordinate who is very responsible and motivated may become apathetic about the work after personal tragedy.

This subordinate would require closer supervision and a developmental intervention designed to boost maturity back to former levels.

Evaluation of Situational Leadership Theory

To date there has been very little research conducted to test Hersey and Blanchard's situational leadership theory. The authors have claimed that the theory can explain the results of earlier research on the results of task-oriented and relationship-oriented leader behavior, but the earlier studies did not attempt to measure maturity as defined in the theory and did not use the kind of analysis needed to evaluate the complex relationships proposed in the theory. Only a few studies (Blank, Weitzel, & Green, 1986; Hambleton & Gumpert, 1982) have attempted to test the theory directly, and these studies find only partial, weak support for it. Various writers have pointed out the following conceptual weaknesses in the theory:

1. There is no coherent, explicit rationale for the hypothesized relationships between leader behavior and effectiveness in different situations. First, there are no explicit intervening variables. The few attempts at explanation involve subordinate ability and motivation, but these are already components of maturity, which is the situational moderator variable. Unnecessary ambiguity and confusion is caused by the failure to differentiate clearly between situational moderators and intervening variables in a manner consistent with the bulk of the literature on performance determinants and leadership. Moreover, some of the explanations proposed by Hersey and Blanchard are inconsistent with other research on leadership and motivation (Graeff, 1983).

2. Maturity is defined too broadly and is conceptually ambiguous (Barrow, 1977). It is a composite situational variable with diverse components, and little guidance is provided for weighting and combining these different components. For example, a confident, responsible subordinate with a difficult task is not equivalent to an insecure, irresponsible subordinate with an easy task, or to a moderately confident and responsible subordinate with a moderately difficult task. The three conditions represent qualitatively different variations of medium maturity. In their most recent version of the theory, Hersey and Blanchard (1982) attempt to deal with this deficiency by suggesting that ability is weighted more in determining overall maturity for the first two quadrants, and motivation is weighted more in the last two quadrants. This proposal makes the questionable assumption that a person is less mature if skilled but unmotivated than if motivated but unskilled (Graeff, 1983). Such assumptions could be avoided if different components of maturity were treated as separate moderator variables, rather than as a single composite variable.

3. Leader behavior is not defined consistently from quadrant to quadrant. For example, relations behavior is described primarily in terms of "socioemotional support" in quadrant M2, whereas in M3 it is "participative decision making" (Graeff, 1983). Task behavior is described primarily as "clarifying the subordinate's role" in quadrant M1, whereas in M4 it is described as "delegation." Once again, unnecessary ambiguity and confusion result from the way the model is formulated. The attempt to explain leadership effectiveness with more specific aspects of behavior indicates that the broad task and relations behaviors may not be necessary or desirable. If the model contained a larger number of more narrowly defined behaviors, the authors could explicitly consider how each behavior should be handled in each situation.

4. The manner in which leader behavior is operationalized in their LEAD questionnaire is deficient in several respects (Blake & Mouton, 1981; Graeff, 1983). Managers are presented with short incidents and asked to select one of several predetermined responses. These choices are biased in favor of the theory and do not allow the option of selecting the type of behavior considered appropriate by competing theories. This deficiency is especially serious when the questionnaire is used as the major basis for testing the theory or as a basis for assessing and improving managerial skills.

5. The theory ignores many important situational variables, as the authors themselves admit. This omission is serious, because some other situational variables are pertinent to the determination of task and relations behavior. Situational variables contained in competing theories are likely to be just as important, if not more important, than subordinate maturity.

Despite its deficiencies, situational leadership theory has made some positive contributions. One contribution was an emphasis on flexible, adaptable leader behavior. Hersey and Blanchard reminded us that it is essential to treat different subordinates differently and to treat the same subordinate differently as the situation changes. Moreover, they advanced the important proposition that leaders should be aware of opportunities to build the skills and confidence of subordinates and not just assume that a particular subordinate with deficiencies in skills or motivation must forever remain a "problem employee." A final contribution of the theory is the recognition that leader behavior can be exhibited in a more or less skillful fashion, although skill is considered only in a general sense, and not explicitly incorporated into the model.

LEADERSHIP SUBSTITUTES THEORY

Kerr and Jermier (1978) developed a model to identify aspects of the situation that reduce the importance of managerial leadership. These researchers were mostly concerned with identifying limiting conditions for leader behaviors already found to influence subordinates, rather than on identifying new aspects of leader behavior that may be important. The model makes a distinction between two kinds of situational variables: *substitutes* and *neutralizers*. Substitutes make leader behavior unnecessary and redundant. They include any characteristics of the subordinates, task, or organization that ensure subordinates will clearly understand their roles, know how to do the work, be highly motivated, and be satisfied with their jobs. Neutralizers are any characteristics of the task or organization that prevent a leader from acting in a specified way, or that nullify the effects of the leader's actions. For example, a leader's lack of authority to reward effective performance is a situational constraint that serves as a neutralizer, whereas subordinate lack of interest in an incentive offered by the leader is a condition that makes the behavior pointless. The theory does not explicitly identify intervening variables, but they are implicit in the assumptions of the model. Substitutes are aspects of the situation that cause intervening variables to be at optimal levels, whereas neutralizers are constraints that prevent the leader from doing anything to improve existing deficiencies in intervening variables.

A preliminary list of substitutes and neutralizers for supportive and instrumental leadership is shown in Table 6-1. Supportive leadership is defined in a way similar to consideration, and instrumental leadership is similar to initiating structure.

TABLE 6-1   Specific Substitutes and Neutralizers for Supportive and Instrumental Leadership

SUBSTITUTE OR NEUTRALIZER	SUPPORTIVE LEADERSHIP	INSTRUMENTAL LEADERSHIP
A. *Subordinate Characteristics:*		
1. Experience, ability, training		Substitute
2. "Professional" orientation	Substitute	Substitute
3. Indifference toward rewards offered by organization	Neutralizer	Neutralizer
B. *Task Characteristics:*		
1. Structured, routine, unambiguous task		Substitute
2. Feedback provided by task		Substitute
3. Intrinsically satisfying task	Substitute	
C. *Organization Characteristics:*		
1. Cohesive work group	Substitute	Substitute
2. Low position power (leader lacks control over organizational rewards)	Neutralizer	Neutralizer
3. Formalization (explicit plans, goals, areas of responsibility)		Substitute
4. Inflexibility (rigid, unyielding rules and procedures)		Neutralizer
5. Leader located apart from subordinates with only limited communication possible	Neutralizer	Neutralizer

Based on Kerr and Jermier, 1978

According to Kerr and Jermier a number of subordinate characteristics may serve as substitutes and/or neutralizers for support and instrumental leadership. Extensive prior experience or training of subordinates serves as a substitute for instrumental behavior by the leader. Little direction is necessary because subordinates already possess the skills and knowledge to know what to do and how to do it. For example, medical doctors, airline pilots, accountants, electricians, and other professionals and craftspeople do not require close supervision. Likewise, most professionals are internally motivated by their values, needs, and ethics, so they do not need to be influenced by the leader to do high-quality work.

Various task attributes also serve as substitutes for instrumental leader behavior. If the task is simple and repetitive, subordinates can learn the appropriate skills quickly without extensive training and direction by the leader. If the task automatically provides feedback on how well the work is being performed, then feedback from the leader is unnecessary. If the task is interesting and enjoyable, there is no need for supportive leadership to make the job situation tolerable for subordinates.

Like prior experience and simple tasks, organizational formalization is a substitute for instrumental leadership behavior. In organizations with detailed written rules, regulations, and policies, little direction is necessary once the rules and policies have been learned by subordinates. Rules and policies can serve as a neutralizer as well as a substitute if they are so inflexible they prevent a leader from making changes in job assignments or work procedures to facilitate subordinate effort. Lack of position power tends to neutralize the use of rewards and punishments by the leader to motivate subordinates. Both supportive and instrumental leader behavior are neutralized when subordinates are geographically dispersed and have only infrequent contact with their leader, as in the case of most field-sales representatives. Finally, the existence of a highly cohesive group of subordinates who work together can serve as a substitute for supportive leadership, since subordinates can obtain psychological support from each other rather than from the leader.

Kerr and Jermier suggest the interesting possibility that leaders are sometimes altogether superfluous. Although the overall influence of a leader on subordinate satisfaction and performance may be less in some situations than in others, the possibility of a situation wherein the leader has virtually no influence seems rather remote. It is important to remember that the model was designed to deal only with substitutes for "hierarchical" leadership behavior by a formal leader. For some substitutes, behavior by the designated leader is merely replaced by similar leadership behavior carried out by peers or informal leaders. Various types of research demonstrate that leadership functions may be shared among members of a group, rather than being performed entirely by the formally designated "leader" (Bowers & Seashore, 1966; Manz & Sims, 1987; Slater, 1955).

Evaluation of Leadership Substitutes Theory

Kerr and Jermier's model is fairly new, and only a few studies have been conducted yet to verify its propositions about specific substitutes and neutralizers (Ford, 1981; Howell & Dorfman, 1981, 1986; Jermier & Berkes, 1979; Kerr & Jermier, 1978). Some support was found for some hypotheses, but in view of the limited evidence, it is still too early to assess the validity and utility of the model. However, a number of conceptual weaknesses are evident.

1. The theory fails to provide a detailed rationale for each substitute and neutralizer, with explicit intervening variables. It is essentially a listing of situational variables that moderate two broadly defined leader behaviors rather than a true theory that explains underlying causal relationships. A sharper focus on intervening, explanatory processes would help to differentiate between substitutes that reduce the importance of an intervening process, and substitutes that involve leadership behavior by people other than the leader. For example, the importance of subordinate ability can be reduced by technological improvements, such as automation and artificial intelligence, which reduces the need to develop subordinate ability through coaching and instruction. A quite different situation is one in which ability remains important, but the skill-building behavior is handled by someone besides the leader (e.g., coworkers, outside trainers).

2. The orientation toward discovering substitutes and constraints for particular behaviors by a formal leader tends to result in a narrow perspective on leadership. To the limited extent that intervening variables are discussed, the theory implicitly assumes that only subordinate ability and motivation are important for leadership effectiveness. The theory largely ignores other important processes that affect the performance of an organizational unit, such as shortages of necessary resources, conflicts among subordinates, lack of cooperation from peers and superiors, design problems in the organization of the work, unusual crises and problems that require decisive action, and environmental changes that call for a reshaping of both strategy and organizational culture.

3. Some of the theory's deficiencies in scope and substance are due to preoccupation with highly abstract behavior categories such as supportive and instrumental behavior. It is difficult to identify specific substitutes and neutralizers for broadly defined behavior categories. The theory would be improved by replacing supportive and instrumental behavior with more specific behaviors. A step in the right direction is the research by Howell and Dorfman (1986) and Jermier & Berkes (1979), in which instrumental leadership was replaced by specific component behaviors such as work assignment, role clarification, and specification of procedures.

One positive contribution already made by the theory is to focus more attention on conditions that serve as substitutes or neutralizers. Even

though many of these are the same ones identified as situational moderator variables in earlier theories, the general orientation encourages researchers to search for limiting conditions beyond the obvious ones.

VROOM AND YETTON
NORMATIVE MODEL

We saw in Chapter 5 that participative behavior has been one of the
most frequently studied aspects of leadership behavior. The importance of
using decision procedures that are appropriate for the situation has been
recognized for some time. Tannenbaum and Schmidt (1958) noted that a
leader's choice of decision procedures reflects forces in the leader, forces in
the subordinates, and forces in the situation. Maier (1963) pointed out the
need for leaders to consider both the quality requirements of a decision and
the likelihood of subordinate acceptance before choosing a decision procedure. Vroom and Yetton (1973) build upon these earlier approaches but go
further in specifying which decision procedures will be most effective in
each of several specific kinds of situations. The Vroom-Yetton model is
based on an analysis of how a leader's decision behavior effects decision
quality and subordinate acceptance of the decision. Quality and acceptance
are intervening variables that jointly affect group performance. Various
aspects of the situation moderate the relationship between decision procedures and the intervening variables.

Decision acceptance is the degree of subordinate commitment to implement a decision effectively. In some cases, subordinates are highly motivated to implement a decision made by the leader because it is beneficial
to them or because the leader uses influence tactics to gain acceptance of
the decision. However, there are other decisions that subordinates will
not accept if the decision is made in an autocratic manner. For example,
subordinates may resent not being consulted, they may not understand the
reasons for the decision, and they may see it as detrimental to their interests. A basic assumption of the model is that participation increases
decision acceptance if it is not already high, and the more influence subordinates have, the more they will be motivated to implement a decision.
Thus, decision acceptance is likely to be greater for joint decision making
than for consultation, and for consultation than for an autocratic decision.

Several explanations have been proposed for the effect of participation on decision acceptance (Anthony, 1978; Maier, 1963; Mitchell, 1973;
Strauss, 1963). When subordinates have unwarranted fears and anxieties
about the implications of a decision, participation leads to better understanding of the reasons for the decision and how it will affect them. Participation also allows subordinates an opportunity to exercise some influence
to protect their interests if actually threatened. A decision is more likely
to be consistent with subordinate interests and preferences if subordinates

participate in making it. Moreover, subordinates who have considerable influence in making a decision tend to identify with it and perceive it to be "their decision," which increases their motivation to implement it successfully. When a decision is made by a group process that members consider as legitimate, the group is likely to apply social pressure on members to implement the decision, thereby further reducing the likelihood of resistance by anyone. Decision acceptance is important whenever a decision must be implemented by subordinates or has implications for their work motivation.

Decision quality refers to the objective aspects of the decision that affect group performance aside from any effects mediated by decision acceptance. A high-quality decision is one where the best alternative is selected. For example, an efficient work procedure is selected instead of less efficient alternatives, or a challenging performance goal is set for the group instead of an easy goal. Decision quality is important when there is a great deal of variability among alternatives, and the decision has important consequences for group performance. If the available alternatives are approximately equal in consequences, or if the decision has no important consequences for group performance, then decision quality is not important. Examples of task decisions that are usually important include determination of goals and priorities, assignment of tasks to subordinates who differ in skills, determination of work procedures for complex tasks, and determination of ways to solve technical problems.

The effect of participation on decision quality depends upon the distribution of relevant information and problem solving expertise between leader and subordinates. The model assumes that participation will result in better quality decisions if subordinates possess relevant information and are willing to cooperate with the leader in making a good decision. Cooperation, however, depends in turn on the extent to which subordinates share the leader's task objectives and have a relationship of mutual trust with the leader. The model assumes that consultation is as likely to facilitate decision quality as joint decision making when subordinates share the leader's objectives. When subordinates have incompatible objectives, consultation usually results in higher quality decisions than joint decision making, because the leader retains control over the final choice.

Vroom and Yetton identify five decision procedures for decisions involving multiple subordinates, including two varieties of autocratic decision (AI and AII), two varieties of consultation (CI and CII), and one variety of joint decision making by leader and subordinates as a group (GII). Each of these decision procedures is defined as follows (Vroom and Yetton, 1973, p. 13):

AI. You solve the problem or make the decision yourself, using information available to you at the time.

AII. You obtain the necessary information from your subordinates, then decide the solution to the problem yourself. You may or may not tell your subordinates what the problem is in getting the information from them. The role played by your subordinates in making the decision is clearly one of providing necessary information to you, rather than generating or evaluating alternative solutions.

CI. You share the problem with the relevant subordinates individually, getting their ideas and suggestions, without bringing them together as a group. Then you make the decision, which may or may not reflect your subordinates' influence.

CII. You share the problem with your subordinates as a group, obtaining their collective ideas and suggestions. Then you make the decision, which may or may not reflect your subordinate' influence.

GII. You share the problem with your subordinates as a group. Together you generate and evaluate alternatives and attempt to reach agreement (consensus) on a solution. Your role is much like that of chairman. You do not try to influence the group to adopt "your" solution, and you are willing to accept and implement any solution which has the support of the entire group.

According to the model, the effectiveness of a decision procedure depends on the following aspects of the situation: (1) the amount of relevant information possessed by leader and subordinates, (2) the likelihood that subordinates will accept an autocratic decision, (3) the likelihood that subordinates will cooperate if allowed to participate, (4) the amount of disagreement among subordinates with respect to their preferred alternatives, and (5) the extent to which the decision problem is unstructured and requires creative problem solving. The model provides a set of rules for identifying any decision procedure that is inappropriate in a given situation because decision quality and/or acceptance would be jeopardized by using that procedure. The rules are based on the assumptions discussed earlier about the consequences of different decision procedures under different conditions. The decision rules can be summarized briefly in the following manner.

1. When the decision is important and subordinates possess relevant information lacked by the leader, an autocratic decision (AI, AII) is not appropriate because an important decision would be made without all the relevant, available information.

2. When decision quality is important and subordinates do not share the leader's concern for task goals, a group decision (GII) is not appropriate because these procedures would give too much influence over an important decision to uncooperative or even hostile persons.

3. When decision quality is important, the decision problem is unstructured, and the leader does not possess the necessary information and expertise to make a good decision, then the decision should be made by interaction among the people who have the relevant information (GII).

4. When decision acceptance is important and subordinates are unlikely to accept an autocratic decision, then an autocratic decision (AI, AII) is not appropriate because the decision may not be implemented effectively.

5. When decision acceptance is important and subordinates are likely to disagree among themselves about the best solution to an important problem, autocratic procedures and individual consultation (AI, AII, CI) are not appropriate because they do not provide the opportunity to resolve differences through discussion and negotiation among subordinates and between the subordinates and the leader.

6. When decision quality is not important but acceptance is critical and unlikely to result from an autocratic decision, the only appropriate procedure is a group decision (GII) because acceptance is maximized without risking quality.

7. When decision acceptance is important and not likely to result from an autocratic decision, and subordinates share the leader's task objectives, subordinates should be given equal partnership in the decision process (GII), because acceptance is maximized without risking quality.

For some decision situations, the model prescribes more than one feasible decision procedure. In this case, the choice among remaining procedures in the "feasible set" should be based on other criteria, such as time pressure, desire to develop subordinates, or leader preferences among procedures. Vroom and Yetton have developed decision process flow charts to simplify the application of the rules and assist managers in identifying the optimal decision procedure. Figure 6-6 shows one of these charts.

Vroom and Jago Revision of the Model

Recently, Vroom and Jago (1988) reviewed the findings on the Vroom-Yetton Model and offered a revised version of it. This model was designed to correct some of the weaknesses in the earlier version. The Vroom-Yetton model tells a manager what not to do but does not indicate what to do. The model eliminates only about half of the procedures from the feasible set, and it does not indicate which of the remaining procedures is best. The Vroom-Jago model incorporates features that allow a manager to determine the relative priority of different criteria and reduce the feasible set to a single procedure by applying the criteria.

The Vroom-Yetton model fails to capture some differences among situations by requiring a definite yes-no answer to the situational questions. The new model corrects this deficiency by requiring managers to differentiate among five choices in describing each aspect of the situation. For example, to the question "Do subordinates share the organizational goals?" to be attained in solving this problem managers select one of the following choices: no, probably no, maybe, probably yes, yes.

FIGURE 6-6 Vroom and Yetton Decision Process Flowchart

A. Does the problem possess a quality requirement?
B. Do I have sufficient information to make a high-quality decision?
C. Is the problem structured?
D. Is acceptance of the decision by subordinates important for effective implementation?
E. If I were to make the decision by myself, am I reasonably certain that it would be accepted by my subordinates?
F. Do subordinates share the organizational goals to be attained in solving this problem?
G. Is conflict among subordinates likely in preferred solutions?

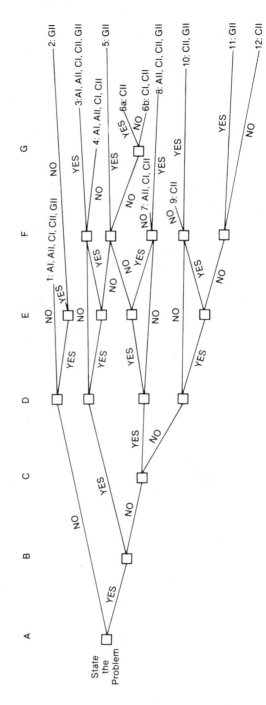

Source: Reprinted, by permission of the publisher, from "Can Leaders Learn to Lead?" by V. H. Vroom, *Organizational Dynamics*, Winter 1976, © 1976 by American Management Associations, New York. All rights reserved.

The Vroom-Yetton model fails to include some important aspects of the situation, such as severe time constraints, amount of subordinate information, and geographical dispersion of subordinates. These attributes are incorporated in the Vroom-Jago model. The Vroom-Yetton model uses only two outcome criteria—decision acceptance and decision quality—in the decision rules. The new model adds concern for subordinate development and concern for decision time as explicit criteria for determining optimal decision procedures. Managers are given more choice in setting the priorities of the criteria in the new model. Decision rules are replaced by mathematical functions. The result of the various changes is to make an already complex model even more complex, and a microcomputer software program is recommended to apply the model in its complete form.

Evaluation of the Vroom-Yetton Model

A number of studies have been conducted to test the Vroom-Yetton model since it first appeared (Crouch & Yetton, 1987; Ettling & Jago, 1988; Field, 1982; Heilman, Hornstein, Cage & Herschlag, 1984; Margerison & Glube, 1979; Jago & Vroom, 1980; Tjosvold, Wedley, & Field, 1986; Vroom & Jago, 1978). Most studies tested the model by comparing effects of decisions made according to the model's prescriptions with effects of decisions made in a way that is inconsistent with the model. The most common procedure has been to ask managers to describe examples of successful and unsuccessful decisions. These decisions are analyzed to determine what situation they represent, and the decision procedure used by the manager is compared to the feasible set recommended by the model. In two laboratory studies with students, leader behavior was manipulated by specifying the decision procedure to be used by a leader in a given situation, and varying the procedures and situations (Field, 1982; Liddel, Elsea, Parkinson & Hackett, 1986, cited in Vroom & Jago, 1988, p. 79–83).

In general, the results in this research have supported the model. Vroom and Jago (1988) computed the mean rate of success across five studies, and they found that for decisions made in accordance with the model, the mean success rate was 62 percent, versus 37 percent for decisions made using a decision procedure outside of the feasible set. According to Vroom and Jago, four studies have tested the decision rules separately. These studies found some decision rules were supported much better than others. Thus, the preliminary results are promising, but more research is clearly needed to test the model and each of its decision rules. The revised version of the model is still too new to have been tested extensively, but Vroom and Jago (1988) report some promising findings.

The Vroom-Yetton model is probably the best supported of the situational leadership theories. It focuses on specific aspects of behavior rather than broadly defined behaviors, it includes meaningful intervening variables, and it identifies important aspects of the situation moderating the relationship between behavior and outcomes. However, the model and its successor deal with only a small part of leadership, and the following weaknesses have been noted for one or both models:

1. Decision processes are treated as a single, discrete episode at one point in time. The descriptive research reviewed in Chapter 4 found that most important decisions involve multiple meetings with a variety of different people at different times, and repeated cycles occur as decisions are returned for revisions necessary for them to be accepted by powerful people not directly involved in the initial process. The theory does not explicitly recognize the possibility that most "thick cycle" decisions require a sequence of different decision procedures with different people at different times.

2. Some important decision procedures are excluded. One of the most important decision procedures used by managers, the so called "trial balloon" approach lies somewhere between AI and CI. The manager makes a tentative (autocratic) decision and then tests its adequacy and acceptability by mentioning it casually to a few carefully selected people. If the proposal is acceptable, it can be announced, and if not, the leader can revise it and try again or shift to a participative procedure such as CII or GII. For a leader with lingering doubts about having the information necessary to make a high quality decision that will be accepted, this procedure allows the initial diagnosis of the situation to be tested without much risk.

3. The models are not parsimonious (Field, 1979). The distinction between AI and AII is unnecessary, since the issue of getting factual and technical information (as opposed to ideas and evaluative reactions) is not a central focus of the model. The descriptive research reviewed in Chapter 4 showed that managers are continually gathering information from a variety of sources. Managers do not need a model to tell them to gather essential information. The distinction between CI and CII injects a separate issue of how a decision procedure should be used. This issue should be the subject of a supplementary model, since it also applies to AI (should the autocratic decision be presented to the group together or separately to individuals?) and GII (should group membership change at different stages of the decision, and should there be subgroups to deal with separate aspects of the decision?). The primary model need distinguish only between autocratic, consultative, and joint decision procedures. Once this choice is made, one or more supplementary models would guide the manager in selecting among the major variations of a decision procedure. The trial balloon procedure could be included as one of the variations of an autocratic decision, along with the distinction between tells and sells used by Hersey and Blanchard (1982) and Tannenbaum and Schmidt (1958).

4. Leaders are assumed to have the skills necessary to apply the model. Not enough guidance is provided to leaders on how to diagnose the sit-

uation, which may be even harder in the Vroom and Jago version than in the Vroom-Yetton version. Managers are also assumed to have sufficient skill to use each of the decision procedures. No guidelines on how to use the procedures are provided, and leader skill is not a factor in determining which procedure is most appropriate (Crouch & Yetton, 1987; Field, 1979). Crouch and Yetton showed that some assumptions of the model are not valid for unskilled leaders. Their study found that in situations with conflict among subordinates, group procedures (CII or GII) were effective for leaders who had conflict management skills but not for leaders lacking these skills. Leaders without these skills are better off using individual consultation (CI), which does not require direct confrontation between subordinates who disagree with each other. The possibility that the potential benefits of group decisions may be nullified by a lack of leader skills is explored further in Chapter 11.

GENERAL EVALUATION
OF SITUATIONAL THEORIES

Table 6-2 summarizes the major features of the four situational theories described in this chapter and the two described in Chapter 9. The table makes it easier to compare the theories with respect to content and validation. All six theories contain situational moderator variables, but the variety of situational variables is greater in some theories than in others. It seems desirable for a situational theory to include many relevant aspects of the situation, but to do so makes a theory very difficult to test. Intervening variables are helpful to explain how leaders influence subordinate performance, but only two of the theories have explicit intervening variables.

In order to support a situational theory, the pattern of results in a study must be consistent with the propositions of the theory. If the theory postulates a causal chain of sequential effects from leader behavior to intervening variable to outcomes, the results must be consistent with this explanation. Unfortunately, most of the situational theories are stated so ambiguously that it is difficult to derive specific, testable propositions. Most of the research provides only an indirect or partial test of the situational theories. In general, the research suffers from lack of accurate measures and reliance on weak research designs that do not permit strong inferences about direction of causality (Korman & Tanofsky, 1975; Schriesheim & Kerr, 1977).

Not all behavioral scientists agree that situational leadership theories are useful. For example, McCall (1977) contends that the hectic, fragmented pace of managerial work and the relative lack of control over it by managers makes it impossible to apply complex theories that specify the optimal behavior for every type of situation. Managers are so busy dealing with problems that they don't have time to stop and analyze the situation with a complicated model. McCall also questions the common underlying assumption of a single "best way" for the manager to act within a given situation. Leaders face an immense variety of rapidly changing situations, and several different patterns of behavior may be equally effective in a given situation.

TABLE 6–2   Summary of Situational Leadership Models

SITUATIONAL MODEL	LEADER TRAITS	LEADER BEHAVIOR	SITUATIONAL VARIABLES	INTERVENING VARIABLES	VALIDATION RESULTS
Path-goal theory	None	Instrumental, supportive, participative, achievement	Many aspects	Expectancies, valences, role ambiguity	Many studies, partial support
Hersey & Blanchard situational leadership	None	Task and relations	Subordinate maturity	None	Few studies, inconclusive
Leadership substitutes	None	Instrumental, supportive	Many aspects	None	Few studies, inconclusive
Vroom-Yetton model	None	Decision procedures	Many aspects	Decision quality and acceptance	Few studies, most supportive
LPC contingency model	LPC	None	Task structure, L-M relations, position power	None	Many studies, partial support
Cognitive resource theory	Intelligence, experience	Directive	Stress, group support task complexity	None	Few studies, inconclusive

The situational models reviewed in this chapter provide some insights, but they do not take us very far toward understanding the nature of effective leader behavior. We saw in Chapter 5 that the universal theories fail to provide guidelines telling managers how to apply general principles differently in different situations. The situational theories suffer from the opposite problem of failing to present general principles to help managers recognize underlying requirements in the myriad of fragmented and varied activities and problems confronting them. What is needed is a theory with both universal and situational elements. The theory should provide managers with general, easily applicable principles, but these must be more concrete than universalistic guidelines such as "allow participation" and "show high concern for both task and people." The general principles should allow a manager some choice in the way they are enacted, yet help managers differentiate between more and less desirable alternatives.

SUMMARY

Situational theories of leader effectiveness are concerned with the moderating influence of situational variables on the relationship between leader behavior and outcomes or between leader traits and outcomes. These theories assume that different situations require different patterns of behavior or traits to be effective.

Hersey and Blanchard's situational leadership theory examines how the effectiveness of task and relations behavior is contingent on subordinate maturity. The theory prescribes different combinations of these behaviors depending on a subordinate's confidence and skill in relation to the task. The theory emphasizes flexible, adaptive leadership that is responsive to changing conditions.

The path-goal theory of Leadership examines how four aspects of leader behavior influence subordinate satisfaction and motivation. In general, leaders motivate subordinates by influencing their perceptions of the likely consequences of different levels of effort. If subordinates believe that valued outcomes can be attained only by making a serious effort and that such an effort will be successful, then they are likely to make the effort. Aspects of the situation such as the nature of the task, the work environment, and subordinate characteristics determine the optimal level of each type of leadership behavior for improving subordinate satisfaction and effort.

Leadership substitutes theory identifies aspects of the situation that make leadership behavior by hierarchical leaders redundant or irrelevant. Various characteristics of the subordinates, task, and organization serve as substitutes for leadership and/or neutralizers of its effects. Substitutes make some types of behavior by the leader unnecessary and redundant, whereas neutralizers are constraints that prevent the leader from doing anything to improve conditions.

Vroom and Yetton's normative model of participation examines the effects of different decision procedures on two intervening variables—decision quality and decision acceptance—which jointly influence group performance. The situational moderator variables are characteristics of the decision situation that determine whether a particular decision procedure will increase or decrease decision quality and acceptance. Leaders are more effective if they use decision procedures that are appropriate in a particular situation. The model has been extended recently by Vroom and Jago.

The situational theories provide some insights into reasons for leadership effectiveness, but they all have conceptual weaknesses that limit their utility. An integrating model that builds on the strengths of these situational theories while avoiding many of their limitations is presented in the next chapter.

REVIEW AND DISCUSSION QUESTIONS

1. What is a situational moderator variable? An intervening variable? How are these two types of variables used in situational or contingency theories of leadership effectiveness?
2. Is there a way to reconcile universal and situational theories of task-oriented and relationship-oriented leadership? Explain.
3. Briefly explain and evaluate path-goal theory of leadership.
4. Briefly explain and evaluate Hersey and Blanchard's situational leadership theory of leadership.
5. Briefly explain and evaluate the Vroom-Yetton normative model of leadership.
6. Briefly explain and evaluate Kerr and Jermier's leadership substitutes theory.
7. Some writers assert that situational leadership theories are not useful for managers. Evaluate this assertion.
8. Compare and contrast the four situational theories in this chapter.

7

AN INTEGRATIVE MODEL
OF EFFECTIVE
MANAGERIAL BEHAVIOR

This chapter builds upon earlier ones and attempts to integrate the diverse findings and theories about effective managerial behavior. We begin by describing a situational model that incorporates major aspects of earlier situational theories, such as path-goal theory, leader substitutes theory, the Vroom-Yetton (1973) normative decision model, and Wofford's (1982) theory of leader-environment-follower interaction. The focus of the model is on the interacting effects of managerial behavior and situational attributes on outcomes. The model is extended in Chapter 12 to include leader traits, power, and situational determinants of leader behavior.

THE MULTIPLE LINKAGE MODEL

Prior to 1970 there were no leadership theories that included intervening variables along with situational variables. Likert (1967) pointed out the desirability of using intervening variables to explain the delayed effects of a manager's behavior on the productivity and profits of the organizational subunit. However, Likert proposed a universal theory that was supposedly applicable to all types of leaders, regardless of the situation. In 1971, Yukl proposed a meta-theory called the multiple linkage model to explain how a leader's behavior affects the performance of an organizational subunit. This model has been revised to incorporate new knowledge about effective managerial behavior. The causal relationships among major types of variables are depicted in Figure 7-1.

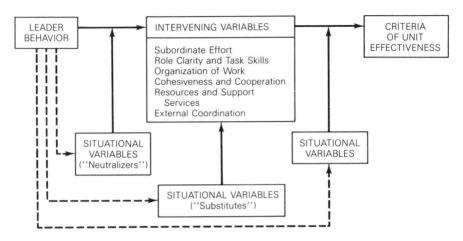

FIGURE 7-1   Causal Relationships in the Multiple Linkage Model

Intervening Variables

There are three sets of intervening variables in the model: two describing individual attributes, two describing group or unit attributes, and two describing the interface with the larger organization. These six intervening variables are defined as follows:

1. *Subordinate effort.* The extent to which subordinates strive to attain a high level of performance and show a high degree of personal responsibility and commitment to task objectives.

2. *Subordinate ability and role clarity.* The extent to which subordinates understand their job responsibilities, know what to do, and have the skills to do it.

3. *Organization of the work.* The extent to which effective performance strategies are used by the group to attain its task objectives and the work is organized to ensure efficient utilization of personnel, equipment, and facilities.

4. *Cooperation and cohesiveness.* The extent to which group members work together smoothly as a team, share information and ideas, help each other, and feel a strong identification with the group.

5. *Resources and Support.* The extent to which the group has the budgetary funds, tools, equipment, supplies, personnel, and facilities needed to do the work, and necessary information or assistance from other units.

6. *External Coordination.* The extent to which the activities and operations of the work unit are synchronized with those of other subunits in

the same organization, thereby avoiding unnecessary delays, disruptions, and wasted effort.

The six intervening variables interact with each other to determine the effectiveness of the organizational unit. A serious deficiency in one intervening variable may lower effectiveness, even though the other intervening variables are not deficient. Individual performance depends on both effort and ability; if either is low, individual performance will be low. Group performance depends on how well the members are organized to use their skills (Hackman, Brousseau, & Weiss, 1976, O'Brien & Habaroff, 1981; Shiflett, 1979.). However, performance will suffer even for a well-organized team with a good performance strategy if there is not a high level of cooperation and teamwork (Hewett, O'Brien, & Hornik, 1974). Performance also depends on getting the necessary resources and cooperation from people outside of the group (Peters, O'Connor, & Rudolf, 1980). A manufacturing plant cannot maintain a high level of production without a dependable supply of raw materials and components and the funds to hire necessary workers. Finally, in organizations with substantial interdependence among subunits, performance for an individual subunit, as well as overall performance for the organization, depends on a high level of coordination among subunits.

Situational Variables

Situational variables in the model exert influence at three points (see Figure 7-1). First, situational variables determine the relative importance of the six intervening variables. For example, group organization and cooperation are less important in coacting groups where subordinates work alone on separate tasks than in interacting groups where subordinates have interdependent tasks. Subordinate ability is less important when the work is simple and repetitive than when the work is complex and nonrepetitive. Resource acquisition is less important when the group needs few resources or has its own reliable sources than when the group is highly dependent upon unreliable sources. External coordination is less important for an autonomous subunit than for one with high lateral and upward dependence (Kotter, 1982; Stewart, 1976).

Second, aspects of the situation influence the current level of each situational variable. This aspect of the model is similar to Kerr and Jermier's "substitutes." Effort is influenced by the formal reward system in the organization and by the intrinsically motivating properties of the work itself. Subordinate effort will be higher if the organization has a reward system that automatically makes rewards contingent upon performance or if the work is naturally interesting and challenging. Subordinate ability will be greater if the organization has effective recruiting and selection procedures, and qualified people are attracted by high salaries.

Ability also depends on the amount of training and preparation a person receives prior to joining the organizational unit.

Work group organization is influenced by technology, geographical distribution of work sites, the policies and procedures imposed by the larger organization, and by informal practices that have evolved over time among subordinates. Cohesiveness and cooperation are influenced by the size of the group, the stability of membership, and similarity among members in values and background. Small groups with a stable, homogeneous membership tend to have more cohesiveness and teamwork. Resources are influenced by higher-level budgetary systems, procurement systems, inventory control systems, availability of alternate sources, and general economic conditions. When organizational practices provide an adequate level of resources and support, the manager's job is less difficult. External coordination is easier to achieve when there are special integrating structural mechanisms, such as integrator positions and committees (Galbraith, 1973; Lawrence & Lorsch, 1967).

A third type of situational variable limits a leader's discretion in making changes and reacting to problems. The extent to which a leader is capable of doing something in the short run to improve any of the intervening variables is limited by position authority, organizational policies, and legal-contractual restrictions. Constraints may prevent a leader from rewarding or punishing subordinates, procuring supplies and equipment, and changing work assignments or procedures. These influences are similar to Stewart's (1976) constraints and Kerr and Jermier's (1978) "neutralizers."

General Propositions

There are two basic propositions in the model, one dealing with short-term actions by the leader and one dealing with long-term actions.

Proposition 1: In the short term, unit effectiveness is greater when the leader acts to correct any deficiencies in the intervening variables.

This feature of the model is similar to the approach used in path-goal theory, situational leadership theory, and Wofford's LEFI theory. The situation determines which intervening variables are most important and which are deficient. A leader who fails to recognize opportunities to correct deficiencies in key intervening variables, who recognizes the opportunities but fails to act, or who acts but is not skilled will be less than optimally effective. An ineffective leader may make things worse by acting in ways that increase rather than decrease the deficiency in one or more intervening variables. For example, a leader who uses coercive influence tactics may lower subordinate effort. A leader who reorganizes the group may reduce efficiency by creating duplication of effort and increasing coordination problems. The multiple-linkage model does not imply that only one particular pattern of managerial behavior is optimal in any given situation. Leaders usually have some choice among intervening variables in need of improvement, and different patterns of behavior are usually possible to correct a particular deficiency. In this respect, the model is similar to Stewart's "choices." However, effectiveness will suffer if a leader's attention is focused on intervening variables that are not deficient or that are not important determinants of unit performance.

Proposition 2: In the longer term, unit effectiveness is greater when the leader acts to make the situation more favorable.

Over a longer period of time, leaders can act to indirectly influence the intervening variables by modifying the situation. These behaviors, shown by the dotted lines in Figure 7-1, occur concurrently with continued efforts to directly influence the intervening variables. In effect, the long-term behaviors attempt to reduce constraints, increase substitutes, and reduce the importance of intervening variables that are not amenable to improvement. Some examples of possible actions to improve the situation are as follows:

1. Developing better relations with superiors to increase their trust and persuade them to provide more authority to deal with task problems.
2. Gain more control over acquisition of resources necessary to do the work by cultivating better relationships with suppliers, finding alternative sources, and reducing dependence on unreliable sources.
3. Gain more control over the demand for the unit's products and services by finding new customers, opening new markets, advertising more, and modifying the products or services to be more acceptable to clients and cusomers.
4. Initiate new, more profitable activities for the work unit that will make better use of personnel, equipment, and facilities.
5. Initiate long-term improvement programs to upgrade personnel, equipment, and facilities in the work unit, such as by replacing old equipment, establishing training programs, reconstructing facilities, and so on.
6. Modify the formal structure of the work unit to solve chronic problems and reduce demands on the leader for short-term troubleshooting, such as by redefining authority relationships, centralizing or decentralizing some decision making, creating or eliminating positions and subunits, modifying information systems, and simplifying or increasing rules and standard procedures.
7. Alter the culture of the organization to emphasize values, beliefs, and norms that are internalized sources of motivation to excel.

The next section of the chapter describes an integrating taxonomy of behaviors used by managers to influence intervening and situational variables.

AN INTEGRATING TAXONOMY
OF MANAGERIAL BEHAVIORS

The earlier behavior taxonomies reviewed briefly in Chapter 5 have deficiencies that limit their utility for developing theories of leadership effectiveness. Many of the taxonomies omit forms of behavior found in empirical research to be related to managerial effectiveness. Other common deficiencies include use of nonbehavioral constructs such as traits and skills, use of behavior constructs that are ambiguous, mixing constructs at different levels of abstraction, and use of behavior categories that are so broadly defined that they obscure important distinctions among component behaviors.

Yukl (1987) proposed an integrating taxonomy based on a combination of approaches, including factor analysis, judgmental classification, and theoretical deduction. The taxonomy is further refined here. The current version has 4 broad categories, 11 middle-range behavior categories, and a much larger number of specific component behaviors. An effort was made to formulate categories that maintained continuity with earlier taxonomies and with major lines of research on leader behavior, such as research on positive reward behavior, participative leadership, supportive leadership, transformational leadership, and so forth.

The broad categories of managerial behavior are the same ones described in Chapter 4: building and maintaining relationships, collecting and disseminating information, making decisions, and influencing people. Within each broad category are behavior categories defined at a middle level of generality (see Figure 7-2). Building and maintaining relationships includes supporting, networking, and team building/managing conflict. Handling information includes monitoring, clarifying, and informing. Making decisions includes planning/organizing, problem solving, and consulting/delegating. Influencing includes motivating and recognizing/rewarding. Table 7-1 gives definitions for each middle-range behavior.

The integrating taxonomy builds on the strengths of earlier taxonomies while avoiding many of their weaknesses. With 11 middle-range categories, the taxonomy is reasonably parsimonious, yet it encompasses most aspects of managerial behavior relevant for understanding managerial effectiveness. The behaviors are generic ones relevant for all managers, although their relative importance varies across situations. Each category includes some behavior that is carried out with subordinates, and some behavior carried out with people outside of the work unit. For example, consulting may occur with subordinates, peers, superiors, or clients. Thus, the taxonomy abandons the earlier tradition among behavior taxonomies of using separate categories to describe internal and external interactions. The behaviors in the taxonomy are measured by a questionnaire called the Managerial Practices Survey (Yukl, 1988).

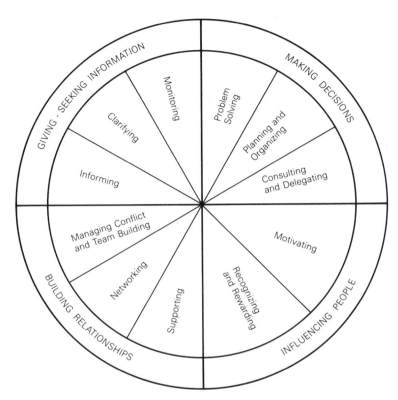

FIGURE 7-2   Integrating Taxonomy of Managerial Behavior

**TABLE 7-1   Definition of Managerial Behavior Categories
in the Integrating Taxonomy**

Networking: Socializing informally, developing contacts with people who are a source of information and support and maintaining relationships through periodic interaction, including visits, telephone calls, and correspondence, and attendance at meetings and social events.

Supporting: Acting friendly and considerate, showing sympathy and support when someone is upset, listening to complaints and problems, looking out for someone's interests, providing helpful career advice, doing things to aid someone's career advancement.

Managing conflict and team building: Encouraging and facilitating constructive resolution of conflict, fostering teamwork and cooperation, and building identification with the organizational unit or team.

Motivating: Using influence techniques that appeal to emotions, values, or logic to generate enthusiasm for the work and commitment to task objectives, or to induce someone to carry out a request for support, cooperation, assistance, resources, or authorization; also, setting an example of proper behavior by one's own actions.

Recognizing and rewarding: Providing praise, recognition, and tangible rewards for effective performance, significant achievements, and special contributions; expressing respect and appreciation for someone's accomplishments.

Planning and Organizing: Determining long-range objectives and strategies for adapting to environmental change, identifying necessary action steps to carry out a project or activity, allocating resources among activities according to priorities, and determining how to improve efficiency, productivity, and coordination with other parts of the organization.

Problem solving: Identifying work-related problems, analyzing problems in a systematic but timely manner to determine causes and find solutions, and acting decisively to implement solutions and deal with crises.

Consulting and delegating: Checking with people before making changes that affect them, encouraging suggestions for improvement, inviting participation in decision making, incorporating the ideas and suggestions of others in decisions, and allowing others to have substantial discretion in carrying out work activities and handling problems.

Monitoring operations and environment: Gathering information about the progress and quality of work activities, the success or failure of activities or projects, and the performance of individual contributors, also, determining the needs of clients or users, and scanning the environment to detect threats and opportunities.

Informing: Disseminating relevant information about decisions, plans, and activities to people who need it to do their work, providing written materials and documents, answering requests for technical information, and telling people about the organizational unit to promote its reputation.

Clarifying roles and objectives: Assigning tasks, providing direction in how to do the work, and communicating a clear understanding of job responsibilities, task objectives, deadlines, and performance expectations.

Each category includes specific examples of behavior that are concerned both with task and people, in varying degrees, even though some categories are more concerned with the task (e.g., monitoring, planning, problem solving), and some categories are more concerned with people relationships (e.g., supporting, networking). Table 7-2 shows the major objectives of each type of behavior in the context of internal and external interactions.

Another general proposition of the multiple-linkage model is that the 11 behaviors interact to determine managerial effectiveness. The taxonomy is used to integrate relevant findings from the diverse and confusing literature on the content of managerial behavior and relate this literature to the model. Each behavior category in the taxonomy is explained, then empirical evidence on the relevance of this behavior to managerial effectiveness is briefly reviewed. Sometimes it was necessary to go outside of the regular leadership and management literature to find relevant empirical evidence, such as the literature on motivation, communication, counseling, decision making, team building, conflict management, training, selection, organization design, and organizational politics. For each behavior category, there is a tentative listing of conditions where the behavior is most likely to be important for managerial effectiveness.

TABLE 7-2   Major Purpose of Managerial Behaviors in the Integrating Taxonomy

MANAGERIAL BEHAVIOR	INTERNAL CONTEXT	EXTERNAL CONTEXT
Networking	Good relations with subordinates	Good relations with peers, superiors, outsiders
Supporting	Good relations with subordinates, stress tolerance by subordinates	Good relations with peers, superiors, outsiders
Managing conflict and team building	Good relations with subordinates, group cohesiveness, cooperation among subordinates	Good relations with peers, superiors, outsiders
Motivating	Subordinate effort	Cooperation and support from peers, superiors, etc.
Recognizing and rewarding	Subordinate effort and role clarity, good relations with subordinates	Cooperation and support from peers, superiors, etc.
Planning and organizing	Unit efficiency and coordination	Adaptation to environment, external coordination
Problem solving	Stability of operations, unit efficiency and coordnation	Adaptation to environment, external coordination
Consulting and delegating	Decision quality, subordinate effort	Decision quality and implementation
Monitoring	Detection of problems, evaluation of performance	Detection of problems and opportunities
Informing	Decision quality, unit efficiency and coordination	External coordination, enhance unit reputation
Clarifying	Role clarity, unit efficiency and coordination	External coordination

Networking

Networking includes a wide variety of behaviors intended to develop and maintain contacts with people who are important sources of information and assistance, both inside and outside of the organization. Some types of behavior within this category are used to maintain relationships with subordinates, particularly "socializing" and informal discussion of subjects not related to the work (e.g., sports, vacations, family, hobbies). However, most networking behavior involves people other than subordinates, such as peers, superiors, and outside clients, customers, and suppliers. Examples include attending social and ceremonial events, sending cards and letters, participating in recreational and leisure activities (e.g., playing handball or golf), joining professional associations or clubs, visiting customers or clients, or meeting them for lunch. Networking also includes behaviors intended to establish an exchange relationship with other managers, such as offering assistance, doing favors that will be appreciated, and providing helpful information. Many episodes of networking involve other behavior categories at the same time, such as informing, consulting, harmonizing, and supporting. Some examples of incidents involving networking are the following:

> The training director met with managers of each product division to find out how we can improve the design of the new training program to better suit their needs.

> The boss visited the new computer facility in another product division to get better acquainted with their new manager and see if we can adapt some features of their management information system for use in our division.

The importance of developing a network has been demonstrated by descriptive studies of managers (Kaplan, 1986; Kotter,1982; Mintzberg, 1973). Networking is likely to be more important under the following conditions:

1. The work unit has high lateral interdependence on many other units.
2. Work unit operations are affected by changing policies, plans, and priorities determined by higher management.
3. The work unit must change its products, services, or timetables to accommodate the needs of outside clients and customers.

Supporting

Supporting includes a wide range of behaviors by which a manager shows consideration, acceptance, and concern for the needs and feelings of others. Supporting also includes backing subordinates in disputes with peers or superiors and doing things to promote their careers, such as telling others about their skills, recommending them for desirable position openings, and providing encouragement when they attempt to learn new skills and meet new challenges. Supporting behaviors aid in building and maintaining effective interpersonal relationships. A manager who is friendly and considerate toward people is more likely to win their friendship and loyalty. The emotional ties that are formed by acting friendly and helpful make it easier to gain cooperation and support from persons upon whom the manager must rely to get the work done. A secondary objective of supporting behavior is to increase the job satisfaction of subordinates and coworkers. It is more satisfying to work with people who are friendly, cooperative, and supportive than to work with people who are cold and impersonal or, worse, people who are hostile and uncooperative. Moreover, being supportive in times of stress helps a person to get over the "rough spots" in a job. Some incidents demonstrating supporting behavior are the following:

> On the day of the big snowstorm, my supervisor told subordinates they could leave early so they wouldn't get caught in the traffic jams.

> The supervisor was very sympathetic and tried to console a subordinate who was upset about something.

Supporting is the major core component of consideration, as defined by Fleishman (1953) and Stogdill (1974), and it is also the core of supportive leadership, as defined by Bowers and Seashore (1966) and House and Mitchell (1974). This type of managerial behavior has been manipulated in laboratory and field experiments, and it has been measured by questionnaire, observation, interview, subordinate diary, and critical incidents. As noted in Chapter 5, the extensive research demonstrates that leaders who are considerate and supportive usually have subordinates that are more satisfied with their leader and with their job. Results for effects on subordinate performance have been inconsistent, and no firm conclusions can be drawn. It si likely that supporting affects performance only indirectly, by improving working relationships with people in the leader's network and increasing the leader's referent power with these people. However, in cases of extremely stressful work, supporting may facilitate performance by helping subordinates cope with stress without resorting to detrimental measures, such as use of drugs, alcohol, or withdrawal (e.g., absenteeism, turnover).

Supporting is important for maintaining good interpersonal relationships in most situations, but it is likely more important under the following conditions, particularly for helping members of the work unit tolerate stress:

1. The work is dangerous, and group members are anxious about their safety.
2. The work is boring and tedious.
3. The work is difficult and frustrating, and group members are likely to become frustrated and discouraged by setbacks and lack of progress.
4. Members must deal with hostile, irate clients or customers.
5. Members work under pressure of difficult deadlines imposed by others.
6. Members lack self-confidence and feel insecure.

Managing Conflict and Team Building

There are a wide variety of behaviors involving development of teamwork and resolution of conflicts. Examples include mediating conflicts between other people, encouraging constructive resolution of conflicts, explaining the importance of cooperation, encouraging sharing of information and ideas, emphasizing common interests, facilitating integrative problem solving that satisfies everyone's needs, holding team building sessions, using ceremonies and symbols to develop identification with the work unit, and encouraging activities such as parties and luncheons to facilitate social interaction among work unit members. The primary purpose of these behaviors is to build and maintain cooperative working relationships with subordinates, peers, superiors, and outsiders. A secondary purpose is to build a cohesive work unit with strong member identification. Some incidents involving this type of behavior are the following:

> The sales manager took the group out to lunch to give everybody a chance to get to know the new sales representative.

> The manager met with two subordinates who were having a dispute about a project and helped them to resolve it in a way that satisfied everyone.

The importance of cooperation, identification with the work unit, and constructive resolution of conflict are central themes in the literature on organizations. This concern is reflected in the group research on cohesiveness and teamwork (Hackman & Morris, 1975), in the organization development research on team building (Dyer, 1977), in the organization design research on "integrators" (Lawrence & Lorsch, 1967), in the conflict management literature (Brown, 1983; Robbins, 1974), and in the literature on effective management in the United States and Japan (Ouchi, 1981; Peters & Waterman, 1982).

Resolution of conflicts involves external relations as well as relations within the manager's work unit. The importance of managing boundary role conflicts has been recognized for a long time in the management literature, and this theme is evident in Likert's (1967) emphasis on the manager as a "linking pin", in Lawrence and Lorsch's emphasis on integrators, in the research on managerial role conflicts (Kahn & Quinn, 1970; Pfeffer & Salancik, 1975), and in some of the conflict management literature that focuses on organizational interfaces (Brown, 1983). Together these diverse literatures provide ample evidence that conflict management behaviors are highly relevant for managerial effectiveness.

Team building and managing conflict are more likely to be important under the following conditions:

1. People have interdependent jobs, requiring considerable cooperation.
2. Differences in values and beliefs are likely to cause suspicion, misunderstanding, and hostility.

3. People must work together in close proximity under stress for long periods of time.
4. People compete against each other for rewards, status, and resources.
5. The work unit has high lateral interdependence with other units.

Motivating

Motivating involves the use of personal power and related influence tactics to generate enthusiasm for the work, commitment to task objectives, and compliance with orders and requests. The major influence tactics include rational persuasion, inspirational appeals, personal appeals, and the symbolic behaviors used by charismatic and transformational leaders. Motivating also includes influence attempts directed at people outside of the manager's work unit with the purpose of promoting and defending work unit interests and obtaining necessary resources, cooperation and political support. Examples of this external form of motivating include lobbying with higher management for necessary resources and financial support, and negotiating with outsiders and managers of other work units to obtain favorable agreements. Some incidents involving motivating behavior are as follows:

> My supervisor held a meeting to talk about how vital the new contract is for the company and said he was confident we could handle it if we all did our part.
>
> The product manager made a presentation with detailed financial information and elaborate graphs to convince the marketing and manufacturing vice presidents that the new product would be profitable.

The leadership and power literature provides evidence that influence behavior is relevant for managerial effectiveness, especially influence attempts that are based on expert and referent power (Kipnis, 1976; Kotter, 1985). The importance of motivating for promoting and defending unit interests is supported by research on the lateral relations of managers (Kanter, 1983; Kotter, 1982; Sayles, 1979; Stewart, 1967; Strauss, 1962) and by research on the upward influence of managers (Cashman, et al., 1976; House, Filley, & Gujarati, 1971; Pelz, 1952).

Motivating is the essence of leadership and is likely to be important in most situations. However, it is especially important when:

1. Errors and mistakes are costly and difficult to correct, or would endanger the lives and health of people.
2. The work is dangerous, and group members are anxious about their safety.
3. The work is boring and tedious.
4. The work is difficult and group members are likely to become frustrated and discouraged by setbacks and lack of progress.
5. The work unit is highly dependent upon resources, cooperation, and political support from superiors, peers, and outsiders.

Recognizing and Rewarding

Recognizing and rewarding is a category of behavior that includes giving tangible and intangible rewards for effective performance, significant achievements, and helpful assistance. Tangible rewards for subordinates include a pay increase, promotion, better work schedule, and better assignments. For peers, tangible rewards include things such as shared resources, faster service, and special favors. Intangible rewards include such things as giving praise, expressing personal appreciation, giving public recognition, holding a special ceremony to honor a person's achievements and contributions, and giving awards such as a special pin or certificate. Recognizing and rewarding has the multiple purpose of motivating subordinates, clarifying performance expectations, and increasing job satisfaction.

As with motivating, one objective of recognizing and rewarding is to increase the target person's effort in doing the work. However, motivating attempts to induce someone to do a task, whereas recognition and rewards are given after a person has performed a task effectively. The motivational aspect comes from the fact that behaviors reinforced by a desirable outcome tend to be repeated, allowing the behavior to be shaped in the desired direction. Some incidents involving recognizing and rewarding are as follows:

> The division vice president recommended a promotion for the product manager with the best record of performance.

> My boss complimented me on the professional manner in which I handled a difficult situation and said I am developing well in my new position.

> In a meeting, the supervisor told us she was very satisfied with our work and said she appreciated the extra effort we made this month.

Positive reinforcement has been the subject of extensive research for several decades in psychology, and a growing interest in positive reward behavior can be found in the leadership literature (Greene, 1975; Keller & Szilagyi, 1976; Oldham, 1976; Podsakoff & Todor, 1985; Podsakoff et al., 1982; Sims & Szilagyi, 1975; Yukl & Clemence, 1984; Yukl & Kanuk, 1979). Evidence on the importance of giving appropriate recognition and rewards to employees comes also from research on behavior modification programs (Hamner & Hamner, 1976; Schneier, 1974) and research on effective organizations (Peters & Waterman, 1982). Together, the related lines of research clearly demonstrate the importance of positive reward behavior for managerial effectiveness. Although results were not significant in every study, they indicate that praise and contingent rewards often increase subordinate motivation and satisfaction.

Recognizing by the leader is more likely to be important when:

1. Performance is determined primarily by an individual's skill rather than luck or uncontrollable events.

2. Members of the work unit are unable to get much direct feedback about their performance from others, such as coworkers and clients.
3. Members lack self-confidence and feel insecure.

Rewarding is more likely to be important when:

1. Performance is determined primarily by skill rather than luck or uncontrollable events.
2. Performance can be measured accurately, or compliance with requests can be confirmed.
3. The leader has authority to dispense desirable rewards.

Planning and Organizing

The behavior category of "planning and organizing" includes managerial decision making about objectives, priorities, strategies, formal structure, allocation of resources, assignment of responsibilities, and scheduling of activities. In other words, planning and organizing means deciding what to do, how to do it, who will do it, and when it will be done. The purpose of the planning and organizing is to ensure efficient organization of the work unit and adaptation to a changing environment.

There are many varieties of planning, ranging from the determination of strategic objectives and broad policies for the organization (*strategic planning*), to the development of detailed action steps and schedules for implementing a change or policy (*operational planning* or *action planning*). Planning includes both the design of formal structure (*organizing*) and the allocation of resources among different activities according to their relative importance (*resource allocation*). Finally, planning includes the development of procedures for avoiding potential problems or disasters (*potential problem analysis*) and the development of procedures for reacting in a quick and effective manner to unavoidable problems and crises (*contingency planning*).

Planning is largely a cognitive activity involving processing of information, analyzing, and deciding. We saw in Chapter 4 that most managerial planning involves the development of informal and implicit agendas, rather than formal, written documents and agreements. Since planning is mostly a cognitive activity and seldom occurs as a single discrete episode, it is difficult to observe (Snyder & Glueck, 1980). Nevertheless, there are some observable aspects such as writing plans, preparing written budgets, developing written schedules, and meeting with others to formulate objectives and strategies. Mintzberg's resource allocator role and his entrepreneur role are components of planning-organizing. Managers use resource allocation to coordinate subordinate actions in support of strategic objectives, and improvement projects are used to initiate planned change.

The importance of planning and organizing has long been recognized in the management literature (Carroll & Gillen, 1987; Drucker, 1974; Fayol, 1949; Urwick, 1952), and new evidence is provided by recent research on managerial competencies relevant to planning (Boyatzis, 1982), as well as by research on strategic management (Quinn, 1980) and project management (Meredith & Mantel, 1985). Descriptive studies of managerial behavior (see Chapter 4) found that effective managers are more likely to develop informal plans and to use their network of political contacts in the organization to get these implemented (Kanter, 1983; Kotter, 1982). Some incidents involving planning-organizing are as follows:

> My supervisor devised a shortcut that allows us to prepare our financial statements in 3 days instead of the 4 days it used to take.

> The sales vice president prepared a staffing plan indicating how many new employees would need to be hired next year for the new sales offices.

Planning is likely to be more important when:

1. The work unit carries out large, complex projects that extend over a period of months or years.
2. The work unit has several different types of tasks to perform, and efficiency depends on how well the work is organized and sequenced.
3. Members of the work unit have interdependent tasks requiring coordination.
4. The work unit has high lateral interdependence with other units, or carries out joint projects with other organizations.

Problem Solving

Like planning, problem solving involves processing information, analyzing, and deciding. However, there are some important differences between the two categories of behavior. Whereas the primary purpose of planning and organizing is to improve work unit efficiency and effectiveness, the primary purpose of problem solving is to maintain orderly, stable operations, and to successfully implement plans and improvement programs.

Problem solving is similar to Mintzberg's disturbance handler role. It occurs in response to some immediate disturbance of normal operations, such as an equipment breakdown, a shortage of necessary materials, a customer with a complaint, a mistake in the work, an accident, or an unusual request by higher management. Problem solving also involves handling of some types of people problems, such as taking necessary disciplinary action when someone's actions threaten to disrupt operations or jeopardize the success of an operation.

Problem solving often involves crises that cannot be ignored, in contrast to planning, which is more likely to be stimulated by the discovery of an opportunity to be exploited, or by the anticipation of a future problem to be avoided. Planning is a proactive behavior with a long-term perspective, whereas problem solving is a reactive behavior with a short-term perspective. Due to the pressure of time, problem solving typically occurs more quickly than planning. The distinction is analogous to that made by McCall, Kaplan, and Gerlach (1982) between "thick" and "thin" decision cycles. Some incidents involving problem solving are as follows:

> The boss held a meeting to let us know that we were behind schedule on a critical project. After we identified the source of the delays, she suggested a way to solve the problem.

> The department was shorthanded due to illness, and we had an important deadline to meet. My boss arranged to borrow two people from other units so we could finish the job today.

Research on crisis management suggests that this type of behavior is important for managerial effectiveness (Stewart, 1967, 1976). The Three Mile Island Nuclear Plant incident and the Union Carbide Bhopal incident provide dramatic evidence of the importance of problem solving in a crisis situation. In both incidents the lack of decisive, skillful problem solving resulted in a disaster. Subordinates expect the leader to take decisive action to deal with a crisis (Mulder, et al.,1970), but it is important to seek a balance between careful analysis of the problem and quick, decisive action to solve it. Kepner and Tregoe, 1965; 1981) have found that many managers fail to use systematic logical analysis to identify the cause of a problem, and they proceed to implement solutions that are ineffective.

Problem solving is more likely to be important when:

1. Disruptions in the workflow are likely, due to equipment breakdowns, technical problems, materials shortages, bad weather, and so on.
2. Operations are disrupted by deliberate interference or the hostile actions of outsiders (e.g., terrorists, military units).
3. Members of the work unit have interdependent tasks requiring continuous coordination.
4. The work unit has high lateral interdependence with other units, or carries out joint projects with other organizations.
5. Work unit operations are frequently affected by changes in policies, plans, or priorities determined by higher management.
6. The work unit must frequently change its products, services, or timetables to accommodate the needs of outside clients and customers.

Consulting and Delegating

Consulting and delegating involve encouragement of participation by others in making decisions for which the manager is responsible. Different degrees of participation are possible, from revising a tentative decision after receiving protests, to consulting with others before making a decision, to asking an individual or group to make the decision within specified guidelines. The latter form of participation provides the maximum amount of power sharing for a decision; when used with an individual subordinate, it is called *delegation*. Consulting and delegating are both intended to improve the quality of decisions and acceptance of decisions by others who must implement them. A secondary purpose is to enrich the job of subordinates and make it more interesting and challenging. Delegation has yet another purpose that is not shared by consultation, namely to reduce a manager's workload by giving subordinates major responsibility for some activities and decisions. This unique purpose does not result in a completely different form of behavior, since consultation between manager and subordinate usually continues, even for delegated decisions. Some incidents involving consulting-delegating are among the following:

> My supervisor asked me to attend a meeting with him and his boss to develop a new production schedule, and he was very receptive to my ideas on the subject.

> My boss gave me a new project and encouraged me to handle it any way I think is best.

As we saw in Chapter 5, participative leadership has been the subject of hundreds of studies, including laboratory and field experiments. These studies find that power-sharing behavior has important implications for managerial effectiveness. Encouraging subordinate participation is more likely to increase satisfaction than performance, but both may be increased under some conditions. The Vroom-Yetton model identifies some of these conditions. Consulting is more likely to be important when:

1. Members of the work unit possess relevant knowledge and information needed by the leader to solve problems and make good decisions.
2. Members of the work unit share the leader's task objectives and are willing to cooperate in making a good decision.
3. There is adequate time for use of consultation.
4. The leader has the skill to manage any conflict among members in a group meeting.

Delegating is more likely to be more important when:

1. The manager is overloaded with responsibilities.
2. The subordinate is competent and shares the leader's task objectives.
3. The subordinate is willing to assume more responsibility.

Monitoring

Monitoring involves gathering information about the operations of the manager's work unit, the progress of the work, the performance of subordinates, the success of projects or programs, and the nature of the external environment. Monitoring can take many forms, and some examples include the following: walking around to observe how the work is going, reading written performance reports, meeting with subordinates or team members to review progress, inspecting the work to check on its quality, using a computer terminal to review information about current operations, and evaluating project performance by getting reactions from clients or customers. Monitoring includes gathering information about the external environment as well as information about internal operations of the work unit (Hambrick, 1981, 1982). Monitoring is facilitated by developing and maintaining a network of contacts with people who can provide timely and relevant information about events affecting the manager's unit. Some incidents involving monitoring are as follows:

> The supervisor walked along the production line checking the indicators on the machines and asking the operators if they had any problems.

> The boss asked me to meet with her today to report on the market test for the new product.

The primary purpose of monitoring is to gather information necessary to evaluate operations and facilitate adjustment in plans to changes in the environment. This dual process of sensing and adjusting is sometimes referred to in the management literature as "controlling." Monitoring is conceptually distinct from planning and problem solving, but it is closely related to them. Monitoring provides much of the information needed for planning and problem solving, and this is the reason why it is so important for managerial effectiveness (Meredith & Mantel, 1985). Monitoring, in turn, may be facilitated by the development of detailed action plans (with schedules, checkpoints, targets, and deadlines) to help a manager identify relevant performance indicators, and to provide a standard against which actual progress can be compared. Observational research by Komaki (1986) found that monitoring was important for the effectiveness of supervisors.

Monitoring is more likely to be more important when:

1. Members of the work unit are inexperienced and likely to make mistakes.
2. Mistakes and accidents would be expensive or would endanger the health and lives of people.
3. Disruptions in the workflow are likely, due to equipment breakdowns, technical problems, materials shortages, bad weather, and so on.
4. Operations are disrupted by deliberate interference or the hostile actions of outsiders (e.g., terrorists, military units).
5. Members of the work unit have interdependent tasks requiring continuous coordination.
6. The work unit has high lateral interdependence with other units, or carries out joint projects with other units or organizations.
7. The work unit has difficult deadlines imposed by higher management.

Informing

Informing involves a manager's communication of task-relevant information needed by subordinates, peers, or superiors to perform their jobs. This behavior may take many forms, such as answering a request for information, calling someone on the telephone to pass on timely news, holding a meeting to brief group members about new developments, writing memos and reports, sending electronic messages, putting messages on the bulletin board, distributing a newsletter, and relaying written documents or reports to people who would otherwise not receive them. The purpose of informing is to facilitate the work of others who depend upon the manager as a source of important information. A secondary purpose is to facilitate power sharing by providing people with the information necessary to participate in making decisions and to carry out delegated duties. As noted in Chapter 2, some managers intentionally limit information in order to increase the dependence of subordinates or superiors and prevent criticism of their decisions. Informing may involve peers, superiors, or outsiders, such as when a manager acts as spokesperson for the work unit, carries out public relations activities to enhance the reputation of the work unit, or recruits and interviews candidates for positions in the work unit. Some incidents involving Informing are as follows:

> The boss held a meeting to tell us when the new machines would arrive and how they would affect our operations.

> The vice president briefed us about some forthcoming changes in policy so we could make any necessary preparations.

The importance of informing was noted by Likert (1967) in his early conception of the manager as a "linking pin." Likert viewed a manager as the central informational link between the work unit and the rest of the organization and outside environment. Managers who serve as a linking pin with other units tend to be more effective than managers who do not serve this function, especially when the nature of the work makes subordinates dependent on the manager for information (Katz & Tushman, 1979). More recently, Mintzberg (1973) described a manager as a "nerve center" in the communication network for an organizational subunit. Informing is similar to Mintzberg's disseminator role, except that it does not include orders and instructions, only technical information and information about events and developments relevant to the work, including objective performance feedback.

Informing is more likely to be important when:

1. Members of the work unit are dependent upon the leader for relevant information because they lack direct access to this information.
2. There is a crisis or emergency, and members of the work unit are anxious and concerned about what is happening.

3. Members of the work unit have interdependent tasks requiring continuous coordination.
4. The work unit has high lateral interdependence with other units, or carries out joint projects with other organizations.
5. Work unit operations are frequently affected by changes in policies, plans, or priorities determined by higher management.
6. The work unit must frequently change its products, services, or timetables to accomodate the needs of outside clients and customers.

Clarifying Roles and Objectives

Clarifying involves the communication of plans, policies, and role expectations to subordinates, and instruction in how to do the work. The purpose of the behavior is to ensure that persons in the manager's work unit know what to do and how to do it. In contrast to motivating, which seeks to energize behavior, clarifying seeks to orient and guide it. Clarifying can take a wide variety of forms, and some examples include the following: explaining job responsibilities, explaining rules and procedures, communicating priorities, making task assignments, setting specific deadlines, setting specific performance goals for a subordinate, endorsing or revising a subordinate's action plans for attaining performance goals, showing someone how to do a task, coaching a person to develop job skills, and having subordinates practice or rehearse complex procedures.

Like informing, clarifying involves communication of information. However, clarifying is an attempt to direct someone's behavior, whereas informing is only intended to facilitate someone's work. This distinction does not imply that the two forms of behavior are unrelated. Sometimes the behaviors occur separately, but many times both forms of behavior are represented in the same behavior incident. For example, in the process of giving a new work assignment to a subordinate or asking a peer to do something, a manager is likely to communicate some specific task information needed to carry out the assignment. Some incidents involving clarifying are as follows:

> The production manager told me about a rush project that must be given top priority, and he gave me some suggestions about how to do the project.

> My boss met with me for 2 hours to establish performance goals for the coming year and discuss my action plans for attaining the goals.

> The sales manager went out on sales calls with a new sales representative last week to provide instruction and advice.

The importance of clarifying for managerial effectiveness is supported by extensive research on goal setting (see Locke & Latham, 1984; Locke, Shaw, Saari, & Latham, 1981). This research finds that subordinate performance is improved if clear, specific, and challenging goals are set by the manager, or jointly by the manager and the subordinate. Specific examples of effective goal setting usually involve both clarifying and motivating. Performance improves in part because specific goals guide subordinate effort into productive activities, and in part because challenging goals energize a higher level of subordinate effort in doing the work (Earley, Wojnaroski, & Prest, 1987).

Despite recent interest in managerial "mentoring" (Hunt & Michael, 1983; Kram, 1985), empirical research on the effects of coaching and training by managers is still very limited. Nevertheless, it is widely accepted in the management literature that developing subordinate skills is important for managerial effectiveness (e.g., Bradford & Cohen, 1984), and the training and development literature tends to support the belief that skill development contributes to the satisfaction and performance of organization members (Guzzo, Jette, & Katzell, 1985; McCauley, 1986; Wexley, 1984).

Clarifying is more likely to be important when:

1. Members of the work unit lack skills and do not know what to do or how to do it.
2. The work is complex and unstructured, causing ambiguity about procedures and priorities.
3. The organization has elaborate rules and regulations that must be observed, and members are not familiar with them.
4. The nature of the work or technology is changing, and members need to learn new skills and procedures.
5. There is a crisis or emergency, and members are confused about how to respond.
6. Members of the work unit have interdependent tasks requiring continuous coordination.
7. Work unit operations are frequently affected by changes in policies, plans, or priorities determined by higher management.

EVALUATION OF THE
MULTIPLE LINKAGE MODEL

The multiple linkage model is more complex and comprehensive than earlier ones because it provides an integrated framework. However, the complexity is reduced by focusing on the intervening variables rather than on the hundreds of potentially relevant behaviors at different levels of abstraction. The model is still incomplete in that it does not specify clearly how each individual behavior affects each intervening variable. However, we can begin to identify these links in two ways: (1) by working backward from an intervening variable to aspects of leader behavior likely to affect that variable or (2) by working forward from the taxonomy of 11 behaviors to the intervening variables, using Table 7-2 as the source of initial hypotheses. Either way, it is obvious that only a few of the linkages have been studied extensively, and there are still large gaps in our knowledge about the way leader behavior affects each intervening variable. Some behaviors stand out as major determinants of a particular intervening variable, but it is unlikely that simple one-to-one relationships will explain much variance in the intervening variables. Instead, patterns of behavior must be considered. For example, motivating is probably the leader behavior with the greatest effect on subordinate effort, but effort is also affected directly by recognizing/rewarding, and consulting/delegating. Several other behavior categories probably influence effort indirectly. At the present time, we know little about which patterns of leader behavior are most useful for improving each intervening variable. This question is a major agenda item for future behavior research. At the present, we can only speculate about most of the linkages between leader behavior and intervening variables.

Specification of situational moderator variables is also incomplete. The listing of conditions in which each type of managerial behavior is likely to be important provides a beginning, but more detailed specification of situational moderators is not yet possible, since most research on situational moderators has considered only broadly defined task and relations-oriented behavior, not middle-range behaviors like those in the integrating taxonomy.

At this stage in the development of the multiple linkage model, the long-term actions of managers are described only in general terms. The middle-range categories of managerial behavior appear equally relevant for short- and long-term actions, but at the level of more specific component behaviors, there are probably some unique forms of behavior used only in long-term actions. The amount of research on long-term managerial behavior is still very limited. Stewart (1976) described how managers exploit different "opportunities" to improve conditions, Mintzberg (1973) described how managers initiate"improvement projects," Kanter (1982) described how middle managers get innovations accepted, Kotter (1982) described how managers get long-term aspects of their agenda implemented, and Gabarro (1985) described how CEOs turn around organizations that are doing poorly. Chapter 10 reviews the literature on transformational leaders, and it includes long-term actions by leaders to change the mission or basic strategy of an organization and to shape the culture of the organization so as to be compatible with the mission and strategy.

SUMMARY

The performance of a work group or organizational subunit can be described by a model of six intervening variables, two involving individual performance, two involving group processes, and two involving the interface with the larger organization and environment. Group performance is highest when members have high task skill and motivation, the group is efficiently organized, there is a high level of member cooperation, adequate resources are acquired, and unit activities are coordinated with those of interdependent units, thereby reducing uncertainty and disruption of internal operations. These intervening variables are affected by a variety of situational variables in addition to the actions of the leader. The multiple linkage model uses this basic model of group performance to integrate the major situational leadership theories and the research literature on determinants and consequences of leadership behavior.

The general propositions are that leaders improve unit effectiveness by enhancing the intervening variables, using the 11 types of managerial behavior. In the short run, the primary orientation of the leader is to correct any deficiencies in the intervening variables. In the longer run, the leader can raise the intervening variables above prior equilibrium levels by actions such as improvement projects, innovations in products or technology, changes in basic strategy, changes in culture, and development of greater political power in the organization. Long-term actions may involve changing the situation to make it more favorable, by reducing constraints, enhancing substitutes, and altering the relative importance of the intervening variables.

Managerial behavior can be described by a multilevel taxonomy, with 4 general categories of behavior and 11 middle-range categories. Each of the behaviors is applicable to internal interactions with subordinates and external interactions with peers, superiors, and outsiders. Relation-building behaviors are used to develop a network of contacts inside and outside of the organization, to develop unit identification and teamwork among subordinates, to facilitate constructive resolution of conflicts and disagreements in both internal and external interactions, and to develop affective links and referent power with people in the leader's network. Information handling and processing behaviors are used to identify problems and opportunites in unit operations and the external environment, to evaluate progress and performance of the unit, to facilitate the work of subordinates, to clarify role expectations and enhance skill levels of subordinates, and to facilitate external coordination with other units. Decision behaviors are used to plan an efficient organization of the work, to determine what resources are needed to do it, and to solve technical problems and handle disturbances. Influencing behaviors are used to increase subordinate effort, to reinforce desirable behavior, and to lobby for resources and support from peers and superiors. Each middle-range behavior is relevant for any manager, but the relative importance of the different behavior categories depends on the situation, including the current state of the intervening variables, the relative importance of the intervening variable as determinants of unit effectiveness, and the opportunites for improving each intervening variable.

REVIEW AND DISCUSSION QUESTIONS

1. Briefly describe the major features of Yukl's multiple linkage model.
2. In what ways is the multiple linkage model similar and different from the situational leadership theories in Chapter 6?
3. Evaluate the multiple linkage model and describe what, if anything, it adds to our understanding of managerial effectiveness.
4. Briefly define the 4 general behaviors and the 11 middle-range behavior categories in Yukl's integrating taxonomy.
5. How does the integrating taxonomy relate to the multiple linkage model?
6. How do the behavior categories in Yukl's integrating taxonomy relate to Mintzberg's managerial roles (Chapter 4)?
7. How do the behavior categories in Yukl's integrating taxonomy relate to Page's behavior categories in the MPDQ (Chapter 4)?
8. How could the multiple linkage model be extended to include leader power and traits (see Chapter 12)?

8

SITUATIONAL
DETERMINANTS
OF
LEADER BEHAVIOR

The three previous chapters were concerned primarily with typical patterns of managerial activity and consequences of managerial behavior for the organization. The present Chapter focuses on situational determinants of managerial behavior. We saw in chapter 2 that influence processes between a leader and another person are reciprocal; the behavior of each party is influenced by the other party. In addition, leaders adjust their behavior to cope with events and changes in the organization and its environment. The present chapter examines research and theory on the major situational determinants of a manager's behavior.

There has been far more research on the consequences of leader behavior than on its determinants. The major reason for this disparity is probably the widespread bias to perceive leaders as causal agents who shape events rather than being shaped by them. It is common for people to attribute more influence to leaders than they actually possess. Leaders usually get more than their fair share of credit when their organization is successful, and are blamed for failures that were not necessarily their fault. Only a few theories have been developed to explain how behavior is influenced by the situation.

ROLE THEORY

A model of behavior determination based on role theory concepts (Merton, 1957) is shown graphically in Figure 8-1. Role expectations are the manager's perception of how other people such as superiors, peers, and subordinates want the managerial role to be carried out (Kahn et al., 1964; Pfeffer & Salancik, 1975). These "role senders" exert pressure on the manager to conform with their beliefs about the proper and necessary way to behave. Role expectations for managers are also influenced by cultural norms and values. Role expectations from subordinates and peers are usually communicated orally, whereas role expectations from superiors are often conveyed by written communication as well as orally. Leaders in organizations are usually provided with a written job description and other documents enumerating the duties, responsibilities, authority, policies and regulations applying to their administrative position. A leader's perception of role requirements is influenced by these prescriptions and prohibitions, as well as by day-to-day requests, orders, and directions from superiors. Role expectations from subordinates are communicated in a more subtle manner, but a socially sensitive leader quickly learns to recognize and consider them.

At times, different people make incompatible demands on the leader, creating *role conflicts*. For example, first-line supervisors often find themselves beset by conflicting demands from superiors and subordinates. Supervisors try to reconcile these conflicting role expectations but are likely to be more responsive to the expectations of superiors, since superiors wield

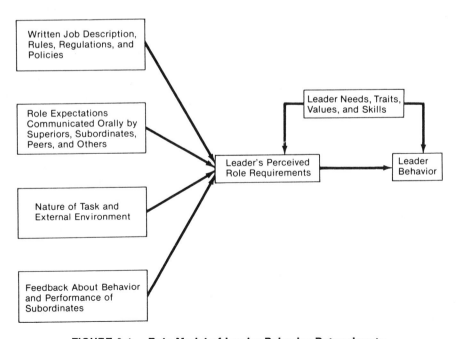

FIGURE 8-1   Role Model of Leader Behavior Determinants

more power over a manager than do subordinates or peers (Kahn, Wolfe, Quinn, & Snolk, 1964). However, the manner in which a role conflict is resolved also depends in part on how important it is to each role sender. In a study of the way military officers reconciled inconsistent expectations of superiors and subordinates, the officers were more responsive either to superiors or subordinates depending on how important the issue was to each party (Salancik, Calder, Rowland, Leblebici, & Conway,1975). Another study found that the task-oriented behavior of managers was influenced more by superiors, whereas social behavior was influenced more by subordinates (Pfeffer & Salancik, 1975). The extent to which a manager is able to reconcile successfully the divergent concerns of superiors and subordinates is related to the manager's effectiveness (Mann & Dent,1954; Mann & Hoffman, 1960; Tsui, 1984).

In addition to role expectations from other people, a leader's perception of role requirements will depend on the nature of the group's mission and tasks. Different kinds of tasks require somewhat different administrative activities by the leader. Role expectations from subordinates or superiors are sometimes inconsistent with objective task requirements, especially when the nature of the task or the external environment has changed while norms and beliefs about proper leader behavior have remained the same. Here again, the leader has a role conflict: conform to expectations from role senders and be less effective in facilitating group performance, or do what is necessary to accomplish the task and take a chance on being initially rejected by role senders?

Role expectations for a leader are seldom absolute or comprehensive, and a leader usually has considerable discretion to shape his or her own role over time. Given enough time, a skillful leader may be able to reconcile role requirements that were initially incompatible. As noted in Chapter 2, leaders with a record of successful decisions and demonstrated loyalty to the organization are given more freedom to redefine their role and initiate innovations. However, flexibility is greater for role expectations that do not involve central values of organization members. Research shows that even high-level leaders must be sensitive to the symbolic importance of some role expectations to peers and subordinates (Biggart & Hamilton, 1984).

It has long been known that a leader's behavior is determined jointly by characteristics of the situation and characteristics of the leader, such as needs, values, and interests (Burke, 1965; Crowe, Bochner, & Clark, 1972). Occasionally, the behavior required for effective leadership is contrary to the leader's needs and values. This situation can be viewed as still another kind of role conflict. In many cases, role senders recognize the objective task requirements and pressure the leader to act accordingly. However, in the absence of strong pressure from role senders, a leader may choose to act in a manner consistent with internal needs and values, even though this behavior is not appropriate for the situation confronting the leader. For example, Kipnis and Lane (1962) found that leaders with low self-confidence were more likely to respond to a problem subordinate by trying to "pass the buck" to superiors, whereas leaders with high self-confidence were more likely to handle the matter themselves and discuss the problem with the subordinate.

In addition to influencing a leader's choice of behavior, leader personality influences the leader's perception of role requirements, thereby exerting an indirect influence on subsequent leader behavior (Kahn & Quinn,1970; Kahn et al., 1964). First, needs and values influence the leader's attention to information and events. For example, a person with a dominant need for affiliation is likely to be especially sensitive to signs of acceptance or rejection by other people; a person with a strong achievement need is likely to be attuned to performance feedback. Second, interpretation of information and events is biased by a leader's needs, values, and attitudes (Mass, 1950). For example, a leader with a negative stereotype about subordinates is likely to attribute performance problems to subordinate incompetence and lack of motivation rather than to factors beyond the subordinates' control, such as deficiencies in the organization of the work. How a leader diagnoses the cause of a performance problem has obvious implications for the way it is handled, and this subject is discussed later in the chapter.

EXPECTANCY THEORY

An alternative conceptual framework for explaining why a leader acts in a particular way is expectancy theory. Nebecker and Mitchell (1974) have proposed that a leader's expectancies about the consequences of various behavior options can be used to explain the leader's choice of behavior. For example, a leader would be predicted to use a moderate amount of a behavior such as coaching subordinates if this level of behavior appeared more likely than either a high or low level to have desirable consequences for the leader (e.g., better group performance, greater subordinate satisfaction). If the same leader also perceived that desired outcomes were more likely with a high level of praise than with a low or moderate level, then the leader would be predicted to use praise frequently and to use it more often than role clarification. If the leader perceived that a low level of some behavior such as criticism were more likely to lead to desired outcomes than greater amounts of the behavior, then the leader would be predicted to use criticism only infrequently, and less often than either praise or role clarification.

Nebecker and Mitchell conducted two studies to test predictions of leader behavior based on the leader's reported perception of expectancies and outcome desirability (valence). Leader behavior was measured with questionnaires filled out by subordinates and by the leaders themselves. Expectancy theory predictions received modest support, indicating that one determinant of leader behavior is the leader's perception of its likely consequences. Leaders select a course of action that they perceive to have a high probability for attaining desired outcomes.

The greatest deficiency of expectancy theory is that it does not explain how leaders formulate expectancies or why some outcomes are valued more than others (e.g., subordinate acceptance more than productivity). Expectancy theory does not take into account the way needs, values, and prior experience shape a leader's expectancies and outcome valences.

OSBORNE AND HUNT'S
MULTIPLE INFLUENCE MODEL

Osborne and Hunt (1975) proposed an "adaptive-reactive theory" of leadership to explain how the behavior of managers in large organizations is influenced by the situation. Subsequently, the theory was modified and renamed "the multiple influence model" of leadership (Hunt & Osborne, 1982). The authors contend that research on the determinants of leadership behavior has neglected "macrovariables" such as the structure of the organization and its external environment. Macrovariables are differentiated from "microvariables," which include things like task characteristics and subordinate characteristics. Macrovariables are assumed to be constant for all of a leader's subordinates, whereas microvariables are likely to be different from subordinate to subordinate. Osborne and Hunt propose that the behavior of leaders is influenced more by macrovariables than by micro variables. Their major premise is that the organizational setting will present the leader with various opportunities and constraints. Some leaders have a great deal of discretion, whereas others are highly constrained in their behavior. Behavior that is initiated by the leader (*discretionary behavior*) is distinguished from behavior that is merely a response to overwhelming pressures from macro variables (*nondiscretionary behavior*).

Leader discretion is reduced by aspects of the environment such as an uncertainty and high dependence on other organizations. For example, the CEO of a small firm with few customers and unpredictable fluctuations in demand for its products has less discretion than the CEO of a large firm with stable demand and many customers. For middle- and low-level managers, discretion is reduced also by aspects of the organization structure such as centralization, formalization, lateral interdependence, and span of control. When there is high centralization, decisions must be approved by superiors. When there is high formalization, behavior must conform to elaborate rules and regulations. When there is substantial lateral interdependence between subunits, the needs of peers must be accommodated. When span of control is large, demands from subordinates are greater, but there is less time available for interacting with each subordinate on a one-to-one basis. Discretion is also affected by micro variables, such as task complexity, task interdependence, subordinate goal orientation, and group cohesiveness. Interaction with individual subordinates is more important when tasks are complex and interdependent, subordinates are inexperienced, and the group is cohesive but hostile toward the leader's goals.

STEWART'S DEMANDS-
CONSTRAINTS-CHOICES MODEL

Stewart (1967, 1976, 1982) has formulated a model for describing managerial jobs and understanding how managers do them. The model was based on extensive research using observation, interviews, and diaries. The model has three components: demands, constraints, and choices.

Demands are what anyone who holds the job must do or risk sanctions and loss of the position. In effect, demands are role expectations from people who have sufficient power to obtain compliance. Demands provide a minimum core of required duties, activities, and responsibilities. Demands include standards, objectives, and deadlines for work that must be met, and bureaucratic procedures that cannot be ignored or delegated, such as preparing budgets and reports, attending certain meetings, authorizing expenditures, signing documents, and conducting performance appraisals. Other demands depend on particular individuals, such as the requirement by the boss that the manager knows operational details, or an important customer's insistence on dealing with the manager instead of a subordinate.

Constraints are characteristics of the organization and external environment limiting what a manager can do. They include legal constraints (e.g., labor laws, environmental regulations, securities regulations, safety regulations, etc.), and bureaucratic rules, policies, and regulations that must be observed. Another type of constraint involves the availability of resources, such as facilities, equipment, budgetary funding, supplies, personnel, and support services. The technology used to do the work constrains the options for how the work will be done. The physical location of facilities and distribution of personnel among work sites limits the opportunities for face-to-face interaction. Market considerations such as the preferences of clients and customers are constraints on the type of products and services that may be provided by the manager's organizational unit.

Choices are the activities that a manager may do but need not do. Choices include the opportunities available to someone in a particular type of managerial position to determine what to do and how to do it. Demands and constraints limit choices in the short run, but over a longer time period, a manager has some opportunities to modify demands and remove or circumvent constraints, thereby expanding choices. Examples of major choices include the objectives for the manager's unit, the priorities attached to different objectives, the strategies selected to pursue objectives, the aspects of the work in which the manager gets personally involved, how and with whom the manager spends time, what responsibility is delegated to whom, and how the manager attempts to influence different people. In a sense, these choices can be described in terms of Kotter's (1982) concepts as what agendas to set, what contacts to make to build a network, and how to influence people to implement the agendas.

Managerial jobs differ greatly in the amount and type of demands and constraints the job holder must face. However, even within the same job, the demands and constraints will vary depending on the perception of the job holder. They are not entirely determined by objective conditions, but result instead from the dynamic interaction between manager and role senders. By their choices, managers influence demands. For example, agreeing to serve on a committee adds to a manager's demands. Moreover, people differ in the way they interpret role expectations from others, and one manager will perceive a demand where another manager may not. For example, one manager may believe that a bureaucratic regulation must be observed exactly, whereas another manager may perceive more flexibility in what can be done.

Demands, constraints, and choices shape the nature of the job and strongly influence the manager's behavior. Based on Stewart's (1967, 1976) research, the following factors were found to be important for comparing managerial jobs with respect to behavioral requirements.

Pattern of Relationships

The demands made on a manager by superiors, subordinates, peers, and persons outside of the organization influence how the manager's time is spent and how much skill is needed to fulfill role requirements. Relationships with subordinates involve the need to coordinate the work of subordinates, the need for frequent assignment of work to them, the need to monitor subordinate performance, and the need to supplement formal authority with other forms of influence to insure subordinate compliance with orders and requests. More time and skill is needed to deal with subordinates when they have interlocking work, new assignments must be made frequently, it is important to monitor subordinate performance but difficult to do so, and automatic compliance with orders and requests is not assured by subordinate respect for legitimate authority.

Relationships with superiors involve the manager's dependence on them for authority, resources, work assignments, and definition of the manager's job scope. The greater the dependence and the more unpredictable the demands made by superiors, the more time and skill is needed to deal with them.

Relationships with peers involve the lateral dependence of the manager on them for services, supplies, and cooperation, and the extent to which the manager must provide services, information, and advice to peers. The more dependent the manager is on peers for inputs or approval of outputs, the more time and skill is needed in dealing with peers.

The extent to which subordinates, peers, and superiors make incompatible demands on a manager determines how much role conflict will be experienced and has obvious implications for the difficulty of satisfying the various demands.

Relationships with external contacts involve the dependence of the manager on clients, customers, suppliers, subcontractors, and so on, and the extent to which it is necessary to develop personal relationships with these people, negotiate agreements, carry out public relations activities, create a good impression, and act discreet. The greater the dependence and the more important it is to engage in these activities, the more time and skill will be needed in dealing with outsiders. Having to establish relationships with many people for short periods of time, as opposed to dealing with the same people repeatedly, further complicates the manager's job, especially when it is necessary to impress and influence people quickly. Finally, the difficulty of handling external demands is increased by incompatible interests between the manager and outsiders.

All managerial jobs require some mix of contacts with subordinates, peers, superiors, and outsiders, but for most jobs there are characteristic patterns of job contacts dictated by differences in the demands made by each party. Jobs with high external dependence include sales managers, purchasing managers, and bank managers. Jobs with high dependence on superiors include hospital administrators and some accounting and staff unit managers. Jobs with high dependence on peers include product managers, production managers, training (personnel) directors, quality control managers, some service managers, and some accounting managers. Jobs with high subordinate demand include retail store managers and managers of other self-contained regional units.

Type of Work Pattern

Several aspects of the work pattern requirements in managerial jobs were studied. The first was the extent to which managerial activities are either self-generating or a response to the requests, instructions, and problems of other people. Much more initiative is required in a predominantly self-generating job (e.g., product manager, research manager, training director) than for a predominantly responding job (e.g., production manager, service manager).

The need to meet deadlines is a second aspect of work pattern requirements. For accounting managers, staff managers, and production managers, meeting deadlines was a primary requirement of the job. For research managers and product managers, it was much less important.

A third aspect is the extent to which the work is recurrent and repetitive rather than variable and unique. For accounting managers and production managers, there was a cyclical pattern of required daily and weekly activities to be performed. For research managers, product managers, and project managers, there was much more flexibility and variety of activities.

A fourth aspect of the work pattern requirements is uncertainty, or the extent to which a manager has to cope with unpredictable problems and workload variations beyond his or her control. Managers faced with frequent crises, like production managers and service managers, must do more troubleshooting and are less able to plan their time than research managers and accounting managers. However, even for a particular category of managers, the amount of uncertainty will depend on the task, technology, and external environment.

A fifth aspect is the typical duration of managerial functions and the extent to which a manager is required to devote sustained attention to activities such as preparing reports, plans, and budgets. Research managers, some product managers, and some managers of staff units require this kind of sustained attention, whereas a pattern of brief, fragmented contracts is more typical of most other kinds of managers, particularly those with high demands from subordinates and peers.

Exposure

Another aspect of a managerial job that determines what behavior and skills are required for the job is called *exposure*. This is related to the "burden of responsibility" borne by a manager but is not merely a question of responsibility alone. Exposure depends in part on the responsibility for making decisions with potentially serious consequences. A manager's job is more exposed if decisions and actions have important consequences for the organization and mistakes or poor judgement can result in loss of resources, disruption of operations, and risk to human health and life. Another determinant of exposure is the time it takes to discover a mistake or poor decision. The longer the delay in evaluating the consequences of a manager's decisions and actions, the lower the exposure. Exposure also depends on a manager's accountability for mistakes. Accountability is reduced when decisions are made by a group or after consultation with others, and poor performance cannot be identified as the fault of the manager.

Product managers, project managers, and managers of profit centers have highly exposed jobs. Product managers recommend expensive marketing programs and product changes that may quickly prove to be a disaster. Project managers may fail to complete projects on schedule, or they may incur massive cost overruns. Managers of profit centers, such as division managers and regional managers, have high exposure when they are held accountable for their profit record. Exposure is relatively low for a research manager or a personnel director.

Core Demands and Managerial Selection

The research on core demands of managerial jobs has important implications for selection and promotion, since different jobs require somewhat different patterns of traits and skills. For example, a person who is very energetic, resourceful, and decisive is more suited to a managerial position characterized by fragmented activities, responding work pattern, need for troubleshooting, and pressure to meet deadlines. A person who has high initiative and strong internal motivation is more suited to a managerial position characterized by self-generating activities, less fragmentation, fewer crises, and activities requiring more sustained attention. Only by first identifying the behavioral demands of a managerial position can the suitability of candidates be evaluated properly.

Stewart suggests that the work pattern associated with some kinds of managerial jobs tends to be habit forming. A person who spends a long time in one position may grow accustomed to acting in a particular way and will find it difficult to adjust to another managerial position with very different behavioral requirements. The transition appears particularly difficult from a "responding" position to a "self-generating" position, or from a position where exercise of authority over subordinates is paramount to a position where influencing peers is the primary requirement. It is important to consider these kinds of issues when a manager is being evaluated for possible promotion to a higher position.

RESEARCH ON MACROLEVEL
SITUATIONAL DETERMINANTS

With the exception of Stewart, research on situational determinants of leader behavior has been rather unsystematic, with somewhat different situational variables and aspects of leader behavior used in each study. Most studies on situational determinants of leader behavior suffer from the lack of a broad perspective on the demands and constraints faced by a leader. Researchers usually investigate only one aspect of the situation at a time. Other aspects are ignored, even though some of these may prove to be far more important than the aspect selected for study. Furthermore, different aspects of the situation are likely to affect leader behavior jointly, and it is not possible to understand these complex interactions unless many situational variables are examined simultaneously. The variety of variables, measures, and approaches used in situational research makes it difficult to compare and integrate results across studies. Nevertheless, the research provides some useful insights into the manner in which leader behavior is shaped by the leadership situation. This section of the chapter reviews research on macro variables found to have substantial influence on managerial activity patterns and behavior content. The variables include managerial level, unit function, unit size, lateral interdependence, and a hostile environment or crisis.

Level in the Authority Hierarchy

Authority level of the manager's position appears to be one of the most important situational influences on leader activity patterns (Mintzberg, 1973; Nealey & Fiedler, 1968). These differences stem from the different job requirements for managers at different levels. Higher-level managers are usually more concerned with exercise of broad authority in making long-range plans, formulating policy, modifying the organization structure, and initiating new ways of doing things. Lower-level managers are more concerned with interpreting and implementing policies and programs (Katz & Kahn, 1978). Thus, as one moves down the authority hierarchy, managers have less discretion and freedom of action. Lower-level managers must operate within the constraints imposed by organizational structure and by policy decisions made at higher levels. Blankenship and Miles (1968) found that lower-level managers had less discretion, were required more often to consult with superiors before taking action on decisions, and made the final choice less often in a decision. For low-level managers, objectives are more specific, issues are less complex and more focused, and a shorter time perspective prevails (Martin, 1956).

Consistent with this difference in job requirements and discretion across levels, is the relative importance and amount of time devoted to different managerial roles (Allan, 1981; Luthans, Rosencrantz, & Hennessey, 1985; McCall & Segrist, 1980; Mintzberg, 1973; Paolillo, 1981). The observational research and related questionnaire research on managerial roles suggest that the resource allocator, spokesman, and figurehead roles are more important for top level managers than for lower-level managers. Results for entrepreneur, liaison, and negotiator roles were not consistent across studies, but these roles are probably more important both for middle and top managers than for low-level managers. Research with job-description questionnaires found that planning, strategic decision making, and public relations activities are more important for top managers than for lower-level managers (Brooks, 1955; Hemphill,1959; Katzell, Barrett,

Vann & Hogan, 1968; Mahoney, Jerdee, & Carroll, 1965; Page & Tornow, 1987; Tornow & Pinto, 1976). Lower-level managers tend to be more concerned with technical matters, staffing(personnel selection and training), scheduling work, and monitoring subordinate performance.

Results for activity patterns are generally consistent with those for activity content (Mintzberg, 1973). The number of activities each day is greater for lower-level managers. For example, executives had an average of 34 activities per day in one study (Kurke & Aldrich, 1983) and 22 in another study (Mintzberg, 1973). In contrast, Thomason (1967) found that superintendents had an average of nearly 300 activities per day, and supervisors had an average of 413 activities per day. As might be expected from their greater number of activities, the time spent on each activity tends to be less for lower-level managers. For example, research found that most activities of supervisors lasted less than 2 minutes (Guest, 1956; Ponder, 1959; Walker, Guest, and Turner, 1956).

A few studies have examined differences in participative leadership across levels. The studies found less use of participative leadership by lower-level managers than by higher-level managers(Blankenship & Miles, 1968; Chitayat & Venezia, 1984; Heller & Yukl, 1969). The reason may be due to time pressure and the perception that subordinates at lower levels have less to contribute and are less concerned about being consulted. Less participation at lower levels may also reflect the fact that lower-level managers have less authority to make important decisions, especially in highly centralized organizations.

Function of the Organizational Unit

Another important source of variation in managerial behavior is the kind of function administered by the manager. Several studies have compared managers in different functionally-specialized departments of business organizations. Except for research on production units and sales units, the number of studies on any one functional area is still very limited. Production managers tend to spend more time with subordinates, have less time alone, and have more variety and fragmentation in their work than sales managers or staff managers (Stewart, 1967). More time is spent resolving workflow problems, and the disturbance handler role is especially important (Mintzberg, 1973). More planning and scheduling of work is done by production managers than by sales managers (Hemphill, 1959; Yukl & Carrier, 1986). Production managers also spend more time engaged in directive behavior such as checking the work, giving orders, and directing the work of subordinates (Hemphill, 1959; Webber, 1972). Decisions are more often made in an autocratic manner without subordinate participation (Heller & Yukl, 1969).

Sales managers tend to emphasize the interpersonal roles (Mintzberg, 1973; McCall & Segrist, 1980; Pavett & Lau, 1983). The importance of external contacts with clients and customers is reflected in the preoccupation of sales managers with the liaison and figurehead roles. Considerable time is spent outside of the company in public relations, promotional activities, image building, and socializing with customers (Stewart, 1967, 1976). The leader role is also important, but it tends to involve primarily selection and training of subordinates, giving them assignments, and encouraging high performance. In one study Yukl and Carrier (1986) found that more motivating and recognizing behavior was reported for sales managers than for production managers. Sales managers spend less time than many types of managers in directing subordinate activities (Hemphill, 1959; Webber, 1972).

The monitor and spokesperson roles are especially important for managers of staff specialists (e.g., legal staff, personnel department, planning department, public relations office, industrial engineering staff) who function as advisors and experts to other units and to higher management (Mintzberg, 1973). Staff managers are expected to keep informed about developments in their technical specialty, and they serve as a technical advisor and representative of their specialty in meetings. These managers tend to spend more time alone, are more involved with paperwork, and have less fragmentation and variety in their work than most other kinds of managers (Mintzberg, 1973; Stewart, 1967, 1976). More of their work is self-initiated than is true for sales or production managers (Stewart, 1976; Webber, 1972). In making decisions, staff managers tend to be more participative than production, sales, or finance managers, which is probably due to the complex nature of their decisions and the greater potential of subordinates to make a significant contribution to the decision (Heller & Yukl, 1969).

A major limitation of the research on unit function is the finding that the effects of function differ depending on other situational variables such as unit size, lateral interdependence, and managerial level. It is difficult to make any broad generalizations about the implications of unit function, because of the complex interactions among situational variables. The sheer number of different functions to be considered makes progress on this type of research difficult. Another complication is the fact that many managerial positions involve organizations or subunits that perform a variety of different functions, rather than a single "pure" function. For example, much of the research on "general managers" (Kotter, 1982; Kaplan, 1986) is concerned with units that include a variety of functions, such as marketing, finance, research and development, operations, and various staff activities. Unit function may not prove to be a very useful situational variable, because it is really a surrogate for other variables such as those described earlier in the discussion of Stewart's research; these other types of variables, must be considered in order to explain differences found between functions.

Size of Organizational Unit

The implications of work unit size or "span of control" for leader behavior have been investigated in several types of research, ranging from studies with small groups to studies on chief executives. Interpretation of the results is complicated by the fact that group size is often confounded with other aspects of the situation, such as task complexity and degree of role interdependence among subordinates. For example, span of control tends to be lower when subordinates have complex and interdependent tasks, because more coordinating and directing by the manager is necessary. A further complication is due to the fact that size can be measured in a variety of ways that may not be consistent. For example, an executive may have few immediate subordinates but many people in his or her organizational unit. Despite all of these complications, some implications of unit size for leader behavior are apparent from the research.

When the number of subordinates is large, it is more difficult to get all of them together for meetings, and it is less feasible to consult individually with each subordinate. Thus, leaders tend to use less participative leadership or to limit it to an "executive committee" or to a few trusted "lieutenants," consistent with vertical-dyad linkage theory(see Chapter 3). Heller and Yukl (1969) found that as span of control increased, upper-level managers made more autocratic decisions, but they also used more delegation. Both decision styles allow a manager who is overloaded with responsibilities to reduce the amount of time needed to make decisions. Lower-level managers in this study also made more autocratic decisions as span of control increased, but they did not use more delegation, perhaps because delegation was less feasible for them. Blankenship and Miles (1968) found that as span of control increased, managers relied more on subordinates to initiate action on decisions, and this trend was much more pronounced for upper-level managers than for lower-level managers.

As the size of the group increases, so does the administrative workload. Managers need to spend more time doing things like planning, coordinating, staffing, and budgeting (Cohen & March, 1974; Hemphill, 1950; Katzell et al., 1968). The increase in coordination requirements is magnified when the subordinates have highly uncertain and interdependent tasks. Sometimes part of the increased administrative burden can be delegated to a second in command, to a coordinating committee composed of subordinates, or to new coordinating specialists who serve as staff assistants. In many cases, however, the leader is expected to assume the administrative responsibility and to provide more overall direction and integration of group activities. In this event, the amount of time available for one-to-one contact with individual subordinates is further reduced.

The decreased opportunity for interacting with individual subordinates in large groups has important implications for the leaders of these groups. There is less time available to provide support and encouragement to each subordinate and to engage in other interpersonal behavior necessary for maintaining effective relationships with subordinates (Ford, 1981). Good performance by individuals is less likely to be recognized and rewarded in large groups (Goodstadt & Kipnis, 1970). Problems with subordinates are likely to be handled in a more formalized, impersonal manner, and managers are more likely to use warnings and punishment (Kipnis & Cosentino, 1969; Kipnis & Lane, 1962). When a subordinate has a performance problem, the leader is less likely to provide individualized instruction and coaching.

Group size also has implications for the team-building activities of a leader. As a group grows larger, separate cliques and factions are likely to emerge. These subgroups often compete for power and resources, creating conflicts and posing a threat to group cohesiveness and teamwork. Thus, the leader of a large group needs to devote more time to building group identification, promoting cooperation, and managing conflict. However, the pressure to carry out more administrative activities in a large group may cause the leader to neglect group maintenance activities until serious problems arise.

Studies on activity patterns for top-level managers find results consistent with other types of research on the effects of unit size. In three studies of chief executives, the executives of large organizations spent more time in scheduled meetings, had fewer unscheduled meetings, made fewer but longer telephone calls, had fewer activities lasting less than 9 minutes, and had more activities lasting longer than an hour (see Kurke & Aldrich, 1983). Kotter studied general managers and concluded that managers of the larger organizational subunits had more demanding jobs in comparison to managers of smaller units. Decisions are more difficult due to the sheer volume of issues and activities and the lack of detailed knowledge a manager is likely to have. Because larger units are likely to have a more bureaucratic structure, managers must cope with more constraints, such as rules and procedures, and staff specialists whose cooperation is needed. Large units are more likely to involve physical separation, such as a boss who is located somewhere else or subordinates scattered across different facilities. Consistent with this analysis, Kotter (1982) found that general managers in larger organizational units had larger networks and attended more scheduled meetings.

Lateral Interdependence

The extent to which a leader's subunit is dependent on other subunits in the same organization or on external groups will affect leader behavior to a considerable extent. As lateral interdependence increases with other subunits, need for external coordination increases, and in uncertain, dynamic environments, it becomes more important but also more difficult for subunit managers to make mutual adjustments in plans, schedules, and activities (Galbraith, 1973; Mintzberg, 1979). Lateral interdependence represents a threat to the subunit because routine activities must be modified more frequently to accommodate the needs of other subunits, with a resulting loss in autonomy and stability (Hunt & Osborne, 1982; Sayles, 1979). Research on activity patterns of managers finds results consistent with this picture. As lateral interdependence increases, the external activities of a leader become more important, managers spend more time in lateral interactions, and they build larger networks with contacts in other parts of the organization (Hammer & Turk, 1987; Kaplan, 1986; Kotter, 1982; Stewart, 1967, 1976; Walker et al., 1956; Yanouzas, 1964).

One type of lateral interdependence occurs when each subunit performs a different step in a series of related operations. Since the work of each subunit depends on the steady flow of materials, parts, or information from other subunits, there is need for close coordination between the subunit managers. Lateral interdependence also occurs when one subunit of an organization is responsible for providing services or advice to other units, evaluating their output, or monitoring their activities (Sayles, 1979). The leader's role in lateral relations includes functions such as gathering information from other subunits, obtaining assistance and cooperation from them, negotiating agreements, reaching joint decisions to coordinate unit activities, defending the unit's interests, promoting a favorable image for the unit, and serving as a spokesperson for subordinates. The extent to which a leader emphasizes each of these activities depends on the nature of the lateral relationship. For example, when a unit provides services on demand to other units, acting as a buffer for subordinates against these external demands is a primary concern of the leader (Sayles, 1979).

Just as the leader tries to reconcile demands from above and below, so also is it also necessary to make compromises in seeking to reach agreements with other units. Subordinates expect the leader to represent their interests, but it will not be possible to maintain an effective working relationship with managers of other units unless the leader is also responsive to their needs. Salancik et al. (1975) conducted a study of managers in an insurance company to investigate this kind of role conflict. Managers with interlocking work activities tended to develop a pattern of similar behavior through a process of mutual reinforcement. They became more responsive to each other's needs in order to maintain a cooperative effort. The greater the number of peers a manager had to interact with on a regular basis, the less responsive the manager was to the desires of subordinates.

Research on the influence tactics used in lateral relations suggests that rational persuasion is commonly employed, as are appeals based on friendship or reciprocity for past favors (Kanter, 1982; Kaplan, 1986; Kipnis et al., 1980; Kotter, 1962; Patchen, 1974; Sayles, 1979; Strauss, 1962). Although a manager usually lacks authority over other subunit managers, legitimate requests are made by appeal to role requirements, organizational policy, or prior tradition. Direct coercion is less common, because managers seldom have much lateral coercive power. However, indirect pressure can sometimes be applied by cultivating high-level supporters and forming coalitions with other subunits. Managers are more likely to spend time in political activities of this kind when there is competition for scarce resources or jurisdictional disputes among subunits (Dalton, 1950; Dutton & Walton, 1965; Seiler, 1963).

Hostile Environment and Crises

When a group is under extreme pressure to perform a difficult task or to survive in a hostile environment, the role expectations for the leader are likely to change in a predictable manner. In this kind of situation, subordinates expect the leader to be more assertive, directive, and decisive (Halpin, 1954; Mulder & Stemerding, 1963). They look to the leader to show initiative in defining the problem, identifying a solution, and directing the group's response to the crisis. Consistent with this proposition, Halpin (1954) found that platoon members were more satisfied with a high structuring leader in combat than in training. A study conducted aboard navy ships showed that navy officers exercised more power in crisis situations and were more directive, autocratic, and goal oriented (Mulder et al., 1970). Officers who showed initiative and exercised power in a confident and decisive manner were rated more effective by superiors. In a similar study of bank managers in the Netherlands (Mulder, de Jong, Koppelaar & Verhage, 1986), consultation with subordinates was used less in crisis situations than in noncrisis situations. Managers rated effective were more likely than less effective managers to use consultation in a noncrisis situation, and were less likely to use it in a crisis situation. Research on survival of air force crews shot down over enemy territory found that a crew was more likely to survive and be rescued if the leader made a quick but adequate analysis of the situation, established a common goal orientation, and kept everybody informed about developments (Torrance, 1954).

Work groups under strong external pressure to meet deadlines or improve performance sometimes show similar but less pronounced changes in leader behavior. The leaders of such groups tend to become more goal oriented, and they display more directive-structuring behavior and less considerate-supportive behavior (Fleishman, Harris, & Burtt, 1955; Guest, 1954; Pfeffer and Salancik, 1975).

RESEARCH ON MICROLEVEL SITUATIONAL DETERMINANTS

Managerial behavior is also influenced by microvariables such as the nature of the task performed by subordinates and subordinate competence. Research on these situational determinants is reviewed next.

Task Characteristics

The characteristics of the tasks performed by subordinates have important implications for leader behavior. It is likely that some of the differences found for unit function are actually due to task attributes. Task characteristics of major interest include task structure, complexity, difficulty, variability, uncertainty, and mechanization. Integration of results from this research is complicated by the proliferation of concepts, measures, and research methods.

Task complexity is a key variable in several situational leadership theories (see Chapter 6). However, the influence of task structure is not as simple as the theories seem to imply. It is easier for a leader to be directive and autocratic when the task is highly structured because the leader is more likely to know the best way to do the task. Nevertheless, the fact that it is easier to act directive and autocratic when the task is highly structured does not imply that it is desirable to do so. Directive, close supervision may be considered redundant and annoying to subordinates who possess adequate skills to perform a highly structured task. Directive, structuring leader behavior is most appropriate in a situation where there is an unstructured task and unskilled, inexperienced subordinates. When the task is unstructured and subordinates are competent and experienced, it is appropriate for a leader to be less directive and to use more consultation and delegation. For example, if subordinates are skilled technicians, craftspeople, or professionals, they will not need much direction from the leader. The importance of directive behavior depends partly on other sources of role clarity such as organizational rules and procedures. If elaborate regulations and standard procedures exist to guide work behavior, less direction from the leader is needed.

In view of these complex relationships, it is not surprising that the results from empirical research on task structure are also inconsistent. Some studies (Ford, 1981; Hill & Hughes, 1974; Vroom & Yetton, 1973) have found that leaders tend to act more directive and autocratic when subordinates have relatively structured tasks to perform (e.g., simple, repetitive, routine, one best procedure). Other studies (Bass, Valenzi, Farrow, & Solomon, 1975; Dessler & Valenzi, 1977; Sheridan & Vredenburgh, 1978) have found no significant effect of task structure on directive or autocratic behavior by leaders.

Another relevant task characteristic is the extent to which different subordinates have interdependent tasks. Such tasks require more coordination and synchronization of activities among subordinates, which may be accomplished either by leader planning and directing, or by other mechanisms such as group meetings or a special integrator role carried out by someone besides the designated leader (Galbraith, 1973). The situation for within-unit interdependence is roughly analogous to the between-unit interdependence discussed earlier in this chapter, except that internal coordination among subordinates is needed rather than external coordination with other subunits. Only a few studies have examined how task interdependence affects managerial behavior. In one laboratory study, Hackman, Brousseau, and Weiss (1976) found that group performance was better for interdependent tasks when performance strategies were discussed to facilitate mutual adjustment. In another laboratory study, Lord and Rowzee (1979) found that group performance was better when the leader did things to coordinate member activity. In a recent study of athletic teams by Fry, Kerr, and Lee (In press), coaches of teams with high interdependence (basketball, ice hockey, football, volleyball) had higher scores on initiating structure than coaches of teams with low interdependence (swimming, tennis, track, golf, wrestling). Moreover, structuring behavior was positively correlated with team performance for high interdependence teams but not for low interdependence teams.

The technology used to perform the work appears to have effects somewhat distinct from those for task structure. Technology involves mechanization and variability of operations sequencing in addition to the complexity, interdependence, and variability of individual subordinate tasks. Many different combinations of these factors are possible, and there is still much confusion about the best way to classify technology. In a study of four types of firms in England, Thurley and Hamblin (1963) found it useful to distinguish between degree of mechanization and degree of variability in operations sequencing. When there was a high degree of mechanization, supervisors spent more time checking machinery and dealing with breakdowns. The greater the variation in operations sequencing, the more time was spent by supervisors in planning, scheduling, and facilitating the work. Yanouzas (1964) compared foremen in an assembly-line plant with foremen in a job-lot plant and found similar results to Thurley and Hamblin. Foremen in the job-lot plant spent more time planning production, scheduling and assigning work, and monitoring operations, whereas foremen in the assembly-line plant spent more time checking quality, dealing with machine breakdowns, and tending to interpersonal relations.

Competence and Performance of Subordinates

In work organizations, one of the most important determinants of leader behavior is the competence and performance of subordinates. Leaders tend to react differently toward subordinates who are performing effectively than toward subordinates whose performance is substandard. More than 20 studies have been conducted on this subject, most of them either laboratory experiments or longitudinal field studies using sophisticated correlational techniques to identify likely causal relationships. A rather consistent pattern of results emerges from these studies. Poor subordinate performance usually causes one or more of the following leader reactions:

1. Closer supervision (Farris & Lim, 1969; James & White, 1983; Lowin & Craig, 1968; McFillen,1978; McFillen & New, 1979).
2. More directive-structuring behavior (Greene, 1975, 1979a, 1979b; Lowin & Craig, 1968).
3. Less considerate-supportive behavior (Barrow, 1976; Dansereau, et al., 1975; Farris & Lim, 1969; Graen & Cashman, 1975; Greene, 1975, 1979b, Herold, 1977; Lowin & Craig, 1968).
4. More critical-punitive behavior (Bankhart & Lanzetta,1970; Barrow, 1976; Curtis, Smith,& Smoll,1979; Greene, 1979b; Herold, 1977; Sims & Manz, 1984; Szilagyi, 1980).
5. More autocratic behavior (Barrow, 1976; Farris & Lim,1969; Greene, 1979b; Heller & Yukl, 1969).
6. More performance emphasis (Barrow, 1976; Farris & Lim, 1969).
7. Less praise and positive rewards (Bankhart & Lanzetta, 1970; Curtis et al., 1979; Farris & Lim, 1969; Kipnis & Vanderveer, 1971; McFillen & New, 1979; Sims, 1977; Sims & Manz, 1984; Szilagyi, 1980).
8. Less delegation (Dewhirst, Metts, & Ladd,1987; Leana, 1986).

Leader behavior is also affected by judgments about the knowledge and dependability of subordinates. Leaders allow more participation by subordinates who have relevant knowledge and can be trusted to cooperate with the leader (Bass, 1976; Dansereau et al., 1975; Graen & Cashman, 1975; Scandura, Graen, & Novak, 1986; Vroom & Yetton, 1973). More responsibility and authority is delegated to subordinates who are perceived to be knowledgeable and dependable (Ashour & England, 1972; Dansereau, Graen, & Haga, 1975; Graen & Cashman, 1975; Heller, 1971).

Lack of subordinate compliance has effects similar to poor performance, although this finding is based on only one study (Green, 1979). When a subordinate fails to comply with rules or orders, a leader is likely to act more punitive, more directive, less considerate, and less participative. These behaviors can be seen as an attempt to pressure the subordinate to comply, or failing that, to isolate and punish him or her. It is interesting to consider that the typical response by a leader to either poor performance or noncompliance is probably not the most effective one. As we saw in Chapter 3, use of coercion, pressure, and hostility by a leader is less effective in most cases than a firm but supportive problem-solving approach, accompanied by any necessary instruction and coaching.

ATTRIBUTION THEORY
AND REACTIONS TO POOR PERFORMANCE

Not all leaders react the same to poor performance by a subordinate. Attribution theory attempts to explain different reactions in terms of situational factors and a leader's cognitive processes. Green and Mitchell (1979) described the reaction of a manager to poor performance as a two-stage process. The first stage is to determine the cause of the poor performance, and the second stage is to select an appropriate response to correct the problem. Several studies have confirmed the major propositions of the model (Green & Liden, 1980; Ilgen, Mitchell, & Fredrickson, 1981; Mitchell & Kalb, 1981; Mitchell & Liden, 1982; Mitchell, Green, & Wood, 1981; Mitchell & Wood, 1980; Wood & Mitchell, 1981).

Managers attribute the major cause of poor performance either to something internal to the subordinate (lack of effort, lack of ability) or to external problems beyond the subordinate's control (e.g., the task had inherent obstacles, resources were inadequate, information was insufficient, other people failed to provide necessary support, or it was just plain bad luck). An external attribution is more likely when (1) the subordinate has no prior history of poor performance on similar tasks, (2) the subordinate performs other tasks effectively, (3) the subordinate is doing as well as other people who are in a similar situation, (4) the effects of failures or mistakes are not serious or harmful, (5) the manager is dependent upon the subordinate for his or her own success, (6) the subordinate is perceived to have other redeeming qualities (popularity, leadership skills), (7) the subordinate has offered excuses or an apology, or (8) there is evidence indicating external causes.

The type of attribution made by a manager influences the response to the problem. When an external attribution is made, the manager is more likely to respond by trying to change the situation, such as providing more resources, providing assistance in removing obstacles, providing better information, changing the task to reduce inherent difficulties, or in the case of bad luck, by showing sympathy or doing nothing. When an internal attribution is made and the manager determines the problem is insufficient ability, the likely response is to provide detailed instruction, monitor the subordinate's work more closely, provide coaching when needed, set easier goals or deadlines, or switch the subordinate to an easier task. If the problem is perceived to be lack of subordinate effort and responsibility, then the likely reaction is to give directive or nondirective counseling, give a warning or reprimand, punish the subordinate, monitor subsequent behavior more closely, or find new incentives.

A number of the studies cited earlier found that managers tend to be biased toward making internal attributions about poor performance, and this leads to greater use of punitive responses directed at the subordinate. At the same time, subordinates tend to blame external factors for their mistakes or failures. These incompatible biases make it especially difficult for the manager to handle performance problems effectively, since punitive actions are all the more resented by subordinates who do not feel responsible for the problem.

The results from the attribution research are generally consistent with research on the effect of leader power on treatment of subordinates (Kipnis, Schmidt, Price, & Stitt, 1981; McFillen & New, 1979). A major implication of both lines of research is that training is needed to help managers become more careful, fair, and systematic about evaluating subordinate performance. Managers need be become more aware of the many options available for dealing with different causes of performance problems, and the importance of selecting an appropriate one. Finally, the attribution research points out another danger of having *out-group* relations with some subordinates (see Chapter 3). Out-group subordinates are likely to get less support, coaching, and resources, yet when they make mistakes or have performance difficulties, the manager is likely to blame them rather than recognizing situational causes and his or her own contribution to the problem.

INDIVIDUAL DISCRETION VERSUS SITUATIONAL REQUIREMENTS

The situational research provides strong evidence that aspects of the situation influence the activity pattern and behavior content of managers. A managerial position makes various demands on the person who occupies it, and the actions of the occupant are constrained by laws, policies, regulations, traditions, and scope of formal authority. Despite these demands and constraints, some choice of behavior remains, particularly with respect to what aspects of the job are emphasized, how much time is devoted to various activities, and how much time is spent with different people. The research showed that even for managers with similar jobs, there was considerable variability of behavior (Kotter, 1982; James & White, 1983; Stewart, 1976, 1982). For example, Stewart found that some bank managers emphasized staff supervision, whereas some others delegated much of the internal management to the assistant manager and concentrated on actively seeking out new business.

In part, variability within the same job reflects the fact that the job has multiple performance dimensions, and within the boundaries imposed by the priorities of higher management, a person may chose to devote more effort to some objectives than to others. For example, activities involving development of new products may get more attention than cost reduction, quality improvements, development of new export markets, or improvement of safety practices. Development of subordinates to groom them for promotion may get more attention than team building or training in skills necessary to improve performance in the present job. The tradeoffs inherent among performance dimensions and lack of time to do everything well make it inevitable that different people will define the same job in different ways. How this is done will reflect a manager's interests, skills, and values, as well as the changing role expectations of the individuals whose destinies are intertwined with the manager's.

IMPLICATIONS FOR
MANAGERIAL EFFECTIVENESS

The research on situational determinants and role expectations provides some useful guidelines for improving a manager's effectiveness (Kanter, 1982; Kieser, 1984; Kotter, 1982; Pfeffer, 1981; Stewart, 1976, 1982). Once again, these are tentative guidelines, not invariable rules, and a manager should exercise considerable judgment in applying them.

1. *Understand the reasons for demands and constraints.* Perception of demands and constraints inevitably involves subjective judgments, but many managers fail to take the time necessary to gather sufficient information on which to base these judgments. It is essential to learn how others perceive the manager's role and what they expect from him or her. Since role expectations are often quite vague and ambiguous, some managers assume that everyone agrees with their perception of the unit's mission, or their implicit theory about effective management. A manager's reputation can be undermined by angry, frustrated peers and subordinates who do not share the manager's vision or priorities. Before a manager can satisfy role senders, or modify their expectations to resolve role conflicts, it is necessary to understand what they really desire. Consistent with the importance of network building and oral interaction, understanding role expectations requires frequent face-to-face interaction, asking questions, listening to others rather than constantly "preaching," being sensitive to negative reactions, including nonverbal cues, and trying to discover the values and needs underlying a person's opinions and preferences.

2. *Expand the range of choices.* Too many managers focus on the demands and constraints and fail to give adequate consideration to opportunities to define the job in different ways. Managers need to remember that different performance criteria may be emphasized, and even for the same criteria, different strategies are possible. It is possible for a manager to be proactive with his or her own boss about defining the job in a way that allows more opportunity and discretion. Choices may be expanded by finding ways to avoid demands and reduce constraints. Role ambiguity due to poorly defined responsibilities can be viewed as an opportunity to have more discretion in the definition of one's job. Part of a manager's planning and agenda development should be a conscious analysis of the demands and constraints limiting current effectiveness, and how they can be reduced, eliminated, or circumvented. The analysis may indicate the need for a slow, difficult political process of initiating improvement programs, building coalitions, shaping expectations, and reinforcing desired behavior.

3. *Understand and influence attributions about your performance.* A manager's reputation depends on attributions made by the boss and other role senders. Thus, it is important to understand how they will interpret

actions and events. Effective managers are adept at impression management and understand the importance of political and symbolic actions, such as (1) showing progress in their projects (e.g., informing others of action steps achieved on schedule, interim improvement targets that were attained, benefits that were realized for others), (2) getting sufficient exposure for your ideas and contributions to successful projects, while simultaneously sharing credit with others whose continued or future support is essential, (3) distancing oneself from projects likely to fail, co-opting others who will judge the success of a risky project to share responsibility for it, and finding positive benefits in failed projects, and (4) appearing cooperative rather than obstructive to peers whose cooperation is needed to accomplish one's own projects.

4. *Be aware your attributions may become self-fulfilling prophecies.* If a manager attributes a subordinate's performance problems to lack of motivation or ability, and then treats the person as lazy or stupid, the attribution may become true, even if it was initially untrue. On the other hand, if a subordinate is initially lacking in ability or responsibility but the manager consistently shows confidence and trust, then the person may change to fit these expectations. Research discussed in Chapter 9 finds that one of the best predictors of advancement in the organization is having a boss who expects that a person will succeed and provides the encouragement, support, coaching, and developmental opportunities necessary for the person to learn new skills and demonstrate them. Chapter 10 reviews some research showing that leader expectations about subordinate competence and success are an important influence on the subordinate's self-perception and development, the so-called Pygmalion effect. This effect extends beyond the dyad to include others, such as peers, who then contribute to a person's reputation by reacting as if it were true.

SUMMARY

Leaders adapt their behavior to the requirements, constraints, and opportunities presented by the leadership situation. Role theory is useful for helping to understand how this process occurs. A leader's perception of role requirements is influenced by role senders, task characteristics, and feedback about subordinate performance. The leader's needs, values, and interests influence perception of role requirements, as well as influencing the leader's choice among behavior alternatives. Expectancy theory provides further insights into the choice of an appropriate behavior. Osborne and Hunt's multiple influence model identifies macro variables such as organization structure that are likely to create demands and constraints on leader behavior. Stewart identified additional influences on leader behavior. The pattern of interactions with subordinates, peers, superiors, and outside persons is affected by the demands they make on a manager. The type of work pattern depends on the nature of the work itself: self-generating or responding, repetitive or variable, uncertain or predictable, fragmented or sustained, and subject to tight deadlines or relatively unhurried.

Comparative research on managers in different situations reveals several aspects of the situation that affect managerial behavior: level of management, size of organizational unit, function of unit, lateral interdependence, task characteristics and technology, and crisis conditions. In addition, managers treat subordinates differently, depending on the perceived competence and performance of each subordinate. Reactions to a subordinate mistake or performance problem depend in part on a manager's attributions about the reason for it. Whether the performance problem is blamed on the subordinate or circumstances is the subject of attribution theory.

Despite all the demands and constraints faced by a manager, some choice of behavior remains. Even managers in similar positions define their roles differently. There are choices in what aspects of the job to emphasize, how to allocate one's time, and with whom to spend it. Managers will be more effective if they understand the demands and constraints in their job situation, work to expand their choices, act to shape the impressions other form about them, and understand how their expectations influence the way others eventually perform.

REVIEW AND DISCUSSION QUESTIONS

1. To what extent are managerial jobs similar and to what extent are they different?
2. How much latitude do managers have in what they do and how they do it? Is it more accurate to view managers as "captains of their destiny" or "prisoners of their fate"?
3. Briefly describe the role theory explanation of how managerial behavior is determined.
4. What macrosituational variables influence managerial behavior?
5. What microsituational variables influence managerial behavior?
6. Briefly describe Stewart's theory of how managerial behavior is influenced by the nature of the job situation.
7. Briefly describe how attribution theory explains a leader's response to a poorly performing subordinate.
8. What are the implications for managerial effectiveness of the research on situational determinants?
9. What points of convergence are there between findings on situational determinants of managerial behavior, findings about typical patterns of managerial behavior (Chapter 4), and findings about power and influence (Chapter 2)?

9

Managerial
Traits and Skills

One of the earliest approaches for studying leadership was the trait approach. Underlying this approach was the assumption that some persons are "natural" leaders. Such persons were assumed to be endowed with certain traits not possessed by other people. The early leadership researchers were not sure what traits would be essential for leadership effectiveness, but they were confident that these traits could be identified by empirical research. Trait research was facilitated by the rapid development of psychological testing during the period from 1920 to 1950. The kinds of traits studied most often in the early leadership research included physical characteristics (e.g., height, appearance), personality (e.g., self-esteem, dominance, emotional stability), and ability (general intelligence, verbal fluency, creativity, social insight).

This chapter will review research on the personal attributes of successful leaders. The emphasis will be on traits and skills that contribute to a person's capacity to perform effectively in a managerial position, rather than on traits that predict who will emerge as a leader in an informal group.

GENERAL REVIEWS OF RESEARCH
ON LEADER TRAITS

Over a hundred studies on leader traits were conducted during the first half of this century. In the majority of studies, the general approach was to compare leaders with nonleaders to see what differences existed with respect to physical characteristics, personality, and ability. A smaller number of studies compared successful leaders with less successful leaders, or correlated measures of traits with measures of leadership effectiveness. Success and leadership effectiveness were sometimes measured in terms of group performance, and sometimes in terms of career advancement. In the latter case, the definition of successful leadership was to advance farther up the authority hierarchy of the organization and to earn a larger salary compared to persons of the same age. Studies in which leaders are rotated among similar work groups are occasionally regarded as part of the trait approach, but these studies (Jackson, 1953; Rosen, 1969; Wyndham & Cooke, 1964) tell us more about the effect of changing leaders than about the specific traits of effective leaders.

The trait research has been reviewed at various times by different scholars (e.g., Bass, 1981; Lord, DeVader, & Alliger, 1986; Mann,1959; Stogdill, 1948, 1974). The two reviews by Stogdill can be compared to discover how conceptions about the importance of leader traits evolved over a quarter of a century.

Stogdill's 1948 Review

In his early review, Stogdill examined the results of 124 trait studies from 1904 to 1948. A number of traits were found to differentiate repeatedly between leaders and nonleaders in several studies. The pattern of results was consistent with the conception of a leader as someone who acquires status through active participation and demonstration of ability to facilitate the efforts of the group in attaining its goals. Traits relevant to the assumption and performance of this role include intelligence, alertness to the needs of others, understanding of the task, initiative and persistence in dealing with problems, self-confidence, and desire to accept responsibility and occupy a position of dominance and control. For a few traits, such as dominance and intelligence, there were some negative correlations, which may indicate a curvilinear relationship.

Despite the evidence that leaders tend to differ from nonleaders with respect to certain traits, Stogdill found that the results varied considerably from situation to situation. In several studies that measured situational factors, there was evidence that the relative importance of each trait depends upon the situation. Thus, Stogdill (1948, p. 64) concluded: "A person does not become a leader by virtue of the possession of some combination of traits . . . the pattern of personal characteristics of the leader must bear some relevant relationship to the characteristics, activities, and goals of the followers."

In effect, the early studies failed to support the basic premise of the trait approach that a person must possess some particular set of traits in order to become a successful leader. Although some traits appeared widely relevant for different kinds of leaders, these traits were neither necessary nor sufficient to insure leadership success. A leader with certain traits could be effective in one situation but ineffective in a different situation. Furthermore, two leaders with different patterns of traits could be successful in the same situation. None of the traits in these studies correlated very highly with leadership effectiveness when considered alone. Various combinations of traits correlated more highly with leader effectiveness, but only within certain limited situations.

Stogdill's 1974 Review

In his 1974 book, Stogdill reviewed 163 trait studies conducted during the period from 1949 to 1970. The research used a greater variety of measurement procedures, including projective tests (e.g., thematic apperception test, the Miner sentence completion scale), situational tests (e.g., in-basket, leaderless group discussion), and forced choice tests (e.g., Ghiselli's self-description inventory, Gordon's survey of interpersonal values). More of the studies involved managers and administrators, as opposed to other kinds of leaders. The 1948 literature review by Stogdill greatly discouraged many leadership researchers from studying traits, but industrial psychologists interested in improving managerial selection continued to conduct trait research. The interest in managerial effectiveness led researchers to extend the list of traits under investigation to include specific administrative and technical skills, and specific aspects of managerial motivation relevant to the requirements of an administrative role.

The difference in methodology and perspective led to stronger, more consistent results in the second set of trait studies. Most of the same traits were again found to be related to leader effectiveness and some additional traits and skills were also found to be relevant (see Table 9-1). Stogdill (1974, p. 81) suggested that the following trait profile is characteristic of successful leaders:

> The leader is characterized by a strong drive for responsibility and task completion, vigor and persistence in pursuit of goals, venturesomeness and originality in problem solving, drive to exercise initiative in social situations, self-confidence and sense of personal identity, willingness to accept consequences of decision and action, readiness to absorb interpersonal stress, willingness to tolerate frustration and delay, ability to influence other persons' behavior, and capacity to structure social interaction systems to the purpose at hand.

TABLE 9-1   Traits and Skills Found Most Frequently to Be
Characteristic of Successful Leaders

TRAITS	SKILLS
Adaptable to situations	Clever (intelligent)
Alert to social environment	Conceptually skilled
Ambitious and achievement-oriented	Creative
Assertive	Diplomatic and tactful
Cooperative	Fluent in speaking
Decisive	Knowledgeable about group task
Dependable	Organized (administrative ability)
Dominant (desire to influence others)	Persuasive
Energetic (high activity level)	Socially skilled
Persistent	
Self-confident	
Tolerant of stress	
Willing to assume responsibility	

In retrospect, it is apparent that many leadership researchers over-reacted to the earlier pessimistic literature reviews by rejecting the relevance of traits entirely. As Stogdill (1974, p. 72) noted:

The reviews by Bird, Jenkins, and Stogdill have been cited as evidence in support of the view that leadership is entirely situational in origin and that no personal characteristics are predictive of leadership. This view seems to overemphasize the situational, and underemphasize the personal, nature of leadership.

However Stogdill makes it clear that recognition of the relevance of leader traits is not a return to the original trait approach. The premise that certain leader traits are absolutely necessary for effective leadership has not been substantiated in several decades of trait research. Today there is a more balanced viewpoint about traits. It is now recognized that certain traits increase the likelihood that a leader will be effective, but they do not guarantee effectiveness, and the relative importance of different traits is dependent on the nature of the leadership situation (Bass, 1981).

MANAGERIAL SELECTION
AND ASSESSMENT

Since some of the most promising results on leader traits have come from studies of managerial assessment and selection, it is worthwhile to examine this line of research more closely. Up until the mid-1960s, attempts to predict managerial effectiveness with measures of personality and ability did not meet with much success. As was characteristic of trait research in general, certain aptitude, personality, and interest measures correlated with effectiveness criteria, but the correlations were sporadic and usually of low magnitude (Ghiselli, 1966; Guion & Gottier, 1965; Korman, 1968). Selection research in this earlier period relied heavily on standardized paper-and-pencil tests. It was common in the earlier research to measure general intelligence, scholastic aptitude, and specific aptitudes such as verbal comprehension, arithmetic computation, numerical reasoning, and perceptual accuracy, but there was seldom any attempt to measure specific, job-relevant technical knowledge or administrative skills. One exception was the use of some mechanical principles tests to predict the effectiveness of production foremen, but even these tests were general in content rather than assessing knowledge of the particular technical processes supervised by the foremen. A few selection studies attempted to assess human relations skills with paper and pencil tests such as the Leadership Evaluation and Development Scale (Mowry, 1964; Tenopyr, 1969) and the How Supervise test (Rosen,1961) However, it is very difficult to measure human relations skills with a written test, and this approach did not prove very useful for predicting managerial effectiveness.

Assessment Center Approach

Around the same time that pessimistic reviews of managerial selection appeared in print, the field was undergoing a major revolution in the methodology of managerial selection. The assessment center approach to managerial selection was being perfected. The term *assessment center* refers to a standardized set of procedures used to identify managerial potential. Although no two programs are exactly alike, they all utilize multiple methods of assessing traits and skills, including projective tests and situational tests in addition to traditional methods like interviews and written tests. Moreover, candidates for selection or promotion to a managerial position are usually given some kind of writing exercise (e.g., a short autobiographical essay) to evaluate their written communication skills and a speaking exercise to evaluate their oral communication skills. The assessment process in the centers typically takes two to three days.

The projective tests used in assessment centers contain ambiguous stimuli such as pictures to be interpreted, or incomplete sentences to be completed by the candidate. Examples of these projective tests are described later in the chapter. Two commonly used situational tests are the in-basket and leaderless group discussion. The in-basket test consists of letters, memos, and reports that supposedly have accumulated in the in-basket of a hypothetical manager. The candidate has a limited amount of time to deal with each of the managerial problems contained in these materials. The leaderless group discussion places candidates in a group situation where there is no designated leader. Sometimes the candidates are asked to represent competing viewpoints, with each candidate trying to persuade the others to adopt his or her viewpoint. Another variation is to have the candidates assume the roles of different managers trying to make a group decision, such as whether to merge with another company. Observers rate each candidate on qualities such as initiative, assertiveness, persuasiveness, dominance, and cooperation.

An overall evaluation of each candidate's management potential is made by several staff members who interview the candidate, examine test scores and biographical information, observe candidate behavior in the situational exercises, and then meet to discuss their assessments and resolve any disagreements. The assessors attempt to integrate the information from these diverse sources into a coherent picture of the motives, skills, and behavior tendencies of each candidate.

Studies on the validity of assessment center predictions of managerial potential usually examine the correlation between this composite evaluation and later managerial success. The research evidence suggests that assessment centers can effectively predict managerial success (Huck, 1973; Wexley & Yukl, 1984). Hundreds of organizations are currently using assessment centers to improve their managerial selection and promotion decisions. However, predictions from an overall measure of management potential do not provide much insight into the relationship of particular skills and traits to managerial success. These insights are gained only from a smaller number of studies that examine the unique predictive power of each trait and skill measured in the assessment center.

One of the best examples of the latter type of assessment center research is the longitudinal study conducted at American Telephone and Telegraph Company (AT&T) by Bray, Campbell, and Grant (1974). Eight years after an early group of candidates was assessed, each candidate's progress in terms of advancement into middle management was related back to the assessment scores, which had been kept confidential so as not to affect promotion decisions. Sixty-four percent of the candidates predicted to reach middle management did so, whereas only 32 percent of the remaining candidates reached middle management. The skills that predicted advancement best were (1) oral communication skill, (2) human relations skill, (3) planning-organizing skill, and (4) creativity. The personality traits that predicted advancement best were (1) desire for advancement, (2) resistance to stress, (3) tolerance of uncertainty, (4) energy/activity level, (5) range of interests, (6) inner work standards, and (7) readiness to make decisions.

An important discovery in the longitudinal research at AT&T was the effect of the job situation on the relevance of individual traits for managerial success. The prediction of success based on a candidate's assessed traits was more accurate if the person had a job situation favorable to individual development. A favorable situation existed when a person was encouraged to develop management skills, was given challenging assignments with increased supervisory responsibility, and had a boss who served as a role model by setting an example of how a successful, achievement-oriented manager should act. Thus, advancement was due to a combination of the relevant personal qualities and the opportunity for these qualities to be translated into competent managerial behavior.

The trait measures in assessment center studies are not independent aspects of personality or ability, so these studies sometimes include a factor analysis to identify a smaller number of distinct traits and skills. Dunnette (1971) reviewed four such studies and found that there was considerable agreement that the following six traits related to managerial success: (1) energy level, (2) organizing and planning skills, (3) interpersonal skills, (4) cognitive skills, (5) work-oriented motivation, and (6) personal control of feelings and resistance to stress. The manner in which these traits jointly influence managerial success can be seen in Bentz's (1967, p. 117–18) description of the successful Sears executive as indicated by that company's assessment center research:

> It would seem that powerful competitive drive for a position of eminence and authority provides a strong impetus for these men: the need to be recognized as men of influence and status, and ambition to govern, and the desire to excel appears to be of primary importance in enabling these men to utilize their talents fully and appropriately. . . . They are fully confident of their abilities to cope with and control unfamiliar situations, have the facility to deal with problems impersonally, and possess the physical vitality to maintain a steadily productive work pace. . . . While they prefer a dominant position within a group, they are also cooperative teamworkers who willingly listen to the ideas and suggestions of others. . . . Their strong power motive is tempered somewhat by consideration for other people, so that they are not likely to run roughshod over others in their efforts to gain success and renown.

The assessment research looks for traits that predict advancement to higher levels of management. A major limitation of this research is the possibility that some traits predicting advancement are not relevant for effective performance of the present managerial job. For example, a manager who is highly ambitious and skilled at impression management may advance faster than other managers who have greater competence in doing the current job but are not as ambitious or adept at selling themselves. Research on traits that differentiate between effective and ineffective leaders at the same level of management is more directly relevant to the objective of understanding how traits relate to effectiveness.

OTHER TRAIT RESEARCH
ON MANAGERIAL SUCCESS

The relationship of traits to managerial success has been investigated in other ways besides the longitudinal assessment studies. Two different research programs are described briefly. These research programs both considered managerial behavior in addition to traits, thereby helping to identify how traits are manifest in behavior.

Managers Who Derail

Researchers at the Center For Creative Leadership (McCall & Lombardo, 1983) have attempted to identify traits and behaviors associated with eventual success or failure of top executives. Interviews were used to gather descriptions of managers who advanced into middle or top management but subsequently failed to perform successfully. These "derailed" managers were dismissed or transferred, opted for early retirement, or simply plateaued, without any chance of further advancement. Descriptions were also obtained of managers who made it to the top successfully. The two sets of descriptions were analyzed to identify similarities and differences between successful and derailed managers. The research did not reveal any foolproof formula for success, but it provided some important insights. Every manager had strengths and weaknesses, and in some cases a weakness was merely an excess of something that had been a strength earlier in a lower-level job. Sometimes there was an obvious reason for derailing, but other times it appeared to be just a matter of bad luck; managers were done in by events beyond their control, such as unfavorable economic conditions or political battles. The major findings about traits were as follows:

1. *Emotional stability and composure.* Managers who derailed were less able to handle pressure and were more prone to moodiness, angry outbursts, and inconsistent behavior, which undermined their interpersonal relationships with subordinates, peers, and superiors. In contrast, the successful managers were calm, confident, and predictable during crises.

2. *Defensiveness.* Managers who derailed were more likely to be defensive about failure and to react by attempting to cover up mistakes or blame other people. The successful managers admitted mistakes, accepted responsibility, then took action to fix the problem. Moreover, having dealt with the problem, they did not continue to dwell on it, but turned their attention to other things.

3. *Interpersonal skills.* Managers who derailed were more likely to be weak in interpersonal skills. This flaw had been tolerated at lower levels of management, especially for managers who had outstanding technical skills, but at higher levels technical skills could not compensate for being

abrasive and offensive. Some of the derailed managers could be charming when they wanted to, but over time it became evident that beneath the facade of charm and concern, the person was selfish, insensitive, and manipulative. In contrast, the successful managers were more sensitive, tactful, and considerate.

4. *Technical and cognitive skills.* For most of the managers who derailed, their technical brilliance was a source of successful problem solving and technical achievement at lower levels of management, where their expertise was usually greater than that of subordinates. However, at higher levels, this strength could become a weakness if it led to overconfidence and arrogance, causing the person to reject sound advice, to offend people by acting superior, and to overmanage subordinates who had equal or greater expertise. In some cases, the managers had technical expertise in only a narrow functional area, and they advanced too quickly to learn other cognitive and technical skills that were needed to perform the higher-level job effectively. Successful managers were more likely to have experience in a variety of different functions and situations where they acquired a broader perspective and expertise in dealing with different types of problems.

Critical Incident Research on Managerial Competencies

Boyatzis (1982) described a program of research conducted in a variety of different private and public sector organizations to discover competencies related to managerial effectiveness. The competencies included motives, traits, skills, self-image, and knowledge. One measure of competencies was the "behavioral event interview," a version of the critical incident method described in Chapter 5. Unlike the usual critical incident study, incidents were obtained in interviews with managers preselected on the basis of effectiveness ratings. The sample included 253 managers at all levels of management, some rated low in effectiveness, some rated medium, and some rated high in effectiveness. Incidents were coded into competency categories, with traits and skills inferred from analysis of behavior in relation to the manager's intentions and the situation. The analysis of variance found nine competencies with a significant trend, such that the mean competency score was highest for effective managers and lowest for ineffective managers. These nine competencies were as follows:

1. *Efficiency orientation.* Demonstrating concern for task objectives, high inner work standards, and high achievement motivation, with behavior such as setting challenging but realistic goals and deadlines, developing specific action plans, determining ways to overcome obstacles, organizing the work efficiently, and emphasizing performance when talking to others.

2. *Concern with impact.* Demonstrating high need for power and concern for power symbols, with behavior such as acting assertively, attempting to influence others, seeking high status positions, and expressing concern about the reputation of the organization's products and services.

3. *Proactivity.* Demonstrating a strong belief in self efficacy and internal locus of control, with behavior such as initiating action rather than waiting for things to happen, taking steps to circumvent obstacles, seeking information from a variety of sources, and accepting responsibility for success or failure.

4. *Self-confidence.* Demonstrating belief in one's own ideas and ability, by behavior such as taking decisive action rather than hesitating or vacillating, and making proposals in a firm, unhesitating manner, with appropriate poise, bearing, and gestures.

5. *Oral presentation skill.* Ability to use symbolic, verbal, and nonverbal behavior, and visual aids to make clear and convincing presentations to others.

6. *Conceptualization.* Ability to identify patterns or relationships in information and events (inductive reasoning), and to convey the meaning by developing a concept, model, or theme, or by using appropriate metaphor and analogy; also the ability to develop creative solutions and new insights into problems.

7. *Diagnostic use of concepts.* Deductive reasoning, using a concept or model to interpret events, analyze situations, distinguish between relevant and irrelevant information, and detect deviations from plans.

8. *Use of socialized power.* Ability to develop networks and coalitions, gain cooperation from others, resolve conflicts in a constructive manner, and use role modeling to influence others.

9. *Managing group process.* Ability to manage group processes to build member identification and team spirit by behavior such as creating symbols of group identity, emphasizing common interests and need for collaboration, facilitating successful teamwork, and providing public recognition of member contributions.

In summary, competencies inferred from descriptions of effective and ineffective behavior incidents distinguished between effective and less effective managers. The competencies included motives, personality traits, cognitive skills, and interpersonal skills. In general, the findings are remarkably similar to those from the earlier trait studies using different research methods.

MINER'S RESEARCH
ON MANAGERIAL MOTIVATION

The importance of managerial motivation as a predictor of managerial advancement and effectiveness has been evident in each type of trait research reviewed in this chapter. Additional evidence is provided by research focused specifically on managerial motivation. Miner (1965) formulated a theory of managerial role motivation to describe the type of motivational traits required for success in most management positions in large, hierarchical organizations. The initial traits selected for investigation were based on an analysis of role requirements common to managerial positions. Miner's theory also reflects some influence from role theory and psychoanalytic theory. The managerial role prescriptions and associated motivational patterns are as follows (Miner, 1978, 1985):

1. *Positive attitude toward authority figures.* Managers should have a generally positive attitude toward superiors in order to develop effective relations with them and obtain necessary resources and support. Any tendency to generalize hatred, distaste, or anxiety in dealings with people in positions of authority will make it extremely difficult to meet job demands.

2. *Desire to compete with peers.* Managers should be favorably disposed toward engaging in competition to benefit themselves and their subordinates. A person who is unwilling to compete for status, advancement, resources, and political support is unlikely to satisfy job demands.

3. *Desire to be actively assertive.* Managers are supposed to take charge, make decisions, take necessary disciplinary actions, and protect other members of a group. A person who becomes upset or disturbed at the prospect of behaving in an assertive manner is unlikely to satisfy job demands.

4. *Desire to exercise power.* Managers must exercise power over subordinates, tell others what to do, and make appropriate use of positive and negative sanctions. A person who finds such behavior difficult and emotionally disturbing or who believes it is wrong to exercise power over others is unlikely to satisfy job demands.

5. *Desire to stand out from the group.* The managerial job requires a person to assume a position of high visibility and do things which inevitably invite attention, discussion, and perhaps criticism. A person who is uncomfortable about assuming a prominent position and taking controversial positions is unlikely to satisfy job demands.

6. *Willingness to carry out routine administrative work.* Managerial work requires a person to perform administrative activities such as preparing budgets, writing reports, and serving on committees, although the specific activities will vary from position to position. A person who strongly dislikes doing these activities and avoids them is unlikely to satisfy job demands.

Managerial motivation is measured with a projective test called the Miner Sentence Completion Scale. The test provides an overall score as well as separate scores on each of the six aspects of managerial motivation. Miner's research over a period of 25 years includes more than 33 studies on the relationship between managerial motivation and managerial advancement (Miner, 1978, 1985). In large bureaucratic organizations, significant correlations were found between a manager's overall score on managerial motivation and advancement to higher levels of management. The particular motivation subscales that correlated most consistently with managerial success included desire to exercise power, desire to compete with peers, and a positive attitude toward authority figures. Desire to stand out from the group and desire to perform routine administrative functions were less frequently associated with managerial success and appear to be less important aspects of managerial motivation. Desire to be assertive has been the least useful component for predicting success.

Miner (1967, 1977) also investigated managerial motivation in samples of leaders who were not in large hierarchical organizations. These samples included managers of branch offices in a consulting firm, administrators in a business school, and educational administrators in small school districts. The managerial motivation of these leaders was not correlated significantly with managerial success. Criterion problems may account for the lack of significant correlations, but it is also possible that the aspects of managerial motivation measured by Miner's test are not important for leadership success in smaller, less bureaucratic organizations. In a recent study on this question, Berman & Miner (1985) found that top executives who had risen up through the ranks in large bureaucratic organizations had higher managerial motivation than top executives of smaller, family-owned companies. However, both samples of executives had higher scores than a comparison group of less successful managers of the same age at lower and middle levels of management.

McCLELLAND'S RESEARCH
ON MANAGERIAL MOTIVATION

Extensive research on managerial motivation has been conducted also by McClelland (1965, 1985) and his associates. In most of the research, need strength was measured with a projective technique called the Thematic Apperception Test (TAT). The test consists of a series of pictures of people in ambiguous situations, and someone who takes the test is asked to make up a story about each picture. The stories reveal the person's daydreams, fantasies, and aspirations, and they are coded by the experimenter to obtain a measure of three underlying needs: power, achievement, and affiliation.

Need for Power

Stories that reveal a person thinks a lot about influencing other people, defeating an opponent or competitor, winning an argument, or attaining a position of greater authority indicate a strong need for power. This need can be satisfied in a variety of ways, including recreational activities that allow a person to outwit or dominate an opponent (e.g., debates, intellectual games, or one-on-one sports), and some vicarious outlets such as watching contact sports, viewing movies with explicit violence, and using alcohol, drugs or mystical rituals to heighten the experience of personal influence over events. Another way to satisfy need for power is to enter an occupation that provides opportunities to exercise influence over the attitudes and behavior of other people. People with a strong need for power prefer occupations such as executive, politician, labor leader, police officer, military officer, and lawyer (McClelland,1975; Winter, 1973).

McClelland proposed that a strong need for power is important for managers and executives in large, established organizations. These jobs require a person to exercise influence over subordinates, peers, and superiors. People who are low in need for power seem to lack the assertiveness and self-confidence necessary to organize and direct group activities effectively. A dominant need for power is desirable, but a manager's effectiveness also depends on how this need finds expression. People with a high need for power tend to have either a "personalized power concern" or a "socialized power concern." A socialized power concern is more likely to result in effective leadership than a personalized power concern.

The people with a personalized power concern have little inhibition or self-control, and they exercise power impulsively. According to McClelland and Burnham (1976, p. 103), "They are more rude to other people, they drink too much, they try to exploit others sexually, and they collect symbols of personal prestige such as fancy cars or big offices." They may provide assistance and advice, but in a way that demonstrates personal superiority and the weakness or dependence of others. Such managers may be able to inspire loyalty and team spirit, but organizational role clarity suffers. Moreover, any subordinate loyalty is to the leader rather than to the organization, and when the leader departs there is likely to be disorder and a breakdown in team spirit.

People with a socialized power concern are more emotionally mature. They exercise power more for the benefit of others, are more hesitant about using power in a manipulative manner, are less egoistic and defensive, accumulate fewer material possessions, have a longer-range view, and are more willing to take advice from experts. In a managerial position, their strong need for power is expressed by using influence to build up the organization and make it successful. A leader with a socialized power concern is more willing to sacrifice self-interest for the welfare of the organization. Because of the orientation toward building organizational commitment, this kind of leader is more likely to use a participative, coaching style of managerial behavior and is less likely to be coercive and autocratic. Such leaders "help make their subordinates feel strong and responsible, bind them less with petty rules, help produce a clear organizational structure, and create pride in belonging to the unit" (McClelland, 1975; p. 302).

Need for Achievement

Stories that reveal a person thinks a lot about attaining a challenging goal, setting new records, successfully completing a difficult task, or doing something never done before, indicate a strong need for achievement. People with a strong need for achievement prefer a job in which success depends on effort and ability rather than chance factors beyond their control. They prefer tasks that are moderately difficult rather than easy or impossible. They like tasks that provide opportunity to use their skills and exercise initiative in solving problems. They desire frequent, concrete feedback about performance so they can enjoy the experience of making progress and successfully attaining objectives. The preferred job characteristics are likely to be found in occupations such as sales representative, real estate agent, producer of entertainment events, and owner-manager of a small business (McClelland, 1965).

Need for achievement motivation is not the most essential motive for managers in large organizations, but it is still important. Need for achievement should be moderately strong, and subordinated to a strong power need, so that it will be expressed in efforts to facilitate team performance rather than in the pursuit of individual success. If achievement is the dominant need, a manager tries to accomplish everything alone, is reluctant to delegate, and fails to develop a strong sense of responsibility and commitment among subordinates (McClelland & Burnham, 1976).

Need for Affiliation

Stories that reveal a person thinks a lot about establishing or restoring close, friendly relationships, joining groups, participating in pleasant social activities, and enjoying shared experiences with family or friends, indicate a strong need for affiliation. People with a strong need for affiliation receive great satisfaction from being liked and accepted by others, and they enjoy working with people who are friendly and cooperative. However, someone with a strong need for affiliation is usually unwilling to allow the work to interfere with harmonious relationships (Litwin & Stringer, 1966; McClelland, 1975).

A moderate degree of affiliation motivation is probably optimal for managerial effectiveness. Managers with a strong need for affiliation avoid making necessary but unpopular decisions and show favoritism to personal friends in dispensing rewards and favors or in permitting exceptions to rules. These managers often disregard procedures and rules, which leaves subordinates feeling "weak, irresponsible, and without a sense of what might happen next, of where they stand in relation to their manager, or even of what they ought to be doing" (McClelland & Burnham, 1976; p. 104). On the other hand, a person who is extremely low in need for affiliation tends to be a "loner" who doesn't like to socialize with others, except perhaps the immediate family or a few close friends. Such a person is likely to lack the motivation to engage in the many social and public relations activities that are essential for a manager, including those involved in establishing effective interpersonal relationships with subordinates, superiors, and peers. As Litwin and Stringer (1966) point out, some basic concern for the needs and feelings of other people seems critical as a source of motivation to build and maintain effective working relationships.

Research on Needs and Managerial Success

A sizeable number of studies have been conducted to investigate how needs are related to managerial advancement and effectiveness. Most of these studies measure needs with the TAT. In general, the results support the proposition that advancement or effectiveness in large, hierarchical organizations is associated with a dominant socialized power concern (Boyatzis, 1982; McClelland, 1975; McClelland & Boyatzis, 1982; McClelland & Burnham, 1976; Winter, 1973).

A study by McClelland and Burnham (1976) provides a good example of research on consequences of different motive patterns, and it is one of the few studies to include measures of intervening variables. In 16 sales districts of a large company, the amount of increase in sales over the prior year was related to team spirit and organizational role clarity within the unit, as reported by subordinates. These intervening variables were related in turn to the motive pattern of the sales managers. Sales managers with higher need for power than for affiliation and with emotional maturity had subordinates with greater team spirit, a stronger sense of personal responsibility, and a clearer understanding of organizational procedures. In other words, these managers were able to create a more effective work climate, which resulted in better group performance.

Some studies using the TAT have found that managerial success is related to a high need for both power and achievement (Cummin, 1967; Varga, 1975). In a study using a job choice measure of needs, Stahl (1983) found that managers high in both need for achievement and power had greater career advancement and higher performance ratings. Still another approach was used by Donley and Winter (1970), who analyzed the inaugural addresses made by several U.S. presidents to determine if the motive patterns reflected in the speech related to the president's administrative style and record of accomplishment. The most dynamic, innovative presidents, such as Theodore Roosevelt, Franklin Roosevelt, John Kennedy, Harry Truman, and Lyndon Johnson, appeared to have a strong need for both power and achievement.

A few studies indicate that a dominant socialized power concern may not be important for all types of managers. In one study by McClelland and Boyatzis (1982), advancement of nontechnical managers to higher levels was predicted by need for power, but advancement through lower levels of management was predicted only by need for achievement. For technical managers, advancement was not predicted either by need for achievement or by need for power; this finding is consistent with results found in an earlier study of navy officers by Winter (1979). Perhaps advancement for technical managers is more dependent upon technical skills and verbal fluency than on motivation.

The optimal pattern of motives appears to be different for entrepreneurial managers, such as owner-managers of small, entrepreneurial organizations and managers of small, autonomous subsidiaries of large organizations. A dominant need for achievement appears to be important for these entrepreneurial managers. Studies of small firms in several countries found that a firm's growth rate was predicted by the achievement motivation of owner-managers and other top executives (Collins, Moore, & Unwalla, 1964; Hundal, 1971; McClelland & Winter, 1969; Wainer & Rubin, 1969). Results for other needs were less clear, but there was some indication that successful entrepreneurs had a high need for independence, a moderately high need for power, and a low need for affiliation. Of course, success depends on ability as well as motivation. An entrepreneurial manager needs relevant technical expertise as an inventor, product designer, promoter, financier, or marketing specialist.

MANAGERIAL INTERESTS
AND VALUES

Another source of information about effective traits is research on interests and values. Some studies compare managers and nonmanagers with respect to their interests and values. Other studies relate a manager's interests and values to measures of managerial effectiveness.

Interests indicate the extent to which a person likes to engage in a particular kind of activity. Interests have been found to be a predictor of both occupational choice and success. It is reasonable to assume that a person who enjoys activities typically associated with a managerial role is more likely to select this role as a career and to be successful at it. Nash

(1965, 1966) reviewed research on the vocational interests of managers and found limited evidence for this premise. Successful managers tend to be interested in verbal and persuasive activities, and they have a strong interest in interacting with people, especially in relationships where the manager is dominant. In addition, successful managers prefer activities that involve independent thought, initiative, and risk. The pattern of results for interests appears consistent with the findings for managerial motivation discussed earlier.

Values are defined by Gordon (1975, p. 2) as "constructs representing generalized behaviors or states of affairs that are considered by the individual to be important." Unlike needs, values may be satisfied by a large variety of behaviors, and they do not dominate behavior in such a compelling manner. Values are important because they influence a person's perception of situations and problems, and they influence preferences, aspirations, and choices (England, 1967; Gordon, 1975). The most widely used measures of values in managerial research are the Allport-Vernon study of values (Allport, Vernon, & Lindsey, 1960) and the Gordon (1976) survey of interpersonal values (SIV). The separate values measured by the SIV are labeled and defined as follows (Gordon, 1975, pp. 22–25):

1. *Support*: Being treated with understanding, receiving encouragement from other people, being treated with kindness and consideration.
2. *Conformity*: Doing what is socially correct, following regulations closely, doing what is accepted and proper, being a conformist.
3. *Recognition*: Being looked up to and admired, being considered important, attracting favorable notice, achieving recognition.
4. *Independence*: Having the right to do whatever one wants to do, being free to make one's own decisions, being able to do things in one's own way.
5. *Benevolence*: Doing things for other people, sharing with others, helping the unfortunate, being generous.
6. *Leadership*: Being in charge of other people, having authority over others, being in a position of leadership or power.

Research on the relationship between values and managerial effectiveness has yielded different results depending on the nature of the administrative position (Nash, 1965; Gordon, 1975, 1976). Several studies using the survey of interpersonal values found that the leadership scale tends to be positively correlated with managerial effectiveness, and the benevolence, support, and conformity scales tend to be negatively related to effectiveness (Gordon, 1976). Gordon also reports results for research comparing leaders and nonleaders on the SIV. Managers and military officers had relatively high leadership scores and low support scores, indicating these leaders place a high value on influencing others and a low value on receiving supportive attention.

A different approach for investigating managerial values was used by England (1967). He conducted a descriptive study of the personal values of 1072 American managers in 1966, and this study was essentially replicated several years later by Lusk and Oliver (1974). These two studies asked managers to rate the importance of different concepts, and the extent to which each concept is perceived to be pleasant, ethical-moral, and instrumental for success. The results indicated that for American managers in general, the primary value orientation is pragmatic rather than moralistic or hedonistic. Managers tended to consider personal qualities such as skill, ambition, achievement, and creativity as both important and instrumental for success. Loyalty, trust, honor, tolerance, dignity, rationality, and individuality were seen as important but not instrumental for success. Rated low in importance but highly instrumental were qualities such as risk, force, power, and aggressiveness.

The Managerial Mind

A different approach for investigating the value orientation and attitudes of managers and administrators is to analyze case histories, biographies, and autobiographies of distinguished executives. Ewing (1964) applied this method and found that successful managers tend to have the following orientation:

1. The primary commitment is to the organization, and though successful managers may criticize certain policies and practices, they remain loyal to the organization as long as they are part of it.
2. The processes of supervising and coordinating are foremost in the thinking of successful managers, but they recognize that an attempt to control people is partly self-defeating because it restricts their spirit and creativity. Thus, they tolerate some forms of tension and disagreement as an essential requirement for creativity, innovation, and adaptation to external change.
3. Successful managers are hesitant about manipulating subordinates or controlling them closely and prefer instead to assign tasks and objectives to subordinates and allow substantial autonomy and self-control in performing the tasks.
4. Successful managers consider it important to establish a climate that encourages subordinates to enlarge their horizons, set high aspirations, be flexible in their behavior, and have less anxiety about mistakes.
5. Successful managers deemphasize personal values such as kindness, gentleness, and sympathy, and instead emphasize getting desired results.

Ewing (1964, p. 209) concludes with the following commentary about the kind of people who flourish in an administrative role:

> As for the administrator himself, I suspect his future is about the same in any organization, in any place. His efforts can never be completely successful: the dilemmas of management and control will always be with him. He has the gift of being able to be absorbed in his work, however, to immerse himself into turning suffering into growth, argument into creativity, defeat into progress. People may say that he "seems to take a beating," but he does not resist the daily give and take. He belongs to it and it to him.

White (1965, p. 366) in writing about U.S. presidents, provides a similar perspective of the kind of person most likely to be successful as a leader:

Whether a man is burdened by power or enjoys power; whether he is trapped by responsibility or made free by it; whether he is moved by other people and outer forces or moves them—this is of the essence of leadership.

MANAGERIAL SKILLS

It is not enough to have the appropriate motivational pattern; a person also needs considerable skill to be an effective leader. The early trait studies uncovered a variety of potentially relevant abilities, and other research described in this chapter has added to the list of relevant managerial skills. The proliferation of skill concepts by different researchers has created a state of conceptual confusion similar to that prevailing for behavior concepts. The next section describes a taxonomy that was developed to group skills into broader categories and reduce some of the confusion.

Three-Skill Taxonomy

The most widely accepted approach for classifying managerial skills is in terms of a three-skill taxonomy. Similar versions of this taxonomy were proposed by Katz (1955) and Mann (1965). The skill categories were defined as follows:

1. *Technical Skills.* Knowledge about methods, processes, procedures, and techniques for conducting a specialized activity, and the ability to use tools and operate equipment related to that activity.

2. *Interpersonal Skills.* Knowledge about human behavior and interpersonal processes, ability to understand the feelings, attitudes, and motives of others from what they say and do (empathy, social sensitivity), ability to communicate clearly and effectively (speech fluency, persuasiveness), and ability to establish effective and cooperative relationships (tact, diplomacy, knowledge about acceptable social behavior).

3. *Conceptual Skills.* General analytical ability, logical thinking, proficiency in concept formation and conceptualization of complex and ambiguous relationships, creativity in idea generation and problem solving, ability to analyze events and perceive trends, anticipate changes, and recognize opportunities and potential problems (inductive and deductive reasoning).

It is evident that technical skills are primarily concerned with things, interpersonal skills are primarily concerned with people, and conceptual skills are primarily concerned with ideas and concepts. Each of the three skill categories is relevant to the role requirements of managers and administrators.

Technical skills are necessary for a manager to solve problems, direct subordinates with specialized activities, evaluate their performance, and provide training. This type of skill is the most concrete and easiest to understand. Technical skills are learned during formal education in specialized subjects (e.g., accounting, finance, marketing, engineering, business law, computer programming, etc.) and through on-the-job training and experience.

Interpersonal or "human relations" skills are important for establishing effective relationships with subordinates, superiors, peers, and outsiders. As Katz (1955, p. 34) points out:

> Real skill in working with others must become a natural, continuous activity, since it involves sensitivity not only at times of decision making but also in the day-by-day behavior of the individual. . . . Because everything a leader says and does (or leaves unsaid or undone) has an effect on his associates, his true self will, in time, show through. Thus, to be effective, this skill must be naturally developed and unconsciously, as well as consistently, demonstrated in the individual's every action.

Conceptual skills are essential for effective planning, organizing, policy formation, problem solving, and program development. A major administrative responsibility is coordination of the separate, specialized parts of the organization. In order to accomplish effective coordination and make necessary modifications in organization structure, a manager needs to understand how the various parts of the organization relate to each other, and how changes in one part of the system affect the other parts. A manager must be sensitive also to the external environment and be able to comprehend how changes in it will affect the organization. The importance of this "external perspective" is explained by Katz and Kahn (1978, p. 541):

> The decision to merge or resist merger, to make a major change in location or to maintain a present position, to launch an entirely new line of products or to stay with the traditional items, to be the first with a new manufacturing process or to wait until others attempt it—these are the kinds of issues that demand the greatest understanding of the environment on the part of management. They are also the kinds of issues that will make the difference between successful and unsuccessful competition, between growth and stagnation, survival and failure.

Skill Importance in Different Situations

Managers need all three kinds of skills to fulfill their role requirements, but the relative importance of the skills depends on the leadership situation. One aspect of the situation influencing skill importance is a manager's position in the authority hierarchy of the organization (Boyatzis, 1982; Katz, 1955; Mann, 1965; Mishauk,1971; Porter & Henry, 1964). Skill priorities at different levels of management are related to the differing role requirements described in Chapter 8.

Since the major responsibility of top executives is making strategic decisions, conceptual skills are more important at this level than at middle or lower levels. The quality of strategic decisions ultimately depends on the conceptual skills of the decision makers, even though some technical knowledge is necessary to make these decisions, and interpersonal skills are necessary for developing relationships, obtaining information, and influencing subordinates to implement decisions (Katz & Kahn, 1978). The role of middle managers as primarily one of supplementing existing structure and developing ways to implement policies and goals established at higher levels. This role requires a roughly equal mix of technical, interpersonal, and conceptual skills. Low-level managers are mainly responsible for implementing policy and maintaining the workflow within the existing organization structure; for these managers, technical skills are usually more important than conceptual skills or interpersonal skills.

Some research indicates the skill requirements for top-level managers vary somewhat, depending on the type of organization, its size, and the degree of centralization of authority (McLennan, 1967). For example, in organizations where operating decisions are highly decentralized, technical skills are of minimal importance for top-level managers. A greater degree of relevant technical skill is needed by executives in organizations where operating decisions are highly centralized, and in organizations where the top executives have functionally specialized roles (e.g., selling to key customers, product design) in addition to general administrative responsibilities.

An interesting question about managerial skills is the extent to which they are transferable from one situation to another. Writers generally agree that lower-level managers cannot easily transfer to a different functional specialty (e.g., from sales manager to engineering manager) because the technical skills at this level of management are so vital and so different across functions. However, there is much less agreement about the transferability of managerial skills at the executive level. Katz (1955) proposed that top-level managers with ample human relations and conceptual skills can be shifted from one industry to another with great ease and no loss of effectiveness. Other writers contend that the transferability of skills for top executives is very limited due to variations in ownership, traditions, organizational climate, and culture (Dale, 1960; Kotter, 1982; McLennan, 1967; Shetty & Peery, 1976). Different industries have unique economic, market, and technological characteristics. Familiarity with technical matters, products, personalities, and tradition is a type of knowledge that is acquired only through long experience in the organization. Only the general components of conceptual and technical skills can be transferred to a different situation; the unique knowledge component of these skills must be relearned. Furthermore, a period of several years may be needed by an outside successor to develop a network of contacts and reciprocal trading relationships, whereas an internal successor already has part of the necessary network in place. In general, it will be more difficult for an executive to make a successful transition to a different industry or type of organization if the difference between situations is great, technical expertise is required in the new position, and the network of internal and external contacts must be extensive (Kotter, 1982; Shetty and Peery; 1976).

CONTINGENCY THEORIES OF TRAITS AND EFFECTIVE LEADERSHIP

In recent years, researchers have increasingly examined traits in relation to situational requirements, but as yet, few situational theories have incorporated traits as a predictor of managerial effectiveness. Two situational theories that focus on traits rather than behavior are Fiedler's LPC contingency model and his cognitive resources theory. These two theories are examined before we turn to practical applications of the trait approach.

Fiedler's LPC Contingency Model

Fiedler's (1964, 1967) LPC contingency model describes how the situation moderates the relationship between leader traits and effectiveness. In 1953, at the University of Illinois, Fiedler began a program of leadership research that attempted to predict leadership effectiveness from a trait measure called the *least preferred coworker score* (LPC). The LPC score is determined by asking a leader to think of all past and present coworkers, select the one with whom he or she could work least well, and rate this person on a set of bipolar adjective scales. The LPC score is the sum of the ratings on all of the bipolar adjective scales. An LPC scale is shown in Appendix C.

A leader who is generally critical in rating the least preferred coworker will obtain a low LPC score, whereas a leader who is generally lenient will obtain a high LPC score. The interpretation of LPC scores has changed several times over the years. According to Fiedler's (1978) most recent interpretation, the LPC score indicates a leader's motive hierarchy. A high-LPC leader is primarily motivated to have close, interpersonal relationships with other people, including subordinates, and will act in a considerate, supportive manner if relationships need to be improved. Achievement of task objectives is a secondary motive that will become important only if the primary affiliation motive is already satisfied by close, personal relationships with subordinates and peers. A low-LPC leader is primarily motivated by achievement of task objectives and will emphasize task-oriented behavior whenever there are task problems. The secondary motive of establishing good relation with subordinates will become important only if the group is performing well and there are no serious task problems.

Rice (1978) reviewed 25 years of research on LPC scores and concluded that the data support a value-attitude interpretation better than a motive hierarchy interpretation. That is, low-LPC leaders value task success, whereas high-LPC leaders value interpersonal success. As with the motive hierarchy interpretation, the pattern of leadership behavior varies with the situation. Rice's interpretation is basically in accord with Fiedler's motive hierarchy interpretation but is more parsimonious and better supported by diverse types of research.

The relationship of between leader LPC score and effectiveness depends on a complex situational variable called *situational favorability* (*or situational control*). Fiedler defines favorability as the extent to which the situation gives a leader control over subordinates. Favorability is measured in terms of three aspects of the situation.

1. *Leader-member relations*: The extent to which the leader has the support and loyalty of subordinates and relations with subordinates are friendly and cooperative.

2. *Position power*: The extent to which the leader has authority to evaluate subordinate performance and administer rewards and punishments.

3. *Task structure*: The extent to which there are standard operating procedures to accomplish the task, a detailed description of the finished product or service, and objective indicators of how well the task is being done.

Favorability is determined by weighting and combining these three aspects of the situation. The weighting procedure assumes that leader-member relations are more important than task structure, which in turn is more important than position power. The possible combinations yield eight levels of favorability, called *octants* (see Table 9–2).

According to the model, the situation is most favorable for the leader (octant 1) when relations with subordinates are good, the leader has substantial position power, and the task is highly structured. When leader-member relations are good, subordinates are more likely to comply with leader requests and directions, rather than ignoring or subverting them. When a leader has high position power, it is easier to influence subordinates. When the task is structured, it is easier for the leader to direct subordinates and monitor their performance. Some examples of this situation include the well-liked commander of an artillery crew and the supervisor of an open-hearth steel shop who has loyal workers. The situation is least favorable for the leader (octant 8) when relations with subordinates are poor, the task is unstructured, and position power is low. Some examples include the unpopular chairperson of a volunteer committee with a vague, problem-solving task, and the disliked chairperson of the board of directors in a small farm-supply cooperative. Examples of a situation with intermediate favorability include the popular leader of a research team who has limited position power (octant 4) and the unpopular new supervisor of a crew of assembly-line workers (octant 5).

TABLE 9-2   Relationships in Fiedler's LPC Contingency Model

OCTANT	L-M RELATIONS	TASK STRUCTURE	POSITION POWER	EFFECTIVE LEADER
1	Good	Structured	Strong	Low LPC
2	Good	Structured	Weak	Low LPC
3	Good	Unstructured	Strong	Low LPC
4	Good	Unstructured	Weak	High LPC
5	Poor	Structured	Strong	High LPC
6	Poor	Structured	Weak	High LPC
7	Poor	Unstructured	Strong	High LPC
8	Poor	Unstrucutred	Weak	Low LPC

The causal relationships in the model are depicted in Figure 9-1. According to the model, when the situation is either favorable (octants 1–3) or very unfavorable (octant 8), low-LPC leaders will be more effective than high-LPC leaders. When the situation is intermediate in favorability (octants 4–7), high-LPC leaders will be more effective than low-LPC leaders. It is important to note the absence of explicit intervening variables in the model to explain how leader LPC affects group performance. Fiedler (1978) proposed a tentative explanation saying, in effect, that the particular motive hierarchy of some leaders makes them more likely to use the kind of leadership behavior that is appropriate for the situation. However, as yet this explanation is very speculative and unsupported.

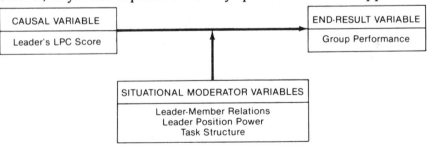

FIGURE 9-1   Causal Relationships in Fiedler's Contingency Theory

A large number of studies have been conducted over the past 20 years to test the model. These studies have been reviewed by Strube & Garcia (1981), and Peters, Hartke, and Pohlmann (1985). The reviewers concluded that the research tends to support the model, although not for every octant and not as strongly for field studies as for laboratory studies. Despite these results, Fiedler's contingency model and the methods used to test it have been severely criticized by a number of writers. The major criticisms are as follows:

1. The LPC score is a "measure in search of a meaning" (Schriesheim & Kerr, 1977: p. 23). Its interpretation has been changed in an arbitrary fashion, and the current interpretation is speculative. LPC scores may not be stable over time and may be more complex than assumed (Yukl, 1970).

2. The model is not really a theory, since it doesn't explain how a leader's LPC score affects group performance (Ashour, 1973).

3. The empirical support for the model is weak because it is based on correlational results that fail to achieve statistical significance in a majority of cases, even though correlations may be in the right direction (Graen, Alvares, Orris, & Martella, 1970; McMahon, 1972; Vecchio, 1983).

4. The weights used to compute situational favorability were determined in an arbitrary manner, and no explicit rationale was presented for them. The model does not explain why three different aspects of the situation should be combined and treated as a single continuum (Shiflett, 1973).

5. The situational measures are probably not independent of the leader's LPC score (Kerr & Harlan, 1973). In most of the studies testing the model, the measure of LPC and the measure of leader-member relations were both obtained from the leaders, and the two may be confounded with each other.

6. The model treats leader-member relations as a situational moderator variable. In view of the evidence from behavior research, it seems more appropriate to treat leader-member relations, which is similar to satisfaction with the leader, as an outcome variable that the leader can influence by acting considerate and supportive.

7. The model and most of the research neglects medium LPC leaders, who probably outnumber the high- and low-LPC leaders. Research suggests that medium-LPC leaders are more effective than either high- or low-LPC leaders in a majority of situations (5 out of 8 octants), presumably because they balance affiliation and achievement concerns more successfully (Kennedy, 1982; Shiflett, 1973).

8. The model treats task structure as a given, whereas in many situations, especially where work is not highly mechanized or unionized, organizing the work is a major responsibility of the manager. Studies suggest that modifying task structure has up to ten times the effect on group per-

formance as leader LPC scores (O'Brien & Kabanoff, 1981). Although the companion training program called "Leader Match" (Fiedler & Chemers, 1982) encourages modification of task structure, the only guideline is to make task structure more compatible with the leader's LPC score. There is no concern for selecting the organization of work that makes most efficient use of group personnel and resources.

9. The model assumes that a structured task is always a more favorable situation for controlling subordinates. However, a leader's power depends in part on the differential between leader and subordinate task knowledge. Leader expert power is highest when the leader has much more experience and information than subordinates, especially when subordinates want the group to perform well. This condition is not likely to continue when the task is so highly structured that it can be learned quickly by subordinates.

Fiedler (1973, 1977) has replied to some of these criticisms, and the debate over the validity of the model is still continuing. However, initial enthusiasm for the model has waned over the years, and it no longer is believed to have much utility for understanding leadership effectiveness.

Cognitive Resource Theory

A different type of situational model developed by Fiedler and his colleagues (Fiedler, 1986; Fiedler & Garcia, 1987) deals with the cognitive abilities of leaders. As noted earlier in this chapter, reviews of trait research find only a weak correlation between leader intelligence and leader effectiveness (Ghiselli, 1966; Stogdill, 1974). The theory examines the conditions under which cognitive resources such as intelligence, experience, and technical expertise are related to group performance. The relation of intelligence and experience to leader effectiveness is an important issue, because organizations use prior experience and intelligence tests in selecting managers. The theory predicts group performance with two situational variables (interpersonal stress and group support), and one type of leader behavior (directive leadership), in addition to leader intelligence and experience.

The first proposition is that leader ability contributes to group performance only when the leader is directive. The theory assumes that intelligent leaders devise better plans and action strategies for doing the work. The theory also assumes that a leader's plans and decisions will be communicated to subordinates through directive behavior. In a problem solving group where the output of the group is a problem solution, the ability of the leader is more directly translated into effective group output if the leader maintains a strong influence over the final choice. In the event that the leader has low ability but group members have high ability and also share the task objectives, a nondirective or participative leader is more effective than a directive, autocratic leader. The rationale so far is consistent with the Vroom-Yetton model and was supported in five studies reported by Fiedler and Garcia (1987, p. 161) and a study by Blyth (1987).

The second proposition is that perceived stress moderates the relation between intelligence and decision quality. Stress may be due to a boss who creates role conflict or demands miracles without providing necessary resources and support. Other sources of stress include frequent work crises and serious conflicts with subordinates. Under low stress, high intelligence results in good plans and decisions, whereas under high stress, there is no relationship, or a negative one. The theory provides several possible explanations why highly intelligent leaders sometimes make terrible task decisions under stress. The most plausible explanation is that stress interferes with decision making. Under high stress, a leader is likely to be distracted and unable to focus on the task. The leader may withdraw and let the group drift or make poor decisions because of the disruptive effects of anxiety about protecting his or her self-image and reputation.

The theory differentiates between leader intelligence and experience. Experience is usually measured in terms of time in the job, and it is assumed to result in habitual behavior patterns for effectively dealing with task problems. It is also assumed that people under stress tend to revert to previously learned behavior to deal with task problems rather than treating them as new problems. Thus, the third proposition is that experience will be positively related to the quality of leader decisions under high interpersonal stress, but it is not related to decision quality under low stress. Presumably, experienced leaders rely mostly on intelligence under low stress, and they rely mostly on experience under high stress. Inexperienced leaders presumably rely on intelligence in both situations, since they don't have much experience. Some evidence supporting these propositions was found in a study of Coast Guard officers (Potter & Fiedler, 1981) and in a study of fire department officers (Frost, 1983).

A final situational variable is the extent to which the task requires leader intelligence or expertise to be performed effectively by subordinates. For a very simple, routine task that subordinates know how to perform, leader intelligence is unlikely to be related to group performance, even for directive leaders. This proposition was not directly tested, but some indirect support was found.

Fiedler attempts to link cognitive resource theory to the contingency model by proposing that leader LPC scores may be the primary determinant of directive behavior under stress and nonstress conditions. However, as yet, little research has been conducted to explore this possible linkage.

The cognitive resources theory is a very new one, and not enough studies have been conducted yet to properly evaluate it. Most of the validation studies have deficiencies that need to be addressed in future research, and the theory has some conceptual weaknesses:

1. Most of the studies cited by Fiedler and Garcia (1987) were laboratory studies with temporary groups or studies of low-level military officers, and the results may not be applicable to executives and middle managers in large organizations.

2. Most of the validation studies were conducted to test the LPC contingency model and only later reanalyzed to test cognitive resource theory. These studies do not provide a simultaneous and complete test of the several propositions in the theory.

3. The most controversial aspect of the theory is the idea that leader effectiveness is predicted by intelligence in low-stress conditions and by experience in high-stress conditions. The theory speculates about possible reasons for poor-quality decisions under stress, but as yet, no study has directly tested the explanations by measuring intervening variables such as decision quality, or by comparing decision processes and outcomes for various combinations of intelligence and experience under stress and non-stress conditions.

4. The validation studies have relied on surrogate measures of experience, such as time on the job, rather than using a direct measure of relevant expertise. This surrogate measure may be contaminated by other differences between managers with short tenure and managers with long tenure. One rival explanation for the results is that "experienced" leaders are higher in stress tolerance because there has been more time to weed out the ones who could not handle the stress (they quit or were dismissed). Another rival explanation is that "experienced" leaders have had more time to develop networks of support relationships that will help them under stressful conditions. The research needs to investigate the various rival explanations.

5. A major trait variable in the theory is general intelligence, as measured by the Wonderlic test. The trend in the trait research over the years has been away from using broad skill categories such as general intelligence, and toward the use of more specific cognitive and administrative skills. No explicit rationale is provided for use of general rather than specific measures.

6. By relying on the old Ohio State measures of directive-structuring leader behavior, the researchers leave themselves open to many of the criticisms discussed in Chapter 5. The measure of directive behavior is inaccurate and it fails to differentiate among important component behaviors such as the difference between how a leader makes a decision and

what the leader does to get it implemented. Before the theory will be useful for explaining leader effectiveness, it needs to be more precise about the behavior of leaders in different situations, how this behavior influences group performance, and how cognitive resources relate to each aspect of behavior in each situation.

PRACTICAL APPLICATIONS
OF TRAIT RESEARCH

Findings from research on leader traits and skills have the greatest potential application to the selection and development of managers and administrators in large organizations. Intensive measurement procedures such as those used in most assessment centers provide moderately accurate information about managerial motivation, personality traits, interpersonal skills, and cognitive skills. When analyzed together with information about someone's prior experience and performance, these assessments can be used to make reasonably good predictions about likely success in a higher managerial position. The accuracy of prediction is increased when the skills, traits, and knowledge especially relevant for a position are determined in advance. Human resource planning, particularly succession planning, is more effective when the skill requirements for each administrative position are determined and considered in relation to the skills of current employees.

Information about a person's traits and skills is very useful for identifying training needs in the current job, as well as for planning management development activities to prepare the person for promotion to higher-level jobs. Assessment centers are one possible source of this information. Other sources include personality and knowledge tests, and ratings by peers or subordinates of the person being assessed. Some people in an organization who aspire to move into a particular kind of management position lack the appropriate pattern of skills and/or motivation to be successful in that position. An individual who is planning a managerial career should consider carefully the match between his/her individual attributes and the requirements of the positions to which the person aspires. Likewise, when a manager provides career counseling to a subordinate, the manager should consider whether the subordinate is able to satisfy the skill requirements for higher-level positions.

Trait research has implications also for organization design and job design. Managers usually think in terms of matching people to jobs, but it is also possible to do some "situational engineering" to match jobs to people. Skill requirements may be affected by a variety of possible changes in design of organization structure, including change from functional to product-based departments, change in the subunit size and diversity of operations, change in reporting relationships, modification of information systems, changes in formal decision processes, and decentralization of operational decisions to subunits. As yet, little research has been conducted on situational engineering to improve utilization of managerial skills.

SUMMARY

The early trait studies attempted to identify physical characteristics, personality traits, and abilities of "natural leaders." Hundreds of trait studies were conducted, but individual traits failed to correlate in a strong and consistent manner with leadership effectiveness. The early trait research did not pay much attention to the question of how traits interact as an integrator of personality and behavior, or how the situation determines the relevance of different traits and skills for leader effectiveness. In recent years, the investigation of leader traits has been more productive, due to the inclusion of more relevant traits, use of better measures of traits, examination of trait patterns, and use of longitudinal research. Some personality traits found to be relevant for effectiveness include self-confidence, emotional stability, energy level, initiative, stress tolerance, and lack of defensiveness.

Managerial motivation is important for effective leadership. The most relevant components of managerial motivation in Miner's research were desire for power, desire to compete with peers, and positive attitude toward authority figures. McClelland found that effective managers have a socialized power orientation and are more interested in building up the organization than in personal aggrandizement or domination over others. Successful managers in large organizations have a strong desire for their group to achieve challenging goals, but they develop a strong sense of responsibility and commitment among subordinates rather than trying to accomplish everything by themselves. Finally, research shows that successful managers are more likely to have values and interests consistent with the requirements of their jobs. They are pragmatic and results-oriented, and they enjoy persuasive activities requiring initiative and risk taking. Their concern for self is subordinated to their concern for task success and effective relationships.

In order to be successful, a leader needs to have considerable ability as well as motivation. Three general categories of skills relevant to all managers are interpersonal skills, cognitive skills, and technical skills. The relative priority of the three types of skills probably depends on the type of organization and level of management. The relative importance of the specific skills within each broad category also depends on the situation. Some skills such as persuasiveness, analytical ability, speaking ability, and memory for details will help a manager be successful in any situation, whereas some other skills are not easily transferred to a different type of position.

Fiedler's LPC contingency model deals with the moderating influence of three situational variables on the relationship between a leader trait (LPC) and subordinate performance. According to the model, leaders with high LPC scores are more effective in moderately favorable situations, whereas leaders with low LPC scores are more favorable in situations that are either very favorable or very unfavorable.

Cognitive resource theory examines the conditions under which cognitive resources such as intelligence, experience, and technical expertise are related to group performance. Situational variables, such as interpersonal stress, group support, and task complexity determine whether a leader's intelligence and experience enhance group performance. Directive leader behavior is an intervening variable used to explain how a leader's cognitive resources affect group performance.

REVIEW AND DISCUSSION QUESTIONS

1. What traits and skills are the best predictors of effective managerial performance and advancement to higher-level positions?
2. What evidence is there of a nonlinear relationship between some traits and leadership effectiveness (with moderate amounts of a trait optimal)?
3. How does consideration of trait patterns advance our understanding beyond what is learned from studying single traits by themselves?
4. What has been learned about managerial motivation, interests, and values of effective managers?
5. How are technical, conceptual, and interpersonal skills important for managerial effectiveness?
6. Why is it important to consider the nature of the managerial job situation when trying to identify essential traits and skills?
7. Briefly explain and evaluate Fiedler's LPC Contingency Model.
8. Briefly explain and evaluate Fiedler's Cognitive Resource Theory of Leadership.
9. What points of convergence are there between the findings of the research on managerial traits and the research on power-influence (Chapters 2 and 3), and managerial behavior (Chapters 4 and 5)?
10. What, if anything, has trait research added to our understanding about leadership effectiveness?

10

CHARISMATIC
AND TRANSFORMATIONAL
LEADERSHIP

In the 1980s management researchers suddenly became very interested in charismatic leadership, the creation of culture in organizations, and the transformation or revitalization of organizations. These subjects are especially relevant at a time when many U. S. companies are suddenly recognizing the need to make major changes in the way things are done in order to survive in the face of increasing economic competition from foreign companies. The terms *transformational leadership* and *charismatic leadership* refer to the process of influencing major changes in the attitudes and assumptions of organization members and building commitment for the organization's mission or objectives. Transformational leadership is usually defined more broadly than charismatic leadership, but there is considerable overlap between the two conceptions. The present chapter will examine major theories and research findings for charismatic and transformational leadership.

THEORIES OF
CHARISMATIC LEADERSHIP

Charisma is a Greek word that means divinely inspired gift, such as the ability to perform miracles or predict future events. The sociologist Max Weber (1947) used the term to describe a form of influence based not on the authority of the position or on tradition but rather on followers' perceptions that the leader is endowed with exceptional qualities. Until recently, charisma was rarely considered within the literature on organizational leadership (Etzioni, 1961; Oberg, 1972). Previously, this subject was mostly the province of researchers studying political leadership (e. g., Burns, 1978; Weber, 1947) and the leadership of social movements and religious cults (e.g., Bromley & Shupe, 1979; Fine, 1982; Friedland, 1964; Kanter, 1968). A number of sociologists and political scientists have attempted to describe charisma and identify the conditions under which it occurs (Berger, 1963; Cohen, 1972; Dow, 1969; Friedland, 1964; Friedrich, 1961; MacIntosh, 1970; Marcus, 1961; Shils, 1965). A major controversy is whether charisma is primarily a result of leader attributes, situational conditions, or an interactive influence process between leader and followers. This controversy resembles the divergent perspectives of the trait, situational, and reciprocal influence approaches within the mainstream leadership literature. Today the term charisma continues to be defined and used in different ways by different writers, but there has been some convergence toward a relational, interactional conception (Bass, 1985; Conger & Kanungo, 1987; Galanter, 1982; House, 1977; Sashkin & Fulmer, 1988; Trice & Beyer, 1986; Willner, 1984). Charisma is believed to result from follower perceptions of leader qualities and behavior. These perceptions are influenced by the context of the leadership situation and the follower's individual and collective needs. Recent theories of charismatic leadership within organizations will be reviewed next.

House's Charismatic Leadership Theory

House (1977) proposed a theory to explain charismatic leadership in terms of a set of testable propositions involving observable processes rather than folklore and mystique. The theory is based on findings from a variety of social science disciplines. The theory identifies how charismatic leaders behave, how they differ from other people, and the conditions where they are most likely to flourish. The inclusion of leader traits, behavior, influence, and situational conditions, makes this theory more comprehensive in scope than most leadership theories. The extent to which a leader is charismatic is determined by the following indicators:

1. Followers' trust in the correctness of the leader's beliefs.
2. Similarity of followers' beliefs to those of the leader.
3. Unquestioning acceptance of the leader by followers.
4. Followers' affection for the leader.
5. Willing obedience to the leader by followers.
6. Emotional involvement of followers in the mission of the organization.
7. Heightened performance goals of followers.
8. Belief by followers that they are able to contribute to the success of the group's mission.

According to the theory, charismatic leaders are likely to have a strong need for power, high self-confidence, and a strong conviction in their own beliefs and ideals. A strong need for power motivates the leader to attempt to influence followers. Self-confidence and strong convictions increase followers' trust in the leader's judgment. A leader without confidence and convictions is less likely to try to influence people, and when an influence attempt is made, it is less likely to be successful.

Charismatic leaders are likely to engage in behaviors designed to create the impression among followers that the leader is competent and successful. This kind of impression management bolsters trust in the leader's decisions and increases willing obedience by followers. In the absence of such behavior, problems and setbacks may erode follower confidence and undermine the leader's influence.

Charismatic leaders are likely to articulate ideological goals relating the mission of the group to deeply rooted values, ideals, and aspirations shared among followers. By providing an appealing vision of what the future could be like, charismatic leaders give the work of the group more meaning and inspire enthusiasm and excitement among followers. The net effect is greater emotional involvement by followers in the mission of the group and greater commitment to its objectives.

Since charismatic leaders rely on appeals to the hopes and ideals of followers, a necessary condition is the possibility of defining task roles in ideological terms that will appeal to followers. It is evident that some work roles have low potential for ideological appeals, particularly simple, repetitive work with little inherent meaning or social significance. However, the story of the two bricklayers illustrates the possibility of making even routine work more meaningful. When asked what he was doing, one bricklayer replied that he was making a wall; the second bricklayer replied that he was building a cathedral.

Charismatic leaders are likely to set an example in their own behavior for followers to imitate. This role modeling involves more than just imitation of leader behavior. If followers admire and identify with a leader, they are likely to emulate the leader's beliefs and values. Through this process, charismatic leaders are able to exert considerable influence on the satisfaction and motivation of followers.

Charismatic leaders are likely to communicate high expectations about follower performance while simultaneously expressing confidence in followers. Leaders with strong referent power can induce followers to set higher performance goals and gain their commitment to these goals. However, such commitment will not occur unless the goals are perceived to be realistic and attainable. If followers lack confidence about meeting the leader's high expectations, they may resist the leader's influence attempts and decline to make a serious effort. The expression of confidence by a highly admired leader is likely to boost follower self esteem and belief in the likelihood of success. Research on the "Pygmalion effect" and "self-fulfilling prophecy" indicates that followers perform better when the leader expresses confidence in them (Eden, 1984; Eden & Shani, 1982; Livingston, 1969).

Charismatic leaders are likely to behave in ways that arouse motives relevant to the group's mission. Arousal of achievement motivation is relevant for complex, challenging tasks requiring initiative, calculated risk taking, personal responsibility, and persistent effort. Arousal of power motivation is relevant for tasks requiring followers to be competitive, persuasive, and aggressive. Arousal of affiliation motivation is relevant for tasks requiring cooperation, teamwork, and mutual support among followers. Motives are aroused by giving inspirational talks with emotional appeals to followers' values, with emphasis on such things as "loyalty," "being the best," and "defeating the enemy."

Bass' Extension of House's Theory

Bass (1985) proposed an extension of House's theory to include some additional antecedent conditions, leader attributes, and consequences of charismatic leadership. According to Bass, charismatic leaders are more than just confident in their beliefs; they see themselves having a supernatural purpose and destiny. Followers, for their part, not only trust and respect the leader, they may idolize and worship the leader as a superhuman hero or spiritual figure. Being viewed as larger than life, a charismatic leader becomes the catalyst for psychodynamic mechanisms of followers, such as projection, repression, and regression. Individual psychodynamics are magnified by group processes. A charismatic leader is especially likely to emerge when followers share norms, beliefs, and fantasies that can serve as the basis for emotional and rational appeals by the leader.

Bass suggests that charismatic leaders differ greatly in their pragmatism, flexibility, opportunism, and manner of appeal. For example, some charismatic leaders rely on emotional appeals, whereas others make extensive use of rational appeals. Charismatic leaders of the latter type are likely to have superior technical expertise and strong persuasive skills. Moreover, the response of people to a charismatic leader is not uniform. In general, the response is likely to be more polarized to a charismatic leader than to a noncharismatic. The same qualities and beliefs that cause some people to adore the leader arouse extreme hatred in other people.

Charismatic leaders are more likely to emerge when an organization is in a state of stress and transition. Charisma is fostered when formal authority has failed to deal with a severe crisis and traditional values and beliefs are questioned. Thus, charismatic leadership is more likely to be found in a new organization struggling to survive, or an old one that is failing, than in an old organization that is highly successful. However, Bass stops short of suggesting that turmoil is a necessary prerequisite for charismatic leadership.

Conger and Kanungo's Charismatic Theory

Conger and Kanungo (1987) recently proposed a theory of charismatic leadership based on the assumption that charisma is an attributional phenomenon. Followers attribute certain charismatic qualities to a leader based on their observations of the leader's behavior. Conger and Kanungo identify aspects of leader behavior responsible for these attributions, drawing on the findings in research comparing charismatic and noncharismatic leaders. The behaviors are not assumed to be present in every charismatic leader to the same extent, and the relative importance of each aspect of behavior for attribution of charisma depends to some extent on the leadership situation. The major features of the theory are summarized in condensed form by the following points:

1. *Extremity of the vision.* Charisma is more likely to be attributed to leaders who advocate a vision that is highly discrepant from status quo, but still within the latitude of acceptance by followers. Noncharismatic leaders typically support the status quo, or advocate only small, incremental changes. A vision that involves only a small deviation from current assumptions and strategies does not clearly set the leader apart from others. However, followers will not accept a vision that is too radical, and the leader may be viewed as incompetent or crazy.

2. *High personal risk.* Charisma is more likely to be attributed to leaders who make self-sacrifices, take personal risks, and incur high costs to achieve the shared vision they espouse. Trust appears to be an important component of charisma, and followers have more trust in a leader who advocates a strategy in a manner reflecting concern for followers rather than self interest. Most impressive is a leader who actually risks substantial personal loss in terms of status, money, leadership position, or membership in the organization (Friedland, 1964).

3. *Use of unconventional strategies.* Charisma is more likely to be attributed to leaders who act in unconventional ways to achieve the shared vision. The leader's strategies for attaining the idealized goal must differ from conventional ways of doing things in order to impress followers that the leader is extraordinary. This proposition reflects the fact that the uniqueness of a leader's vision involves strategies as well as objectives. Use of innovative strategies that appear to be succeeding results in attri-

bution of superior expertise to the leader by followers, consistent with exchange theory (see Chapter 2).

4. *Accurate assessment of the situation.* The risks inherent in use of novel strategies make it important for the leader to have the skills and expertise to make a realistic assessment of environmental constraints and opportunities for implementing the strategies. Timing is critical; the same strategy may succeed at one time and place but fail completely if implemented too soon or too late. Leaders need to be sensitive to the needs and values of followers as well as to the environment in order to identify a vision that is innovative, relevant, timely, and appealing.

5. *Follower disenchantment.* Charismatic leaders are more likely to emerge when there is a crisis requiring major change or followers are otherwise dissatisfied with the status quo. However, an objective crisis is not viewed as a necessary condition for charismatic leadership. Even in the absence of a genuine crisis, a leader may be able to create dissatisfaction with current conditions, and simultaneously provide a vision of a more promising future. The leader may precipitate a crisis where none existed previously, setting the stage for demonstration of superior expertise in dealing with the problem in unconventional ways. Likewise, the impact of unconventional strategies is greater when followers perceive that conventional approaches are no longer effective. Here again, the leader may be able to discredit the old, accepted ways of doing things to set the stage for proposing new ways.

6. *Communication of self-confidence.* Leaders who appear confident about their proposals are more likely to be viewed as charismatic than leaders who appear doubtful and confused. The success of an innovative strategy may be attributed more to luck than to expertise if the leader fails to communicate confidence. A leader's confidence and enthusiasm can be contagious. Followers who believe the leader knows how to attain the shared objective will work harder to implement the leader's strategy, thereby increasing the actual probability of success.

7. *Use of personal power.* Leaders are more likely to be viewed as charismatic if they influence followers with expert power based on advocacy of successful, unconventional changes, and referent power based on perceived dedication to followers. In the absence of an appealing vision, leaders who implement an innovative strategy by use of their authority to obtain compliance may gain more expert power if the strategy is successful, but they are unlikely to appear charismatic. Likewise, a leader who asks followers to meet as a group to develop a consensus strategy may have followers who are satisfied, but the leader will not appear to have extraordinary qualities. This proposition of the theory appears to be at odds with some other theories discussed later in this chapter, such as the theory by Tichy & Devanna (1986).

TRANSFORMATIONAL
LEADERSHIP

Transformational leadership, like charisma, has become a popular topic in the recent literature on leadership in organizations. Some writers use the two terms interchangeably, whereas other writers distinguish between them. This section of the chapter reviews two theories of transformational leadership.

Burns' Theory of Transforming Leadership

Burns (1978, p. 20) described transformational leadership as a process in which "leaders and followers raise one another to higher levels of morality and motivation." Transformational leaders seek to raise the consciousness of followers by appealing to higher ideals and moral values such as liberty, justice, equality, peace, and humanitarianism, not to baser emotions such as fear, greed, jealousy, or hatred. In terms of Maslow's (1954) need hierarchy, transformational leaders activate higher-order needs in followers. Followers are elevated from their "everyday selves" to their "better selves." For Burns, transformational leadership may be exhibited by anyone in the organization in any type of position. It may involve people influencing peers and superiors as well as subordinates. It can occur in the day-to-day acts of ordinary people, but it is not ordinary or common.

Burns contrasts transformational leadership with transactional leadership. The latter type of leadership motivates followers by appealing to their self interest. Political leaders exchange jobs, subsidies, and lucrative government contracts for votes and campaign contributions. Corporate leaders exchange pay and status for work effort. Transactional leadership involves values, but they are values relevant to the exchange process, such as honesty, fairness, responsibility, and reciprocity. Burns also differentiates transactional and transformational leadership from influence based on bureaucratic authority. Bureaucratic organizations emphasize legitimate power and respect for rules and tradition, rather than influence based either on exchange or inspiration.

For Burns, leadership is a process, not a set of discrete acts. Burns (1978, p. 440) described leadership as "a stream of evolving interrelationships in which leaders are continuously evoking motivational responses from followers and modifying their behavior as they meet responsiveness or resistance, in a ceaseless process of flow and counterflow." Transformational leadership can be viewed both as a microlevel influence process between individuals, and as a macrolevel process of mobilizing power to change social systems and reform institutions. At this macrolevel of analysis, transformational leadership involves shaping, expressing, and mediating conflict among groups of people in addition to motivating individuals.

Conflicts among factions make the leader's life more difficult, but at the same time, they can be useful for mobilizing and channeling energy to achieve shared ideological objectives.

Bass' Theory of Transformational Leadership

Bass (1985) defines transformational leaders primarily in terms of the leader's effect on followers. Followers feel trust, admiration, loyalty, and respect toward the leader, and they are motivated to do more than they originally expected to do. A leader can transform followers by: (1) making them more aware of the importance and value of task outcomes, (2) inducing them to transcend their own self interest for the sake of the organization or team, and (3) activating their higher-order needs.

Bass views transformational leadership as more than just another term for charisma. Some charismatic people, such as a rock stars, movie stars, and famous athletes, do not have any systematic transformational effect on followers, even though followers may identify with a celebrity and imitate his or her behavior and appearance. According to Bass (1985, p. 31), "Charisma is a necessary ingredient of transformational leadership, but by itself it is not sufficient to account for the transformational process." Transformational leaders influence followers by arousing strong emotions and identification with the leader, but they may also transform followers by serving as a coach, teacher, and mentor.

The conceptions of transformational leadership proposed by Bass and Burns are similar in many respects, but there are also some differences. First, Burns limits transformational leadership to enlightened leaders who appeal to positive moral values and higher-order needs of followers. In contrast, for Bass a transformational leader is one who activates follower motivation and increases follower commitment, regardless of whether the effects ultimately benefit followers. Bass would not exclude leaders who appeal to lower-order needs such as safety, subsistence, and economic needs. Leaders such as Adolph Hitler and Reverend Jim Jones (of the Jonestown massacre) are considered transformational, despite their negative effects.

With respect to transactional leadership, once again there are similarities but also some differences in the two theorists' conceptions. Like Burns, Bass views transactional leadership as an exchange of rewards for compliance. However, Bass defines transactional leadership in broader terms than Burns. According to Bass, it includes not only the use of incentives and contingent rewards to influence motivation, but also clarification of the work required to obtain rewards. Bass sees theories such as the vertical dyad linkage theory and the path-goal theory (see Chapters 3 and 6) as descriptions of transactional leadership. He views transformational and transactional leadership as distinct but not mutually exclusive processes, and he recognizes that the same leader may use both types of leadership at different times in different situations.

A Conceptual Critique

The distinction between transformational and transactional leadership has some utility for shifting the attention of researchers to leadership processes that have been neglected. However, the distinction is fast becoming a two-factor theory of leadership processes, which is an unwarranted oversimplication of a complex phenomenon. The exchange process in transactional leadership does not have to be limited to tangible benefits. As in social theory it is possible for transformational leadership to include reciprocal influence involving an exchange of commitment for meaning. Furthermore, the vision articulated by transformational leaders usually includes a promise of tangible benefits for followers in addition to ideological elements. Thus, the distinction between the two types of leadership is not as clear as some theorists would have us believe. Differences in leadership process undoubtedly exist, but the nature of these differences should be determined by empirical research, not predetermined by theoretical definitions that make unnecessary assumptions and bias subsequent research.

LEADERSHIP AND
ORGANIZATION CULTURE

An important source of insight into the dynamics of transformational leadership is provided by research and theory on organizational culture. Schein's (1985) book provides the most comprehensive review and integration of this literature. Schein defines culture as the basic assumptions and beliefs shared by members of a group or organization. The assumptions and beliefs involve the group's view of the world and their place in it, the nature of time and space, human nature, and human relationships. Schein distinguishes between underlying assumptions, which may be unconscious, and espoused values, which may or may not be consistent with these values. Espoused values that are not consistent with underlying beliefs based on prior learning will not accurately reflect the culture. For example, a company may espouse open communication, but the underlying assumption may be that any expression of criticism or disagreement is detrimental and should be avoided. It is often difficult to dig beneath the superficial layer of espoused values to discover the underlying beliefs and assumptions, some of which may be unconscious.

The underlying beliefs representing the culture of a group or organization are learned responses to problems of survival in the external environment and problems of internal integration. The primary external problems are the core mission or reason for existence of the organization, concrete objectives based on this mission, strategies for attaining these objectives, and ways to measure success in attaining objectives. Most organizations have multiple objectives with differing priorities, and some objectives may not be as obvious as others. For example, the primary espoused objective of public schools is to educate students, but less obvious objectives include providing employment for teachers and keeping children busy and out of the labor market until there is room for them (Merton, 1957). Agreement on a general mission does not imply agreement about specific objectives or their relative priority. Schein (1985, p. 56) provides an example of a company in which there was consensus about having a line of winning products, but disagreement about how to allocate resources among different product groups, or how to market the products:

> One group thought that marketing meant better image advertising, another group thought it meant developing the next generation of products, while a third group emphasized merchandizing and sales support as the key goals.

In contrast to these task-oriented problems, the organization also needs to solve problems of internal integration. Objectives and strategies cannot be achieved effectively without cooperative effort and reasonable stability of membership in the organization. Internal problems include the criteria for determining membership in the organization, the basis for determining members' relative status and power, criteria and procedures for allocating rewards and punishments, an ideology to explain unpredictable and uncontrollable events, rules or customs about how to handle interpersonal relationships and deal with aggression and intimacy, and a shared consensus about the meaning of words and symbols. The beliefs that develop about these issues serve as the basis for role expectations to guide behavior, help people know what is proper and improper, and help people maintain comfortable relationships with each other.

A major function of culture is to help us understand the environment and determine how to respond to it, thereby reducing anxiety, uncertainty, and confusion. The internal and external problems are closely interconnected, and organizations must deal with them simultaneously. As solutions are developed through experience, they become shared assumptions that are passed on to new members. Over time, the assumptions may become so familiar that members are no longer consciously aware of them.

How Leaders Shape Culture

According to Schein (1985), leaders have the greatest potential for embedding and reinforcing aspects of culture with the following five primary mechanisms:

1. *Attention.* Leaders communicate their priorities, values, and concerns by their choice of things to ask about, measure, comment on, praise, and criticize. Much of this communication occurs during monitoring and planning activities, such as planning meetings, progress review meetings, and

"management by walking around." Emotional outbursts by leaders have an especially strong effect in communicating values and concerns. An example is a leader who reprimands a subordinate for not knowing what is happening in his or her unit. Not responding to something also carries a message, namely, that it is not important.

2. *Reactions to crises.* Crises are significant because the emotionality surrounding them increases potential for learning about values and assumptions. For example, a company faced with drastically lower sales avoided layoffs by having all employees (including managers) work less hours and take a pay cut, thereby communicating a strong concern for preserving employee jobs.

3. *Role modeling.* Leaders can communicate values and expectations by their own actions, especially actions showing special loyalty, self-sacrifice, and service beyond the call of duty. A leader who institutes a policy or procedure but fails to observe it is communicating the message that it is not really important or necessary.

4. *Allocation of rewards.* Criteria used as the basis for allocating rewards such as a pay increase or promotion communicate what is valued by the leader and organization. Formal recognition in ceremonies and informal praise also communicate a leader's concerns and priorities. Failure to recognize contributions and achievements communicates that they are not important. Finally, awarding of status symbols affirms the relative importance of some members compared to others. Of course, obvious status differentials are contrary to egalitarian values. In comparison to most American companies, Japanese companies use far fewer status symbols and privileges of rank such as special dining rooms and parking spaces.

5. *Criteria for selection and dismissal.* Leaders can influence culture by recruiting people who have particular values, skills, or traits, and by promoting them to positions of authority. Unsuitable applicants can be screened out by formal and informal selection procedures, and there are also procedures to increase self-selection, such as giving applicants realistic information about the criteria and requirements for success in the organization. The criteria and procedures used to expel or dismiss members of an organization also communicate the leader's values and concerns.

In addition to these primary mechanisms, Schein described five secondary mechanisms that are useful for embedding and reinforcing culture when they are consistent with the primary mechanisms:

1. *Design of organization structure.* The design of structure is often influenced more by assumptions about internal relationships or implicit theories of management than by actual requirements for effective adaptation to the environment. A centralized structure reflects the belief that

only the leader can determine what is best, whereas a decentralized structure reflects a belief in individual initiative and shared responsibility.

2. *Design of systems and procedures.* Formal budgets, planning sessions, reports, performance reviews, and management development programs can formalize attention to some activities and criteria, while also helping to reduce role ambiguity.

3. *Design of facilities.* Although it is rarely done as an intentional strategy, leaders can design facilities to reflect basic values. For example, an open office layout is consistent with a value for open communication. Having similar offices for managers at different levels, and similar dining facilities for all employees is consistent with egalitarian values.

4. *Stories, legends, and myths.* Stories about important events and people in the organization help to transmit values and assumptions. However, the potential use of this mechanism may be quite limited for leaders of business organizations. A story that is ambiguous does not communicate clear values, and one that is obviously fabricated may backfire. Stories and myths may be more a reflection of culture than an intentional mechanism for influencing it.

5. *Formal statements.* Public statements of values by the leader and written creeds, charters, and philosophies are not very important except as a supplement to other mechanisms. This mechanism usually communicates only a small portion of an organization's cultural assumptions and beliefs.

Culture and Growth Stages of Organizations

The influence of a leader on the culture of an organization varies depending on the developmental stage of the organization. The founder of a new organization has a strong influence on its culture. The founder typically has a vision of a new enterprise and proposes ways of doing things that, if successful in accomplishing objectives and reducing anxiety, will gradually become embedded in the culture. However, creating culture in a new organization is not necessarily a smooth process; it may involve considerable conflict if the founder's ideas are not successful, or if there are other powerful members of the organization who have competing ideas. In order to succeed, the founder needs an appropriate vision and the ability and persistence to influence others to accept it. If the founder does not articulate a consistent vision and act consistently to reinforce it, the organization may develop a dysfunctional culture reflecting the inner conflicts of the founder (Kets de Vries & Miller, 1984).

One of the most important elements of culture in new organizations is the set of beliefs about the distinctive competence of the organization that differentiates it from other organizations. The beliefs are likely to include the reason why the organization's products or services are unique or superior, and the internal processes that account for continued ability to provide these products and services. Implications for the relative status of different functions in the organization and the strategies for solving crises differ depending on the source of distinctive competence. For example, in a company that is successful due to its development of innovative products, the research and development function is likely to have higher status than other functions, and the likely response to a recent decline in sales is to introduce some new products. In a company that has been able to provide a common product at the lowest price, manufacturing will have higher status, and the response to a decline in sales is likely to involve the search for ways to reduce costs below those of competitors.

The culture in young, successful organizations is likely to be very strong because it is instrumental to the success of the organization, the assumptions have been internalized by current members and transmitted to new members, and the founder is still present to symbolize and reinforce the culture. The culture of such an organization will evolve slowly over the years as experience reveals that some assumptions need to be modified. Eventually, as the organization matures and people other than the founder or his or her family occupy leadership positions, the culture will become more unconscious and less uniform. Different subcultures develop in different subunits, and these may lead to conflicts and power struggles. Segments of the culture that were initially functional may become dysfunctional, preventing the organization from adapting successfully to a changing environment. However, cultural assumptions justify the past and are a matter of pride, making them more difficult to change. Moreover, culture will influence the selection of leaders and the role expectations for them, making it more difficult to make drastic changes, unless there is a major crisis threatening the welfare and survival of the organization. In general, it is more difficult to change culture in a mature organization than to create it in a new organization. Considerable insight and skill on the part of the leader is needed to understand the culture in a mature organization and implement changes successfully. Changes may require selection of an outside successor to lead the organization, and assistance may be needed from outside consultants to diagnose the problem and plan changes.

RESEARCH BY
TICHY AND DEVANNA

Tichy and Devanna (1986) conducted a study of 12 CEOs in a variety of organizations, most of which were large corporations. The primary method of data collection was to conduct interviews with the leaders and occasionally with other people in the organizations. The focus of the study was on leaders of large organizations who must transform and renew those organizations to adapt successfully to a changing and increasingly competitive environment characterized by rapid technological change, widespread social and cultural change, intense competition from foreign companies, and increasing interdependence among the economies of different nations. Leadership of these organizations must somehow deal with the paradox of the need for stability versus the need for adaptation, and the hope for improvement versus the fear of change.

Based on the findings of their study, Tichy and Devanna describe the processes that occur when leaders transform organizations, the behaviors that facilitate these processes, and the traits and skills characteristic of transformational leaders. The processes are viewed as a sequence of phases, beginning with recognition of the need for change, followed by creation of a new vision and then institutionalization of change.

Recognizing the Need for Change

The first requirement for transformational leaders is to recognize the need for change. When changes in the environment are gradual, many leaders fail to recognize the threats to their organization. Examples include the steel industry and the auto industry in the United States during the 1960s. An important role of the leader is to persuade other key people in the organization of the seriousness of the threat and the need for major changes rather than incremental adjustments. The task is more difficult when the environmental changes are gradual and the organization is still prosperous than when there is an obvious, abrupt crisis. For example, Lee Iacocca assumed the leadership of Chrysler at a time when a crisis was obvious, whereas John Akers attempted to make changes at IBM at a time when the company was more prosperous than ever before. The task of transforming organizations is more difficult when necessary changes in strategy are incompatible with the existing culture than when the leader can build on existing values and assumptions that are still appropriate. For example, it is more difficult to convince people that their basic values are wrong and must be abandoned than it is to justify changes as a return to basic values that have been corrupted or neglected.

Tichy and Devanna suggest some approaches for leaders to increase sensitivity of key members of the organization to environmental changes and threats:

1. Challenge current assumptions by encouraging objective critique and dissenting opinions or proposals. For example, use "devil's advocates" in decision processes (see Chapter 11). Don't assume that everybody who disagrees is wrong, and avoid the tendency of some top management groups to congratulate themselves constantly on how good they are or to revel in past successes while ignoring current weaknesses.

2. Improve monitoring of the environment by developing better external networks that include people who can provide an objective evaluation of the organization's strength's and weaknesses. Examples include having a diverse set of outside members on the organization's board of directors, and having technical and operations people accompany sales representatives to meetings with customers to aid in discovering their needs and concerns.

3. Encourage members of the organization to visit other organizations, including those in other countries, to find out how they operate and how they deal with problems. These visitors should include middle managers and technical people as well as executives. For example, "when General Electric began taking manufacturing people to Japan, the managers had feelings that bordered on terror when they realized that Japanese companies were frequently turning out [competitive] products with half the number of employees and significantly lower defect rates . . ." (Tichy & Devanna, p. 54).

4. Measure performance against that of competitors, not just against last year's performance. The evaluation of organizational performance should be based on a variety of economic indicators (e.g., earnings, market share, return on investment) and noneconomic indicators (product quality, customer satisfaction, rate of product innovation, employee turnover). Information about the performance of the overall organization and its major subunits should be distributed widely in the organization to keep attention focused on the objectives and avoid the dangers of complacency and insulation.

After people recognize the old ways of doing things are no longer effective and major changes are necessary, the next task of the transformational leader is to manage the transition process. This process includes diagnosis of the problem to determine what changes are necessary. A major danger for transformational leaders to avoid is the desire of people for a "quick fix" that will not involve major changes. Another important function of the leader at this stage is to help people deal with the emotional turmoil of rejecting old beliefs and values. It is difficult for people to accept the failure of past decisions and policies. Changes will alter the distribution of power and status in the organization, threaten some peoples' career opportunities, and require people to learn new behavior patterns. Transformational leaders help people to accept the need for change without feeling that they are personally responsible for failure. At the same time, these leaders increase followers' self-confidence and optimism about making a successful transition.

Creating a New Vision

When a leader discovers the need for major revitalization of the organization, it becomes necessary to find ways to inspire people with a vision of a better future that is sufficiently attractive to justify the costs of changing familiar ways of doing things. In contrast to new organizations founded by a visionary entrepreneur, Tichy and Devanna discovered that successful visions in large, mature organizations are rarely the product of a single individual. The vision evolves over a longer period of time and is the product of a participative process involving important people in the organization who must embrace the vision for it to be successful. Of course, if there is an severe crisis or a long tradition of centralized leadership, people may expect the leader to propose a solution. Even in this situation, some participation may be better, since there is a tendency for people to regress to the old ways of doing things when the immediate crisis has passed unless new values and assumptions have been internalized. Participation facilitates this process of internalization.

To be motivating, a vision must be a source of self-esteem and common purpose for members. The vision should convey an intuitive, appealing picture of what the organization can be in the future. The core of the vision is the organization's mission statement. The mission statement is a general picture rather than a detailed blueprint, and it should reflect the major themes and values in the vision. It should be expressed in ideological terms, not just in economic terms, in order to help people develop a sense of purpose about their membership in the organization. Examples of mission statements for a repair facility and a newspaper, respectively, are "Fix it right the first time" and "All the news that people want to read" (Harrison, 1987). The general mission statement must be supplemented eventually by the more detailed answers to basic questions such as what kinds of products will be made, how will decisions be made, who will have power, how will rewards be allocated, how will managers be selected, how will people treat each other, and what values will influence decisions? Beginning with the mission statement, an agenda of priority objectives should be developed, followed by strategies for attaining them.

Tichy and Devanna suggest some techniques to help executives develop a shared vision of what the organization should be like. One technique is to ask the executives to write a magazine article in journalistic style describing the organization as they would like it to be five years in the future. A variation of this technique is a role play in which half of the executives are "reporters," who interview the remaining executives and ask them to describe how they would like the organization to be in five or ten years. Still another technique is to have people describe a fictitious organization that would be able to compete effectively with the leading companies in a specified market. The group then determines how the current organization differs from the fictitious one and looks for ways to close the gaps.

Institutionalizing the Changes

In order to implement major changes in a large, complex organization, the leader needs the help of top-level executives, and a plan for getting the support of other important people in the organization. Once again, participation in strategic planning helps to develop commitment to the plans. In effect, the transformational leader must develop a new coalition of important people, both inside and outside the organization, who will be committed to the vision. An analysis should be made to determine whose commitment is necessary for changes in structure, policies, or strategies. The leader will depend on his or her network of relationships with key people in the organization, and the network may need to be expanded to include other people who are influential. In some cases, the leader will have to make personnel changes to replace people in key positions with others who have the skills and commitment necessary to implement the changes successfully. A large variety of techniques can be employed to facilitate the change process, including special task forces, planning meetings, management-development workshops, team-building interventions, reorganization of subunits, creation of new positions, change in reward systems and appraisal procedures, and design of facilities.

At each stage of the transformational process, success will depend in part on the leader's attitudes, values, and skills. The effective transformational leaders in this study had the following attributes: (1) They saw themselves as change agents, (2) they were prudent risk takers, (3) they believed in people and were sensitive to their needs, (4) they were able to articulate a set of core values which guided their behavior, (5) they were flexible and open to learning from experience, (6) they had cognitive skills and believed in disciplined thinking and the need for careful analysis of problems, and (7) they were visionaries who trusted their intuition.

RESEARCH BY
BENNIS AND NANUS

Bennis and Nanus (1985) conducted a 5-year study with 90 effective leaders, including 60 corporate leaders and 30 leaders of public sector organizations. The researchers collected data with unstructured interviews lasting 3 to 4 hours, sometimes supplemented with observation. Leaders were asked about their strengths and weaknesses, and the major decision points in their career, events that influenced their management philosophy or style. There was a great amount of diversity among the leaders, and few fit a common stereotype of the charismatic leader. Most were very ordinary in appearance, personality, and general behavior. Nevertheless, some similarities in the interview protocols provided insights about the nature of effective transformational leadership. This section summarizes common themes Bennis and Nanus found in the way chief executives reshape organizational practices to adapt to environmental changes, and how they build employee confidence and mastery of new ways of doing things.

Developing a Vision

All of the leaders had a vision of a desirable and possible future for their organization. It was sometimes just a vague dream, and at other times it was as concrete as a written mission statement. Transformational leaders channel the collective energies of organizational members in pursuit of a common vision. These leaders "move followers to higher degrees of consciousness, such as liberty, freedom, justice, and self-actualization" (p. 218). Examples from historical leaders include Martin Luther King, Jr. ("I have a dream"), and President John Kennedy's goal of "putting a man on the moon by 1970." Bennis and Nanus (1985, p. 88–89) reached the following conclusion about the effective leaders in their study:

> They paid attention to what was going on, they determined what parts of the events at hand would be important for the future of the organization, they set a new direction, and they concentrated the attention of everyone in the organization on it. . . . This was a universal principle of leadership, as true for orchestra conductors, army generals, football coaches, and school superintendents as for corporate leaders.

A clear and appealing vision serves some important functions. One function is to inspire followers by giving their work meaning and appealing to their fundamental human need to be important, to feel useful, and to be part of a worthwhile enterprise. A second function of a vision is to facilitate decision making, initiative, and discretion by employees at all levels. Knowing the organization's central purpose and objectives helps people determine what is good or bad, important or trivial.

How do leaders arrive at a vision? Bennis and Nanus found that the leaders in their study did not develop a vision through some mysterious inner process, and indeed the leader was rarely the person who first conceived of a vision. The leaders established a network of formal and informal contacts with people, including outsiders as well as members of the organization. They were attentive to the ideas and opinions of others, especially people who advocated new or different viewpoints. The vision was selected from among those to which the leader was exposed, or was a composite of them. The genius of the leader was to articulate a vision simple enough to be understood, appealing enough to evoke commitment, and credible enough to be accepted as realistic and attainable. An effective vision is "right for the times, right for the organization, and right for the people who are working in it" (p. 107). Judgment and analytical ability are needed to synthesize such a vision, but intuition and creativity are important as well.

According to Bennis and Nanus, lack of a clear vision is a major reason for the declining effectiveness of many organizations in recent years. A similar argument has been made by others, such as Peters and Waterman (1982). During the past two decades, many organizations have been unable to maintain a clear vision, due in part to changing social values, internationalization of business, rapid technological change, increased diversification caused by mergers and acquisitions, and a short-term, "bottom-line" mentality among many executives and powerful external coalitions (e.g., stockholders, owners, bankers).

Developing Commitment and Trust

It is not enough to identify a coherent and appealing vision, it must be communicated and embodied in the culture of the organization. A vision must be transmitted by persuasion and inspiration, not by edict or coercion. Effective leaders use a combination of captivating rhetoric, metaphor, slogans, symbols, and rituals. President Reagan is an example of a leader who made effective use of anecdotes and metaphors, in contrast to President Carter, who "never made the meaning come through the facts" (Bennis, 1985, p. 17). The vision must be repeated in different variations and at different levels of specificity, from a vague mission statement to detailed plans and policies. The vision must be reinforced by the decisions and actions of the leader. Changes must be made in organization structure and management processes, consistent with the values and objectives contained in the new vision. The process of mobilizing commitment should begin at the top of the organization with the inner circle of executives. Other executives should participate in the process of reshaping the organization's culture and embodying the vision in it. However, the primary responsibility for this difficult leadership task should never be delegated to others, or the effort is unlikely to succeed.

Commitment to the vision is closely related to follower trust in the leader. It is unlikely that an untrusted leader can successfully achieve commitment to a new vision for the organization. Trust is dependent on the perceived expertise of the leader, but it also depends on the leader's consistency in statements and actions. Leaders who shift positions frequently and express contradictory values undermine the trust and confidence of followers. Inconsistency reduces the clarity of the vision, and lack of confidence in the leader reduces the appeal of the vision. Leaders demonstrate commitment to values by their own behavior and by the way they reinforce the behavior of others.

Bennis and Nanus describe a procedure called "quest" that is useful both for developing strategies and obtaining commitment to them. Quest is a 2-day exercise held with executives and relevant outsiders to discuss long-range opportunities and risks, and possible reactions by the organization. During the first day, participants are asked to identify important stakeholders, relevant indicators of effectiveness, and important environmental events. Participants also estimate the probability that each event will occur during the next ten to twenty years, they identify relationships among the environmental events, and they identify relationships between events and each indicator of organizational effectiveness. Next, the leader uses the results to develop some short scenarios describing how the organization could possibly evolve during the next two decades. The scenarios represent a diverse set of possible futures, each plausible in terms of the expectations of the participants. A written report is prepared and circulated to participants to study. At a second meeting, participants identify strategy choices for the organization, including options for reacting to environmental events, options for changing the organization, options for changing the environment, and options for making coordinated changes in both the organization and the environment. Then the group determines which proposals appear most promising for the organization. For each promising option, a separate task force is formed to study the feasibility, costs, and benefits of pursuing that option; the task forces report back to the larger group at a third meeting.

Facilitating Organizational Learning

One prominent theme found by Bennis and Nanus was the importance of both individual and organizational learning. Effective leaders did a number of things to develop their skills and increase the knowledge gained from experience of success and failures. They recognized the necessity of continually gathering information about changing, uncertain events. They engaged in exercises to force themselves to examine their assumptions, and they tested their ideas by getting reactions from colleagues and outside experts. They created an information network and initiated special studies to gather information needed for strategic planning. They used experimentation to encourage innovation and to test new products and procedures. They viewed mistakes as a normal part of doing things and used them as opportunities to learn and develop. In order to facilitate learning by other members of the organization, the leaders encouraged subordinate managers to set longer time horizons (e.g., by requiring them to make five-year plans), and sponsored seminars to develop planning skills and awareness of environmental changes and trends (e.g., by using the quest exercise).

OTHER RESEARCH ON
TRANSFORMATIONAL LEADERSHIP

As yet, the amount of empirical research on charismatic and transformational leadership is still very limited. The interview studies by Tichy and Devanna and Bennis and Nanus represent one type of research methodology for studying transformational leadership. A variety of other methods have been used as well, including content analysis of biographies, content analysis of critical incidents, laboratory experiments, field studies comparing charismatic to noncharismatic leaders, questionnaire studies, and intensive case studies on individual leaders. Four studies were selected to illustrate the varied approaches and also the immense difficulties in studying transformational leadership.

Most of the questionnaire research on transformational leadership up to this time has been conducted by Bass and his colleagues (Bass, 1985; Bass, Avolio, & Goodheim, 1987; Bass, Waldman, Avolio, & Bebb, 1987). Based on factor analysis of a new leadership questionnaire, Bass (1985) identified three aspects of leadership behavior that he believes account for transformational leadership: (1) charismatic behavior, (2) individualized consideration, and (3) intellectual stimulation. The research method selected to identify transformational behavior was an unfortunate choice. It is difficult to base behavior constructs on questionnaire research when our knowledge of transformational behavior is still so primitive that we cannot identify good examples to use as items in a questionnaire. Most items in the charismatic and intellectual stimulation scales describe the outcomes of leadership (e.g., followers become more enthusiastic about the work and view problems in novel ways), rather than specific, observable actions by the leader to cause these outcomes. The scale for individualized consideration has some behavioral items, but they appear no different than consideration items in questionnaires from the 1950s. These deficiencies and other limitations of behavior description questionnaires (see Chapter 5) make it doubtful that questionnaire research will provide much useful insight into the nature of transformational leadership in the immediate future. Descriptive research using interviews and observation is more promising for discovering what leaders actually do to transform followers.

House and his colleagues conducted a study of charisma in former U. S. Presidents (House, Woycke, & Fodor, 1987). Nine historians were asked to classify the Presidents as charismatic or noncharismatic in relation to their cabinets. The classification procedure identified six effective charismatics (Jefferson, Jackson, Lincoln, T. Roosevelt, F. Roosevelt, Kennedy), six ineffective noncharismatics (Arthur, Tyler, Pierce, Buchanan, Harding, Coolidge), and three effective noncharismatics (Truman, Cleveland, Polk). Next the biographies of two or more members of each president's cabinet were content-analyzed for charismatic behavior and positive influence by the president on the cabinet member. Compared to ineffective noncharismatics, effective charismatics were significantly higher in expression of self-confidence, ideological goals, expectations for subordinate performance, confidence in subordinates, and individualized consideration. However, effective charismatics did not differ significantly from effective noncharismatics. Motive strength for power, achievement, and affiliation needs was obtained from an analysis of the first inaugural address made by each president. Effective charismatics had significantly higher needs for power and achievement than the other two groups, and there was no significant difference in need for affiliation. Of the charismatic Presidents, only the inaugural address of Lincoln did not fit the pattern, perhaps because of the Civil War.

Howell and Frost (1988) conducted a laboratory study of charismatic leadership with college students. Charismatic leaders were compared to directive leaders and considerate leaders. The leaders were actors who were coached in how to behave toward "subordinates." In each work group, a leader supervised three subordinates, two of whom were always confederates who exerted peer influence on the real subjects. Confederates showed interest in the work in half of the work groups and expressed boredom in the remaining work groups. Subordinates worked separately so that the influence of the leader on the real subjects could be determined. The charismatic leader explained the importance of the work, indicated high performance expectations, expressed confidence that subordinates would achieve these high expectations, empathized with the needs of subordinates, and acted confident and dynamic (e.g., used a captivating tone of voice, maintained eye contact, leaned toward the subject, alternately paced or sat on the edge of the desk). Subordinates of the charismatic leader had higher performance, greater satisfaction, and less role conflict than subordinates of directive or considerate leaders. However, the study fails to demonstrate that a charismatic leader is necessarily any better than a noncharismatic leader who shows concern both for the task and for people, since a high-high condition was not included in the study. Despite this design defect, the study succeeds in demonstrating that aspects of charismatic leadership can be manipulated.

The final study, by Roberts (1984) is an intensive case analysis of a single transformational leader—the superintendent of a public school district. Data were collected by archival searches, analysis of newspaper articles, participant observation of formal and informal meetings, and interviews with the superintendent, other administrators, board members, staff, teachers, parents, and students. The superintendent in this study was deemed to be effective, because she was able to implement large, mandated budget cuts in a way that satisfied diverse stakeholders and still allowed progress on implementing desirable educational innovations. The teachers gave her a standing ovation for her efforts, even though the plan required program cuts and elimination of jobs. She was described as a "visionary" who had almost a "cult like following" in the district.

Some key steps in the transformational process resulting in a successful outcome were the following: (1) the leader formulated a mission statement and made frequent reference to it during the change process, (2) a strategic vision was developed during a series of meetings and workshops involving district personnel, (3) some personnel in key positions were replaced with more competent, dynamic people to support the change effort,

(4) performance objectives and action plans were developed for immediate subordinates (the school principals) and progress monitored by reports and meetings; extensive participation and initiative by subordinates was encouraged during this process, (5) temporary task forces were created to involve all stakeholders in recommendating where to make the budget cuts and how to deal with other budget and educational issues, (6) staff members received training in how to run structured public meetings in which task forces made presentations and solicited suggestions about budget cuts.

Roberts characterized the transformational process as more a matter of creating and managing energy than of shaping culture or managing meaning. The leader was energetic, created enthusiasm, channeled emotions aroused by the budget crisis, and galvanized others to action. The leader helped people to feel like they made a difference, and she helped them to recognize the value of working together toward common objectives. The transformation process occurred in a highly bureaucratic type of organization, contrary to Weber's (1947) assertion that charisma and bureaucracy are incompatible. The following episode shows the richness of the behavioral data provided by this type of descriptive research (Roberts, p. 24–25):

> After a scheduled 40-minute presentation to district staff, teachers besieged the stage to ask for more of her time to discuss the various initiatives the district was pursuing. Their requests turned into a four-hour dialogue with 800 people, in which the superintendent shared her hopes, her dreams, her past, her disappointments. Many people were moved to tears, including the superintendent. A critical point in the exchange came in answer to a question of how people could be certain that what she and the School Board promised would indeed occur. The superintendent's response was, "Well, I guess you just have to trust us. I trust you." Dead silence followed as people drew in their breaths and held them for a moment or two. Upon being asked what this silence meant, people responded that the superintendent had proven her point. That was what the dialogue and the honesty were all about. She had trusted them with her thoughts, hopes, and feelings, and they in turn would trust her. Mutual trust had created a bond between the superintendent and her audience.

When the superintendent was appointed to her position, she was not initially perceived as a charismatic leader; this occurred only after the change process was well underway. Roberts concludes that charisma was attributed as a result of the crisis situation and the leader's handling of the change process, rather than being an inevitable result of the leader's personal qualities. This conclusion is consistent with the position taken by some other theorists such as Conger and Kanungo (1987) and Bradley (1984).

THE DARK SIDE OF CHARISMA

The study of great historical leaders reveals both positive and negative aspects of charisma. Franklin Roosevelt lifted the United States out of the Great Depression, implemented major social programs such as social security, and mobilized the nation for World War II. In the same historical period, Adolph Hitler transformed Germany in a manner resulting in paranoid aggression, persecution, destruction, and the death of millions of people. For every example of a positive charismatic leader such as Mohandas Gandhi and Martin Luther King, Jr., one can find an example of a negative charismatic such as Charles Manson and Reverend Jim Jones. How to account for the difference between positive and negative charismatic leaders has been a problem for leadership theory.

One approach is to examine the consequences for followers; did they ultimately benefit or lose as a result of the charismatic leader's influence? As was noted in Chapter 1, a limitation of this approach is that evaluation of outcomes depends on the values and assumptions of the person making the judgment. Sometimes there is disagreement about whether outcomes are beneficial or detrimental, and outcomes may benefit some stakeholders but harm others. For example, some people would regard leaders such as Mao Tse Tung and Ayatollah Khomeini as positive charismatics, whereas others would regard them as negative charismatics.

Musser (1987) recommended a different criterion for classifying charismatic leaders. He proposed that all charismatics intentionally seek to instill commitment to ideological goals, and either consciously or unconsciously, they also seek to instill devotion to themselves. Negative charismatics emphasize devotion to themselves more than to ideals. Indeed, they often use ideology merely as a means to gain power, and afterward, the ideology is ignored or arbitrarily changed to serve the leader's personal objectives. Decisions of these leaders reflect a greater concern for self-glorification and maintaining power than for the welfare of followers. In contrast, positive charismatics seek to instill devotion to ideology more than devotion to themselves. As a result, the outcomes of their leadership are more likely to be beneficial to followers, although this is not inevitable if the strategies encouraged by the leader are inappropriate. Musser proposed that some leaders fall between the two extremes. These "neutral charismatics" may become negative charismatics if they have certain personality defects that cause them to become intoxicated by the devotion and adulation of followers.

Musser's conception of positive and negative charismatics is consistent with the ideas and findings of some other leadership theorists. In Chapter 9 we saw that McClelland differentiated between leaders with a personalized power concern and leaders with a socialized power concern. The behavior pattern typical for these two different types of leaders is referred to by McClelland (1970) as the "two faces of power." Personalized power leaders seek to dominate and subjugate followers by keeping them weak and dependent on the leader. For example, many cult leaders increase the dependency of followers on the leader by making them break their social ties to family and friends outside of the cult and by requiring donation of all of material assets to the cult as a condition for continued membership. Rewards and punishments are used to manipulate and control followers. Authority for making important decisions is centralized in the leader, and information is restricted and used to maintain an image of leader infallibility, and sometimes to exaggerate external threats to the group or organization. In contrast, socialized power leaders seek to build commitment to the organization and its ideals rather than to themselves. Authority is delegated to a considerable extent, information is shared openly, participation in decisions is encouraged, and rewards are used to reinforce behavior consistent with the mission and objectives of the organization.

The identification of personality bases for negative charismatics has been advanced by researchers with a background in clinical psychology and psychoanalysis. Kets de Vries and Miller (1984, 1985) review this literature and describe the causes and behavior patterns of highly narcissistic leaders. People whose parents have been emotionally unresponsive and rejecting come to believe that they cannot depend upon anyone's love or loyalty. In an effort to cope with their deprivation and inner loneliness, extreme narcissists become preoccupied with establishing their power, status, and prestige. They have fantasies of success and power. They have a grandiose sense of their own self-importance and unique talents. To support this self-deception, they seek continuous attention and admiration from others. They tend to oversimplify human relationships and motives and see everything in extreme good and bad terms. Relationships are polarized between loyal supporters and enemies. Any criticism by others is interpreted as a sign of rejection and disloyalty. They have little empathy or concern for the feelings and needs of others. They exploit and manipulate others to indulge their desire for self-aggrandizement.

Leaders who are extreme narcissists have a number of characteristic flaws. They surround themselves with subordinates who are loyal and uncritical. They make decisions without gathering adequate information about the environment. In the belief that they alone are sufficiently informed and talented to decide what is best, objective advice is not sought or accepted from subordinates and peers. They tend to undertake ambitious, grandiose projects to glorify themselves, but in the absence of an adequate analysis of the situation, the projects are likely to be risky and unrealistic. When a project is not going well, the leader ignores negative information, thereby reducing the likelihood that corrections can be made in time to avert a disaster. When failure is evident, the leader refuses to admit any responsibility, but instead finds scapegoats to blame.

With all of these weaknesses, is the negative charismatic leader doomed to failure? Here again, it all depends on the definition of success and failure. Although many people may suffer or die along the way, it is not necessarily the case that a narcissistic, transformational leader will lose power, or that the organization created by the person will be dissolved during the leader's tenure. History is full of examples of narcissistic charismatics who established political empires, founded prosperous companies, or initiated new religious sects, and retained control of them throughout their lifetimes. Continued success is possible if the leader has the expertise to make good decisions, if the environment does not pose serious threats that can overwhelm the organization, and if the leader has the political skill to maintain power. For this type of organization, the crisis will come when it is time to find a successor. Many organizations founded by an autocratic charismatic leader fail to survive after the leader dies (Mintzberg, 1983).

Followers are likely to be much better off with a positive charismatic leader than they would have been with a negative charismatic. They are more likely to experience psychological growth and development of their abilities, and the organization is more likely to adapt to an environment that is dynamic, hostile, and competitive. The effect of a positive charismatic leader is usually the creation of an "achievement-oriented" culture (Harrison, 1987), "high performing system" (Vaill, 1978), or "hands-on, value-driven" organization (Peters & Waterman, 1982). The organization has a clearly understood mission that embodies social values beyond mere profit or growth, members at all levels are empowered to participate in making important decisions about how to accomplish the mission and how to implement strategies, communication is open and information shared, and organization structures and systems support the mission. Such an organization has obvious advantages, but Harrison (1987, p. 12) contends there are also some potential costs that proponents usually overlook:

> In their single-minded pursuit of noble goals and an absorbing task, people lose their sense of balance and perspective; the end can come to justify the means. The group or organization exploits its environment, and its members—to the detriment of their health and quality of life—willingly exploit themselves in the service of the organization's purpose.

If prolonged as a normal operating mode, a single-minded achievement culture creates excessive stress, and members who are unable to tolerate this stress experience psychological disorders. An achievement culture created within one subunit of a larger organization may result in elitism, isolation, and lack of necessary cooperation with other subunits. Harrison concludes that subordinating member needs to the mission can be justified in a severe crisis, the moral equivalent of war, but under less demanding conditions the culture should have a better balance between task concerns and people concerns. This conclusion is consistent with the general pattern of findings for effective leadership.

SUMMARY

We still have much to learn about charismatic and transformational leadership, but some progress has been made during the past decade. Charisma appears to be an attribution resulting from the interactive process between leader and followers. Some leader attributes such as self-confidence, strong convictions, poise, speaking ability, and a dramatic flair increase the likelihood of attributed charisma, but more important is a context that makes the leader's attributes and vision especially relevant to follower needs. The same traits perceived as charismatic in one person may cause another person with a less relevant and credible vision to be perceived as insane.

The process by which charismatic leaders arouse enthusiasm and commitment in followers is still not clear, but an important component is the leader's articulation of an appealing vision that taps the conscious or unconscious needs, values, and feelings of followers. Emotional appeals are enhanced by use of symbols, metaphors, and dramatic staged events, and they may be supplemented with rational persuasion to convince followers that the leader's strategy for attaining the shared ideological goal is feasible. Commitment is likely to be greater if the leader bolsters follower confidence that they can achieve challenging performance objectives. Leader credibility is increased by apparent success of initial follower efforts to achieve the shared objective. The more innovative and unconventional the leader's strategy, and the more personal risk to the leader in advocating it, the more likely it is that the leader will be perceived as charismatic.

Transformational leadership increases follower motivation by activating higher needs of followers, appealing to moral ideals, and empowering followers. An important source of insight into the dynamics of transformational leadership is provided by research and theory on organizational culture. The basic assumptions and beliefs shared by members of a group or organization are learned responses to problems of survival in the external environment and problems of internal integration. Culture is influenced by several aspects of a leader's behavior, including examples set by the leader, what the leader attends to, how the leader reacts to crises, how the leader allocates rewards, and how the leader makes selection, promotion, and dismissal decisions. Supplementary mechanisms for shaping culture include the design of organization structure, management systems, facilities, formal statements of ideology, and informal stories, myths, and legends. It is much easier for founders to embed culture in new organizations than to change the culture of mature organizations.

Research by Tichy and Devanna and Bennis and Nanus provides insights into the way transformational leaders change the culture and strategies of an organization. In general, transformational leaders formulate a vision, develop commitment to it among internal and external stakehold-ers, implement strategies to accomplish the vision, and embed the new values and assumptions in the culture of the organization.

Charismatic leaders can have a tremendous influence on an organi-zation, but the consequences are not always beneficial. History is full of accounts of charismatic leaders who caused untold death, destruction, and misery in the process of building an empire, leading a revolution, or founding a new religion. Many entrepreneurs who founded prosperous com-panies were tyrants and egomaniacs. Negative charismatics are likely to have a narcissistic personality and a personalized power orientation. They emphasize devotion of followers to themselves rather than to ideo-logical goals, which are used only as a means to manipulate followers. Positive charismatics seek to instill devotion to ideological goals, but the achievement culture fostered by these leaders can produce undesirable con-sequences if individual needs of followers are ignored.

REVIEW AND DISCUSSION QUESTIONS

1. What are the major controversies about charismatic leadership and major differences between theorists in the way they view it?
2. Is charismatic leadership different from transformational leader-ship, and if so, how?
3. What is the relationship of transformational leadership to organi-zational culture?
4. How, if at all, does the behavior of charismatic leaders differ from the behavior of effective noncharismatic leaders?
5. Briefly describe what Tichy and Devanna found about transforma-tional leaders.
6. Briefly describe what Bennis and Nanus found about transformational leaders.
7. What is the relationship of transformational leadership to strategic planning?
8. What skills and traits are important for transformational leaders? Charismatic leaders?
9. Does the effectiveness of transformational (or charismatic) leader-ship depend on the situation?
10. What is the "dark side" of charismatic leadership?

11

LEADERSHIP
IN DECISION-MAKING
GROUPS

Group meetings, whether formal or informal, are used frequently to solve problems and make decisions in organizations. Leaders meet with subordinates to make a group decision, committees meet to coordinate the activities of different subunits in an organization, and teams meet to plan project activities and solve technical problems. In general, the reason for holding group meetings is to solve problems and make decisions that cannot be handled as well by a single individual. Groups are used when relevant information and expertise are distributed among different people, when participation is needed to obtain necessary commitment, when it is inappropriate to concentrate power in a single individual, or when unpopular decisions need to be made.

What leaders should do to make their meetings effective has been the subject of research by behavioral scientists over the last three decades. Consultants and practitioners have also contributed to our knowledge about meeting leadership. Since meetings are such an important part of the managerial job, the subject of how to run them effectively is examined in more detail in this chapter.

DETERMINANTS OF EFFECTIVE
GROUP DECISIONS

When the relevant information necessary to solve a problem is distributed among several persons, a group decision is potentially superior to a decision made by a single individual. However, there are many things that can prevent a group from effectively utilizing the information and achieving its full potential. Whether a group decision is superior to an individual decision depends on the internal group processes that occur during each stage of problem solving and decision making. The quality of a group decision depends on the contribution of information and ideas by group members, the clarity of communication, the accuracy of prediction and judgments, the extent to which the discussion is focused on the problem, and the manner in which disagreement is resolved. Group processes are influenced by the size and composition of the group, member cohesiveness, status differentials, member knowledge and personality, the immediate environment, and the leader's skill and behavior (Filley, 1970). Let us look more closely at the way each of these factors can facilitate or impede group decisions.

Group Size and Composition

The size of a decision group can affect group processes in several ways (Shull, Delbecq, & Cummings, 1970). Communication becomes more difficult as the number of members increases and less time is available for each person to speak. In large groups, it is common for a few talkative and aggressive members to dominate the discussion. The rest of the members are less willing to initiate contribution and tend to feel threatened and dissatisfied. As groups get larger, cliques and coalitions are likely to develop, creating greater potential for conflict. Meetings require more time, and a consensus agreement becomes more difficult to achieve. Clearly, there are some potential disadvantages of meetings with large groups. On the other hand, some benefits result from increasing group size, at least up to a point. A larger group usually has the advantage of more collective knowledge and a greater variety of perspectives on a problem. Thus, there is a trade-off between costs and benefits as a group size increases, and the trick is to determine what size is optimal in a given situation.

If a leader is able to determine who will attend a particular meeting, the choice should be based on who has relevant knowledge and who needs to be there to ensure effective implementation of the decision. As the size of a group increases beyond eight members, the potential contribution of any additional persons should be carefully weighed against the added difficulty of running an effective meeting. If possible, persons who are not needed but who might expect to attend should be tactfully excluded. If a large group is absolutely necessary, the leader should plan to use subgroups and subcommittees whenever they are feasible (Bradford, 1976).

Status Differentials

Obvious status differences among members inhibit information exchange and accurate evaluation of ideas. Low-status members are usually reluctant to criticize or disagree with high-status persons. Moreover, the ideas and opinions of high-status persons have more influence and tend to be evaluated more favorably, even when the basis of their status is irrelevant to the decision problem (Berger, Cohen, & Zelditch, 1972; Harvey, 1953). In a group where each member has relevant knowledge and nobody has a monopoly on ideas, it is desirable to minimize the influence of status differences on group decisions. One way to do this is to keep meetings free of obvious status symbols such as insignias, titles, and seating privileges. Another approach is to develop a norm of mutual respect and appreciation for each person's ideas and contributions, regardless of member status.

Group Cohesiveness and Groupthink

Cohesiveness is the degree of mutual affection among members and their attraction to the group. Cohesiveness is a characteristic of the group, but it is dependent on individual characteristics of the members. A group is much more likely to be cohesive if its members have similar values, attitudes, and cultural backgrounds. A high degree of group cohesiveness can be a mixed blessing. A cohesive group is more likely to agree on a decision, but members tend to agree too quickly without a complete, objective evaluation of the alternatives. Members of a cohesive group are less willing to risk social rejection for questioning a majority viewpoint or presenting a dissenting opinion. Consequently, the critical evaluation of ideas is inhibited during decision making, and creativity is reduced during problem solving.

Highly cohesive groups sometimes foster a phenomenon called "groupthink" (Janis, 1972). Groupthink involves certain kinds of illusions and stereotypes that interfere with effective decision making. Members develop an illusion of invulnerability, which is supported by an unfavorable stereotype of outsiders. Critics are ridiculed, and opponents or competitors are underestimated. As a result, the group is likely to overestimate the probability of success for a risky course of action. In the group discussion, any expression of doubt about a preferred but risky alternative is inhibited by "self-censorship" as well as by social pressure from other members. The group strives to maintain the illusion of internal harmony by avoiding open expression of disagreement. Factual information not consistent with the preferred alternative is prevented from being seriously considered in the meeting ("mindguarding"), or it is discounted through a process of rationalization. If ethical issues are involved in the decision, the group's illusion of moral superiority makes it easy to justify a course of action that would normally be considered unethical by the members.

Groupthink can result in disastrous decisions. An example is the decision made by the Kennedy administration in 1961 to invade Cuba at the Bay of Pigs (Janis, 1972, p. 19).

"The group that deliberated on the Bay of Pigs decision included men of considerable talent. Like the President, all of the main advisors were shrewd thinkers, capable of objective rational analysis, and accustomed to speaking their minds. But collectively they failed to detect the serious flaws in the invasion plans."

The group seriously overestimated the likelihood of overthrowing Castro with only a small brigade of 1400 Cuban exiles, in part because they erroneously assumed that the Cuban people would rise up and join the invaders in overthrowing Castro. The planners also underestimated the risks involved if the invasion failed. They did not anticipate that an unsuccessful invasion would eventually lead to the transformation of Cuba into a Soviet base with nuclear missiles and more than 5000 Soviet troops only 90 miles from the United States. If the group had seriously considered this possibility, they would have rejected the CIA invasion plan as too risky.

The adverse effects of groupthink can be avoided if the leader is aware of the potential problem and takes steps to increase critical evaluation of alternatives under consideration. A number of procedures to do this are described later in this chapter.

Member Personality

Each member of a group brings to a meeting certain needs, attitudes, values, knowledge, and experience. Some of these characteristics of the members have obvious implications for group processes. We have already seen that the information and knowledge of members is a major determinant of decision quality. Another important determinant is the goal orientation of group members. If the members have personal objectives that are inconsistent with the leader's task objectives, the two parties will be working at cross-purposes. Members may openly promote their point of view in a debate with the leader, but it is more likely that they will become apathetic and uninvolved in the meeting, letting the leader dominate the group decision but later resisting or sabotaging the decision.

The traits and values of group members can also affect group processes and the quality of decisions. Research has shown that groups with compatible members are more productive, especially when agreement is necessary under conditions of time pressure (Liddell & Slocum, 1976; Shutz, 1955). Group process is affected by the maturity and emotional stability of group members. Groups with a high proportion of immature and neurotic members tend to have more disruptive self-oriented behavior such as attention seeking (e.g., making provocative comments, clowning, bragging, showing off) and domination (e.g., interrupting other members, "shouting them down," threatening to withdraw support to get one's own way). This kind of behavior reduces group cohesiveness and effectiveness (Bradford,

1976; Fouriezos et al., 1950). When such behavior occurs, a leader can ignore it, try to suppress it, or point out its dysfunctional effects and help the person learn more appropriate behavior.

Immediate Physical Environment

Meetings occur in a physical environment that helps to determine the psychological climate and indirectly influences group processes (Bradford, 1976; Golde, 1972). One of the most obvious physical factors is the seating arrangement. Some arrangements create psychological separation between the leader and other members, resulting in a climate of stiff formality. Examples are when the leader stands at a lectern, sits behind a desk, or sits at the head of a long rectangular table. A long rectangular table may emphasize status differentials for other members besides the leader if sitting close to the head of the table is based on status (Bradford, 1976; Jay, 1976). This kind of seating arrangement also inhibits conversation among the members if they cannot see each other without leaning inward or moving their chairs outward (Golde, 1972). A round table or a circular arrangement of chairs is more conducive to open communication and informality.

A second important aspect of the physical environment is the presence or absence of distractions, such as outside noise, ringing telephones, and interruptions by the leader's secretary or boss. The leader should try to schedule meetings in a quiet location and plan ways to prevent any interruptions except for emergencies. Visitors, television crews, and reporters should be avoided if their presence is not absolutely necessary.

Quality of Leadership

Quality of leadership is one of the most important determinants of meeting success. The leadership role can be shared, to some extent, but studies of decision-making groups find that members usually prefer a "take-charge" leader who performs many of the essential leadership functions, and such leaders tend to have more satisfied and productive groups (Berkowitz, 1953; Schlesinger, Jackson, & Butman, 1960). On the other hand, a leader who dominates the discussion ("content control") rather than merely ensuring that it proceeds in a systematic manner ("process control") will likely discourage the contribution of ideas and the critical evaluation of proposals. Clearly, the job of meeting leader is a difficult one. The group will be ineffective if the leader is either too passive or too domineering. A considerable amount of skill is needed to achieve a delicate balance between these two extremes. The behaviors and procedures used to achieve this balance are discussed in the remaining sections of the chapter.

LEADERSHIP FUNCTIONS
IN DECISION GROUPS

We saw in Chapter 5 that leadership behavior can be classified into task-oriented behavior and relationship-oriented behavior. A similar distinction can be made for leadership behavior in the context of group meetings. Of course, specific aspects of leadership behavior often involve both task and relationship concerns simultaneously, but the two-factor taxonomy helps to remind group leaders how important it is to balance task and relationship concerns in leading meetings. Several writers have proposed two-factor taxonomies of group leader behavior, and a simplified composite of these earlier taxonomies will be presented here (Bales, 1950; Benne & Sheats, 1948; Bradford, 1976; Lord, 1977; Schein, 1969).

Task-Oriented Behavior

Task-oriented leadership behavior in a group meeting facilitates systematic communication, evaluation, and analysis of information and ideas, and aids problem solving and decision making. There are five major types of task-oriented behavior.

1. *Process Structuring:* To present a problem to the group, to propose an objective and get the group's approval, to introduce a procedure for the group to use in solving a problem or making a decision, to develop an agenda listing topics to be discussed and issues to be decided, to suggest that the group is ready to proceed to a different activity, to direct the discussion back to the task after it has wandered off track, to recess or end the meeting. Some specific examples are as follows:

> It looks like we are ready to start suggesting solutions.
>
> Why don't we decide first whether to accept the new contract and discuss the other items at the next meeting?
>
> Let's break up into four smaller groups and have each group develop solutions.

2. *Stimulating Communication:* To seek specific information from group members, to ask members for their opinions, to encourage members to contribute their ideas, to provide specific information yourself. Some specific examples are as follows:

> What are the latest sales figures for product X?
>
> Does anyone know more about this new development?
>
> My survey shows that production costs increased by 20 percent in the last year.

3. Clarifying Communication: To reduce confusion or clear up a misunderstanding by asking a member to elaborate, by restating in a different way what someone has said, by asking a group member how he or she interpreted another member's comment, by interpreting ideas and defining terms, or by integrating separate ideas to show how they are related. Some specific examples are as follows:

> Are you suggesting that we change the amount spent on different advertising media rather than increase the overall budget?
>
> Some of us seem to be using the same term in two different ways.
>
> I'm not sure that I understand what you mean. Can you give us some specific examples?

Clarifying is especially important in groups whose members are not proficient in listening skills. Many people try to quickly identify the theme or essence of what is being said, after which the remainder of the message is tuned out as the person formulates a reply or thinks about something else. This kind of listening pattern can result in hasty and erroneous initial impressions, which will tend to persist because the person ignores later information that would have cleared up the misunderstanding.

4. Summarizing: To review what has been said or accomplished so far, to review ideas and facts offered during a lengthy period of discussion, to list or post ideas as they are suggested and ask the group to review them. Some specific examples are as follows:

> So far we have heard three different ideas of ways to reduce costs. They are . . .
>
> We have considered the pros and cons of the first three proposals, but the fourth proposal has not been discussed yet.
>
> In the meeting today we agreed that it is desirable to go ahead with the new project. We decided that Bob and John should meet tomorrow to draft the revised proposal, and Linda said she would work on the specifications. We also decided . . .

Summarizing has several important benefits, including (a) checking and aiding understanding after a complex discussion, (b) avoiding loss of ideas, (c) organizing contributions, (d) assessing progress to maintain interest, (e) keeping a discussion on course, and (f) demonstrating "nonevaluative listening" by the person making the summary (Maier, 1963). Summarizing is especially important at the end of a meeting to ensure that members leave with an understanding of what has been decided and what each person is supposed to do next.

5. Consensus Testing: To check on the amount of agreement among group members with respect to objectives, interpretation of information, evaluation of different alternatives, and readiness to reach a decision. Some specific examples are the following:

Are we in agreement that layoffs are the best way to cut labor costs?

Perhaps someone has doubts about the market survey for the new product. Let's check and see if we agree about the meaning of the figures.

There seems to be a feeling that we need to get a lot more information before this issue can be resolved. Are we in agreement with Bill's suggestion to postpone the decision until the next meeting?

The five types of behavior seem to be the most essential aspects of task-oriented leadership in meetings. Bradford (1976) reminds us that it is not sufficient for a leader simply to engage in task-oriented behaviors; a sense of proper timing is also essential. Any task-oriented behavior can be useless or even detrimental if it is premature or overdone. For example, summarizing too soon may discourage contribution of additional ideas on a subject. A discussion may be excessively prolonged if the leader keeps on stimulating communication instead of testing for a consensus. It is also important for the leader to have considerable skill in the use of each kind of task-oriented behavior. For example, an unskilled leader who tries to clarify a member's statement may succeed only in creating more confusion. A leader who is unskilled in summarizing may make a summary that leaves out key points and fails to organize contributions in a meaningful way.

Group-Maintenance Functions

Task-oriented leadership behavior in a meeting is essential for group effectiveness, but group-maintenance (relationship-oriented) behavior is also important. Group maintenance includes leadership behavior that increases cohesiveness, improves interpersonal relations, aids resolution of conflict, and satisfies the personal needs of members for acceptance, respect, and involvement. Just as machines need periodic maintenance to keep them running smoothly, so also do human relationships in a group. As with machines, preventative maintenance should be carried out frequently rather than waiting to do corrective maintenance after a serious breakdown. Group maintenance should be an ongoing activity designed to build teamwork and prevent the development of chronic apathy, withdrawal, interpersonal conflict, and power-status struggles. If allowed to develop, these problems will disrupt the task-oriented activity in a group and reduce group effectiveness. There are five major types of group-maintenance behavior.

1. Gatekeeping: To regulate and facilitate the participation of group members, to suggest ways of increasing participation, to encourage contributions by quiet members and prevent dominant members from monopolizing the discussion. Some specific examples are as follows:

> That is an interesting point, Fred. I'd like to hear more about what you have in mind.

> We haven't heard anything yet from the production people. It might be helpful to get their reaction to this proposal.

> George, why don't you hold off giving us all those technical details until later, so that we can find out what other kind of general approaches the group wants to consider.

2. Harmonizing: To smooth over conflict between members or mediate it by suggesting compromises, to reduce tension with humor, to ask members to reconcile their differences in a constructive manner, to discourage personal attacks, insults, and threats. Some specific examples are as follows:

> Let's try to keep personalities out of this discussion.

> Let's not allow this difference to be blown out of proportion. We seem to be in agreement on all of the other points.

> Is there some way we can combine the best features of both proposals rather than having to make a choice between them?

3. Supporting: To be friendly and supportive to group members, to be responsive to their needs and feelings, to come to the aid of a member or help the person save face, to show appreciation for the contributions of members. Some specific examples are as follows:

> I think your idea is a very creative one, Carol, despite Tom's doubts about its feasibility. Why don't we all try to think of some ways to overcome the limitation pointed out by Tom?

> I would like to express the appreciation of the group for Nancy's special efforts in preparing this report.

> You seem very upset about this aspect of the proposal, Joe. I can see how you might have some doubts about it.

4. Standard Setting: To suggest norms and standards of behavior (e.g., objectivity, fairness), to encourage the group to establish norms, to remind the group of norms that it established previously, to point out implicit group norms and check how members really feel about them. Some specific examples of this are the following:

> Didn't we agree before not to blame individual members for this problem?

I think we should all agree to be completely candid about our feelings, rather than holding back or making up phony reasons for objecting to a proposal.

We should agree to find something positive about a person's idea before pointing out any weaknesses.

5. *Process Analyzing*: To examine group processes in order to identify process problems and dysfunctional member behavior, to point out process problems to the group, to ask members for their perception of the group meetings (e.g., openness of communication, degree of trust, amount of cooperation, effectiveness of procedures). Some specific examples of this are the following:

Let's spend the last 15 minutes discussing how well the meeting has gone and see if we're satisfied with the new procedure for evaluating alternative proposals.

The group has avoided dealing with the tough issues in this meeting. Why is this happening?

I get the impression that people are not really leveling with each other on this subject. Has communication been as open as it should be?

Some group-maintenance behavior occurs in any meeting, but it is neglected by many leaders who are unaware of its importance. Standard setting and process analyzing are the aspects of behavior least likely to occur, perhaps because they require an explicit recognition of maintenance needs. As in the case of task-oriented behaviors, the group-maintenance behaviors require skill and sense of proper timing to be performed effectively. Table 11-1 summarizes the objectives of each kind of task-oriented and group-maintenance behavior discussed in this chapter.

TABLE 11-1   Major Types of Leadership Behavior in Decision Groups

TASK-ORIENTED BEHAVIOR	SPECIFIC OBJECTIVE
1. Process structuring	Guide and sequence discussion
2. Stimulating communication	Increase information exchange
3. Clarifying communication	Increase comprehension
4. Summarizing	Check understanding and assess progress
5. Consensus testing	Check on agreement

GROUP-MAINTENANCE BEHAVIOR	SPECIFIC OBJECTIVE
1. Gatekeeping	Increase and equalize participation
2. Harmonizing	Reduce tension and hostility
3. Supporting	Prevent withdrawal
4. Standard setting	Regulate behavior
5. Process Analyzing	Discover and resolve process problems

ROLE OF THE LEADER
IN DECISION GROUPS

Behavioral scientists generally agree that task-oriented behavior and group-maintenance behavior are both essential for the effectiveness of decision groups. However, there is some disagreement about who should perform these functions and about their relative priority. One part of the controversy began when some behavioral scientists proposed that the two functions are basically incompatible and should be performed by separate task and maintenance leaders in each group (e.g., Slater, 1955). Other behavioral scientists took the position that it is best for the designated leader in a group to perform both roles if capable of doing so (Borgotta, Couch, & Bales, 1954). This early controversy has been largely superseded by a debate over whether leaders should perform both kinds of functions alone or encourage group members to share responsibility for performing them.

Bradford (1976) suggests that there are two opposing viewpoints regarding the proper role of a discussion leader. He refers to these viewpoints as the "traditional approach" and the "group-centered" approach. A summary comparison of the two approaches is shown in Table 11-2, and each approach is described in more detail in the following sections.

TABLE 11-2   Comparison of Traditional and Group-Centered Leadership

BASIS FOR COMPARISON	TRADITIONAL	GROUP-CENTERED
1. Responsibility for group effectiveness	Leader responsible	Responsibility shared by group
2. Control over final choice	Control held by leader	Control vested in group
3. Importance of position power as source of leader influence	Emphasized and guarded carefully	Deemphasized
4. Leader perceives group	As set of individuals	As interacting, collective entity
5. Task-oriented functions	Performed by leader only	Shared by group
6. Group-maintenance functions	Not performed systematically	Emphasized and shared by group
7. Socioemotional processes and interactions	Mostly ignored by leader	Observed closely by leader
8. Expression of member needs and feelings	Discouraged by leader; emphasis on objective analysis	Encouraged by leader and dealt with in meetings

Based on Bradford, 1976.

Traditional Leadership

The traditional view is that leaders should have "the initiative, and power to direct, drive, instruct, and control those who follow" (Bradford, 1976; p. 8). This definition of the leader's role points to the following prescriptions:

1. The leader should focus on the task and ignore personal feelings and relationships whenever possible.
2. The leader should seek opinions and try to get agreement but never relinquish the right to make final choices.
3. The leader should stay in control of the group discussion at all times and should politely but firmly stop disruptive acts and irrelevant discussion.
4. The leader should discourage members from expressing their feelings and should strive to maintain a rational, logical discussion without any emotional outbursts.
5. The leader should guard against threats to his or her authority in the group and should fight if necessary to maintain it.

According to Bradford, this kind of group leadership produces some favorable results but at an unacceptable price. Meetings are orderly and decisions get made, but members become apathetic and resentful, which leads to a loss of potential contributions and a reduction in quality of decisions. Acceptance of decisions by group members may also be reduced, if members feel manipulated and unable to influence the decisions significantly.

Group-Centered Leadership

Bradford (1976) contends that much better results can be attained by using group-centered leadership in meetings. The group-centered conception of leadership is an outcome of extensive experience with T-groups and process consultation by behavioral scientists associated with the NTL Institute of Applied Behavioral Science, beginning in 1947. According to this view of leadership, the group as a whole must share the responsibility for its effectiveness. Group-maintenance functions are considered to be as important as task-oriented functions because feelings and interactions profoundly affect the problem-solving and decision-making processes in a group. Performance of both kinds of functions should be shared with the members, because no one person can be sensitive to all of the process problems and needs of the group. Sharing the responsibility for leadership functions will make members more satisfied with the group, according to Bradford. The following prescriptions for leaders are indicated by group-centered leadership:

1. The leader should listen attentively and observe nonverbal cues to be aware of member needs, feelings, interactions, and conflict. In doing so, the leader should view the group as a collective entity or social system rather than as merely a collection of individuals.

2. The role of the leader should be to serve as a consultant, advisor, teacher, and facilitator, rather than as a director or manager of the group.
3. The leader should model appropriate leadership behaviors and encourage members to learn to perform these behaviors themselves by imitation.
4. The leader should establish a climate of approval for expression of feelings as well as ideas.
5. The leader should encourage the group to deal with any maintenance needs and process problems within the context of the regular group meetings. However, the leader should not try to move too quickly in encouraging group self-evaluation.
6. The leader should relinquish control to the group and allow the group to make the final choice in all appropriate kinds of decisions.

Evaluation of the Group-Centered Approach

Bradford (1976) recognizes some difficulties in implementing group-centered leadership. He notes that this kind of leadership requires considerable skill on the part of both the leader and group members, and the necessary skill is learned only gradually. Leaders who are used to the traditional approach may be afraid to risk sharing control with group members or dealing openly with emotional behavior. There may be concern by such leaders that the new approach will make them appear weak or incompetent. Resistance to the new approach may come also from group members who are afraid of dealing openly with emotions or who prefer to avoid assuming more responsibility for leadership functions in the group. The traditional approach is often reinforced by ritual and tradition, which represent additional obstacles to the introduction of group-centered leadership. In some kinds of organizations, decision groups are legally required by their charter or bylaws to follow cumbersome procedural rules more appropriate for very large, formal groups (e.g., Robert's Rules of Order).

Despite these many obstacles, Bradford is optimistic about the prospects for successful implementation of group-centered leadership. In his book, he provides examples that show how the new approach has been used effectively in a variety of different kinds of groups. Nevertheless, there remain some questions about the applicability of group-centered leadership. Like other humanistic ideas for improving employee satisfaction (e.g., job enrichment, industrial democracy, participative management), the approach is based on rather optimistic assumptions about human nature. It is doubtful that all groups have members with sufficient maturity and emotional stability to respond favorably to group-centered leadership. It is also doubtful that some groups can achieve the high degree of interpersonal skill and sensitivity needed by members to make the approach successful. Many committees are only temporary and do not meet over a long enough time to develop the necessary trust and skills. Other committees are composed of persons who represent competing constituent groups, and these persons may be unwilling to support committee activities that are incompatible with constituent interests. Still other committees have no real authority or power, and are staffed by unwilling members who are required to fulfill committee duties. In such committees, members usually prefer to meet as seldom as possible and to assume as little responsibility as possible for committee activities.

Group-centered leadership sounds very appealing, and it has been found to be effective in some groups, but further research is needed to determine the limits of its usefulness. This research is likely to indicate the need for a contingency theory of meeting leadership. Such a theory would prescribe more sharing of leadership functions in some situations than in others. The contingency approach may also indicate a need to modify the relative priority of task-oriented and group-maintenance functions in different kinds of groups and in different stages of development within the same group.

GUIDELINES FOR FACILITATING PROBLEM DIAGNOSIS

Up to now we have discussed conference leadership in terms of general types of behavior that a leader or other group members can use (e.g., clarifying or supporting). There are also some standardized procedures that can be used by a leader to improve group effectiveness in solving problems and making decisions.

Preparation for the Meeting

In preparation for a meeting, it is usually advisable to plan an agenda and circulate it a few days before the meeting (Jay, 1976). If the agenda is circulated too far in advance, it may be forgotten or lost, and if circulated too late, some group members may not have a chance to study it. The agenda can be of help in planning what items to include in the meeting and how much time to devote to each item. The time allocated to each item and the purpose of the item (e.g., "for information," "for discussion," "for decision") can be indicated on the agenda next to the item (Jay, 1976). When there is an important problem to solve or decision to make, it is best to devote an entire meeting to it, rather than try to cram too many items into a single meeting. If there are reports and proposals to be studied by members in preparation for the meeting, they should be circulated in advance with the agenda. Of course, if the information is highly sensitive or confidential, it may be advisable to present this information at the meeting rather than circulating written reports.

Presentation of the Problem

The first step in a problem-solving meeting is to present the problem to the group. The manner in which the problem is presented can either hinder or facilitate group problem solving. A presentation that is vague and ambiguous creates confusion, misunderstanding, and possibly even anxiety. A presentation that implies the group is to blame for the problem stimulates defensiveness. A presentation that implies a favored solution by the leader tends to discourage consideration of other solutions and may engender resentment by group members. Maier (1963, p. 76) offers several recommendations about the way a problem should be presented to the group.

1. Use situational terms. The problem should be stated in situational terms rather than in behavioral terms. Describing the problem in situational terms avoids the implication that certain persons are behaving improperly and is less likely to threaten group members and make them defensive. The leader asks for help in solving a mutual problem rather than making an accusation. Examples of behavioral problem statements and corresponding situational problem statements are as follows:

> How can we get people to stop their excessive use of the duplicating machines? (Behavioral)
>
> How can we reduce duplicating expenses? (Situational)
>
> How can we get employees to do more work? (Behavioral)
>
> How can we increase productivity in our department? (Situational)

2. Avoid suggesting causes. The problem statement should not suggest the reasons for the problem or possible solutions to it. This kind of statement would limit the consideration of different problem diagnoses by the group. Instead, the problem statement should be worded in a way that encourages exploration of a variety of causes and a variety of possible solutions. Examples of restrictive and less restrictive problem statement are the following:

> How can we introduce incentives to increase employee productivity?
>
> How can we increase employee productivity?

The first problem statement implies that the cause of low productivity is poor motivation, whereas the second statement leaves it up to the group to discover the cause of low productivity and generate solutions.

3. Invoke mutual interests. The problem statement should incorporate mutual interests of group members. Problem solving will be more effective if the members are interested in the problem and perceive that its solution will benefit them as well as the organization. Consider the following examples:

How can we hold down production costs?

How can we protect our jobs by keeping our production costs from rising above those of competitors?

The second problem statement will be more effective with group members who are initially concerned about holding down production costs, because it indicates how this objective is relevant to their interests.

4. Specify one primary objective. The problem statement should specify only one major objective. Other objectives should be regarded as secondary, and any benefits and costs relevant to these objectives should be treated as positive or negative byproducts of achieving the primary objective. This guideline is intended to facilitate diagnosis of the problem and simplify the evaluation of solutions. Consider the following example:

How can we reduce errors and delays in deliveries to customers?

Two objectives are stated, but it is not clear which one is paramount. It is also unclear whether there is one complex problem or two unrelated ones. It is easier to make an initial problem diagnosis for each objective to see if errors and delays have different and completely unrelated causes, with a need for different kinds of solutions. If a common cause is found for the two problems, then they can be solved together.

5. Be brief. In most cases, it should be possible to present the problem in no more than 5 minutes. It is common for leaders to spend too much time introducing the problem before inviting discussion. Long introductions give the impression that the leader is trying to sell his or her own point of view. Another disadvantage of long introductions is that they usually create confusion and misunderstanding. Too much information at one time "overloads" people, and they are unable to digest all of it. The leader should briefly introduce the problem, then pause and wait for the group to respond. If the problem statement is not clear, someone will ask questions indicating a lack of understanding. At that point, the leader can make a more detailed description of the problem or call upon an expert member to do so. Sometimes the group will request the leader's opinion about the cause of the problem. If this occurs, the leader should point out that the purpose of the meeting is to obtain the group's ideas, not to promote his or her own ideas.

6. Share essential information. When the problem is presented, essential facts should be reviewed briefly. Things that the group needs to know to solve the problem are how long the problem has been evident, the nature of the problem symptoms, and what if anything has been done about the problem up to that time. The amount of information that should be presented depends on the nature of the problem and on how well informed the group members are already. The leader should be careful to present facts with as little interpretation as possible. For example, if the problem is how to increase sales, it is better simply to review sales figures for each district than to make judgments such as "sales are terrible in the central district." If there are definite constraints on solutions available to the group, such as spending limits or legal restrictions, these should also be mentioned briefly when the problem is presented.

Problem Diagnosis

After the problem is presented to the group, the next step is to determine the cause of the problem. There are basically two different kinds of problems: *control-deviation problems* and *goal-attainment problems*.

In a control-deviation problem, the objective is to restore conditions to a previously satisfactory state. For example, some equipment that was operating properly suddenly starts having defective output. The cause of a control-deviation problem is determined by a logical analysis of data on the exact nature of the deviation from normal, satisfactory conditions and the exact timing of the deviations (e.g., when did they start, how often do they occur, how long do they last?). The main reason for holding a meeting to solve a control-deviation problem is that the leader does not have all the information needed to determine the nature and cause of the problem. In making the problem diagnosis, the leader should have the group follow a systematic procedure to describe the deviations and identify single or multiple changes that occurred prior to the onset of the deviations (Kepner & Tregoe, 1965, 1981).

In a goal-attainment problem, a new or higher goal has been established, and the problem is how to attain the goal. The problem is caused by obstacles that prevent the goal from being attained in some easy, obvious manner. The meeting is held because the leader does not have all the relevant information about the nature of the problem, and the group has the collective knowledge to diagnose the problem and generate more creative solutions than the leader could.

As a first step in problem diagnosis for a goal-attainment problem, Maier (1963) recommends the leader should stimulate group members to express different conceptions of the problem. Since a complex problem has many elements to be considered, alternative problem diagnoses help to identify different parts of the problem and suggest different ways of solving it. To avoid dominating and inhibiting the group's thinking, the leader should refrain from offering ideas about the nature of the problem until other group members have presented their ideas. This guideline can be waived, however, if the leader uses a procedure for anonymous idea generation (e.g., brainstorming, nominal group technique).

Several common errors occur in problem diagnosis, regardless of whether the diagnosis is made by an individual or a group. These common errors include: (1) confusing facts with opinions or assumptions, (2) confusing symptoms with causes, (3) looking for scapegoats to blame, (4) proposing solutions before the problem is clearly understood, (5) defining the problem in a way that implies a choice must be made between two particular solutions, and (6) defining the problem in such a way that it could not be solved without exceeding the discretion and authority of the leader and group. The leader can help the group avoid making these types of errors.

Comparison of alternative problem statements is easier if members are encouraged to provide supporting facts and explain the logic behind their inferences and hypotheses. In making this comparison, it may be possible for the group to agree which problem statement is the most accurate and useful one. However, it is not absolutely necessary for the group to agree on a single problem statement. In some cases, where there is disagreement about the nature of the problem, it is advisable to adjourn the meeting to collect additional information needed to understand the problem. In other cases, where additional information is unnecessary or unavailable, the group can select one problem statement that appears especially promising and consider possible solutions in an effort to make further progress. Sometimes in the course of exploring solutions the understanding of the problem will change (Gordon, 1961).

GUIDELINES FOR FACILITATING
SOLUTION GENERATION

Some common mistakes made by groups when generating solutions to a problem include the following: (1) discussing what should have been done in the past instead of what can be done in the present, (2) dwelling on solutions that exceed the discretion and authority of the group, (3) focusing on solutions that have been used in the past without any attempt to create novel solutions, and (4) evaluating solutions as they are generated instead of waiting until after everyone has had an opportunity to suggest solutions. The leader can help the group avoid making these common mistakes. As in problem diagnosis, the leader should be careful to avoid dominating the discussion of solutions with his or her own ideas and preferences.

Creative idea generation is a vital element of problem solving for goal-attainment problems. It is important both for development of alternative problem definitions and for development of potential solutions to the problem. As noted earlier in this chapter, the contribution of ideas by group members can be inhibited in many ways. Much of the problem stems either from domination of the discussion by certain individuals or from members' fears that their ideas will be evaluated unfavorably. Research on problem solving in groups has found that idea generation is less inhibited when it is separated from idea evaluation (Maier & Hoffman, 1960;

Maier & Maier, 1957; Maier & Solem, 1952). Based on this and other research, some new procedures have been developed to facilitate idea generation in groups. The procedures are applicable to problem diagnosis as
well as to solution generation.

Brainstorming

Brainstorming is a procedure wherein members are encouraged to suggest any idea about the problem that comes to mind. The ideas are written
on a blackboard or flip chart, and no positive or negative evaluation of
ideas is permitted, including scowls, groans, sighs, or gestures. Contribution of ideas is supposed to be completely spontaneous, and members are
encouraged to build on each other's ideas.

Brainstorming was the first of the new procedures devised to reduce
inhibition and facilitate idea generation. It was hoped that inhibition
would be reduced by deferring evaluation of ideas, domination would be
reduced by making contributions brief and spontaneous, and creativity
would be increased by mutual facilitation of ideas and a climate of acceptance for strange and novel ideas. Brainstorming was only partially successful. It is likely to improve idea generation in comparison with a regular
interacting group, but some inhibition continues to occur when ideas are initially suggested out loud in a face-to-face meeting.

Nominal Group Technique

The nominal group technique for idea generation was undoubtedly inspired by research that found more and better ideas were generated by a
set of persons working separately ("nominal group") than by the same persons or the same number of persons working together in an interacting
group, even when the interacting group used brainstorming (Dunnette,
Campbell, & Jaastad, 1963; Van de Ven & Delbecq, 1971; White, Dittrich,
& Lang, 1980). The nominal group technique attempts to capitalize on the
advantages of both nominal and interacting groups, while avoiding their
limitations. The approach is applicable to complex problems requiring
original solutions, but it may not be appropriate for problems requiring
group acceptance of a convergent solution (Stumpf, Freedman, & Zand,
1979).

The conditions for a nominal group are simulated by having members
first write their ideas on a slip of paper without discussing them. A period
of from 5 to 15 minutes is usually required to write ideas, and the leader
insures that there is no talking during this time. The next step in the procedure recommended by Delbecq, Van de Ven, and Gustafson (1975) is
a round-robin contribution of ideas. Each member in turn is asked to contribute one idea. As an idea is suggested, it is written by the leader on a
blackboard or flip chart. No evaluation of ideas or discussion of them is

permitted during the posting. As the round-robin continues, some members may pass if they have no additional ideas differing from those already posted. A person may suggest ideas not on his or her original list, and members are encouraged to build on each other's ideas. After all ideas are posted, the leader reviews the list of ideas and asks if there are any questions, statements of clarification, or statements of agreement or disagreement regarding the relevance of the ideas to the problem. The procedure is applicable for groups of up to nine persons, but it should not be used in larger groups unless carried out within subgroups (ideas can be combined after the subgroups are finished).

An alternative approach to the one recommended by Delbecq et al. (1975) is simply to have members write their ideas, then have all ideas posted at the same time. After the ideas are posted, they are discussed and additional ideas that occur to members can be added. The advantage of this procedure over the round-robin procedure is that the anonymity of contributors is maintained, which may or may not be important, depending on how sensitive the topic is and how worried members are about rejection for suggesting bizarre, silly, or controversial ideas. A disadvantage is that many of the same ideas are likely to occur on each list. Either the leader will have to merge and simplify the lists before posting, or the group will have to spend some time doing this after the sheets are posted.

Synectics Techniques

Synectics techniques utilize fantasy and analogy to facilitate creativity and encourage new ways of looking at a problem (Gordon, 1961). Some of the techniques can be used by an individual problem solver, but they are more appropriate for use in a diverse group of people who can take advantage of mutual stimulation and acceleration of the "kind of semi-conscious mental activity which might take months of incubation for a single person" (Gordon, 1961; p. 11). Groups can stimulate more daring and psychological risk taking in abandonment of familiar ways of looking at things and temporary suspension of tendencies to organize perception in a rational manner. The primary objective of synectics technique is to stimulate creativity by overcoming internal inhibitions resulting from normal, rational ways of perceiving and thinking. Inhibition of contributions due to group processes is regarded as a secondary barrier to creative idea generation, and procedures comparable to brainstorming and the nominal group technique are used together with special training to minimize this additional source of inhibition.

According to Prince (1969, 1970), the following steps should be followed in a problem-solving meeting. First, the leader makes a brief statement of the problem. One or more members with specialized knowledge about the problem are asked to provide a more detailed explanation and answer any questions. Then all members are asked to write one or more restatements of the problem as they understand it. In making these problem restatements, members are encouraged to use fantasy and think in terms of wishful goals, regardless of how unrealistic these are. For example, in a group working on the problem of how to "enter the pet food market with an advantage over the competition," some of the problem restatements were as follows (Prince, 1969; p. 102):

> Why don't we devise a pet food that makes addicts out of pets?
>
> How can we make pet food that perfectly fits the buyer's image of what the pet needs and loves?
>
> Why can't we devise a pet food that the pet will choose every time in a taste test?

The problem restatements are collected and posted on a blackboard or flip chart. After the group has had an opportunity to study them, the leader selects one to focus on initially. No attempt is made to get the group to agree on a single definition of the problem. Prince (1970) argues that it is not only impossible but also undesirable to achieve consensus about the nature of a highly complex problem. Members will naturally view it differently, and once these differences are recorded, the group can tolerate the differences and go on to find a solution that will be acceptable to everyone.

The next step is called an "excursion." Its purpose is to get group members to put the problem out of mind temporarily, but at the same time to use imagery and knowledge about other subjects as a source of creative solutions. In one type of excursion, the leader asks for images from some field of natural science and selects a promising example for the group to discuss. Another kind of excursion is generation of two-word phrases that capture the essence of a paradox (e.g., aggressive-surrender, familiar-surprise, disciplined-freedom). A third kind of excursion is a "personal analogy," in which members discuss what it would feel like to be a physical object, such as a tree, wall, or cloud.

The leader asks members to apply their metaphorical images or their two-word phrases to the problem restatement, regardless of how irrelevant they first appear to be. If this "force fit" is successful, it is considered as a possible solution. A number of fantasy excursions may be necessary to develop a viable set of solutions.

The leader of a synectics group plays an important role, although the leadership can be rotated among group members from meeting to meeting if desired. The leader's role is to ensure appropriate procedures are followed, everyone has an opportunity to participate, members are not put on the defensive, enthusiasm is maintained, communication is effective, and incomplete new ideas are protected and nurtured.

One of the most useful supplementary techniques is to ask members to restate another member's idea and find something worthwhile about it before saying anything critical. A member who points out a deficiency or limitation of another's idea is also encouraged to suggest a way to correct the deficiency or overcome the limitation. The emphasis is on careful listening and constructive, helpful behavior. This technique is applicable in any decision group, regardless of whether the other synectics procedures are used. The amount of published research on synectics techniques is quite limited, but the available evidence suggests the techniques can be very effective (Bouchard, 1971).

GUIDELINES FOR IMPROVING
SOLUTION CHOICE

After a set of alternative solutions has been generated by a group or by a leader acting alone, the alternatives must be evaluated and the best one selected. When a group is involved in this process, the leader should be aware of certain process problems that are likely to reduce group effectiveness: (1) hasty decisions, (2) incomplete participation, (3) polarization, and (4) superficial action planning. This section of the chapter will describe some procedures for avoiding or correcting each process problem.

Hasty Decision

A *hasty decision* is one made without an adequate evaluation of the available alternatives. We saw earlier in the chapter that highly cohesive groups are likely to agree too quickly because nobody is willing to disagree strongly with other members or to criticize a popular alternative. Even when there are uninhibited critics and dissenters in a group, a strong majority coalition may ram through a decision quickly before the critics have an opportunity to explain its weaknesses and gather support. The pressure of time is another reason for hasty decisions. Such decisions commonly occur when a meeting is about to end and members desire to resolve matters quickly so they can adjourn and also avoid another meeting.

When alternatives are not carefully evaluated, the result is likely to be a poor quality decision. Careful consideration of the possible consequences of each alternative course of action is necessary to identify adverse consequences not foreseen when the alternative was proposed. Sometimes the actions taken to solve a problem create new problems that are worse than the original one. When a solution is selected without due consideration to the cost of implementing it, the cost may prove to be greater than the benefits.

There are several things the leader can do to prevent hasty decisions and improve the accuracy of the solution evaluation process. One important step is to plan meetings in which enough time is available to explore adequately the implications and consequences of each alternative. If an important decision is being considered and the meeting must end before solutions can be properly evaluated, the leader should try to postpone the decision until another meeting. If an immediate decision is not necessary and it is obvious that more information is needed, the leader may want to adjourn the meeting and arrange for additional information to be obtained. For very important decisions, another option is to have a completely independent decision group make a separate recommendation or to use outside experts as consultants to provide an independent report on the feasibility of various alternatives.

A number of procedures have been devised to identify implicit assumptions and facilitate careful consideration of the positive and negative aspects of each alternative. These procedures are especially appropriate when a cohesive group is reluctant to disagree, or an impatient group is pushing for a quick decision. Some of the procedures are complex, highly sophisticated methods of analyzing quantitative data (e.g., mathematical models, linear programming, nonlinear programming, policy capturing models, etc.). Only four of the less complex approaches are described here.

1. Two-column method. This procedure is recommended by Maier (1963) when there is no single solution that is clearly superior to all others, and each solution has both positive and negative features. The procedure is feasible only if the number of solutions under consideration is small. If more than four solutions are available, the list should first be reduced, otherwise the procedure will be too time-consuming. Each solution is written on a blackboard or flip chart. Under each solution, the leader makes two columns and labels one "advantages" and the other "disadvantages." Then the leader asks members to work together as a group in exploring the advantages and disadvantages of each alternative. The alternatives can be discussed one at a time, or they can all be discussed together. The important point is to involve every group member in the identification of both the advantages and the disadvantages of each alternative. The procedure is intended to avoid the usual tendency people have to support their preferred alternative and criticize competing ones. As the group members point out advantages and disadvantages, the leader abbreviates each comment and writes it in the appropriate column. After the posting of comments is completed, objections to any items are considered by the group, and items that lack factual support or are irrelevant can be deleted.

2. Cost-benefit analysis. This procedure is appropriate when the consequences of each solution are fairly certain, and it is possible to make reasonably accurate estimates of the benefits and costs involved. The analysis consists of identifying benefits and costs in monetary terms, using cost accounting and other quantitative techniques. It is important for the leader to insure that this analysis is as objective as possible. The analysis should be conducted in a systematic manner, and care should be taken to avoid biasing estimates of costs and benefits to support a preferred solution. After the alternatives have all been analyzed, the group selects the best one by using whatever economic criterion seems most appropriate (e.g., maximize net benefit, maximize return on investment).

3. *Devil's advocate procedure.*   When a preliminary evaluation of alternatives reveals that one alternative is strongly favored, there is danger of a groupthink type of decision, especially in a highly cohesive group. In this situation, the leader should try to postpone the decision until a later meeting and assign some group members to serve as "devil's advocates" who investigate possible weaknesses of the proposed solution (Janis,1972). The process can be formalized by having one part of the group prepare a formal proposal supported by all the key underlying assumptions, facts, and data. Then the devil's advocates prepare a formal critique and present it to the group. In making the critique, the devil's advocates examine all of the assumptions, facts, and recommendations in the proposal, looking for weaknesses such as faulty logic, doubtful inferences, questionable assumptions, overlooked information, biased forecasts, and misinterpreted data. Finally the group considers whether the proposal can be revised to deal with the criticisms in a satisfactory manner. If not, the group may try to generate additional solutions or postpone the decision. Research shows that a devil's advocate approach for evaluating a proposed solution is better than the usual interacting/consensus procedure where the role of critic is diffused among group members (Cosier, 1978, 1982; Schweiger, Sandberg, & Ragan, 1986).

4. *Dialectical inquiry procedure.*   This procedure is most applicable to complex, unstructured problems when it is possible to identify two completely different and contrary approaches for dealing with a problem. The group is divided into two subgroups, each of which prepares a written proposal explaining its proposed solution and explicitly identifies underlying assumptions and supporting data. Each subgroup meets separately to analyze the opposing proposal, then the subgroups meet together to debate the proposals. The objective is to arrive at a list of assumptions, facts, and data that are acceptable to both sides and that can be used to develop a final solution. Research finds that the procedure improves the solution evaluation process for executives making strategic decisions (Lourenco & Glidewell, 1974; Mitroff, Barabba, & Kilman, 1977). However, a weakness of the procedure is that it tends to undermine group cohesiveness and create dissatisfaction with the group (Schweiger et al., 1986).

Incomplete Participation

Just as group members may be inhibited during problem solving, they may be inhibited about contributing their opinions and knowledge during solution evaluation and choice. Incomplete participation sometimes results in a "false consensus." When some members loudly advocate a particular solution and other members remain silent or fail to take a position, the silent ones are usually assumed to be in agreement. In fact, silence may indicate dissent rather than agreement. A false consensus will result in a lower-quality decision if the inhibited members have important information indicating that the alternative favored by the more vocal members is actually deficient. This information is likely to be suppressed by members who are afraid to oppose openly the vocal minority, especially if the leader or other high-status persons support the dominant position. A false consensus will also lead to a low level of decision acceptance by members of the "silent majority."

The leader can do much to facilitate complete participation by engaging in appropriate gatekeeping behavior. Each member should be encouraged to contribute to the evaluation of solutions, and members should be discouraged from using social-pressure tactics (e.g., threats, derogatory comments) to intimidate persons who disagree with them. The leader should be careful to continue discussion long enough to provide minority factions with ample opportunity to influence the decision.

The procedure used to make the final choice of the best alternative has important implications for the acceptance of the decision by group members.

Two kinds of procedures can be used to insure that members have an equal influence over the final choice.

1. Voting. With this technique, each group member is asked to indicate his or her single preferred choice from among the alternatives being considered. Voting can be done by a show of hands, by going around the group to hear each member's preference, or with a secret written ballot. The secret ballot is appropriate if there is indication that members will be inhibited about revealing their real preferences. A voting procedure is easy to use when there are only a few alternatives, but it is not very effective when there are many alternatives. As the number of alternatives increases, it is more and more likely that the votes will be widely distributed among them without a clear majority or even a strong plurality for any one alternative. Rather than go through successive ballots when there are many alternatives, it is better initially to reduce the list by some other procedure besides regular voting. Maier (1963) suggests having each member write his or her three most preferred alternatives on a slip of paper, after which the leader posts the tally for each alternative. In studying decision groups, Maier finds that invariably three or four solutions stand out by getting well over half of the votes, and each group member is likely to have at least one of his or her preferred choices among them. The list of alternatives can be reduced to these three or four most popular ones, and it then becomes feasible to make the final choice with a regular voting procedure.

When voting is used with a short list of alternatives, the leader should encourage the group to try to reach a consensus rather than deciding on the basis of a simple majority. A consensus occurs when all members of the group agree that a particular alternative is acceptable to them. This alternative is not necessarily the first choice of every member, but any members who do not regard it as their first choice are willing to accept it and support the group decision (Schein, 1969). A consensus decision usually generates more commitment than a majority decision, but a group consensus is not easy to achieve, and it usually takes more time to make the decision. When the group has a large majority in support of one alternative, but there are still a few dissenters, the leader should carefully weigh the possible benefits of winning them over against the cost of spending additional discussion time. If adequate time has been devoted already to discussion of alternatives, it is usually not worthwhile to prolong the discussion merely to persuade one or two stubborn members. In this situation, the leader should take the initiative and declare that a group decision has been reached.

2. Ranking and ratings.   A variation of the "nominal group technique" can be used to make a final choice among alternative solutions to a problem. The consequences of each alternative solution are discussed by the group, but group members do not openly indicate their preferences among alternatives. Then preference judgments are made privately. When rankings are to be used, Delbecq et al. (1975) suggest the following procedural steps.

a. The leader posts the alternatives and assigns each a code number.
b. Each member selects five preferred alternatives and writes the code number of each alternative on a different 3 x 5 card.
c. Each member ranks the alternatives by ordering the cards from most to least preferable and then writes on each card the rank assigned to that alternative.
d. The rank scores are tallied by the leader on the blackboard or flip chart.
e. If the group is generally in agreement, the alternative with the highest tally of rank scores is selected as the final choice.
f. If there is substantial disagreement, the group discusses the results and explores reasons why members have different preference. During the discussion, some members may change their preferences, leading to general agreement.
g. If necessary, a final ballot can be used to determine which alternative has the most support.

A similar procedure is followed if ratings are used instead of rankings. Rather than ranking their five preferred alternatives, the members rate them on a scale of from 0 (least desirable) to 10 (most desirable). Otherwise, the same sequence of steps is followed (Delbecq et al., 1975)

Polarization

Polarization occurs when group members form two opposing factions, each strongly committed to its own preferred alternative. When this happens, each faction tends to ignore the good features of the opposing position. Discussion is focused on differences between positions, while similarities are ignored. As each faction concentrates on attacking the weaknesses of the opposing position, emotional debate replaces objective analysis. Each faction selects different fact or makes a different interpretation of facts to support its own position. Loud arguments are likely to ensue as people struggle to be heard or try to interrupt opposing speakers to refute their arguments. Since members are not listening carefully to opposing speakers, they seldom understand what is being said (Blake, Shepard, & Mouton, 1964).

Polarization may lead to a number of undesirable outcomes. One possible outcome is a prolonged stalemate in which the group is unable to reach a decision. Another outcome is a forced decision in which the politically stronger faction imposes its choice on the weaker faction. If this happens, it is unlikely that members of the weaker faction will be committed to implement the decision. Another possible outcome is that the two factions will agree on a compromise decision that is only marginally acceptable to either faction, in which case there is unlikely to be much commitment to the decision (Schein, 1969).

Sometimes polarization can be prevented by an alert leader who is sensitive to its early signs. The leader can try to reduce tension and hostility by use of "harmonizing" behavior, such as discouraging derogatory comments, pointing out areas of agreement, and interjecting some humor into the discussion. Misunderstandings due to poor listening can be minimized by restating comments ("clarifying communication") or asking a group member to restate the comment made by someone in the opposing faction. The leader can point out to the group that they appear to be drifting toward polarization and ask them to discuss ways to avoid it ("process-analyzing" behavior). When there are rival alternatives and the group is having difficulty reaching agreement, the following procedures can be used to prevent polarization or resolve a stalemate.

1. Posting advantages. If the group has not already used the two-column method to evaluate alternatives, a variation of this procedure can be helpful for preventing polarization (Maier, 1963). Instead of posting both the advantages and the disadvantages for two competing alternatives, only the positive aspects of each alternative are posted. This procedure delays criticism and requires each member to consider positive aspects of the alternative not favored. When negative aspects of each alternative are eventually considered, they can be restated as positive aspects of the other alternative. The procedure tends to depersonalize the discussion, minimize tension and hostility, and develop and understanding and appreciation of both alternatives. However, the success of the procedure depends greatly on the skill of the leader in using it. The leader plays an important role in getting members to participate actively in development of a supporting case for each alternative, and in preventing intrusion of critical judgements during posting of positive aspects.

2. *Solution integration.*   The group is encouraged to develop an integrative solution that encompasses the rival solutions or at least their principal features. One way to begin this procedure is to examine both alternatives closely to identify what features they have in common and how they differ. This comparison develops a better understanding and appreciation of the opposing alternative, especially if all group members become actively involved in the discussion. The leader should encourage participation, keep the discussion analytical rather than critical, and post the results of the comparison to provide a visual summary of the similarities and differences.

When members disagree about which alternative is best, it is helpful to determine whether the disagreement is due primarily to different objectives or to a different estimate of consequences. Members may disagree because they do not have the same objectives or priorities, and each faction prefers the alternative most consistent with its own objectives or priorities. Finding a single solution to satisfy different objectives is very difficult, especially if the objectives are essentially incompatible. It is usually necessary to resolve this kind of disagreement by a compromise in which each faction makes some concessions. The process of finding an integrative solution, or at lease a good compromise, is facilitated by having members separately rate the importance of each objective being used as a criterion for evaluating the alternatives. The results can be posted by the leader and examined by the group to see how much agreement there is in objectives and priorities. If there is substantial disagreement, a discussion of the reasons for the differences is sometimes helpful in reducing disagreement, or at least in developing a better understanding of why other people feel the way they do.

When members have the same objectives and priorities but disagree about the likely outcomes of each alternative, the discussion should focus on the reasons for the different estimates. The facts and inferences used in making each estimate about the consequences of an alternative should be reviewed carefully to see if more agreement can be achieved. It is easier to find an integrative solution if the disagreement is over means rather than objectives. The process of finding an integrative solution requires a return to the use of problem-solving procedures such as those described earlier. In effect, the group is asked to generate either a composite solution using the best features of the rival solutions, or a completely new solution that both factions can agree is superior to the initial solutions.

3. Experimentation. When a group is sharply divided in support of competing alternatives, it is sometimes feasible to conduct a limited test of one or both of them to evaluate their likely consequences. Whether such a test is feasible will depend on time pressures, the cost of experimentation, and the possibility of conducting a limited, reversible trial for either alternative. Experimentation is highly desirable when it is likely to provide accurate information about consequences, and different estimates of the consequences are the primary source of the disagreement over which alternative is better. The most direct procedure is to conduct a limited test of both alternatives simultaneously, and then compare the results. It is also possible to use a sequential strategy in which only one alternative is tested initially. If the consequences are satisfactory to both factions, the other alternative does not need to be tested.

4. Leader decision. Another way for the leader to resolve a stalemate is to make the final choice himself or herself after carefully considering the ideas and preferences of group members. In effect, the leader reverts to use of "consultation" rather than "group decision making." Some leaders make it clear to group members in advance that this will be done if the group cannot reach agreement in a specified time period. A leader decision is sometimes necessary when a decision needs to be reached quickly, experimentation is not feasible, and other methods of resolving the deadlock are unsuccessful.

Superficial Action Planning

The final step in decision making is planning how the decision will be implemented. Detailed action steps should be specified, and procedures for monitoring progress should be established. Some good decisions are unsuccessful simply because nobody bothers to ensure that action plans are made.

One important part of action planning is what Kepner and Tregoe (1981) call "potential problem analysis." It is the process of anticipating what may go wrong with the chosen alternative, planning how to prevent undesirable but avoidable events, and planning how to minimize any damage caused by unavoidable events. In their book, Kepner and Tregoe recommend detailed procedures for carrying out a potential problem analysis.

Another important part of action planning is the assignment of responsibility for different tasks involved in implementing the decision. If the group members are going to implement the decision, it is necessary to determine who will be responsible for which tasks. Group members may be asked to select tasks, or the leader may make the task assignments. If the decision is to be implemented by persons not involved in making it, they may not understand why the decision was made, and the decision may not be implemented in an enthusiastic manner (Bass, 1970). The best way to avoid this potential problem is to invite some of the persons responsible for implementing the decision to participate in making it. If it is not feasible to involve some of these persons directly, they should at least be informed in detail about the reasons for the decision (Schein, 1969).

SUMMARY

For some kinds of problems, a group decision is potentially superior to a decision made by a single individual such as the leader, but many things can prevent a group from realizing its potential. Group problem-solving is affected by group size, cohesiveness, status differentials, member characteristics, and the physical environment. A major determinant of group effectiveness is the quality of leadership. The leadership role is difficult, because the decision process will be adversely affected if the leader is either too passive or too domineering.

Task-oriented leadership functions in the context of decision groups include: structuring activities, stimulating communication, clarifying communication, summarizing, and consensus testing. Group-maintenance functions include: gatekeeping, harmonizing, providing support, standard setting, and process analyzing. Both categories of group leadership behavior appear essential for the success of a decision group. Each of the specific functions requires skill and a sense of proper timing to be effective.

There is some disagreement about letting subordinates share in performing group leadership functions. Proponents of traditional leadership emphasize the need to direct and control group activities. Proponents of group-centered leadership contend that better results are obtained when group-maintenance functions are given equal priority with task-oriented functions, and group members share in carrying out both kinds of leadership. Group-centered leadership sounds appealing, but it requires considerable skill and maturity on the part of both the leader and group members. Additional research is needed to resolve the controversy and determine if one style of leadership is universally superior, or if the optimal style varies depending on the situation.

Research suggests a number of ways to improve group problem solving, such as presenting the problem in an unbiased manner, considering alternative conceptions of the problem, and deferring solution generation until the problem diagnosis is completed. Procedures for increasing idea generation, including brainstorming, the nominal group technique, and synectics techniques. Typical obstacles encountered during the evaluation and choice of alternatives include: hasty decisions, incomplete participation, polarization, and superficial action planning. There are several techniques a skilled leader can use to deal with these obstacles and improve group decision processes.

REVIEW AND DISCUSSION QUESTIONS

1. How are group decisions affected by the size and composition of the group?
2. What is groupthink, and under what conditions is it most likely to occur?
3. What are the major types of task-oriented leadership functions in decision groups and their objectives?
4. What are the major types of group-maintenance leadership functions in decision groups and their objectives?
5. What is group-centered leadership and how does it differ from the so-called traditional view of group leadership?
6. What are common errors in problem diagnosis by groups, and how can a leader help to avoid these errors?
7. What are common errors in evaluating and selecting a solution in decision groups, and how can a leader help to avoid these errors?
8. Briefly compare brainstorming, nominal group procedure, and synectics procedures for idea generation.
9. How does leadership in decision groups relate to other aspects of managerial leadership described in earlier chapters?

12

OVERVIEW
AND
INTEGRATION

This final chapter summarizes the major findings from earlier chapters and examines convergence across different approaches for studying leadership, including power research, behavior research, trait research, and situational research. Two basic questions about the field are considered: (1) how important is leadership to organizational survival and effectiveness, and (2) how much do we really know about leadership effectiveness? The major approaches for improving leadership in organizations are discussed briefly.

HOW IMPORTANT IS LEADERSHIP?

Some writers argue that leadership is a major determinant of organizational effectiveness (e.g., Chandler, 1962; Katz & Kahn, 1978; Peters & Waterman, 1982), whereas other writers express doubts that leaders have any substantial influence on the performance of their organization (e.g., Meindl, Ehrlich, & Dukerich, 1985; Pfeffer, 1977b). The essence of Pfeffer's argument is that organizational effectiveness depends primarily on factors beyond the leader's control, such as the economic conditions, market conditions, governmental policies, and technological change. The new CEO of a mature company inherits an organization with various strengths and weaknesses, and the potential for making improvements is severely limited by internal political constraints and uncontrollable external conditions. A similar argument has been made for lower-level leaders (see

Kerr, Hill, & Broedling, 1986). As constraints have magnified over the years, the discretion of first-line supervisors has become too limited for them to have much influence on subordinate performance. Calder (1977) argued that the importance of leadership is exaggerated by the need for people to explain events in a way that fits their assumptions and implicit theories. Two lines of research relevant to the question of leadership importance include research on leadership succession and research on attributional processes. Each type of research will be reviewed briefly.

Consequences of Leadership Succession

The succession studies examine changes in performance occurring after changes in leadership. It is assumed that if leadership is important, changes in top leadership should be associated with changes in the performance of the organization. These studies demonstrate the difficulty of doing research on leadership importance, and selection of an appropriate criterion of organizational performance has been a particular problem. A weakness in some studies is the use of stock prices as the criterion of company performance rather than a criterion more directly influenced by the company leadership. Day and Lord (1985, 1988) found that some results from succession research have been understated due to methodological problems such as failure to correct for the effects of organization size, failure to correct dollar-denominated criteria for effects of inflation, and failure to allow enough time for new leaders to influence quantitative performance outcomes. For example, Lieberson and O'Connor (1972) examined the relative effects of year, industry, and company CEO on the earnings of 167 companies in 13 industries. Leadership succession accounted for only 7.5 percent of the variance in net income with no lag time or correction for size, but leadership explained 32 percent of profit margin (i.e., net income corrected for size of organization) for a 3 year lagged effect. Salancik and Pfeffer (1977b) examined the relative effects of city, year, and mayor on budget variables for 30 U.S. cities. Mayor effects accounted for only 10 percent of budget outcomes when results were not corrected for city size, but when city size was controlled, mayor effects accounted for over 24 percent of budget outcomes. Day and Lord pointed out that writers such as Pfeffer (1977b), Brown (1982), and Mcindl et al. (1985) have erroneously interpreted these studies as demonstrating that leadership is not important.

The substantial effect of leadership on appropriate criteria in the studies by Lieberson and O'Connor and Salancik and Pfeffer is consistent with results in more recent research. Weiner and Mahoney (1981) examined 193 manufacturing companies over a 19-year period and found that leadership explained 44 percent of the variance in profits as a percentage of assets. The succession studies cannot demonstrate the importance of leadership unless the new leaders differ considerably in skill from the leaders they replace. The influence of successor ability on organizational effectiveness was examined in two studies, one on church ministers (Smith, Carson, and Alexander,1984) and the other on basketball coaches in the NBA (Pfeffer & Davis-Blake, 1986). In both studies, leadership succession predicted performance only for leaders with a previous record of effectiveness. The amount of influence a new leader has on organizational performance also depends on other factors, such as whether there is a performance crisis at the time of succession, whether there is an inside or outside successor, and how much support the successor has from key stakeholders (e.g., owners, board of directors, employees, creditors, etc.) to make major changes in strategy (Brady & Helmich, 1984).

In summary, the succession studies demonstrate that leadership is indeed an important determinant of organizational performance. However, research on CEO's is still very limited, and we know little about the attributes and behavior of successors who are successful, how they exercise power, or the conditions that determine how much influence a particular leader will have (House & Singh, 1987).

Attribution Research on Leader Importance

Organizations are complex social systems of patterned interactions among people. In their effort to understand the causes, dynamics, and outcomes of organizational processes, people interpret events in simple, human terms. Stereotypes, implicit theories, and simplified assumptions about causality aid people in making sense out of events that would otherwise be incomprehensible. One especially strong and prevalent explanation of organizational events is to attribute causality to the influence of leaders (Pfeffer, 1977b; Calder, 1977). Leaders are pictured as heroic figures who are capable of determining the fate of their organizations. There is a mystical, romantic quality associated with leadership, similar to that for other stereotyped heroes in our culture, such as the lone cowboy who single-handedly vanquishes the bad guys, and the secret agent who acts on his or her own to save the world from nuclear destruction. The emphasis on leadership as a cause of organizational events reflects a common cultural bias toward explaining experience primarily in terms of the rational actions of people, as opposed to uncontrollable natural forces, actions by supernatural beings, or random events not susceptible to human comprehension. A related cause is the widespread faith in human organizations as rational, goal-oriented systems that fulfill the needs of members and contribute to the general welfare of society. The people who occupy positions of top leadership in organizations symbolize the promise of organizations in modern civilization (Meindl et al., 1985).

The attributional biases about leaders are exploited by many political leaders and top executives who seek to create the impression that they are in control of events. Symbols and rituals, such as elaborate inaugural ceremonies, reinforce the perceived importance of leaders (Pfeffer, 1977b, 1981). Successes are announced and celebrated; failures are suppressed or downplayed. Symbolic action is most likely when situational constraints and unpredictable events make it impossible for management to exert much influence over organizational performance. It is all the more important in this situation to maintain the impression that organizational leaders know what they are doing and are making good progress toward attaining organizational objectives. For example, national political leaders engage in highly publicized activities that appear "presidential." Coaches of sports teams are commonly replaced as a form of "ritualistic scapegoating" when the team has a losing season (Gamson & Scotch, 1964).

Impression management is important for the CEO of publicly owned corporations, because stock prices and ratings for the corporation's bonds are strongly influenced by perception of company performance. Research on the content of annual reports to shareholders provides interesting insights into impression management by the leaders of large corporations (Bettman & Weitz, 1983; Staw, McKechnie, and Puffer,1983). Salancik and Meindl (1984) analyzed annual reports for 18 corporations over an 18-year period and found that managers rather consistently credited themselves for positive outcomes and blamed negative outcomes on aspects of the environment. The variability in company performance influenced the pattern of attributions. Companies with highly variable performance took more credit for good performance, but also blamed external conditions less for poor performance, in effect accepting responsibility in order to enhance the illusion of control. These companies also made greater use of symbolic actions such as shuffling executives and restructuring when performance was unfavorable.

The attributional research demonstrates a bias for people to exaggerate the importance of leadership as a cause of organizational performance, but this research fails to show that leaders have no influence on performance. Together with the succession research, the attribution research demonstrates that an accurate conception of leadership importance lies between the two extremes of heroic leader and impotent figurehead. How an organization performs is determined by a variety of external and internal factors. The internal factors include leadership processes at all levels, not just the competence and actions of the CEO. Indeed, Bradford and Cohen (1984) contend that the stereotype of the "heroic leader" undermines effective leadership by a chief executive. The heroic manager is expected to be wiser and more courageous than anyone else in the organization and to know everything that is happening in it. However, these expectations are unrealistic, and leaders are seldom able to live up to them. Shared responsibility for leadership functions and empowerment of subordinates is more effective than heroic leadership, but it is unlikely to occur as long as people expect the leader to take full responsibility for the fate of the organization.

HOW MUCH DO WE KNOW?

The field of leadership is presently in a state of ferment and confusion. Most of the widely known theories are beset with conceptual weaknesses and lack strong empirical support. Several thousand empirical studies have been conducted on leader traits, behavior, power, and situational variables as predictors of leadership effectiveness, but most of the results are contradictory and inconclusive. The confusion in the field is nothing new. As early as 1959, Bennis (1959, p. 259) made the following observation:

> Of all the hazy and confounding areas in social psychology, leadership theory undoubtedly contends for the top nomination. And, ironically, probably more has been written and less known about leadership than about any other topic in the behavioral sciences.

In 1974, after making an extensive review of more than three thousand leadership studies, Stogdill (1974, p. vii) concluded:

> Four decades of research on leadership have produced a bewildering mass of findings. . . . The endless accumulation of empirical data has not produced an integrated understanding of leadership.

Lombardo and McCall (1978, p. 3) made the following observations about the leadership literature:

> . . . the number of unintegrated models, theories, prescriptions, and conceptual schemes of leadership is mind-boggling . . . much of the literature is fragmentary, trivial, unrealistic, or dull . . .

Salancik et al. (1975, p. 81) are even more critical:

> There is perhaps no area of study in organizational behavior which has more blind alleys and less critical knowledge than the area of leadership. Practitioners and researchers alike have groped for years with such questions as: What is leadership? How does it work? How does one become an effective leader? Yet after many years of investigation, it appears we have no ready, useful answers.

Miner (1975, p. 200) concluded that "the concept of leadership has outlived its usefulness," and he suggested a moratorium on traditional leadership research.

The leadership literature currently includes over 5000 studies, and the number continues to increase by several hundred each year. The confused state of the field can be attributed in large part to the sheer volume of publications, the disparity of approaches, the proliferation of confusing terms, the narrow focus of most researchers, the high percentage of irrelevant or trivial studies, and the absence of an integrating conceptual framework. As the old adage goes, it is difficult to see the forest for the trees. A primary objective of this book was to determine what we actually know about leadership. The conclusion reached after carefully reviewing the literature is that we know much more about leadership than is usually recognized.

An Integrating Conceptual Framework

When the sets of variables from different approaches are viewed as part of a larger network of interacting variables, they appear to be interrelated in a meaningful way. Figure 12-1 provides an integrating conceptual framework that encompasses each of the important sets of variables relevant for leadership effectiveness. The model combines less comprehensive models presented in earlier chapters (see Figures 3-1, 7-1, and 8-1). In effect, it is an extension of the model presented in Chapter 7 to include power and traits in addition to leader behavior, intervening variables, situational variables, and end-result variables. The conceptual framework also builds on earlier attempts to catalog the variables essential for understanding leadership effectiveness (Bass, 1981, Barrow, 1977; Halal, 1974; Karmel & Egan, 1976; Melcher, 1977; Van Fleet & Yukl, 1986a).

The model, like the one in Chapter 7, is based on the assumption that organizational effectiveness, in terms of end-result variables, is mediated by the core set of intervening variables. These in turn are determined by a complex interaction among leader traits, power, influence, and situational variables. Leaders can directly influence intervening variables in a variety of ways, and by taking actions to make the situation more favorable, they can indirectly influence the intervening variables. Transformational leaders probably do both. The model recognizes the fact that leadership is only one of many determinants of organizational performance, and the possibility that these other influences may overwhelm the leader's influence. The model allows for reciprocal influence processes; leader behavior is both an independent and dependent variable at the same time. Leader behavior is influenced by a variety of factors, including leader attributes, situational demands and constraints, and information about the intervening variables and end results. In Figure 12-1, the numbers in parentheses indicate the chapters emphasizing each causal linkage.

Unfortunately, few researchers consider all of these variable sets simultaneously. The dominant tendency is to study one or two variable sets and ignore the others. Moreover, researchers usually include only one or two variables within a variable set in the same study. The interface between traits, behavior, and power variables has been the subject of only a limited amount of research (see for example, House, 1988; Podsakoff, 1982). Thus, we have learned something about the different pieces but have little information about the way the pieces fit together. Until more integrative research is conducted, it will not be possible to develop the sketchy conceptual framework into a full-fledged leadership theory. In the meantime, the best way to see how the variables are interrelated is to find points of convergence in results from the different approaches. First, however, the most important findings in each line of research will be reviewed briefly.

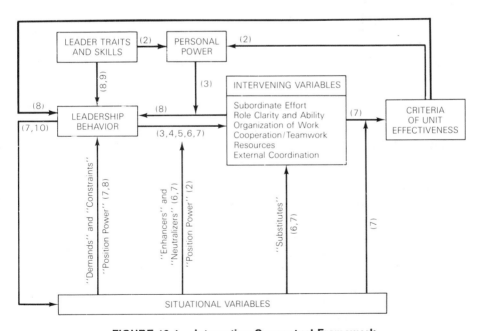

FIGURE 12-1   Integrating Conceptual Framework

OVERVIEW OF FINDINGS
FROM DIFFERENT APPROACHES

Power and Influence

The study of reciprocal influence processes between leader and followers has been an important line of research for learning about emergent leadership and the acquisition of power by leaders. Leaders gain expert power and eventually legitimate power by demonstrating competence in solving problems that are important to the organization. The power acquired by solving important problems is greater for a leader who occupies a central position in the workflow of the organization and has unique abilities that cannot be replaced or routinized. Demonstration of exceptional expertise may result in attributions of charisma by subordinates if the leader implements innovative strategies that involve high risk of personal loss. Referent power is developed during repeated interactions in which the leader provides appropriate benefits and treats subordinates in a fair and considerate manner.

Effective leaders develop referent and expert power to supplement their position power and use it to make nonroutine requests and motivate commitment to tasks that require high effort, initiative, and persistence. The manner in which a leader exercises power largely determines whether it results in enthusiastic commitment, passive compliance, or stubborn resistance. Both position power and personal power are exerted in a subtle, easy fashion that minimizes status differentials and avoids threats to the self-esteem of subordinates. Effective leaders select influence tactics that are appropriate for the situation. The choice of influence tactics varies somewhat with the status of the target person and the objective of the influence attempt. The influence tactics used most often by managers include legitimate requests, exchange of favors, rational persuasion, pressure tactics, ingratiation, consultation, and inspirational appeals. In addition to overt influence attempts, indirect tactics such as intentional role modeling and ecological control may be used to influence subordinates. Leaders also use political tactics such as forming coalitions, co-opting opponents, gaining control over key decisions, and institutionalizing power.

Leaders are better off if they have at least a moderate amount of position power, especially the authority to make necessary changes and dispense tangible rewards and benefits. The capacity to provide satisfactory benefits and facilitate the work of the group depends on the leader's upward and lateral influence in the organization. Upward influence can be viewed as a source of position power, but it is also as a way of bypassing the constraints of formal authority to get things accomplished. Too much position power entails the risk that the leader will be tempted to rely on it and neglect more effective forms of influence for building commitment, such as persuasion, participation, and inspirational appeals.

Traits and Skills

The primary focus of the trait research has been on the implications of leader attributes for leadership effectiveness. Managerial motivation is one of the most promising predictors of effectiveness. Effective leaders in large, hierarchical organizations tend to have a strong need for power, a fairly strong need for achievement, and a somewhat weaker need for affiliation. Related traits include high self-confidence, energy, emotional maturity, stress tolerance, and a favorable attitude toward authority figures. Effective managers are inclined to be pragmatic and result-oriented, and they enjoy persuasive activities requiring initiative and moderate risk taking. The optimal pattern of managerial motivation is somewhat different for entrepreneurs. They tend to have a strong need for achievement and a strong need for independence, and they are less likely to have a favorable attitude toward authority figures. Otherwise, the same trait pattern is probably relevant for entrepreneurial managers as for managers in large organizations.

Skills are another promising predictor of leader effectiveness. Technical skills, conceptual skills, and interpersonal skills are all necessary for most leadership roles. However, the relative importance of the three types of skills varies greatly from situation to situation. In addition, the optimal mix of specific component skills and the nature of the technical expertise required by a leader vary greatly from one type of organization to another. However, some specific skills such as analytical ability, persuasiveness, speaking ability, memory for details, empathy, tact, and charm are probably useful in all leadership positions.

One of the key principles coming out of the trait approach is the idea of balance. In some cases balance means a moderate amount of some trait, such as need for achievement, need for affiliation, self confidence, risk taking, initiative, decisiveness, assertiveness and so forth, rather than either a very small or a very great amount of the trait. In other cases, balance means tempering one trait with another, such as tempering a high need for power with the emotional maturity required to ensure that subordinates are empowered rather than dominated. Sometimes balance must be achieved between competing values (Quinn & Rohrbaugh, 1983). Concern for the task must be balanced against concern for people. Concern for a leader's own needs must be balanced against concern for organizational needs. Concern for the needs of subordinates must be balanced against concern for the needs of peers, superiors, and outsiders. Desire for change must be balanced against need for continuity and predictability.

Effective leaders are people able to achieve an appropriate balance in these inevitable role conflicts.

Leadership Behavior

One line of behavior research has been concerned with discovering the nature of managerial work. The typical pattern of managerial activity reflects the dilemmas faced by most managers. Relevant information exists only in the heads of people who are widely scattered within and outside of the organization. Managers need to make decisions based on information that is both incomplete and overwhelming and to get cooperation from many people over whom they have no formal authority. The descriptive research shows that managerial work is inherently hectic, varied, fragmented, reactive, and disorderly. Many activities involve brief oral interactions that provide an opportunity to obtain relevant, up-to-date information, discover problems, and influence people to implement plans. Many interactions involve people besides subordinates, such as lateral peers, superiors, and outsiders.

Decision processes are highly political, and most planning is informal and adaptive to changing conditions. Effective managers develop a mental agenda of short- and long-term objectives and strategies. The network of relationships inside and outside of the manager's unit is used to implement plans and strategies. For plans that affect the distribution of power and resources or involve significant innovations, it is necessary for the manager to forge a coalition of supporters and sponsors, which may involve expanding the network of contacts and allies. Effective managers are able to recognize relationships among the streams of problems, issues, and opportunities they encounter. By relating problems to each other and to informal objectives, a manager is more likely to recognize opportunities to solve more than one problem at the same time.

Another line of behavior research has attempted to identify differences in behavior between effective and ineffective leaders. Progress has been impeded by difficulties in the conceptualization and measurement of leadership behavior. Confusion has been created by a proliferation of behavior constructs and competing taxonomies. There has been little agreement about what categories of behavior are meaningful, except at the most abstract level of conceptualization, where the relevance of task-oriented and relationship-oriented behavior is widely recognized. Hundreds of empirical studies have examined the implications of task-oriented behavior and relationship-oriented behavior for leader effectiveness, usually measured in terms of subordinate satisfaction and performance. The results of these studies have been contradictory and inconclusive except for the generally positive effect of considerate-supportive behavior on subordinate satisfaction.

Results from other types of research including critical incident studies and observational studies reveal important underlying relationships that are masked by the deficiencies of the questionnaire-correlational studies. Effective leaders show concern for both task and relationships, but these concerns are reflected in the pattern of specific day-to-day actions of the leader. The behavior pattern of effective leaders also reveals a concern both for internal relations with subordinates and external relations with peers, superiors, and outsiders.

Further progress in the behavior research requires a shift in focus to more specific aspects of behavior. A promising taxonomy that is capable of integrating most earlier behavior research differentiates between three aspects of decision making (consulting-delegating, planning, problem solving), three aspects of information exchanging (monitoring, informing, clarifying), two aspects of influencing behavior (motivating, recognizing/rewarding), and three aspects of relationship-building behavior (supporting, networking, and managing conflict/team building). The behavior categories are generic ones applicable to all types of leaders and organizations, and they may occur in interactions with subordinates, peers, superiors, or outsiders. Of course, the specific form of the behavior varies from context to context. Some of the behaviors are more concerned with accomplishing task objectives and some are more concerned with maintaining relationships, but both concerns are balanced in the pattern of specific actions used by an effective leader to enact the behaviors. All 11 behaviors are relevant for leadership effectiveness, but their relative importance varies across situations.

In the context of leading problem-solving groups, effective leaders once again show concern both for task objectives and relationships. Leadership functions that are primarily task-oriented include structuring activities, stimulating communication, clarifying communication, summarizing, and consensus testing. Leadership functions primarily concerned with maintaining relationships include gatekeeping, harmonizing, supporting, standard setting, and process analyzing. Each function requires skill and a proper sense of timing to be effective.

Situational Approaches

One type of situational theory describes the situational determinants of managerial behavior. Leaders adapt their behavior to role requirements, constraints, and demands of the leadership situation, and they seek to exploit opportunities and expand the range of choices. The role expectations from superiors, peers, and subordinates are a major influence on a leader's behavior. Effective leaders are able to reconcile the role conflicts caused by incompatible role expectations from different role senders, and they take advantage of role ambiguity as an opportunity for discretionary action. The pattern of interactions and how much time is spent with subordinates, peers, superiors, and outsiders depends on the nature of the work, and whether it is self-generating or reactive, repetitive or variable, uncertain or predictable, fragmented or sustained, hurried or unhurried. The work pattern is affected by attributes of the managerial position such as level of authority in the organization, size of work unit, function of work unit, technology and task characteristics, lateral interdependence, and existence of a hostile or unstable environment that causes frequent crises. Despite the situational demands and pressures, managers have choices in what aspects of the job to emphasize, how to allocate time, and with whom to interact. Effective managers seek to understand the demands and constraints and work to expand their choices, exploit opportunities, and shape the impressions formed by others about their competence and expertise.

A second line of situational theories and research examines how aspects of the situation moderate the relationship between leader behavior (or traits) and outcomes. Despite a great deal of research effort, these theories have done little to advance our understanding of managerial effectiveness. Even with respect to the broad categories of task-oriented and relations-oriented behavior, there has been a continuing controversy for more than two decades between universalistic and situational theories of leadership effectiveness. A way to resolve this controversy can be found if theorists recognize that leadership behavior can be described at different levels of abstraction, and that behavior categories are merely abstractions based on complex, multidimensional behavior incidents. Rather than being incompatible, both theories are correct when they are stated in terms of appropriate behavior constructs. The appropriate universal hypothesis is that effective leaders act in ways reflecting a concern for both task and relationships in each specific situation. The appropriate situational hypothesis is that aspects of the situation determine which specific leader behaviors are more likely to result in achievement of task objectives and maintenance of effective relationships. Further progress in developing situational theories requires use of behavior categories that are narrower and more concrete than task-oriented and relationship-oriented behavior.

The leadership model presented in Chapter 7 was developed to help advance theory and research on effective leadership behavior in different situations. The model incorporates the best features of earlier situational theories, but it also includes variables not included in these theories. The model begins with the assumption that work unit performance depends primarily on six unit characteristics: member effort, member ability, organization of the work, teamwork and cooperation, procurement of essential resources, and external coordination with other parts of the organization. The relative importance of these six factors varies from situation to situation. Leaders can influence these intervening variables in a number of ways. In the short term, most leader actions are intended to correct deficiencies in the intervening variables, whereas in the longer term, leaders seek to make the situation more favorable by actions such as implementing improvement programs, initiating new or activities or products, forming coalitions to gain more control over resources, modifying the formal structure, and changing the culture of the organizational unit. The short-term actions are intended to raise the intervening variables up to their short-term maximum levels, whereas the longer-term actions are intended to raise this "ceiling" to higher levels.

POINTS OF CONVERGENCE AMONG APPROACHES

Studies on leader power, behavior, traits, and situation have generated a number of convergent results. That is, the findings from different lines of research are consistent and mutually supportive. Several interesting points of convergence are examined in this section. The points are organized according to the four general categories of managerial behavior identified earlier, namely, maintaining effective relationships, gathering and using information, making decisions, and influencing people.

Leader-Subordinate Relations

Effective leaders establish cooperative relationships with subordinates, characterized by high levels of mutual trust and loyalty. The power research indicated the importance of referent power as a source of influence over the effort and commitment of subordinates. Referent power is developed gradually over time as a result of dyadic social exchange processes in which the leader demonstrates trust and provides benefits to a subordinate, while avoiding forms of influence that cause resentment. Referent power is stronger for leaders who are attributed to be charismatic.

The behavior research found that the strongest determinant of subordinate satisfaction with the leader is considerate-supportive behavior. Favorable leader-subordinate relations are much more likely for leaders who act friendly, open, sympathetic, and helpful toward subordinates, treat them fairly, show respect, demonstrate concern for their needs and feelings, and do things to advance their careers. Consideration does not necessarily imply that the leader has an intimate relationship with subordinates; it is possible to be supportive and still maintain some social distance if the leader chooses to do so. Relationships with subordinates also depend on other aspects of leader behavior such as providing recognition and equitable rewards, representing subordinate interests in relations with people outside of the work unit, and allowing participation in making decisions when appropriate.

The situational research showed that the effect of leader behavior depends in part on the needs and values of subordinates and the type of role expectations they have for the leader. The effect of supportive behavior on subordinate satisfaction is likely to be stronger when the subordinate has a stressful, difficult task and lacks self-confidence and experience in doing it. In this type of situation, subordinates need and appreciate more encouragement and support from the leader and/or coworkers. If a subordinate is performing poorly, the leader's reaction will be influenced by attributions about the cause of the poor performance. Less sympathy and support are likely for a subordinate perceived to be indifferent about the work than for one who is perceived to be highly motivated but lacking skill or having bad luck. The situation also determines the importance of leader-subordinate relations. Labor-intensive work involving highly skilled subordinates who are difficult to replace due to a tight labor market or the uniqueness of their skills increases leader dependence on subordinates and makes relations with them all the more important.

Several of the traits and skills predictive of leadership effectiveness appear important for developing favorable relationships with subordinates. Relevant interpersonal skills include tact and diplomacy, empathy for peoples' needs and feelings, listening skills, social sensitivity, and counseling skills. Personal charm, presence, and dramatic ability are relevant for charismatic influence, which is another source of subordinate identification with the leader. A narcissistic leader with a strong, personalized power concern is not likely to develop a relationship of mutual trust and respect with subordinates. However, some narcissistic leaders are able to establish a close working relationship with select subordinates based on exchange of status and rewards in return for subordinate adulation and unquestioning loyalty.

Relationship with Peers and Superiors

The importance of good relationships with subordinates is mirrored by the importance of lateral and upward relationships. Research on downward and upward power indicates that the two are related. Without sufficient upward power to obtain necessary resources, protect subordinate interests, and gain approval for necessary changes, a leader is unlikely to develop a favorable exchange relationship with subordinates. A leader without the "clout" to represent his or her unit effectively in competition with other organizational units for scarce resources will lose status and influence with subordinates. Although not as important as upward influence, lateral influence determines the amount of cooperation and support a leader can obtain from other units and the extent to which a leader can buffer subordinates from disruptive changes and unreasonable demands. The amount of upward and lateral power possessed by a unit depends in part on its centrality in the workflow of the organization and the extent to which the unit performs a vital function that cannot be easily replaced or routinized. The leader's power derives in part from unit power and in part from the individual's demonstrated expertise in solving important problems and facilitating the work of the unit. Expert and referent power and political tactics such as coalitions are especially important in lateral relations, since managers seldom have direct authority over peers whose cooperation is needed to get the work done.

Research on managerial activities shows a high incidence of interaction with peers, superiors, and outsiders. Much of the managerial behavior in these external interactions involves monitoring of events in the organization and its environment, network building and maintenance, and the leader's role as representative of the organizational unit. Behaviors involving maintenance of relationships include networking, supporting, and harmonizing. Networks of contacts are established and maintained through meetings, visits, telephone calls, and correspondence. The essence of these activities includes keeping in touch, doing favors, joining groups and professional allocations, attending meetings and ceremonial events, socializing before and after meetings, going out to lunch, playing golf or racquetball, entertaining visitors, and so forth. Supporting behavior strengthens mutual trust and friendship in a leader's other relationships, just as it does in relationships with subordinates. The management of conflict between a leader and other people is especially important in relationships with peers and superiors. Some conflicts are due to misunderstandings, role ambiguity, and communication breakdowns, and these conflicts are less likely if a leader makes extensive use of information exchange and consultative decision making. Effective managers are careful to consult with appropriate people and keep them informed about discretionary actions and changes in plans in order to avoid misunderstandings and embarrassing "surprises."

Several traits and skills predictive of managerial success are especially relevant for relations with peers, superiors, and outsiders. Need for affiliation and positive regard for others increase the likelihood that a leader will seek to develop friendly relationships with people. As in the case of relationships with subordinates, interpersonal skills such as tact, diplomacy, social insight, empathy, and charm aid managers in developing effective working relationships outside of their organizational unit. Relations with superiors are likely to be better if a leader has a positive attitude toward authority figures. Leaders who have a personalized power concern or who are preoccupied with personal ambition invariably do things that jeopardize relationships with people. For example, they may use others as scapegoats to protect their own reputation; they may betray a trust or renege on a promise in order to increase their personal gain.

The relative importance of relationships with peers, superiors, outsiders, and subordinates depends on aspect of the situation, such as the work pattern and dependencies involving the different parties. High lateral interdependence with other work units in the organization increases the importance for middle managers of lateral relations with peers. The upward dependence of middle managers is increased by high centralization of authority in top management. For top managers and some middle- and lower-level managers, high dependence on a small number of external parties such as clients, suppliers, and government regulators increases the importance of interactions with these outsiders. Situational factors also affect the difficulty of developing and maintaining effective relationships with people outside of the work unit. A close, working relationship is more difficult to maintain with people who are located in widely dispersed facilities, such as plants or offices in a different part of the country, or overseas, especially when communication media are primitive and unreliable.

Importance of Information Processes

The power research indicates that control over important information is a major source of downward, lateral, and upward power in organizations. Control over technical information and knowledge of procedures for solving problems enhances a person's expert power. Control over information about the performance of the organization allows a leader to exaggerate the success of initiatives and cover up mistakes, thereby enhancing and protecting a reputation of expertise. Control over information about events and developments outside of the organization makes other members of the organization more dependent on the leader to interpret events and define reality in a meaningful way, thereby increasing the leader's influence over strategic decisions.

The behavior research indicates that a large part of managerial activity involves gathering, analyzing, and disseminating information. Effective managers develop and maintain a large network of information sources inside and outside of the organization. Since relevant, timely information often exists only in the heads of people, many of a manager's activities involve face-to-face interactions and oral communication. Interaction with people in a manager's network also provides information about the role expectations others hold for the manager. Behavior categories that emphasize information exchange include monitoring, informing, and clarifying. Monitoring includes gathering information about the operations of their work unit and scanning events in the external environment to detect problems, threats, and opportunities, to evaluate progress in implementing plans and strategies, and to evaluate the performance of the work unit and of individual subordinates. Informing behavior involves the manager's role as a "linking pin" or "nerve center" to mediate information flows among subordinates and between subordinates and people outside of the manager's organizational unit. Managers are an important source of technical information necessary to facilitate the work of subordinates. Effective managers keep subordinates informed about relevant changes in plans, policies, and strategies. Clarifying involves communication of role expectations to others, especially subordinates. Effective managers communicate clear expectations about task objectives and standards for evaluating results. In decision groups, many of the key leadership functions involve facilitating information exchange among members of the group during problem solving.

Information about the nature of the external environment is essential for formulating plans, strategies, and a captivating vision of the organization's proper mission. The more dynamic and turbulent the environment, the more important it is for a leader to monitor and interpret events for other members of the organization. Opportunity for greater power is provided by a dynamic, hostile environment if the leader has the expertise and information needed to develop innovative strategies to help the organization adapt and prosper. However, this situation also offers contenders more opportunity to remove a leader who appears uninformed and incompetent in the face of a growing crisis.

Various traits and skills found to be predictive of leader effectiveness are relevant for the information handling activities of managers. Several cognitive skills such as deductive and inductive reasoning are especially relevant for analyzing information, detecting patterns and trends, differentiating between relevant and irrelevant information, and developing concepts or models to help convey the meaning to others. Cognitive and technical skills are also relevant for group leadership functions such as clarifying meaning and summarizing. Oral presentation skills such as verbal fluency, knowledge of technical language, and ability to use visual aids are relevant for communicating information to subordinates, peers, and superiors. Proactivity and belief in internal locus of control are probably associated with more information gathering activity by a leader. Leaders with high need for achievement are probably more attuned to task information and performance feedback. Leaders with a personalized power orientation are more likely to control the dissemination of information and use information distortion as tactics to manipulate people. The unrealistically high self confidence of paranoid narcissistic leaders tends to make them indifferent about scanning the environment and unreceptive to unfavorable feedback.

Importance of Managerial Decision Making

In the power-influence research, decision making is viewed as both a source and object of power. People who effectively solve problems or develop successful strategies gain in status and power as a result, especially if the solutions are innovative. Attributions of charisma are likely in a crisis situation where the leader confidently proposes unorthodox strategies or takes untraditional actions involving personal risk to himself or herself. The reputation for expertise gained from successful decisions made in the past gives a person greater influence over current decisions of the same type. When individuals or coalitions seek to influence decisions to benefit themselves, the decisions become an object of power rather than a source of it. Current power is often used to protect or enhance future power, by employing a variety of political tactics to influence important decisions involving strategic plans, allocation of scarce resources, membership on key committees, selection of the CEO, control of assets, division of responsibilities, and scope of authority.

Much of the activity of managers involves decision making, but managers are seldom observed to make important decisions as a discrete action at a single point in time, except for those involving a manager's response to immediate crises and disruptions. Much of a manager's planning involves informal agendas that exist in the manager's head rather than in a written planning document. Organizational decision processes are highly political, and important decisions typically require the endorsement and authorization of many different people at different levels of management and in different subunits of the organization. These decisions may drag on for months or years as the decision is sidetracked or cycled back for revisions needed to gain the support of key stakeholders.

Decision processes are usually characterized more by confusion, disorder, and emotionality than by rationality. Information is often distorted or suppressed, wishful thinking is common, and search for solutions is unnecessarily limited. Problems in making individual decisions are compounded when decisions are made by a group. The effectiveness of a group in making decisions depends to a considerable extent on whether essential leadership functions are carried out and whether the group is able to avoid common process problems such as incomplete participation, hasty decisions, groupthink, and polarization.

Situational theories and research on group decision making suggest the conditions under which participation is most likely to be beneficial. Participation results in better decisions when the participants have relevant information and ideas lacked by the leader, when they are willing to cooperate in finding a good solution, and when there is ample time for the participative process to be carried out properly. Acceptance of the decision and commitment to implement it is more likely when participants are in initial agreement about objectives and priorities, and when participants perceive that the decision process allowed them ample opportunity to present their ideas and influence the outcome. Consultation is more important for innovations and major changes in policies and strategies than for routine decisions.

Several of the traits and skills predictive of leadership effectiveness are relevant for decision making. Managers with extensive technical knowledge and cognitive skills are more likely to make high-quality decisions. These skills are important for analyzing problems, identifying causal patterns and trends, and forecasting likely outcomes of different strategies for attaining objectives. Managers high in proactivity and efficiency orientation are more likely to take the initiative in discovering problems and acting decisively to solve them. Managers with strong achievement motivation are willing to assume responsibility for solving task-related problems, and they prefer solutions that involve moderate levels of risk. In contrast, less effective managers are more likely to make decisions that are either too risky or too conservative. Self-confidence, tolerance of ambiguity, and stress tolerance help managers cope with the heavy responsibility for making momentous decisions on the basis of incomplete information. Managers with high regard for others and optimistic assumptions about human nature are more likely to use participation than managers who hold negative stereotypes of human nature or who are obsessed with protecting their own status and power. A variety of cognitive and interpersonal skills are relevant for leader effectiveness in conducting meetings of problem solving groups.

Importance of Motivating and Influencing

The research on power showed that some forms of power are more likely than others to result in commitment rather than compliance or resistance. Skillful use of legitimate power, reward power, or coercive power is likely to result in compliance but only rarely results in commitment. Commitment is more likely for influence attempts based on expert and referent power, but the outcome could be compliance or even resistance if the timing and execution of the influence attempt is handled poorly. Power-sharing tactics such as consultation are likely to result in commitment if the target persons share the leader's objectives and perceive the participative process to be legitimate. Effective leaders develop and use a variety of power bases, including the occasional use of coercion when necessary. Indirect forms of influence such as ecological control and the design of reward systems are used also to shape the behavior of subordinates and reinforce desired behavior.

Much of the activity of managers involves attempts to influence the attitudes and behavior of people, including subordinates, peers, superiors, and outsiders. Managers act as the representative of their organizational unit, promoting and defending the unit's interests and obtaining necessary information, resources, support, and cooperation. Managers organize coalitions of supporters to gain approval for a major innovation or to implement a program or policy that requires the cooperation of people outside of the manager's work unit. Major types of influence behavior include motivating and recognizing/rewarding. Motivating behavior includes a variety of social influence techniques for developing commitment to organizational objectives and compliance with requests and orders. Much of the influence behavior of charismatic leaders falls into the motivating category, including inspiring commitment to new objectives and strategies, modeling exemplary behavior for followers to imitate, activating needs for achievement and power, and appealing to values such as "serving justice," "being the best," "doing a noble deed," or serving God and country." Recognition and rewards are used by managers to reinforce desirable behavior and increase the likelihood that it will be repeated.

Situational factors determine the importance of leader efforts to motivate subordinates. Leader influence on subordinate motivation is most critical when the task is not intrinsically motivating, such as a tedious task that leaves subordinates bored and apathetic, a very difficult task that frustrates and discourages subordinates, or a dangerous task that makes them fearful. In these situations, subordinate performance will suffer unless the leader intervenes to arouse enthusiasm and confidence. The amount of position power a leader possesses depends on aspects of the situation such as amount of formal authority, control over distribution of rewards and punishments, control over information, and access to important people. Aspects of the situation also determine which forms of influence are most likely to be effective for a given purpose. The situational factors include subordinate education and professionalism, cultural values regarding obedience to authority figures and submission to the collective will, organizational norms regarding participation in decision making, and legal or policy constraints on improper use of power.

Some of the traits and skills that are predictive of leader effectiveness are relevant to the use of power. Leaders with high self-confidence, need for power, and relevant expertise make more influence attempts. These three attributes, together with persuasive ability and political insight, facilitate the effectiveness of influence attempts. Leaders whose need for power is combined with a high need for achievement are more likely to use their influence to accomplish task objectives. Leaders with a personalized power orientation and/or an extreme narcissistic personality exercise power in a manipulative, impulsive, domineering manner intended to aggrandize themselves and foster personal loyalty from subordinates. In contrast, leaders with a socialized power orientation use their influence to build commitment to idealized goals, and they seek to empower subordinates by using more consultation, delegation, and development of subordinate skills and confidence.

IMPLICATIONS
FOR IMPROVING LEADERSHIP

The knowledge gained from extensive research on leadership effectiveness has important implications for improving managerial leadership. There are three general approaches for improving leadership: (1) selection and placement, (2) training and development, (3) situational engineering. It is beyond the scope of this book to review these approaches in detail, but a brief description is provided.

Selection and Placement

When there is a vacant leadership position in an organization, the need to find someone to fill this position provides an opportunity to influence the quality of leadership in the organization. The objective is to find a close match between position requirements and manager attributes. Aspects of the situation to be considered in determining what type of person is needed are discussed in Chapter 8. Various types of job analysis procedures are sometimes useful for identifying the duties and responsibilities required in a managerial position. The position description questionnaires described in Chapter 4 provide this type of information. Additional clues about the type of managerial behaviors important for a particular administrative position can be found in Chapter 7. Required skills and traits can be inferred from the role requirements and critical behaviors identified in the job analysis, although the process is still quite subjective and inexact. Chapter 9 describes traits and skills likely to be relevant. For selection of executives who manage a strategic business unit, the strategy of the unit should be considered in addition to other position requirements. The matching of managers to strategies has been a topic of growing interest in recent years (Gersein & Reisman, 1983; Gupta & Govindarajan, 1984; Leontiades, 1982; Szilagyi & Schweiger, 1984).

Candidates for a management position are assessed on the key skills and traits needed to do the job. The process is easier for internal candidates, since ratings of traits and skills can be obtained from superiors, peers, and even subordinates. Assessment for both internal and external candidates may involve written tests, interviews, situational tests, and recommendations. Assessment centers like those described in Chapter 9 have been quite effective for identifying persons with high potential, but they have been used mostly for selecting lower-level managers. Rather than directly assessing candidate skills and traits, an alternative approach is to evaluate the match between the requirements of the vacant position and each candidate's prior experience. The objective here is to select someone with a demonstrated record of effective performance (e.g., based on ratings and recommendations) in earlier positions requiring the same types of skills and behavior.

Selection decisions for executive positions are likely to involve organizational politics, and sometimes the politics undermine any efforts to objectively evaluate qualifications of candidates. For example, a dominant coalition may seek to install one of its own people in the top leadership position, even if other candidates are more qualified. If external candidates are considered, the selection process may be biased toward candidates who do not appear to threaten the power and status of current executives and directors.

Training and Development

Training is the most widely used approach for improving leadership. Most large companies have management development programs of one kind or another, and many organizations send their managers to outside seminars and workshops. Technical skills are learned by training methods such as technical books, procedural manuals, videotaped demonstrations, slide-audio programs, equipment simulators, and computer tutorial programs. Coaching and instruction from the boss or a coworker is another way technical skills are learned (Wexley & Latham, 1981).

Conceptual skills are more difficult to acquire through short-term training. Some specialized training methods for conceptual skills include cases, business games, simulations, and problem-solving exercises. Texts, films, and videotapes are used to present procedures for problem analysis, forecasting, planning, solution generation, and solution evaluation. Creativity can be enhanced by specialized training, such as instruction in how to use the idea generation techniques described in Chapter 11.

Interpersonal skills are also difficult to acquire. More than just a lecture or textbook description is needed to increase human relations skills such as social sensitivity, charm, tact, persuasiveness, and the ability to provide praise and criticism, handle conflict, negotiate agreements, and enhance group cohesiveness. Films and videotapes are used to demonstrate effective and ineffective behavior involving interpersonal skills. Cases and short incidents are used to stimulate discussion about appropriate and inappropriate behavior in sensitive situations such as dealing with a problem subordinate, conducting a performance appraisal, or resolving a conflict between subordinates. The most effective methods involve opportunities to practice skills and obtain feedback about what is done well and what is not. Role-play exercises can be very useful if they are properly designed and feedback from observers and other participants is provided during or after the role play (e.g., Lawshe, Bolda, & Brune, 1959; Wexley & Nemeroff, 1975). A modern variation is to videotape the role play and have the trainee observe and analyze his or her own behavior. Role-modeling training is a procedure that combines several of these features. After viewing a videotape or film demonstrating effective behavior, trainees practice doing it themselves in the context of a role play, then receive reinforcement and coaching from the trainer and other trainees. A number of training experiments have demonstrated the effectiveness of role modeling training for managers (e.g. Burnaska, 1976; Goldstein & Sorcher, 1974; Latham & Saari, 1979; Porras & Anderson, 1981; Smith, 1976). In each of these experiments, a trained group was compared to a control group without training (or with a "placebo" treatment), and interpersonal skills were measured before and after training.

Occasionally studies have been conducted to evaluate training programs designed to increase managerial motivation rather than skills. An example is the managerial motivation workshop developed by Miner (1988). In one study of research and development managers, the managers who were trained had stronger managerial motivation and advanced to higher positions of authority than a comparison group of untrained managers (Miner, 1965).

An alternative for skill training is a feedback intervention in which managers receive information about their behavior from questionnaires filled out by subordinates or peers. The intervention is most likely to be effective if managers actively set goals to improve aspects of behavior for which deficiencies have been revealed, and monitor themselves afterward as they implement their improvement plans back on the job. An example of this type of developmental intervention is provided in a study by Nemeroff and Cosentino (1979). Insurance office managers received feedback from subordinates about their behavior during an earlier performance appraisal meeting. In comparison to the control group, managers who received feedback and set improvement goals demonstrated more favorable behavior in subsequent performance appraisal meetings with subordinates. Another example of a feedback intervention is a developmental workshop based on the management behaviors described in Chapter 7 (see Yukl & Lepsinger, 1989).

Some organizations track the managerial skills of lower-level managers and develop these skills to ensure that a pool of qualified candidates exists to fill higher-level positions when they become vacant. Sophisticated human resource planning systems have been developed to facilitate this process. A variety of developmental experiences can be used, including rotation among managerial jobs in different functional subunits of the organization, special projects requiring new skills, understudy assignments, junior boards, formal mentors, and career counseling sessions. More detailed descriptions of these developmental procedures can be found in specialized articles and books on management development (e.g., Broderick, 1983; Hunt & Michael, 1983; Klauss, 1981; Kram, 1985; Wexley & Latham, 1981).

Much of the management development in organizations is conducted informally by individual managers working with their subordinates. Managers are more likely to learn relevant leadership skills and values if they are are exposed to a variety of developmental experiences on the job, with appropriate coaching and mentoring by superiors and peers. Some characteristics of experiential learning found to be predictive of later success for managers include diverse experiences that require adaptation to new situations, assignments that broaden a person's perspective, challenges that the manager must face alone, and opportunities to make mistakes and learn to handle failure (Davies & Easterby-Smith, 1984; McCauley, 1986). Managers also learn appropriate values and behaviors from superiors who provide positive role models for them to emulate (Manz & Sims, 1981). Developing subordinates is a major responsibility of most managerial positions, but it seldom receives the attention it deserves from managers preoccupied with immediate problems and crises.

Situational Engineering

The third approach for improving leadership in organizations is situational engineering. Instead of trying to select or train leaders to fit the existing job requirements, the situation is changed to make it more compatible with the leader. This type of "situational engineering" was discussed briefly in Chapter 9. Aspects of the situation that help to determine role requirements for managers were described in Chapter 7 and 8. The design of organization structure is influenced by a variety of factors, including technology, politics, and historical events. Explicit consideration of the match between structure and managerial attributes rarely occurs in high-level strategic planning. Situational engineering, when it occurs, is more likely to involve an individual manager who modifies some aspects of a subordinate manager's job. Typical examples include an increase or decrease in position responsibilities, a change in reporting relationships, delegation of more authority, modification of information systems, modification of the appraisal process, and modification of the formal planning process.

A variation of situational engineering is the "leader match" training program developed by Fiedler and his associates (Fiedler & Chemers, 1982). A programmed text shows leaders how to modify their own situations to make them compatible with their motive hierarchy, as specified by Fiedler's contingency model (see Chapter 9). A number of studies found that the training improved leader performance, but the research did not determine how much situational engineering actually occurred or whether any changes were consistent with the model (Csoka & Bons, 1978; Fiedler & Mahar, 1979). A study by Burke and Day (1986) found change consistent with the model for managers trained with leader match, but the managers did not differ in performance from the untrained control group.

SUMMARY

Critics bemoan the absence of strong and consistent findings in the literature on leadership effectiveness. They argue that if leaders really make a difference, their influence should be detected, even with weak measures. Succession studies on effects of changing the leadership of organizations are cited as one form of evidence that leaders have little impact on organizational performance. However, critics have cited inappropriate statistics in making this argument. When artifacts are eliminated, the succession studies actually demonstrate a moderately strong influence of leaders on organizational performance.

Attacks on leadership theory from another quarter are made by critics who argue that leadership is merely a simplistic explanation for complex events that we are unable to understand. These critics cite findings from attribution research that show people are biased toward exaggerating the importance of individual leaders and de-emphasizing other explanations such as industry performance, the state of the general economy, and systems dynamics of the organization. Here again, the research demonstrates that leaders have less influence over organizational events than is often assumed, but it does not support the conclusion that leadership is unimportant or that leaders are unnecessary.

Confusion and contradictions in the literature appear to be due in part to narrow research, lack of integrating conceptual frameworks, and a high percentage of seriously flawed studies. The selective, critical review of research and theory made in this book supports the conclusion that we know much more about leadership effectiveness than is commonly realized. Nevertheless, much yet remains to be learned. The development of the field has been slower than would be expected from the large volume of publications and the immense amount of effort expended to study leadership and managerial effectiveness. The last decade has witnessed an increase in the variety of research questions and research methods, and the field appears to be undergoing an accelerating pace of discovery. With such a vital subject as this one, it is imperative that we continue to upgrade the quality of leadership research. With dedicated effort, and researchers who value discovery of useful knowledge more than publishing trivial studies, there are good prospects for rapid progress in the coming years.

REVIEW AND DISCUSSION QUESTIONS

1. Briefly summarize major findings in research on leadership succession.

2. Briefly summarize major findings in research on attributions about leadership as a determinant of organizational effectiveness.

3. How important is top-level leadership in organizations? Defend your position.

4. How important is leadership by managers at middle and lower levels in large organizations? Defend your position.

5. Briefly summarize major findings in trait research, power-influence research, behavior research, and situational research.

6. What are major points of convergence among the different approaches? Can you find some additional points of convergence not mentioned in the chapter?

7. Briefly describe the selection, development, and situational engineering approaches for improving leadership in organizations.

8. What are some major gaps in our knowledge about leadership?

9. What types of future research would contribute the most to our understanding of leadership effectiveness?

REFERENCES

ALDAG, R. J., & BRIEF, A. P. (1979). *Task design and employee motivation.* Glenview, IL: Scott, Foresman.

ALLAN, P. (1981). Managers at work: A large-scale study of the managerial job in New York City government. *Academy of Management Journal, 24,* 613–619.

ALLPORT, G. W., VERNON, P. E., & LINDZEY, G. (1960). *A study of values* (3 ed). Boston: Houghton Mifflin.

ANDERSON, B., & NILSSON, S. (1964). Studies in the reliability and validity of the critical incident technique. *Journal of Applied Psychology, 48,* 398–413.

ANTHONY, W. P. (1978). *Participative management.* Reading, MA: Addison-Wesley.

ARGYRIS, C. (1964). *Integrating the individual and the organization.* New York: Wiley.

ARVEY, R. D., & IVANCEVICH, J. M. (1980). Punishment in organizations: A review, propositions, and research suggestions. *Academy of Management Review, 5,* 123–132.

ASHOUR, A. S. (1973). The contingency model of leadership effectiveness: An evaluation. *Organizational Behavior and Human Performance, 9,* 339–355.

ASHOUR, A. S., & ENGLAND, G. (1972). Subordinates' assigned level of discretion as a function of leader's personality and situational variables. *Journal of Applied Psychology, 56,* 120–123.

BACHMAN, J. G., SMITH, C. G., & SLESINGER, J. A. (1966). Control, performance, and satisfaction: An analysis of structural and individual effects. *Journal of Personality and Social Psychology, 4,* 127–136.

BALES, R. F. (1950). A set of categories for the analysis of small group interaction. *American Sociological Review, 15,* 257–263.

BANKHART, C. P., & LANZETTA, J. (1970). Performance and motivation as variables affecting the administration of rewards and punishments. *Representational Research in Social Psychology, 1,* 1–10.

BARNARD, C. I. (1952). A definition of authority. In R. K. Merton, A. P. Gray, B. Hockey, and H. C. Selven (Eds.), *Reader in bureaucracy.* New York: Free Press.

BARROW, J. C. (1976). Worker performance and task complexity as causal determinants of leader behavior style and flexibility. *Journal of Applied Psychology, 61,* 433–440.

BARROW, J. C. (1977). The variables of leadership: A review and conceptual framework. *Academy of Management Review, 2,* 231–251.

BASS, B. M. (1970). When planning for others. *Journal of Applied Behavioral Science, 6,* 151–171.

BASS, B. M. (1976). A systems survey research feedback for management and organizational development. *Journal of Applied Behavioral Science, 12,* 215–229.

BASS, B. M. (1981). *Handbook of leadership: A survey of theory and research.* New York: Free Press.

BASS, B. M. (1985). *Leadership and performance beyond expectations.* New York: Free Press.

BASS, B. M., AVOLIO, B. J., & GOODHEIM, L. (1987). Biography and the assessment of transformational leadership at the world class level. *Journal of Management, 13,* 7–20.

BASS, B. M., VALENZI, E. R., FARROW, D. L., & SOLOMAN, R. J. (1975). Management styles associated with organizational, task, personal, and interpersonal contingencies. *Journal of Applied Psychology, 60,* 720–729.

BASS, B. M., WALDMAN, D. A., AVOLIO, B. J., & BEBB, M. (1987). Transformational leadership and the falling dominoes effect. *Group and Organization Studies, 12,* 73–87.

BAUER, R. (1968). The study of policy formation: An introduction. In R. Bauer and K. Gergen (Eds.), *The study of policy formation.* New York: Free Press.

BEHLING, D., & STARKE, F. A. (1973). The postulates of expectancy theory. *Academy of Management Journal, 16,* 373–388.

BENNE, K. D., & SHEATS, P. (1948). Functional roles of group members. *Journal of Social Issues, 2,* 42–47.

BENNIS, W. G. (1959). Leadership theory and administrative behavior: The problem of authority. *Administrative Science Quarterly, 4,* 259–260.

BENNIS, W. G. (1984). The four competencies of leadership. *Training and Development Journal, 38* (8), 14–19.

BENNIS, W. G., & NANUS, B. (1985). *Leaders: The strategies for taking charge.* New York: Harper & Row.

BENTZ, V. J. (1967). The Sears experience in the investigation, description, and prediction of executive behavior. In F. R. Wickert and D. E. McFarland (Eds.), *Measuring executive effectiveness.* New York: Appleton-Century-Crofts.

BERGER, P. L. (1963). Charisma and religious innovation: The social location of Israelite prophecy. *American Sociological Review, 28,* 940–949.

BERGER, J., COHEN, B. P., & ZELDITCH, M. (1972). Status characteristics and social interaction. *American Sociological Review, 37,* 241–255.

BERKOWITZ, L. (1953). Sharing leadership in small decision-making groups. *Journal of Abnormal and Social Psychology, 48*, 231–238.

BERLEW, D. E. (1974). Leadership and organizational excitement. In D. A. Kolb, I. M. Rubin, and J. M. McIntyre (Eds.), *Organizational psychology: A book of readings.* Englewood Cliffs, NJ: Prentice Hall.

BERMAN, F. E., & MINER, J. B. (1985). Motivation to manage at the top executive level: A test of the hierarchic role-motivation theory. *Personnel Psychology, 38*, 377–391.

BETTMAN, J. R., & WEITZ, B. A. (1983). Attributions in the board room: Causal reasoning in corporate annual reports. *Administrative Science Quarterly, 28*, 165–183.

BIGGART, N. W., & HAMILTON, G. G. (1984). The power of obedience. *Administrative Science Quarterly, 29*, 540–549.

BLADES, J. W., & FIEDLER, F. E. (1973). *The influence of intelligence, task ability and motivation on group performance.* Seattle: University of Washington, Organizational Research Technical Report #76–78.

BLAKE, R. R., & MOUTON, J. S. (1964). *The managerial grid.* Houston: Gulf Publishing.

BLAKE, R. R., & MOUTON, J. S. (1982). Management by grid principles or situationalism: Which? *Group and Organization Studies, 7*, 207–210.

BLAKE, R. R., SHEPARD, H. A., & MOUTON, J. S. (1964). *Managing intergroup conflict in industry.* Houston: Gulf Publishing.

BLANK, W., WEITZEL, J. R., & GREEN, S. G. (1986). Situational leadership theory: A test of underlying assumptions. Paper presented at the Academy of Management Meeting, Chicago.

BLANKENSHIP, L. V., & MILES, R. E. (1968). Organizational structure and managerial decision making. *Administrative Science Quarterly, 13*, 106–120.

BLAU, P. M. (1956). *Bureaucracy in modern society.* New York: Random House.

BLAU, P. M. (1974). *Exchange and power in social life.* New York: Wiley.

BLYTH, D. E. (1987). Leader and subordinate expertise as moderators of the relationship between directive leader behavior and performance. Unpublished doctoral dissertation, University of Washington, Seattle.

BORGOTTA, E. G., ROUCH, A. S., & BALES, R. F. (1954). Some findings relevant to the great man theory of leadership. *American Sociological Review, 19*, 755–759.

BOUCHARD, T. J. (1971). Whatever happened to brainstorming? *Journal of Creative Behavior, 5*, 182–189.

BOWERS, D. G. (1975). Hierarchy, function, and the generalizability of leadership practices. In J. G. Hunt and L. L. Larson (Eds.), *Leadership frontiers.* Kent, OH: Kent State University Press.

BOWERS, D. G., & SEASHORE, S. E. (1966). Predicting organizational effectiveness with a four-factor theory of leadership. *Administrative Science Quarterly, 11*, 238–263.

BOYATZIS, R. E. (1982). *The competent manager.* New York: John Wiley.

BRADFORD, D. L., & COHEN, A. R. (1984). *Managing for excellence: The guide to developing high performance organizations.* New York: John Wiley.

BRADFORD, L. P. (1976). *Making meetings work.* La Jolla, CA: University Associates.

BRADLEY, R. T. (1984). *The structural properties of charismatic organization.* Paper presented to the Academy of Management Meeting, Boston.

BRADY, G. F., & HELMICH, D. L. (1984). *Executive succession: Toward excellence in corporate leadership.* Englewood Cliffs, NJ: Prentice Hall.

BRAGG, J., & ANDREWS, I. R. (1973). Participative decision making: An experimental study in a hospital. *Journal of Applied Behavioral Science, 9,* 727–735.

BRASS, D. J. (1984). Being in the right place: A structural analysis of individual differences in an organization. *Administrative Science Quarterly, 29,* 518–539.

BRASS, D. J. (1985). Technology and the structuring of jobs: Employee satisfaction, performance, and influence. *Organizational Behavior and Human Decision Processes, 35,* 216–240.

BRAY, D. W., CAMPBELL, R. J., & GRANT, D. L. (1974). *Formative years in business: A long term AT&T study of managerial lives.* New York: Wiley.

BRODERICK, R. (1983). How Honeywell teaches its managers to manage. *Training,* January, 18–22.

BROMLEY, D. G., & SHUPE, A. D. (1979). *Moonies in America: Cult, church, and crusade.* Beverly Hills, CA: Sage.

BROOKS, E. (1955). What successful executives do. *Personnel, 32,* 210–225.

BROWN, L. D. (1983). *Managing conflict at organizational interfaces.* Reading, MA: Addison-Wesley.

BROWN, M. C. (1982). Administrative succession and organizational performance: The succession effect. *Administrative Science Quarterly, 29,* 245–273.

BURKE, M. J., & DAY, R. R. (1986). A cumulative study of the effectiveness of managerial training. *Journal of Applied Psychology, 71,* 232–246.

BURKE, W. W. (1965). Leadership behavior as a function of the leader, the follower, and the situation. *Journal of Personality, 33,* 60–81.

BURNASKA, R. F. (1976). The effects of behavior modeling training on managers' behaviors and employee's perceptions. *Personnel Psychology, 29,* 329–335.

BURNS, J. M. (1978). *Leadership.* New York: Harper & Row.

CALDER, B. J. (1977). An attribution theory of leadership. In B. M. Staw and G. R. Salancik (Eds.), *New direction in organizational behavior.* Chicago: St. Clair.

CAMPBELL, J. P. (1977). The cutting edge of leadership: An overview. In J. G. Hunt and L. L. Larson (Eds.), *Leadership: The cutting edge.* Carbondale, IL: Southern Illinois University Press.

CAMPBELL, J. P., DUNNETTE, M. D., ARVEY, R. D., & HELLERVIK, L. W. (1973). The development and evaluation of behaviorally based rating scales. *Journal of Applied Psychology, 57,* 15–22.

CARROLL, S. J. JR., & GILLEN, D. J. (1987). Are the classical management functions useful in describing managerial work? *Academy of Management Review, 12,* 38–51.

CARTWRIGHT, D. (1965). Leadership, influence, and control. In J. G. March (Ed.), *Handbook of organizations.* Chicago: Rand McNally.

CASHMAN, J., DANSEREAU, F. JR., GRAEN, G., & HAGA, W. J. (1976). Organizational understructure and leadership: A longitudinal investigation of the managerial role-making process. *Organizational Behavior and Human Performance, 15,* 278–296.

CHANDLER, A. D. (1962). *Strategy and structure.* Cambridge, MA: M.I.T. Press.

CHITAYAT, G., & VENEZIA, I. (1984). Determination of management style in business and nonbusiness organizations. *Journal of Applied Psychology, 69,* 437–447.

COCH, L., & FRENCH, J. R. P. JR. (1948). Overcoming resistance to change. *Human Relations, 1,* 512–532.

COHEN, D. L. (1972). The concept of charisma and the analysis of leadership. *Political Studies, 20*, 299–305.

COHEN, M. D., & MARCH, J. G. (1974). *Leadership and ambiguity*. New York: McGraw-Hill.

COLLINS, O. F., MOORE, D. G., & UNWALLA, D. B. (1964). *The enterprising man*. East Lansing, MI: Bureau of Business and Economic Research, Michigan State University.

CONGER, J. A. & KANUNGO, R. (1987). Toward a behavioral theory of charismatic leadership in organizational settings. *Academy of Management Review, 12*, 637–647.

COSIER, R. A. (1978). The effects of three potential aids for making strategic decisions on prediction accuracy. *Organizational Behavior and Human Performance, 22*, 295–306.

COSIER, R. A. (1982). Methods for improving the strategic decision: Dialectic versus the devil's advocate. *Strategic Management Journal, 3*, 373–374.

CROUCH, A., & YETTON, P. (1987). Manager behavior, leadership style, and subordinate performance: An empirical extension of the Vroom-Yetton conflict rule. *Organizational Behavior and Human Decision Processes, 39*, 384–396.

CROWE, B. J., BOCHNER, S., & CLARK, A. W. (1972). The effects of subordinates' behavior on managerial style. *Human Relations, 25*, 215–237.

CSOKA, L. S., & BONS, P. M. (1978). Manipulating the situation to fit the leader's style: Two validation studies of Leader Match. *Journal of Applied Psychology, 63*, 295–300.

CUMMIN, P. C. (1967). TAT correlates of executive performance. *Journal of Applied Psychology, 51*, 78–81.

CURTIS, B., SMITH, R. E., & SMOLL, F. L. (1979). Scrutinizing the skipper: A study of leadership behavior in the dugout. *Journal of Applied Psychology, 64*, 391–400.

DAHL, R. A. (1957). The concept of power. *Behavioral Science, 2*, 201–218.

DALE, E. (1960). Management must be made accountable. *Harvard Business Review, 38*, 49–59.

DALTON, M. (1950). Conflicts between staff and line managerial officers. *American Sociological Review, 15*, 342–351.

DANSEREAU, F., JR., GRAEN, G., & HAGA, W. J. (1975). A vertical dyad linkage approach to leadership within formal organizations: A longitudinal investigation of the role making process. *Organizational Behavior and Human Performance, 13*, 46–78.

DAVIES, J., & EASTERBY-SMITH, M. (1984). Learning and developing from managerial work experiences. *Journal of Management Studies, 2*, 169–183.

DAVIS, K. (1968). Attitudes toward the legitimacy of management efforts to influence employees. *Academy of Management Journal, 11*, 153–162.

DAY, D. V., & LORD, R. G. (1985). Leadership and organizational performance: A critical review of current data and theory. Paper presented at the Academy of Management Meeting, Chicago.

DAY, D. V., & LORD, R. G. (in press). Executive leadership and organizational performance. *Journal of Management*, In Press.

DAY, R. C. (1971). Some effects of combining close, punitive, and supportive styles of supervision. *Sociometry, 34*, 303–327.

DAY, R. C., & HAMBLIN, R. L. (1964). Some effects of close and punitive styles of supervision. *American Journal of Sociology, 69*, 499–510.

DELBECQ, A. L., VAN DE VEN, A. H., & GUSTAFSON, D. H. (1975). *Group techniques for program planning: A guide to nominal and delphi processes.* Glenview, Illinois: Scott, Foresman.

DESSLER, G., & VALENZI, E. R. (1977). Initiation of structure and subordinate satisfaction: A path analysis test of path-goal theory. *Academy of Management Journal, 20,* 251–259.

DEWHIRST, D., METTS, V., & LADD, R. T. (1987). Exploring the delegation decision: Managerial responses to multiple contingencies. Paper presented at the Academy of Management Meetings, New Orleans.

DIENESH, R. M., & LIDEN, R. C. (1986). Leader-member exchange model of leadership: A critique and further development. *Academy of Management Review, 11,* 618–634.

DONLEY, R. E., & WINTER, D. G. (1970). Measuring the motives of public officials at a distance: An exploratory study of American presidents. *Behavioral Science, 15,* 227–236.

DOW, T. E. (1969). The theory of charisma. *Social Quarterly, 10,* 306–318.

DRUCKER, P. F. (1974). *Management: Tasks, responsibilities, practices.* New York: Harper & Row.

DUBIN, A. J. (1978). *Human relations: A job-oriented approach.* Reston, VA: Reston.

DUCHON, D., GREEN, S. G., & TABER, T. D. (1986). Vertical dyad linkage: A longitudinal assessment of antecedents, measures, and consequences. *Journal of Applied Psychology, 71,* 56–60.

DUNNETTE, M. D. (1971). Multiple assessment procedures in identifying and developing managerial talent. In P. McReynolds (Ed.), *Advances in psychological assessment,* (Vol. 2). Palo Alto, CA: Science and Behavior Books.

DUNNETTE, M. D., CAMPBELL, J., & JAASTAD, K. (1963). The effect of group participation on brainstorming effectiveness for two industrial samples. *Journal of Applied Psychology, 47,* 30–37.

DUTTON, J. M., & WALTON, R. E. (1965). Interdepartmental conflict and cooperation: Two contrasting studies. *Human Organization, 25* (3), 207–220.

DYER, W. G. (1977). *Team building: Issues and alternatives.* Reading, MA: Addison-Wesley.

EARLEY, P. C., WOJNAROSKI, P., & PREST, W. (1987). Task planning and energy expended: Exploration of how goals influence performance. *Journal of Applied Psychology, 72,* 107–114.

EDEN, D. (1984). Self-fulfilling prophecy as a management tool: Harnessing Pygmalion. *Academy of Management Review, 9,* 64–73.

EDEN, D., & LEVIATAN, U. (1975). Implicit leadership theory as a determinant of the factor structure underlying supervisory behavior scales. *Journal of Applied Psychology, 60,* 736–741.

EDEN, D., & SHANI, A. B. (1982). Pygmalion goes to boot camp: Expectancy, leadership and trainee performance. *Journal of Applied Psychology, 67,* 194–199.

ENGLAND, G. W. (1967). Personal value systems of American managers. *Academy of Management Journal, 10,* 53–68.

ETTLING, J. T., & JAGO, A. G. (1988). Participation under conditions of conflict: More on the validity of the Vroom-Yetton model. *Journal of Management Studies, 25*(1), 73–83.

ETZIONI, A. (1961). *A comparative analysis of complex organizations.* New York: Free Press.

EVAN, W. M., & ZELDITCH, M. (1961). A laboratory experiment on bureaucratic authority. *American Sociological Review, 26,* 883–893.

EVANS, M. G. (1970). The effects of supervisory behavior on the path-goal relationship. *Organizational Behavior and Human Performance, 5,* 277–298.

EVANS, M. G. (1974). Extensions of a path-goal theory of motivation. *Journal of Applied Psychology, 59,* 172–178.

EVANS, M. G. (1986). Path-goal theory of leadership: A meta analysis. Unpublished paper, Toronto: University of Toronto.

EWING, D. W. (1964). *The managerial mind.* New York: Free Press.

FARRIS, G. F., & LIM, F. G., Jr. (1969). Effects of performance on leadership, cohesiveness, satisfaction, and subsequent performance. *Journal of Applied Psychology, 53,* 490–497.

FAYOL, H. (1949). *General and industrial management.* London: Pitman.

FIEDLER, F. E. (1964). A contingency model of leadership effectiveness. In L. Berkowitz (Ed.), *Advances in experimental social psychology.* New York: Academic Press.

FIEDLER, F. E. (1967). *A theory of leadership effectiveness.* New York: McGraw-Hill.

FIEDLER, F. E. (1970). Leadership experience and leader performance—Another hypothesis shot to hell. *Organizational Behavior and Human Performance, 5,* 1–14.

FIEDLER, F. E. (1971). Validation and extension of the contingency model of leadership effectiveness: A review of empirical findings. *Psychological Bulletin, 76,* 128–148.

FIEDLER, F. E. (1973). The contingency model: A reply to Ashour. *Organizational Behavior and Human Performance, 9,* 356–368.

FIEDLER, F. E. (1977). A rejoinder to Schriesheim and Kerr's premature obituary of the contingency model. In J. G. Hunt and L. L. Larson (Eds.), *Leadership: The cutting edge.* Carbondale, IL: Southern Illinois University Press.

FIEDLER, F. E. (1978). The contingency model and the dynamics of the leadership process. In L. Berkowitz (Ed.), *Advances in experimental social psychology.* New York: Academic Press.

FIEDLER, F. E. (1986). The contribution of cognitive resources to leadership performance. *Journal of Applied Social Psychology, 16,* 532–548.

FIEDLER, F. E., & CHEMERS, M. M. (1982). *Improving leadership effectiveness: The leader match concept* (2nd ed). New York: Wiley, 1982.

FIEDLER, F. E., & GARCIA, J. E. (1987). *New approaches to leadership: Cognitive resources and organizational performance.* New York: Wiley.

FIEDLER, F. E., & MAHAR, L. (1979). The effectiveness of contingency model training: A review of the validation of Leader Match. *Personnel Psychology, 32,* 45–62.

FIELD, R. H. G. (1979). A critique of the Vroom-Yetton contingency model of leadership behavior. *Academy of Management Review, 4,* 249–257.

FIELD, R. H. G. (1982). A test of the Vroom-Yetton normative model of leadership. *Journal of Applied Psychology, 67,* 523–532.

FILLEY, A. C. (1970). Committee management: Guidelines from social science research. *California Management Review, 13* (1), 13–21.

FINE, G. A. (1982). The Manson family: The folklore traditions of a small group. *Journal of the Folklore Institute, 19,* 47–60.

FLANAGAN, J. C. (1951). Defining the requirements of an executive's job. *Personnel, 28,* 28–35.

FLEISHMAN, E. A. (1953). The description of supervisory behavior. *Personnel Psychology, 37,* 1–6.

FLEISHMAN, E. A., & HARRIS, E. F. (1962). Patterns of leadership behavior related to employee grievances and turnover. *Personnel Psychology, 15,* 43–56.

FLEISHMAN, E. A., HARRIS, E. F., & BURTT, H. E. (1955). *Leadership and supervision in industry.* Columbus: Bureau of Educational Research, Ohio State University.

FORD, J. D. (1981). Departmental context and formal structure as constraints on leader behavior. *Academy of Management Journal, 24,* 274–288.

FOURIEZOS, N. T., HUTT, M. L., & GUETZKOW, H. (1950). Measurement of self-oriented needs in discussion groups. *Journal of Abnormal and Social Psychology, 45,* 682–690.

FRENCH, J. R. P. (1950). Field experiments: Changing group productivity. In J. G. Miller (Ed.), *Experiments in social process.* New York: McGraw-Hill.

FRENCH, J. R. P., ISRAEL, J., & AS, D. (1960). An experiment on participation in a Norwegian factory. *Human Relations, 13,* 3–19.

FRENCH, J., & RAVEN, B. H. (1959). The bases of social power. In D. Cartwright (Ed.), *Studies of social power.* Ann Arbor, MI: Institute for Social Research.

FRIEDLAND, W. H. (1964). For a sociological concept of charisma. *Social Forces, 43* (1), 18–26.

FRIEDRICH, C. J. (1961). Political leadership and the problem of the charismatic power. *Journal of Politics, 23,* February, 3–24.

FROST, D. C. (1983). Role perceptions and behaviors of the immediate superior moderating effects on the prediction of leadership effectiveness. *Organizational Behavior and Human Performance, 31,* 123–142.

FRY, L. W., KERR, S., & LEE, C. (in press). Effects of leader behaviors under different levels of task interdependence. *Human Relations.*

FULK, J., & WENDLER, E. R. (1982). Dimensionality of leader-subordinate interactions: A path-goal investigation. *Organizational Behavior and Human Performance, 30,* 241–264.

GABARRO, J. J. (1985). When a new manager takes charge. *Harvard Business Review,* May-June, 110–123.

GALANTER, M. (1982). Charismatic religious sects and psychiatry: An overview. *American Journal of Psychiatry, 139,* 1539–1548.

GALBRAITH, J. (1973). *Designing complex organizations.* Menlo Park, CA: Addison-Wesley.

GAMSON, W. A., & SCOTCH, N. A. (1964). Scapegoating in baseball. *American Journal of Sociology, 70,* 69–72.

GELLERMAN, S. W. (1976). Supervision: Substance and style. *Harvard Business Review,* March–April, 89–99.

GEORGOPOULOS, B. S., MAHONEY, G. M., & JONES, N. W., Jr. (1957). A path-goal approach to productivity. *Journal of Applied Psychology, 41,* 345–353.

GERSEIN, M., & REISMAN, H. (1983). Strategic selection: Matching executives to business conditions. *Sloan Management Review, 24* (2), 33–49.

GHISELLI, E. E. (1966). *The validity of occupational aptitude tests.* New York: Wiley.

GILMORE, D. C., BEEHR, T. A., & RICHTER, D. J. (1979). Effects of leader behaviors on subordinate performance and satisfaction: A laboratory experiment with student employees. *Journal of Applied Psychology, 64,* 166–172.

GIOIA, D. A., & SIMS, H. P. Jr. (1985). On avoiding the influence of implicit leadership theories in leader behavior descriptions. *Journal of Educational and Psychological Measurement, 45,* 217–237.

GOLDE, R. A. (1972). Are your meetings like this one? *Harvard Business Review,* January–February, 68–77.

GOLDNER, F. H. (1970). The division of labor: Processes and power. In M. N. Zald (Ed.), *Power in organizations.* Nashville, TN: Vanderbilt University Press.

GOLDSTEIN, A. P., & SORCHER, M. (1974). *Changing supervisory behavior.* New York: Pergamon Press.

GOODSTADT, B., & KIPNIS, D. (1970). Situational influences on the use of power. *Journal of Applied Psychology, 54,* 201–207.

GORDON, L. V. (1975). *The measurement of interpersonal values.* Chicago: Science Research Associates.

GORDON, L. V. (1976). *Survey of interpersonal values: Revised manual.* Chicago: Science Research Associates.

GORDON, W. J. (1961). *Synectics.* New York: Collier Books.

GRAEFF, C. L. (1983). The situational leadership theory: A critical review. *Academy of Management Review, 8,* 285–296.

GRAEN, G., ALVARES, K. M., ORRIS, J. B., & MARTELLA, J. A. (1970). Contingency model of leadership effectiveness: Antecedent and evidential results. *Psychological Bulletin, 74,* 285–296.

GRAEN, G., & CASHMAN, J. F. (1975). A role making model of leadership in formal organizations: A developmental approach. In J. G. Hunt and L. L. Larson (Eds.), *Leadership frontiers.* Kent, OH: Kent State University Press.

GREEN, S. G., & LIDEN, R. C. (1980). Contextual and attributional influences on control decisions. *Journal of Applied Psychology, 65,* 453–458.

GREEN, S. G., & MITCHELL, T. R (1979). Attributional processes of leaders in leader-member exchanges. *Organizational Behavior and Human Performance, 23,* 429–458.

GREENE, C. N. (1975). The reciprocal nature of influence between leader and subordinate. *Journal of Applied Psychology, 60,* 187–193.

GREENE, C. N. (1979a). Questions of causation in the path-goal theory of leadership. *Academy of Management Journal, 22,* 22–41.

GREENE, C. N. (1979b) A longitudinal investigation of modifications to a situational model of leader effectiveness. *Proceedings of the Academy of Management,* Chicago.

GRIMES, A. J. (1978). Authority, power, influence, and social control: A theoretical synthesis. *Academy of Management Review, 3,* 724–735.

GUEST, R. H. (1956). Of time and the foreman. *Personnel, 32,* 478–486.

GUEST, R. H. (1964). *Organizational change: The effect of successful leadership.* Homewood, IL: Irwin-Dorsey.

GUION, R. M., & GOTTIER, R. F. (1965). Validity of personality measures in personnel selection. *Personnel Psychology, 18,* 135–164.

GUPTA, A. K., & GOVINDARAJAN, V. (1984). Business unit strategy, managerial characteristics, and business unit effectiveness at strategy implementation. *Academy of Management Journal, 27,* 25–41.

GUZZO, R. A., JETTE, R. D., & KATZELL, R. A. (1985). The effects of psychologically based intervention programs on worker productivity: A meta-analysis. *Personnel Psychology, 38,* 275–291.

HACKMAN, J. R., BROUSSEAU, K. R., & WEISS, J. A. (1976). The interaction of task design and group performance strategies in determining group effectiveness. *Organizational Behavior and Human Performance, 16,* 350–365.

HACKMAN, J. R., & MORRIS, C. G. (1975). Group tasks, group interaction process, and group performance effectiveness: A review and proposed integration. In L. Berkowitz (Ed.), *Advances in experimental social psychology.* New York: Academic Press.

HACKMAN, J. R., & OLDHAM, G. R. (1976). Motivation through the design of work: Test of a theory. *Organizational Behavior and Human Performance, 16,* 250–279.

HACKMAN, J. R., & OLDHAM, G. R. (1980). *Work redesign.* Reading, MA: Addison-Wesley.

HAIMANN, T., & HILERT, R. L. (1977). *Supervision: Concepts and practices of management.* Cincinnati: South-Western.

HALAL, W. E. (1974). Toward a general theory of leadership. *Human Relations, 27,* 401–416.

HALPIN, A. W. (1954). The leadership behavior and combat performance of airplane commanders. *Journal of Abnormal and Social Psychology, 49,* 19–22.

HALPIN, A. W., & WINER, B. J. (1957). A factorial study of the leader behavior descriptions. In R. M. Stogdill and A. E. Coons (Eds.), *Leader behavior: Its description and measurement.* Columbus, OH: Bureau of Business Research, Ohio State University.

HAMBLETON, R. K., & GUMBERT, R. (1982). The validity of Hersey and Blanchard's theory of leader effectiveness. *Group and Organization Studies, 7,* 225–242.

HAMBRICK, D. C. (1981). Environment, strategy, and power within top management teams. *Administrative Science Quarterly, 26,* 253–276.

HAMBRICK, D. C. (1982). Environmental scanning and organizational strategy. *Strategic Management Journal, 3,* 159–174.

HAMNER, T. H., & TURK, J. M. (1987). Organizational determinants of leader behavior and authority. *Journal of Applied Psychology, 72,* 647–682.

HAMNER, W. C., & HAMNER, E. P. (1976). Behavior modification on the bottom line. *Organizational Dynamics, 4* (4), 2–21.

HAMNER, W. C., & ORGAN, D. W. (1978). *Organizational behavior: An applied approach.* Dallas: Business Publications.

HAND, H., & SLOCUM, J. (1970). Human relations training for middle management: A field experiment. *Academy of Management Journal, 13,* 403–410.

HAND, H., & SLOCUM, J. (1972). A longitudinal study of the effect of a human relations training program on managerial effectiveness. *Journal of Applied Psychology, 56,* 412–418.

HARRISON, R. (1987). Harnessing personal energy: How companies can inspire employees. *Organizational Dynamics,* Autumn, 4–21.

HARVEY, O. J. (1953). An experimental approach to the study of status relationships in informal groups. *American Sociological Review, 18,* 357–367.

HEILMAN, M. E., HORNSTEIN, H. A., CAGE, J. H., & HERSCHLAG, J. K. (1984). Reactions to prescribed leader behavior as a function of role perspective: The case of the Vroom-Yetton Model. *Journal of Applied Psychology, 69,* 50–60.

HEIZER, J. H. (1972). Manager action. *Personnel Psychology, 25,* 511–521.

HELLER, F. (1971). *Managerial decision making: A study of leadership style and power sharing among senior managers.* London: Tavistock.

HELLER, F., & YUKL, G. (1969). Participation, managerial decision making, and situational variables. *Organizational Behavior and Human Performance, 4,* 227–241.

HELMICH, D. L. (1974). Organizational growth and succession patterns. *Academy of Management Journal, 4,* 771–775.

HEMPHILL, J. K. (1950). Relations between the size of the group and the behavior of "superior" leaders. *Journal of Social Psychology, 32,* 11–22.

HEMPHILL, J. K. (1959). Job descriptions for executives. *Harvard Business Review, 37,* September-October, 55–67.

HEMPHILL, J. K. (1960). *Dimensions of executive positions.* Columbus, OH: Bureau of Business Research, Ohio State University.

HEMPHILL, J. K., & COONS, A. E. (1957). Development of the leader behavior description questionnaire. In R. M. Stogdill and A. E. Coons (Eds.), *Leader behavior: Its description and measurement.* Columbus, OH: Bureau of Business Research, Ohio State University.

HEROLD, D. (1977). Two way influence processes in leader-follower dyads. *Academy of Management Journal, 20,* 224–237.

HERSEY, P., & BLANCHARD, K. H. (1969). Life cycle theory of leadership. *Training and Development Journal, 23* (2), 26–34.

HERSEY, P., & BLANCHARD, K. H. (1977). *Management of organizational behavior.* (3rd ed.). Englewood Cliffs, NJ: Prentice Hall.

HERSEY, P., & BLANCHARD, K. H. (1984). *The management of organizational behavior.* (4th ed.). Englewood Cliffs, NJ: Prentice Hall.

HEWETT, T. T., O'BRIEN, G. E., & HORNIK, J. (1974). The effects of work organization, leadership, and member compatibility of small groups working on a manipulative task. *Organizational Behavior and Human Performance, 11,* 283–301.

HICKSON, D. J., HININGS, C. R., LEE, C. A., SCHNECK, R. S., & PENNINGS, J. M. (1971). A strategic contingencies theory of intra-organizational power. *Administrative Science Quarterly, 16,* 216–229.

HILL, W. A., & HUGHES, D. (1974). Variations in leader behavior as a function of task type. *Organizational Behavior and Human Performance, 11,* 83–96.

HILLS, F. S., & MAHONEY, T. A. (1978). University budgets and organizational decision making. *Administrative Science Quarterly, 23,* 454–465.

HININGS, C. R., HICKSON, D. J., PENNINGS, J. M., & SCHNECK, R. E. (1974). Structural conditions of intra-organizational power. *Administrative Science Quarterly, 19,* 22–44.

HOLLANDER, E. P. (1958). Conformity, status, and idiosyncracy credit. *Psychological Review, 65,* 117–127.

HOLLANDER, E. P. (1960). Competence and conformity in the acceptance of influence. *Journal of Abnormal and Social Psychology, 61,* 361–365.

HOLLANDER, E. P. (1961). Some effects of perceived status on responses to innovative behavior. *Journal of Abnormal and Social Psychology, 63,* 247–250.

HOLLANDER, E. P. (1978). *Leadership dynamics: A practical guide to effective relationships.* New York: Free Press.

HOLLANDER, E. P. (1979). Leadership and social exchange processes. In K. Gergen, M. S. Greenberg, and R. H. Willis (Eds.), *Social exchange: Advances in theory and research.* New York: Winston-Wiley.

HOLLANDER, E. P., & JULIAN, J. W. (1970). Studies in leader legitimacy, influence, and innovation. In L. Berkowitz (Ed.), *Advances in experimental social psychology,* (Vol. 5). New York: Academic Press.

HOLLANDER, E. P., & JULIAN, J. W. (1978). A further look at leader legitimacy, influence, and motivation. In L. Berkowitz (Ed.), *Group processes.* New York: Academic Press.

HOMANS, G. C. (1958). Social behavior as exchange. *American Journal of Sociology, 63,* 597–606.

HOUSE, R. J. (1971). A path-goal theory of leader effectiveness. *Administrative Science Quarterly,16,* 321–339.

HOUSE, R. J. (1977). A 1976 theory of charismatic leadership. In J. G. Hunt and L. L. Larson (Eds.), *Leadership: The cutting edge.* Carbondale, IL: Southern Illinois University Press.

HOUSE, R. J. (1988). Power and personality in organizations. *Research in Organizational Behavior,* (Vol. 10). Greenwich, CT: JAI Press, pp. 305–357.

HOUSE, R. J., & DESSLER, (1974). The path-goal theory of leadership: Some post hoc and a priori tests. In J. Hunt and L. Larson (Eds.), *Contingency approaches to leadership.* Carbondale IL: Southern Illinois Press.

HOUSE, R. J., FILLEY, A. C., & GUJARATI, D. N. (1971). Leadership style, hierarchical influence, and the satisfaction of subordinate role expectations. *Journal of Applied Psychology, 55,* 422–432.

HOUSE, R. J., & MITCHELL, T. R. (1974). Path-goal theory of leadership. *Contemporary Business, 3,* Fall, 81–98.

HOUSE, R. J., & SINGH, J. V. (1987). Organizational behavior: Some new directions for I/O psychology. *Annual Reviews of Psychology, 38,* 669–718.

HOUSE, R. J., WOYCKE, J., & FODOR, E. M. (1987). Motive patterns, perceived behavior and effectiveness of charismatic and noncharismatic U. S. presidents. Unpublished paper, University of Toronto.

HOWELL, J. M., & FROST, P. (in press). A laboratory study of charismatic leadership. *Organizational Behavior and Human Decision Processes.*

HOWELL, J. P., & DORFMAN, P. W. (1981). Substitutes for leadership: Test of a construct. *Academy of Management Journal, 24,* 714–728.

HOWELL, J. P., & DORFMAN, P. W. (1986). Leadership and substitutes for leadership among professional and nonprofessional workers. *Journal of Applied Behavioral Science, 22,* 29–46.

HUCK, J. R. (1973). Assessment centers: A review of external and internal validities. *Personnel Psychology, 26,* 191–212.

HUNDAL, P. S. (1971). A study of entrepreneurial motivation: Comparison of fast and slow progressing small scale industrial entrepreneurs in Punjab, India. *Journal of Applied Psychology, 55,* 317–323.

HUNT, J. G., & MICHAEL, C. (1983). Mentorship: A career training and development tool. *Academy of Management Review, 8,* 475–485.

HUNT, J. G., & OSBORN, R. N. (1982). Toward a macro-oriented model of leadership: An odyssey. In J. G. Hunt, U. Sekaran, & C. Schriesheim (Eds.), *Leadership: Beyond establishment views* (pp. 196–221). Carbondale, IL: Southern University University Press.

ILGEN, D. R., MITCHELL, T. R., & FREDRICKSON, J. W. (1981). Poor performers: Supervisor's and subordinate's responses. *Organizational Behavior and Human Performance, 27,* 386–410.

INDVIK, J. (1986). Path-goal theory of leadership: A meta-analysis. In *Proceedings of the Academy of Management Meetings,* 189–192.

ISENBERG, D. J. (1984). How senior managers think. *Harvard Business Review,* November-December, 81–90.

JACKSON, J. M. (1953). The effect of changing the leadership of small work groups. *Human Relations, 6,* 25–44.

JACOBS, T. O. (1970). *Leadership and exchange in formal organizations.* Alexandria, VA: Human Resources Research Organization.

JAGO, A. G., & VROOM, V. H. (1980). An evaluation of two alternatives to the Vroom/Yetton normative model. *Academy of Management Journal, 23,* 347–355.

JAMES, L. R., & WHITE, J. F. (1983). Cross situational specificity in manager's perceptions of subordinate performance, attributions, and leader behaviors. *Personnel Psychology, 36,* 809–856.

JANDA, K. F. (1960). Towards the explication of the concept of leadership in terms of the concept of power. *Human Relations, 13,* 345–363.

JANIS, I. L. (1972). *Victims of groupthink.* Boston: Houghton Mifflin.

JANIS, I. L., & MANN, L. (1977). *Decision making: A psychological analysis of conflict, choice, and commitment.* New York: Free Press.

JAY, A. (1976). How to run a meeting. *Harvard Business Review,* March-April, 43–57.

JERMIER, J. M., & BERKES, L. J. (1979). Leader behavior in a police command bureaucracy: A closer look at the quasi-military model. *Administrative Science Quarterly, 24,* 1–23.

KAHN, R. L., & QUINN, R. P. (1970). Role stress: A framework for analysis. In A. McLean (Ed.), *Mental health and work organizations.* Chicago: Rand McNally.

KAHN, R. L., WOLFE, D. M., QUINN, R. P., & SNOEK, J. D. (1964). *Organizational stress: Studies in role conflict and ambiguity.* New York: Wiley.

KANTER, R. M. (1968). Commitment and social organizations: A study of commitment mechanisms in utopian communities. *American Sociological Review, 33* (4), 499–518.

KANTER, R. M. (1979). Power failures in management circuits. *Harvard Business Review, 57,* July-August, 65–75.

KANTER, R. M. (1982). The middle manager as innovator. *Harvard Business Review,* July-August, 95–105.

KANTER, R. M. (1983). *The change masters.* New York: Simon & Schuster.

KAPLAN, R. E. (1984). Trade routes: The manager's network of relationships. *Organizational Dynamics,* Spring, 37–52.

KAPLAN, R. E. (1986). *The warp and woof of the general manager's job.* (Technical Report No. 27, pp. 1–32). Greensboro, NC: Center For Creative Leadership.

KARMEL, B. (1978). Leadership: A challenge to traditional research methods and assumptions. *Academy of Management Review, 3,* 475–482.

KARMEL, B., & EGAN, D. M. (1976). Managerial performance: A new look at underlying dimensionality. *Organizational Behavior and Human Performance, 15,* 322–334.

KATZ, D., & KAHN, R. L. (1952). Some recent findings in human relations research. In E. Swanson, T. Newcomb, and E. Hartley (Eds.), *Readings in social psychology.* New York: Holt, Rinehart & Winston.

KATZ, D., & KAHN, R. L. (1978). *The social psychology of organizations.* (2nd ed.). New York: John Wiley.

KATZ, D., MACCOBY, N., GURIN, G., & FLOOR, L. (1951). *Productivity, supervision, and morale among railroad workers.* Ann Arbor, MI: Survey Research Center, University of Michigan.

KATZ, D., MACCOBY, N., & MORSE, N. (1950). *Productivity, supervision, and morale in an office situation.* Ann Arbor, MI: Institute For Social Research.

KATZ, D., & TUSHMAN, M. (1979). Communication patterns, project performance, and task characteristics: An empirical evaluation and integration in an R & D laboratory. *Organizational Behavior and Human Performance, 23,* 139–162.

KATZ, R. L. (1955, January–February). Skills of an effective administrator. *Harvard Business Review,* 33–42.

KATZELL, R. A., BARRETT, R. S., VANN, D. H., & HOGAN, J. M. (1968). Organizational correlates of executive roles. *Journal of Applied Psychology, 52,* 22–28.

KAY, B. R. (1959). Factors in effective foreman behavior. *Personnel, 36,* 25–31.

KELLER, R. T., & SZILAGYI, A. D. (1976). Employee reactions to leader reward behavior. *Academy of Management Journal, 19,* 619–627.

KENNEDY, J. K. Jr. (1982). Middle LPC leaders and the contingency model of leadership effectiveness. *Organizational Behavior and Human Performance, 30,* 1–14.

KEPNER, C., & TREGOE, B. (1965). *The rational manager.* New York: McGraw-Hill.

KEPNER, C., & TREGOE, B. (1981). *The new rational manager.* Princeton, NJ: Kepner-Tregoe.

KERR, S., & HARLAN, A. (1973). Predicting the effects of leadership training and experience from the contingency model: Some remaining problems. *Journal of Applied Psychology, 57,* 114–117.

KERR, S., HILL, K. D., & BROEDLING, L. (1986). The first-line supervisor: Phasing out or here to stay? *Academy of Management Review, 11,* 103–117.

KERR, S., & JERMIER, J. M. (1978). Substitutes for leadership: Their meaning and measurement. *Organizational Behavior and Human Performance, 22,* 375–403.

KERR, S., & SCHRIESHEIM, S. (1974). Consideration, initiating structure, and organizational criteria—an update of Korman's 1966 review. *Personnel Psychology, 27,* 555–568.

KETS DE VRIES, M. F. R., & MILLER, D. (1984). *The neurotic organization: Diagnosing and changing counter-productive styles of management.* San Francisco: Jossey-Bass.

KETS DE VRIES, M. F. R., & MILLER, D. (1985). Narcissism and leadership: An object relations perspective. *Human Relations, 38,* 583–601.

KIESER, A (1984). How does one become an effective manager? In J. G. Hunt, D. Hosking, C. A. Schriesheim, & R. Stewart (Eds.), *Leaders and managers: International perspectives on managerial behavior and leadership* (pp. 90–95). New York: Pergamon Press.

KIM, K. I., & ORGAN, D. W. (1982). Determinants of leader-subordinate exchange relationships. *Group and Organization Studies, 7,* 77–89.

KIPNIS, D. (1972). Does power corrupt? *Journal of Personality and Social Psychology, 24,* 33–41.

KIPNIS, D. (1976). *The powerholders.* Chicago: University of Chicago Press.

KIPNIS, D., & COSENTINO, J. (1969). Use of leadership powers in industry. *Journal of Applied Psychology, 53,* 460–466.

KIPNIS, D., & LANE, W. P. (1962). Self confidence and leadership. *Journal of Applied Psychology, 46,* 291–295.

KIPNIS, D., SCHMIDT, S. M., PRICE, K., & STITT, C. (1981). Why do I like thee: Is it your performance or my orders? *Journal of Applied Psychology, 66,* 324–328.

KIPNIS, D., SCHMIDT, S. M., & WILKINSON, I. (1980). Intra-organizational influence tactics: Explorations in getting one's way. *Journal of Applied Psychology, 65,* 440–452.

KIPNIS, D., & VANDERVEER, R. (1971). Ingratiation and the use of power. *Journal of Personality and Social Psychology, 17,* 280–286.

KLAUSS, R. (1981). Formalized mentor relationships for management and executive development programs in the federal government. *Public Administration Review, 41,* 489–496.

KOMAKI, J. (1986). Toward effective supervision: An operant analysis and comparison of managers at work. *Journal of Applied Psychology, 71,* 270–278.

KORDA, M. (1975). *Power! How to get it, how to use it.* New York: Ballantine Books.

KORMAN, A. K. (1968). The prediction of managerial performance: A review. *Personnel Psychology, 21,* 295–322.

KORMAN, A. K., & TANOFSKY, R. (1975). Statistical problems of contingency models in organizational behavior. *Academy of Management Journal, 18,* 393–397.

KOTTER, J. P. (1982). *The general managers.* New York: Free Press.

KOTTER, J. P. (1985). *Power and influence: Beyond formal authority.* New York: Free Press.

KOTTER, J. P., & LAWRENCE, P. (1974). *Mayors in action: Five studies in urban governance.* New York: John Wiley.

KRAM, K. E. (1985). *Mentoring at work: Developmental relationships in organizational life.* Glenview, IL: Scott, Foresman.

KUHN, A. (1963). *The study of society: A unified approach.* Homewood, IL: Richard D. Irwin.

KUHNERT, K. W., & LEWIS, P. (1987). Transactional and transformational leadership: A constructive/developmental analysis. *Academy of Management Review, 12,* 648–657.

KURKE, L., & ALDRICH, H. (1983). Mintzberg was right: A replication and extension of the nature of managerial work. *Management Science, 29,* 975–984.

LARSON, L. L., HUNT, J. G., & OSBORN, R. N. (1976). The great hi-hi leader behavior myth: A lesson from Occam's razor. *Academy of Management Journal, 19,* 628–641.

LATHAM, G. P., & SAARI, L. (1979). The application of social learning theory to training supervisors through behavioral modeling. *Journal of Applied Psychology, 64,* 239–246.

LATHAM, G. P., & WEXLEY, K. N. (1977). Behavioral observation scales for performance appraisal purposes. *Personnel Psychology, 30,* 255–268.

LAU, A. W., NEWMAN, A. R., & BROEDLING, L. A. (1980). The nature of managerial work in the public sector. *Public Management Forum, 19,* 513–521.

LAWRENCE, P. R., & LORSCH, J. W. (1967). New management job: The integrator. *Harvard Business Review, 45,* November-December, 142–151.

LAWRENCE, P., & LORSCH, J. (1969). *Organization and environment: Managing differentiation and integration.* Homewood, IL: Richard D. Irwin.

LAWSHE, C. H., BOLDA, R. A., & BRUNE, R. L. (1959). Studies in management training evaluation: The effect of exposures to role playing. *Journal of Applied Psychology, 43,* 287–292.

LEANA, C. R. (1986). Predictors and consequences of delegation. *Academy of Management Journal, 29,* 754–774.

LEE, J. A. (1977). Leader power for managing change. *Academy of Management Review, 2,* 73–80.

LEONTIADES, M. (1984). Choosing the right manager to fit the strategy. *The Journal of Business Strategy, 3* (2), 58–69.

LEWIN, K., LIPPITT, R., & WHITE, R. K. (1939). Patterns of aggressive behavior in experimentally created social climates. *Journal of Social Psychology, 10,* 271–301.

LIDDELL, W. W., & SLOCUM, J. W. Jr. (1976). The effects of individual role compatibility upon group performance: An extension of Shutz's FIRO theory. *Academy of Management Journal, 19,* 413–426.

LIEBERSON, S., & O'CONNOR, J. F. (1972). Leadership and organizational performance: A study of large corporations. *American Sociological Review, 37,* 117–130.

LIKERT, R. (1961). *New patterns of management.* New York: McGraw-Hill.

LIKERT, R. (1967). *The human organization: Its management and value.* New York: McGraw-Hill.

LITWIN, G. H., & STRINGER, P. A. (1966). *Motivation and organizational climate.* Boston: Division of Research, Harvard Business School.

LIVINGSTON, J. S. (1969). Pygmalion in management. *Harvard Business Review,* July–August, 81–89.

LOCKE, E. A., & LATHAM, G. P. (1984). *Goal setting: A motivational technique that works.* Englewood Cliffs, NJ: Prentice Hall.

LOCKE, E. A., SHAW, K. N., SAARI, L. M., & LATHAM, G. P. (1981). Goal setting and task performance. *Psychological Bulletin, 90,* 125–152.

LOMBARDO, M. M., & MCCALL, M. W. Jr. (1978). Leadership. In M. W. McCall Jr. and M. M. Lombardo (Eds.), *Leadership: Where else can we go?* (pp. 1–2). Durham, NC: Duke University Press.

LORD, R. G. (1977). Functional leadership behavior: Measurement and relation to social power and leadership perceptions. *Administrative Science Quarterly, 22,* 114–133.

LORD, R. G., BINNING, J. F., RUSH, M. C., & THOMAS, J. C. (1978). The effect of performance cues and leader behavior on questionnaire ratings of leader behavior. *Organizational Behavior and Human Performance, 21,* 27–39.

LORD, R. G., DEVADER, C. L., & ALLIGER, G. M. (1986). A meta-analysis of the relation between personality traits and leadership: An application of validity generalization procedures. *Journal of Applied Psychology, 71,* 402–410.

LORD, R. G., & ROWZEE, M. (1979). Task interdependence, temporal phase, and cognitive heterogeneity as determinants of leadership behavior-performance relationships. *Organizational Behavior and Human Performance, 23,* 182–200.

LOURENCO, S. V., & GLIDEWELL, J. C. (1974). A dialectical analysis of organizational conflict. *Administrative Science Quarterly, 20,* 489–508.

LOWIN, A., & CRAIG, J. R. (1968). The influence of level of performance on managerial style: an experimental object lesson in the ambiguity of correlational data. *Organizational Behavior and Human Performance, 3,* 440–458.

LOWIN, A., HRAPCHAK, W. J., & KAVANAGH, M. J. (1969). Consideration and initiating structure: An experimental investigation of leadership traits. *Administrative Science Quarterly, 14,* 238–253.

LUSK, E. J., & OLIVER, B. L. (1974). American managers' personal value systems— revisited. *Academy of Management Journal, 17,* 549–554.

LUTHANS, F., & LOCKWOOD, D. L. (1984). Toward an observation system for measuring leader behavior in natural settings. In J. G. Hunt, D. Hosking, C. A. Schriesheim, & R. Stewart (Eds.), *Leaders and managers: International perspectives on managerial behavior and leadership.* New York: Pergamon Press.

LUTHANS, F., ROSENKRANTZ, S. A., & HENNESSEY, H. W. (1985). What do successful managers really do? An observational study of managerial activities. *Journal of Applied Behavioral Science, 21,* 255–270.

MACINTOSH, D. (1970). Weber and Freud: On the nature and source of authority. *American Sociological Review, 35,* 901–912.

MAHONEY, T. A., JERDEE, T. H., & CARROLL, S. J., Jr. (1963). *Development of managerial performance: A research approach.* Cincinnati: South-Western.

MAHONEY, T. A., JERDEE, T. H., & CARROLL, S. J., Jr. (1965). The jobs of management. *Industrial Relations, 4,* 97–110.

MAIER, N. R. F. (1963). *Problem-solving discussions and conferences: Leadership methods and skills.* New York: McGraw-Hill.

MAIER, N. R. F., & HOFFMAN, L. R. (1960). Using trained "developmental" discussion leaders to improve further the quality of group decisions. *Journal of Applied Psychology, 44,* 247–251.

MAIER, N. R. F., & MAIER, R. A. (1957). An experimental test of the effects of "developmental" versus "free" discussions on the quality of group decisions. *Journal of Applied Psychology, 41,* 320–323.

MAIER, N. R. F., & SOLEM, A. R. (1952). The contribution of a discussion leader to the quality of group thinking: The effective use of minority opinions. *Human Relations, 5,* 277–288.

MANN, F. C. (1965). Toward an understanding of the leadership role in formal organization. In R. Dubin, G. C. Homans, F. C. Mann, and D. C. Miller (Eds.), *Leadership and productivity.* San Francisco: Chandler.

MANN, F. C., & DENT, J. (1954). The supervisor: Member of two organizational families. *Harvard Business Review, 32* (6), 103–112.

MANN, F. C., & HOFFMAN, L. R. (1960). *Automation and the worker: A study of social change in power plants.* New York: Holt, Rinehart & Winston.

MANN, R. D. (1959). A review of the relationships between personality and performance in small groups. *Psychological Bulletin, 56,* 241–270.

MANZ, C. C., & SIMS, H. P., Jr. (1981). Vicarious learning: The influence of modeling on organizational behavior. *Academy of Management Review, 6,* 105–113.

MANZ, C. C., & SIMS, H. P., Jr. (1987). Leading workers to lead themselves: The external leadership of self-managing work teams. *Administrative Science Quarterly, 32,* 106–128.

MARCH, J. G., & SIMON, H. A. (1958). *Organizations.* New York: Wiley.

MARCUS, J. T. (1961). Transcendence and charisma. *The Western Political Quarterly, 14,* 236–241.

MARGERISON, C., & GLUBE, R. (1979). Leadership decision making: An empirical test of the Vroom and Yetton Model. *Journal of Management Studies, 16* 45–55.

MARTIN, N. H. (1956). Differential decisions in the management of an industrial plant. *Journal of Business, 29*, 249–260.

MARTINKO, M. J., & GARDNER, W. L. (1984). *The behavior of high performing educational managers: An observational study.* Tallahassee: Florida State University, Department of Management.

MASLOW, A. (1954). *Motivation and personality.* New York: Harper & Row.

MASS, H. S. (1950). Personal and group factors in leaders' social perception. *Journal of Abnormal and Social Psychology, 45*, 54–63.

McCALL, M. W., Jr. (1977). Leaders and leadership: Of substance and shadow. In J. Hackman, E. E. Lawler Jr., L. W. Porter (Eds.), *Perspectives on behavior in organizations.* New York: McGraw-Hill.

McCALL, M. W., & SEGRIST, C. A. (1980). *In pursuit of the manager's job: Building on Mintzberg* (Technical Report No. 14) Greensboro, NC: Center For Creative Leadership.

McCALL, M. W., Jr., & KAPLAN, R. E. (1985). *Whatever it takes: decision makers at work.* Englewood Cliffs, NJ: Prentice Hall.

McCALL, M. W., Jr., KAPLAN, R. E., & GERLACH, M. L. (1982). *Caught in the act: Decision makers at work* (Technical Report No. 20) Greensboro, NC: Center For Creative Leadership.

McCALL, M. W. Jr., & LOMBARDO, M. M. (1983). *Off the track: Why and how successful executives get derailed* (Technical Report No. 21) Greensboro, NC: Center For Creative Leadership.

McCALL, M. W. Jr., MORRISON, A. M., & HANNAN, R. L. (1978). *Studies of managerial work: Results and methods* (Technical Report No. 9) Greensboro, NC: Center For Creative Leadership.

McCAULEY, C. D. (1986). *Developmental experiences in managerial work* (Technical Report No. 26) Greensboro, NC: Center For Creative Leadership.

McCLELLAND, D. C. (1965). N-achievement and entrepreneurship: A longitudinal study. *Journal of Personality and Social Psychology, 1*, 389–392.

McCLELLAND, D. C. (1970). The two faces of power. *Journal of International Affairs, 24* (1), 29–47.

McCLELLAND, D. C. (1975). *Power: The inner experience.* New York: Irvington.

McCLELLAND, D. C. (1985). *Human motivation.* Glenview, IL: Scott, Foresman.

McCLELLAND, D. C., & BOYATZIS, R. E. (1982). Leadership motive pattern and long term success in management. *Journal of Applied Psychology, 67*, 737–743.

McCLELLAND, D. C., & BURNHAM, D. H. (1976, March-April). Power is the great motivator. *Harvard Business Review*, 100–110.

McCLELLAND, D. C., & WINTER, D. G. (1969). *Motivating economic achievement.* New York: Free Press.

McFILLEN, J. M. (1978). Supervisory power as an influence in supervisor-subordinate relations. *Academy of Management Journal, 21*, 419–433.

McFILLEN, J. M., & NEW, J. R. (1979). Situational determinants of supervisor attributions and behavior. *Academy of Management Journal, 22*, 793–809.

McGREGOR, D. (1960). *The human side of enterprise.* New York: McGraw-Hill.

McLENNAN, K. (1967). The manager and his job skills. *Academy of Management Journal, 3*, 235–245.

McMAHON, J. T. (1972). The contingency theory: Logic and method revisited. *Personnel Psychologyy, 25*, 697–711.

MECHANIC, D. (1962). Sources of power of lower participants in complex organizations. *Administrative Science Quarterly, 7*, 349–364.

MEINDL, J. R., EHRLICH, S. B., & DUKERICH, J. M. (1985). The romance of leadership. *Administrative Science Quarterly, 30*, 78–102.

MELCHER, A. J. (1977). Leadership models and research approaches. In J. G. Hunt and L. L. Larson (Eds.), *Leadership: The cutting edge*. Carbondale, IL: Southern Illinois University Press.

MEREDITH, J. R., & MANTEL, S. J., Jr. (1985). *Project management: A managerial approach*. New York: John Wiley.

MERTON, R. K. (1957). *Social theory and social structure*. New York: Free Press.

MILLER, K. I., & MONGE, P. R. (1986). Participation, satisfaction, and productivity: A meta-analytic review. *Academy of Management Journal, 29*, 727–753.

MINER, J. B. (1965). *Studies in management education*. Atlanta: Organizational Measurement Systems Press.

MINER, J. B. (1967). *The school administrator and organizational character*. Eugene, OR: Center for the Advanced Study of Educational Administration.

MINER, J. B. (1975). The uncertain future of the leadership concept: An overview. In J. G. Hunt and L. L. Larson (Eds.), *Leadership frontiers*. Kent, OH: Kent State University Press.

MINER, J. B. (1977). *Motivation to manage: A ten-year update on the "studies in management education" research*. Atlanta: Organizational Measurement Systems Press.

MINER, J. B. (1978). Twenty years of research on role motivation theory of managerial effectiveness. *Personnel Psychology, 31*, 739–760.

MINER, J. B. (1985). Sentence completion measures in personnel research: The development and validation of the Miner Sentence Completion Scales. In H. J. Bernardin & D. A. Bownas (Eds.), *Personality assessment in organizations* (pp. 145–176). New York: Praeger.

MINER, J. B. (in press). Managerial role motivation training. *Journal of Management Psychology*.

MINTZBERG, H. (1973). *The nature of managerial work*. New York: Harper & Row.

MINTZBERG, H. (1975). The manager's job: Folklore and fact. *Harvard Business Review*, July-August, 49–61.

MINTZBERG, H. (1979). *The structuring of organizations*. Englewood Cliffs, NJ: Prentice Hall.

MINTZBERG, H. (1983). *Power in and around organizations*. Englewood Cliffs, NJ: Prentice Hall.

MINTZBERG, H., RAISINGHANI, D., & THEORET, A. (1976). The structure of unstructured decision processes. *Administrative Science Quarterly, 21*, 246–275.

MISHAUK, M. J. (1971). Supervisory skills and employee satisfaction. *Personnel Administration*, July-August, 29–33.

MISUMI, J. (1985). *The behavioral science of leadership: An interdisciplinary Japanese research program*. Ann Arbor, MI: The University of Michigan Press.

MISUMI, J., & PETERSON, M. (1985). The performance-maintenance (PM) theory of leadership: Review of a Japanese research program. *Administrative Science Quarterly, 30*, 198–223.

MISUMI, J., & SHIRAKASHI, S. (1966). An experimental study of the effects of supervisory behavior on productivity and morale in a hierarchical organization. *Human Relations, 19*, 297–307.

MITCHELL, T. R. (1973). Motivation and participation: An integration. *Academy of Management Journal, 16,* 660–679.

MITCHELL, T. R. (1974). Expectancy models of job satisfaction, occupational preference, and effort: A theoretical, methodological, and empirical appraisal. *Psychological Bulletin, 81,* 1053–1077.

MITCHELL, T. R., & KALB, L. S. (1981). Effects of outcome knowledge and outcome valence on supervisor's evaluation. *Journal of Applied Psychology, 66,* 604–612.

MITCHELL, T. R., GREEN, S. C., & WOOD, R. E. (1981). An attributional model of leadership and the poor performing subordinate: Development and validation. In L. L. Cummings and B. M. Staw (Eds.), *Research in organizational behavior,* (Vol. 3). Greenwich, CT: JAI Press.

MITCHELL, T. R., LARSON, J. R. Jr., & GREEN, S. G. (1977). Leader behavior, situational moderators, and group performance: An attributional analysis. *Organizational Behavior and Human Performance, 18,* 254–268.

MITCHELL, T. R., & LIDEN, R. C. (1982). The effects of social context on performance evaluations. *Organizational Behavior and Human Performance, 29,* 241–256.

MITCHELL, T. R., & WOOD, R. E. (1980). Supervisor's responses to subordinate poor performance: A test of an attributional model. *Organizational Behavior and Human Performance, 25,* 123–138.

MITROFF, I. I., BARABBA, V. P., & KILMAN, R. H. (1977). The application of behavioral and philosophical technologies to strategic planning: A case study of a large federal agency. *Management Science, 24,* 44–58.

MORSE, J. J., & WAGNER, F. R. (1978). Measuring the process of managerial effectiveness. *Academy of Management Journal, 21,* 23–35.

MORSE, N. C., & REIMER, E. (1956). The experimental change of a major organizational variable. *Journal of Abnormal and Social Psychology, 52,* 120–129.

MOWDAY, R. (1978). The exercise of upward influence in organizations. *Administrative Science Quarterly, 23,* 137–156.

MOWRY, H. W. (1964). *Leadership evaluation and development scale casebook.* Los Angeles: Psychological Services.

MULDER, M., DEJONG, R. D., KOPPELAAR, L., & VERHAGE, J. (1986). Power, situation, and leaders' effectiveness: An organizational study. *Journal of Applied Psychology, 71,* 566–570.

MULDER, M., RITSEMA VAN ECK, J. R., & DE JONG, R. D. (1970). An organization in crisis and non-crisis conditions. *Human Relations, 24,* 19–41.

MULDER, M., & STEMERDING, A. (1963). Threat, attraction to group, and need for strong leadership. *Human Relations, 16,* 317–334.

MUSSER, S. J. (1987). The determination of positive and negative charismatic leadership. Working Paper, Grantham, PA: Messiah College.

NASH, A. V. (1965). Vocational interest of effective managers: A review of the literature. *Personnel Psychology, 18,* 21–38.

NASH, A. V. (1966). Development and evaluation of a SVIB key for selecting managers. *Journal of Applied Psychology, 50,* 250–254.

NEALY, S. M., & FIEDLER, F. E. (1968). Leadership functions of middle managers. *Psychological Bulletin, 5,* 313–329.

NEBECKER, D. M., & MITCHELL, T. R. (1974). Leader behavior: An expectancy theory approach. *Organizational Behavior and Human Performance, 11,* 355–367.

NEMEROFF, W., & COSENTINO, J. (1979). Utilizing feedback and goal setting to increase performance appraisal interviewer skills of managers. *Academy of Management Journal, 22,* 566–576.

NEUSTADT, R. E. (1960). *Presidential power.* New York: Wiley.

OBERG, W. (1972). Charisma, commitment, and contemporary organization theory. *MSU Business Topics, 20,* 18–32.

O'BRIEN, G. E., & KABANOFF, B. (1981). The effects of leadership style and group structure upon small group productivity: A test of a discrepancy theory of leader effectiveness. *Australian Journal of Psychology, 33* (2), 157–168.

O'BRIEN, R. M., DICKINSON, A. M., & ROSOW, M. (Eds.), (1981). *Industrial behavior modification: A learning-based approach to business management.* New York: Pergamon Press.

OLDHAM, G. R. (1976). The motivational strategies used by supervisors: Relationships to effectiveness indicators. *Organizational Behavior and Human Performance, 15,* 66–86.

OSBORN, R. N. (1974). Discussant comments. In J. G. Hunt and L. L. Larson (Eds.), *Contingency approaches to leadership.* Carbondale, IL: Southern Illinois University Press.

OSBORN, R. N., & HUNT, J. G. (1975). An adaptive-reactive theory of leadership: The role of macro variables in leadership research. In J. G. Hunt and L. L. Larson (Eds.), *Leadership Frontiers.* Kent, OH: Kent State University Press.

OUCHI, W. G. (1981). *How American business can meet the Japanese challenge.* Reading, MA: Addison-Wesley.

PAGE, R. (1985). *The position description questionnaire.* Unpublished paper, Minneapolis: Control Data Business Advisors.

PAGE, R., & TORNOW, W. W. (1987). Managerial job analysis: Are we farther along? Paper presented at the Second Annual Conference of the Society for Industrial and Organizational Psychology, Atlanta.

PAOLILLO, J. G. (1981). Role profiles for managers at different hierarchical levels. *Proceedings of the Academy of Management Meetings* (pp. 91–94).

PATCHEN, M. (1974). The locus and basis of influence on organizational decisions. *Organizational Behavior and Human Performance, 11,* 195–221.

PAVETT, C., & LAU, A. (1983). Managerial work: The influence of hierarchical level and functional specialty. *Academy of Management Journal, 26,* 170–177.

PELZ, D. C. (1952). Influence: A key to effective leadership in the first-line supervisor. *Personnel, 29,* 209–217.

PETERS, L. H., HARTKE, D. D., & POHLMAN, J. T. (1985). Fiedler's contingency theory of leadership: An application of the meta-analysis procedures of Schmidt and Hunter. *Psychological Bulletin, 97,* 274–285.

PETERS, L. H., O'CONNOR, E. J., & RUDOLF, C. J. (1980). The behavioral and affective consequences of performance-relevant situational variables. *Organizational Behavior and Human Performance, 25,* 79–96.

PETERS, T. J., & AUSTIN, N. (1985). *A passion for excellence: The leadership difference.* New York: Random House.

PETERS, T. J., & WATERMAN, R. H., Jr. (1982). *In search of excellence: Lessons from America's best-run companies.* New York: Harper & Row.

PETTIGREW, A. (1972). Information control as a power resource. *Sociology, 6,* 187–204.

PETTIGREW, A. (1973). *The politics of organizational decision making.* London: Tavistock.

PFEFFER, J. (1977a). Power and resource allocation in organizations. In B. Staw and G. Salancik (Eds.), *New directions in organizational behavior.* Chicago: St. Clair Press.

PFEFFER, J. (1977b). The ambiguity of leadership. *Academy of Management Review, 2,* 104–112.

PFEFFER, J. (1981). *Power in organizations.* Marshfield, MA: Pittman.

PFEFFER, J., & DAVIS-BLAKE, A. (1986). Administrative succession and organizational performance: How administrator experience mediates the succession effect. *Academy of Management Journal, 29,* 72–83.

PFEFFER, J., & MOORE, W. L. (1980). Average tenure of academic department heads: The effects of paradigm, size and department demography. *Administrative Science Quarterly, 25,* 387–406.

PFEFFER, J., & SALANCIK, G. R. (1974). Organizational decision making as a political process: The case of a university budget. *Administrative Science Quarterly, 19,* 135–151.

PFEFFER, J., & SALANCIK, G. R. (1975). Determinants of supervisory behavior: A role set analysis. *Human Relations, 28,* 139–153.

PODSAKOFF, P. M. (1982). Determinants of a supervisor's use of rewards and punishments: A literature review and suggestions for future research. *Organizational Behavior and Human Performance, 29,* 58–83.

PODSAKOFF, P. M., & SCHRIESHEIM, C. A. (1985). Field studies of French and Raven's bases of power: Critique, reanalysis, and suggestions for future research. *Psychological Bulletin, 97,* 387–411.

PODSAKOFF, P. M., TODOR, W. D. (1985). Relationships between leader reward and punishment behavior and group processes and productivity. *Journal of Management, 11,* 55–73.

PODSAKOFF, P. M., TODOR, W. D., GROVER, R. A., & HUBER, V. L. (1984). Situational moderators of leader reward and punishment behavior: Fact or fiction? *Organizational Behavior and Human Performance, 34,* 21–63.

PODSAKOFF, P. M., TODOR, W. D., & SKOV, R. (1982). Effects of leader contingent and noncontingent reward and punishment behaviors on subordinate performance and satisfaction. *Academy of Management Journal, 25,* 810–821.

PONDER, Q. D. (1957). The effective manufacturing foreman. In E. Young (Ed.), *Proceedings of the Industrial Relations Research Association Meetings* (pp. 41–54). Madison, WI.

PONDER, Q. D. (1959). Supervisory practices of effective and ineffective foremen. Unpublished doctoral dissertation, Columbia University. *Dissertation Abstracts, 20,* 3983.

PORRAS, J. I. & ANDERSON, B. (1981). Improving managerial effectiveness through modeling-based training. *Organizational Dynamics,* Spring, 60–77.

PORTER, L. W., ALLEN, R. W., & ANGLE, H. L. (1981). The politics of upward influence in organizations. In L. L. Cummings and B. M. Staw (Eds.), *Research in Organizational Behavior* (Vol. 3). Greenwich, CT: JAI Press.

PORTER, L. W., & HENRY, M. M. (1964). Job attitudes in management: Perceptions of the importance of certain personality traits as a function of job level. *Journal of Applied Psychology, 48,* 31–36.

POTTER, E. H., & FIEDLER, F. E. (1981). The utilization of staff member intelligence and experience under high and low stress. *Academy of Management Journal, 24,* 361–376.

PRESTON, P., & ZIMMERER, T. W., (1987). *Management for supervisors*. Englewood Cliffs, NJ: Prentice Hall.

PRINCE, G. M. (1969). How to be a better meeting chairman. *Harvard Business Review*, January-February, 98–108.

PRINCE, G. M. (1970). *The practice of creativity*. New York: Harper & Row.

QUINN, J. B. (1980). Formulating strategy one step at a time. *Journal of Business Strategy, 1,* 42–63.

QUINN, R. E., & ROHRBAUGH, J. (1983). A spatial model of effectiveness criteria: Towards a competing values approach to organizational analysis. *Management Science, 29,* 363–377.

REITZ, H. J. (1977). *Behavior in organizations*. Homewood, IL: Richard Irwin.

RICE, R. W. (1978). Construct validity of the least preferred co-worker score. *Psychological Bulletin, 85,* 1199–1237.

ROACH, C. F., & BEHLING, O. (1984). Functionalism: Basis for an alternate approach to the study of leadership. In J. G. Hunt, D. M. Hosking, C. A. Schriesheim, & R. Stewart (Eds.), *Leaders and managers: International perspectives on managerial behavior and leadership*. Elmsford, NY: Pergamon Press.

ROBBINS, S. P. (1974). *Managing organizational conflict: A nontraditional approach*. Englewood Cliffs, NJ: Prentice Hall.

ROBERTS, N. C. (1984). Transforming leadership: Sources, processes, consequences. Paper presented at the Academy of Management, Boston.

ROSEN, N. A. (1961). How supervise? 1943–1960. *Personnel Psychology, 14,* 96–97.

ROSEN, N. A. (1969). *Leadership change and work group dynamics: An experiment*. Ithaca, NY: Cornell University Press.

RUSH, M. C., THOMAS, J. C., & LORD, R. G. (1977). Implicit leadership theory: A potential threat to the internal validity of leader behavior questionnaires. *Organizational Behavior and Human Performance, 20,* 93–110.

SALANCIK, G. R., CALDER, B. J., ROWLAND, K. M., LEBLEBICI, H., & CONWAY, M. (1975). Leadership as an outcome of social structure and process: A multidimensional analysis. In J. C. Hunt and L. L. Larson (Eds.), *Leadership Frontiers*. Kent, OH: Kent State University Press.

SALANCIK, G. R., & MEINDL, J. R. (1984). Corporate attributions as strategic illusions of management control. *Administrative Science Quarterly, 29,* 238–254.

SALANCIK, G. R., & PFEFFER, J. (1977a). Who gets power and how they hold on to it: A strategic contingency model of power. *Organizational Dynamics, 5,* 3–21.

SALANCIK, G. R., & PFEFFER, J. (1977b). Constraints on administrative discretion: The limited influence of mayors on city budgets. *Urban Affairs Quarterly, 12,* 474–498.

SAMUELSON, B. A., GALBRAITH, C. S., & MCGUIRE, J. W. (1985). Organizational performance and top-management turnover. *Organizational Studies, 6,* 275–291.

SASHKIN, M., & FULMER, R. M., (1988). Toward an organizational leadership theory. In J. G. Hunt, B. R. Balinga, H. P. Dashler, and C. A. Schiesheim (Eds.), *Emerging leadership vistas*. Lexington, MA: Lexington Books, 51–66.

SAYLES, L. R. (1979). *What effective managers really do and how they do it*. New York: McGraw-Hill.

SCANDURA, T. A., & GRAEN, G. B. (1984). Moderating effects of initial leader-member exchange status on the effects of leadership intervention. *Journal of Applied Psychology, 69,* 428–436.

SCANDURA, T. A., GRAEN, G. B., & NOVAK, M. A. (1986). When managers decide not to decide autocratically: An investigation of leader-member exchange and decision influence. *Journal of Applied Psychology, 71,* 579–584.

SCHACHTER, S., WILLERMAN, B., FESTINGER, L., & HYMAN, R. (1961). Emotional disruption and industrial productivity. *Journal of Applied Psychology, 45,* 201–213.

SCHEIN, E. (1969). *Process consultation: Its role in management development.* Reading, MA: Addison-Wesley.

SCHEIN, E. H. (1985). *Organizational culture and leadership.* San Francisco: Jossey-Bass.

SCHLESINGER, L., JACKSON, J. M., & BUTMAN, J. (1960). Leader-member interaction in management committees. *Journal of Abnormal and Social Psychology, 61,* 360–364.

SCHNEIER, C. E. (1974). Behavior modification in management: A review and critique. *Academy of Management Journal, 17,* 528–548.

SCHOEN, S. H., & DURAND, D. E. (1979). *Supervision: The management of organizational resources.* Englewood Cliffs, NJ: Prentice Hall.

SCHRIESHEIM, C. A., & KERR, S. (1977). Theories and measures of leadership: A critical appraisal. In J. G. Hunt and L. L. Larson (Eds.), *Leadership: The cutting edge.* Carbondale, IL: Southern Illinois University Press.

SCHRIESHEIM, C. A., KINICKI, A. J., & SCHRIESHEIM, J. F. (1979). The effect of leniency on leader behavior descriptions. *Organizational Behavior and Human Performance, 23,* 1–29.

SCHRIESHEIM, C. A., & STOGDILL, R. M. (1975). Differences in factor structure across three versions of the Ohio State leadership scales. *Personnel Psychology, 28,* 189–206.

SCHILIT, W. K., & LOCKE, E. A. (1982). A study of upward influence in organizations. *Administrative Science Quarterly, 27,* 304–316.

SCHWARTZ, K. B., & MENON, K. (1985). Executive succession in failing firms. *Academy of Management Journal, 26,* 680–686.

SCHWEIGER, D. M., ANDERSON, C. R., & LOCKE, E. A. (1985). Complex decision making: A longitudinal study of process and performance. *Organizational Behavior and Human Decision Processes, 36,* 245–272.

SCHWEIGER, D. M., & LEANA, C. R. (1985). Participation in decision making. In E. A. Locke (Ed.), *Generalizing from laboratory to field settings.* Boston: Heath-Lexington.

SCHWEIGER, D. M., SANDBERG, W. R., & RAGAN, J. W. (1986). Group approaches for improving strategic decision making: A comparative analysis of dialectical inquiry, devil's advocacy, and consensus. *Academy of Management Journal, 29,* 51–71.

SEILER, J. A. (1963). Diagnosing inter-departmental confict. *Harvard Business Review, 41,* September-October, 121–132.

SHERIDAN, J. E., & VREDENBURGH, D. J. (1978). Usefulness of leadership behavior and social power variables in predicting job tension, performance, and turnover of nursing employees. *Journal of Applied Psychology, 63,* 89–95.

SHETTY, Y. K., & PEERY, N. S. (1976). Are top executives transferable across companies? *Business Horizons, 19* (3), 23–28.

SHIFLETT, S. C. (1973). The contingency model of leadership effectiveness: Some implications of its statistical and methodological properties. *Behavioral Science, 18* (6), 429–440.

SHIFLETT, S. C. (1979).   Toward a general model of small group productivity. *Psychological Bulletin, 86,* 67–79.

SHILS, E. (1965). Charisma, order, and status. *American Sociological Review, 30,* 199–213.

SHULL, F. A., DELBECQ, A. L., & CUMMINGS, L. L. (1970). *Organizational decision making.* New York: McGraw-Hill.

SHUTZ, W. C. (1955). What makes groups productive? *Human Relations, 8,* 429–465.

SIMON, H. (1987). Making managerial decisions: The role of intuition and emotion. *Academy of Management Executive, 1,* 57–64.

SIMS, H. P., Jr. (1977). The leader as a manager of reinforcement contingencies: An empirical example and a model. In J. G. Hun and L. L. Larson (Eds.), *Leadership: The cutting edge.* Carbondale, IL: Southern Illinois University Press.

SIMS, H. P., Jr., & MANZ, C. C. (1984). Observing leader verbal behavior: Toward reciprocal determinism in leadership theory. *Journal of Applied Psychology, 69,* 222–232.

SIMS, H. P., Jr., & SZILAGYI, A. D. (1975). Leader reward behavior and subordinate satisfaction and performance. *Organizational Behavior and Human Performance, 14,* 426–437.

SKINNER, E. W. (1969). Relationships between leadership behavior patterns and organizational-situational variables. *Personnel Psychology, 22,* 489–494.

SLATER, P. E. (1955). Role differentiation in small groups. In A. P. Hare, E. F. Borgatta, and R. F. Bales (Eds.), *Small groups: Studies in social interactions.* New York: Knopf.

SMITH, C. G., & TANNENBAUM, A. S. (1963). Organizational control structure: A comparative analysis. *Human Relations, 16,* 299–316.

SMITH, J. E., CARSON, K. P., & ALEXANDER, R. A. (1984). Leadership: It can make a difference. *Academy of Management Journal, 27,* 765–776.

SMITH, P. E. (1976). Management modeling training to improve morale and customer satisfaction. *Personnel Psychology, 29,* 351–359.

SNYDER, N., & GLUECK, W. F. (1980). How managers plan: The analysis of manager's activities. *Long Range Planning, 13,* 70–76.

STAHL, M. J. (1983). Achievement, power and managerial motivation: Selecting managerial talent with the job choice exercise. *Personnel Psychology, 36,* 775–789.

STAW, B. M., MCKECHNIE, P. I., & PUFFER, S. M. (1983). The justification of organizational performance. *Administrative Science Quarterly, 28,* 582–600.

STEVENSON, W. B., PEARCE, J. L., & PORTER, L. W. (1985). The concept of coalition in organization theory and research. *Academy of Management Review, 10,* 256–268.

STEWART, R. (1967). *Managers and their jobs.* London: Macmillan.

STEWART, R. (1976). *Contrasts in management.* Maidenhead, Berkshire, England: McGraw-Hill UK.

STEWART, R. (1982). *Choices for the manager: A guide to understanding managerial work.* Englewood Cliffs, NJ: Prentice Hall.

STINSON, J. E., & JOHNSON, T. W. (1975). The path goal theory of leadership: A partial test and suggested refinement. *Academy of Management Journal, 18,* 242–252.

STOGDILL, R. M. (1948). Personal factors associated with leadership: A survey of the literature. *Journal of Psychology, 25,* 35–71.

STOGDILL, R. M. (1963). *Manual for the Leader Behavior Description Questionnaire—Form XII.* Columbus: Ohio State University, Bureau of Business Research.

STOGDILL, R. M. (1974). *Handbook of leadership: A survey of the literature.* New York: Free Press.

STOGDILL, R. M., GOODE, O. S., & DAY, D. R. (1962). New leader behavior description subscales. *Journal of Psychology, 54,* 259–269.

STRAUSS, G. (1962). Tactics of lateral relationship: The purchasing agent. *Administrative Science Quarterly, 7,* 161–186.

STRAUSS, G. (1963). Some notes on power equalization. In H. J. Leavitt (Ed.), *The social science of organizations: Four perspectives.* Englewood Cliffs, NJ: Prentice Hall.

STRAUSS, G. (1977). Managerial practices. In J. R. Hackman and J. L. Suttle (Eds.), *Improving life at work.* Santa Monica, CA: Goodyear.

STRUBE, M. J., & GARCIA, J. E. (1981). A meta-analytic investigation of Fiedler's contingency model of leadership effectiveness. *Psychological Bulletin, 90,* 307–321.

STUMPF, S. A., FREEDMAN, R. D., & ZAND, D. E. (1979). Judgmental decisions: A study of interactions among group membership, group functioning, and decision situation. *Academy of Management Journal, 22,* 765–782.

SZILAGYI, A. D. (1980). Causal inferences between leader reward behavior and subordinate goal attainment, absenteeism, and work satisfaction. *Journal of Occupational Psychology, 53,* 195–204.

SZILAGYI, A. D., & SCHWEIGER, D. M. (1984). Matching managers to strategies: A review and suggested framework. *Academy of Management Review, 9,* 626–637.

TANNENBAUM, A. S., & ALLPORT, F. H. (1956). Personality structure and group structure: An interpretive study of their relationship through an event structure hypothesis. *Journal of Abnormal and Social Psychology, 53,* 272–280.

TANNENBAUM, R., & SCHMIDT, W. H. (1958). How to choose a leadership pattern. *Harvard Business Review, 36,* March-April, 95–101.

TANNENBAUM, R., WESCHLER, I. R., & MASSARIK, F. (1961). *Leadership and organization.* New York: McGraw-Hill.

TAYLOR, J., & BOWERS, D. (1972). *The survey of organizations: A machine-scored standardized questionnaire instrument.* Ann Arbor: MI: Institute for Social Research, University of Michigan.

TENOPYR, M. L. (1969). The comparative validity of selected leadership scales related to success in production management. *Personnel Psychology, 22,* 77–85.

THAMBAIN, H. J., & GEMMILL, G. R. (1974). Influence styles of project managers: Some project performance correlates. *Academy of Management Journal, 17,* 216–224.

THIBAUT, J. W., & KELLEY, H. H. (1959). *The social psychology of groups.* New York: Wiley.

THOMASON, G. F. (1967). Managerial work roles and relationships (Part 2). *Journal of Management Studies, 4,* 17–30.

THURLEY, K. E., & HAMBLIN, A. C. (1963). *The supervisor and his job.* London: Her Majesty's Stationery Office, Department of Scientific and Industrial Research.

TICHY, N. M. & DEVANNA, M. A. (1986). *The transformational leader.* New York: Wiley.

TJOSVOLD, D., WEDLEY, W. C., & FIELD, R. H. G. (1986). Constructive controversy: The Vroom-Yetton model and managerial decision making. *Journal of Occupational Behavior, 7,* 125–138.

TORNOW, W. W., & PINTO, P. R. (1976). The development of a managerial job taxonomy: A system for describing, classifying, and evaluating executive positions. *Journal of Applied Psychology, 61,* 410–418.

TORRANCE, E. P. (1954). The behavior of small groups under stress conditions of survival. *American Sociological Review, 19,* 751–755.

TRICE, H. M., & BEYER, J. M. (1986). Charisma and its routinization in two social movement organizations. *Research in Organization Behavior,* Vol. 8 (pp. 113–164). Greenwich, CT: JAI Press.

TSUI, A. (1984). A role set analysis of managerial reputation. *Organizational Behavior and Human Performance, 34,* 64–96.

URWICK, L. F. (1952). *Notes on the theory of organization.* New York: American Management Association.

VAILL, P. B. (1978). Toward a behavior description of high-performing systems. In M. W. McCall, Jr. and M. M. Lombardo (Eds.), *Leadership: Where else can we go?* Durham, NC: Duke University Press.

VAN DE VEN, & A. H. DELBECQ, A. L. (1971). Nominal versus interacting group processes for committee decision making effectiveness. *Academy of Management Journal, 14,* 203–212.

VAN FLEET, D. D., & YUKL, G. (1986a). A century of leadership research. In D. A. Wren (Ed.), *One hundred years of management* (pp. 12–23). Chicago: Academy of Management.

VAN FLEET, D. D., & YUKL, G. (1986b). *Military leadership: An organizational perspective.* Greenwich, CT: JAI Press.

VARGA, K. (1975). N-achievement, n-power, and effectiveness of research development. *Human Relations, 28,* 571–590.

VECCHIO, R. P. (1983). Assessing the validity of Fiedler's contingency model of leadership effectiveness: A closer look at Strube and Garcia. *Psychological Bulletin, 93,* 404–408.

VECCHIO, R. P., & GOBDEL, B. C. (1984). The vertical dyad linkage model of leadership: Problems and prospects. *Organizational Behavior and Human Performance, 34,* 5–20.

VROOM, V. H. (1964). *Work and motivation.* New York: Wiley.

VROOM, V. H., & JAGO, A. G. (1978). On the validity of the Vroom-Yetton model. *Journal of Applied Psychology, 63,* 151–162.

VROOM, V. H., & JAGO, A. G. (1988). *The new leadership: Managing participation in organizations.* Englewood Cliffs, NJ: Prentice Hall.

VROOM, V. H., & YETTON, P. W. (1973). *Leadership and decision making.* Pittsburgh: University of Pittsburgh Press.

WAGNER, J. A., & GOODING, R. Z. (1987). Shared influence and organizational behavior: A meta-analysis of situational variables expected to moderate participation-outcome relationships. *Academy of Management Journal, 30,* 524–541.

WAINER, H. A., & RUBIN, I. M. (1969). Motivation of research and development entrepreneurs: Determinants of company success. *Journal of Applied Psychology, 53,* 178–184.

WAKABAYASHI, M., & GRAEN, G. B. (1984). The Japanese career progress study: A seven-year followup. *Journal of Applied Psychology, 69,* 603–614.

WALKER, C. R., GUEST, R. H., & TURNER, A. N. (1956). *The foreman on the assembly line.* Cambridge, MA: Harvard University Press.

WARREN, D. I. (1968). Power, visibility, and conformity in formal organizations. *American Sociological Review, 6,* 951–970.

WEBBER, R. A. (1972). *Time and management.* New York: Van Nostrand-Reinhold.

WEBBER, R. A. (1975). *Management: Basic elements of managing organizations.* Homewood, IL: Richard D. Irwin.

WEBER, M. (1947). *The theory of social and economic organizations.* (T. Parsons, trans.). New York: Free Press.

WEINER, N., & MAHONEY, T. A. (1981). A model of corporate performance as a function of environmental, organizational, and leadership influences. *Academy of Management Journal, 24,* 453–470.

WEXLEY, K. N. (1984). Personnel training. In M. R. Rosenweig and L. W. Porter (Eds.), *Annual review of psychology.* Palo Alto, CA: Annual Reviews.

WEXLEY, K. N., & LATHAM, G. P. (1981). *Developing and training human resources in organizations.* Glenview, IL: Scott, Foresman.

WEXLEY, K. N., & NEMEROFF, W. F. (1975). Effects of positive reinforcement and goal setting as methods of management development. *Journal of Applied Psychology, 60,* 446–450.

WEXLEY, K. N., & YUKL, G. A. (1984). *Organizational behavior and personnel psychology.* Homewood, IL: Richard D. Irwin.

WHITE, J. H. R. (1975). *Successful supervision.* London: McGraw-Hill.

WHITE, T. H. (1965). *The making of the president, 1960.* New York: Atheneum.

WHITE, S. E., DITTRICH, J. E., & LANG, J. R. (1980). The effects of group decision-making process and problem-situation complexity on implementation strategies. *Administrative Science Quarterly, 25,* 428–440.

WHYTE, W. F. (1969). *Organizational behavior: Theory and applications.* Homewood, IL: Richard D. Irwin.

WILLIAMS, R. E. (1956). A description of some executive abilities by means of the critical incident technique. Unpublished doctoral dissertation, Columbia University.

WILLNER, A. R. (1984). *The spellbinders: Charismatic political leadership.* New Haven: Yale University Press.

WINTER, D. G. (1973). *The power motive.* New York: Free Press.

WINTER, D. G. (1979). *Navy leadership and management competencies: Convergence among tests, interviews, and performance ratings.* Boston: McBer.

WOFFORD, J. C. (1982). An integrative theory of leadership. *Journal of Management, 8,* 27–47.

WOFFORD, J. C., & SRINIVASAN, T. N. (1984). Experimental tests of leader-environment-follower interaction theory of leadership. *Organizational Behavior and Human Performance, 32,* 33–54.

WOOD, R. E., & MITCHELL, T. R. (1981). Manager behavior in a social context: The impact of impression management on attributions and disciplinary actions. *Organizational Behavior and Human Performance, 28,* 356–378.

WYNDHAM, C. H., & COOKE, H. M. (1964). The influence of quality of supervision on the production of men engaged in moderately hard work. *Ergonomics, 9* (2), 139–149.

YANOUZAS, J. N. (1964). A comparative study of work organization and supervisory behavior. *Human Organization, 23,* 245–253.

YUKL, G. A. (1970). Leader LPC scores: Attitude dimensions and behavioral correlates. *Journal of Social Psychology, 80,* 207–212.

YUKL, G. A. (1971). Toward a behavioral theory of leadership. *Organizational Behavior and Human Performance, 6,* 414–440.

YUKL, G. A. (1981). *Leadership in organizations.* Englewood Cliffs, NJ: Prentice Hall.

YUKL, G. A. (1983). Development of a taxonomy of managerial behavior by factor analysis. Paper presented at the Society For Organizational Behavior Annual Meeting, Minneapolis, MN.

YUKL, G. A (1987). A new taxonomy for integrating diverse perspectives on managerial behavior. Paper presented at the American Psychological Association Meeting, New York.

YUKL, G. A. (1988). Development and validation of the managerial practices questionnaire. Technical report, State University of New York at Albany.

YUKL, G. A., & CARRIER, H. (1986). An exploratory study on situational determinants of managerial behavior. *Proceedings of the Eastern Academy of Management Meetings,* 174–177.

YUKL, G. A., & CLEMENCE, J. (1984). A test of path-goal theory of leadership using questionnaire and diary measures of behavior. *Proceedings of the twenty-first annual meeting of the Eastern Academy of Management,* 174–177.

YUKL, G. A., & KANUK, L. (1979). Leadership behavior and effectiveness of beauty salon managers. *Personnel Psychology, 32,* 663–675.

YUKL, G. A., & LEPSINGER, R. (1989). An integrating taxonomy of managerial behavior: Implications for improving managerial effectiveness. In J. W. Jones, B. D. Steffy, and D. W. Bray (Eds.), *Applying psychology in business: The manager's handbook.* Lexington, MA: Lexington Press.

YUKL, G. A., & NEMEROFF, W. (1979). Identification and measurement of specific categories of leadership behavior: A progress report. In J. G. Hunt and L. L. Larson (Eds.), *Crosscurrents in leadership.* Carbondale, IL: Southern Illinois University Press.

YUKL, G. A., & VAN FLEET, D. (1982). Cross-situational, multi-method research on military leader effectiveness. *Organizational Behavior and Human Performance, 30,* 87–108.

ZALEZNIK, A. (1970). Power and politics in organizational life. *Harvard Business Review,* May-June, 47–60.

ZALEZNIK, A. (1977). Managers and leaders: Are they different? *Harvard Business Review, 55,* (5), 67–78.

Appendix A
A Day in the Life of Michael Richardson,
President of an Investment Management Firm*

7:35 A.M.	He arrives at work (he does not have a long commute), unpacks his briefcase, gets some coffee, and begins a "to-do" list for the day.
7:40	Jerry Bradshaw, a subordinate, arrives. Bradshaw's office is right next to Richardson's; he has two sets of duties, one of which is an assistant to Richardson.
7:45	Bradshaw and Richardson have an informal conversation on a number of topics. Richardson shows Bradshaw some pictures he recently took at his summer home.
8:00	Bradshaw and Richardson talk about a schedule and priorities for the day. In the process, they touch on a dozen different subjects and issues relating to customers, other subordinates, and suppliers.
8:20	Frank Wilson, another subordinate, drops in. He asks a few questions about a personnel problem and then joins in the previous discussion. The discussion is straightforward, rapid, and occasionally is punctuated with humor.
8:30	Fred Holly, Richardson's boss, stops in and joins in the conversation. He also asks about an appointment at 11:00 and brings up a few other topics.
8:40	Richardson leaves to get more coffee. Bradshaw, Holly and Wilson continue their conversation.
8:42	He's back. A subordinate of a subordinate stops in and says hello, the others leave.
8:43	Bradshaw drops off a report, gives Richardson instructions to go with it, and leaves.
8:45	His secretary arrives. They discuss her new apartment and arrangements for a meeting later in the morning.
8:49	He gets a phone call from a subordinate who is returning his call of the day before. They talk primarily about the subject of the report he just received.
8:55	He leaves his office and goes to a regular morning meeting that one of his subordinates runs. There are about thirty people there. Richardson reads during the meeting.
9:09	The meeting is over. Richardson grabs one of the people there and talks to him briefly.

*Reprinted with permission of The Free Press, a Division of Macmillan, Inc. From *The General Managers*, by John P. Kotter, pp. 81–85. Copyright © 1982 by The Free Press.

9:15	He walks over to the office of one of his subordinates (corporate counsel). His boss is there, too. They discuss a phone call the lawyer just received. While standing, the three talk about possible responses to a problem. As before, the exchange is quick and occasionally includes some humor.
9:30	Richardson goes back to his office for a meeting with the vice chairman of another firm (a potential customer and supplier). One other person, a liaison with that firm and a subordinate's subordinate, also attends the meeting. The discussion is cordial and covers many topics from their products to foreign relations.
9:50	The visitor leaves. Richardson opens the adjoining door to Bradshaw's office and asks a question.
9:52	His secretary comes in with five items.
9:55	Bradshaw drops in with a question about a customer and then leaves.
9:58	Frank Wilson and one of his people arrive. He gives Richardson a memo and then the three begin to talk about the important legal problem. Wilson does not like a decision that Richardson has tentatively made and is arguing for him to reconsider. The discussion goes back and forth for twenty minutes until they agree on the next action and schedule it for 9:00 tomorrow.
10:35	They leave. Richardson looks over papers on his desk, then picks one up and calls his boss's secretary regarding the minutes of the last board meeting. He asks her to make a few corrections.
10:41	His secretary comes in with a card to sign for a friend who is sick. He writes a note to go with the card.
10:50	He gets a brief phone call, then goes back to the papers on his desk.
11:03	His boss stops in. Before they can start, he gets a brief call. After the call he tells his secretary that someone didn't get a letter he sent and to please send another.
11:05	Holly brings up a couple of issues, and then Bradshaw comes in. The three start talking about Jerry Phillips, who has become a difficult personnel problem. Bradshaw leads, telling the others about what he has done over the last few days regarding this issue. Richardson and Holly ask questions. After a while, Richardson begins to take notes. The exchange, as before, is rapid and straightforward. They try to define the problem and outline alternative next steps. Richardson is not sure what is best so he lets the discussion go on, roaming around and in and out of the topic again and again. Finally, they agree on a next step.
12:00	Richardson orders some lunch for himself and Bradshaw. Bradshaw comes in and generally goes over twelve items. Wilson stops by to say that he had already followed up on their earlier conversation.

12:10	A staff person stops by with some calculations Richardson has requested. He thanks her and has a brief pleasant conversation.
12:20	Lunch arrives. Richardson and Bradshaw go into the conference room to eat. Over lunch they pursue business and nonbusiness subjects; they laugh often at each other's humor. They end the lunch focusing on a major potential customer.
1:15	Back in his office, they continue this discussion of the customer. Bradshaw gets a pad and they discuss a presentation to the customer in detail. Then Bradshaw leaves.
1:40	Working at his desk, Richardson looks over a new marketing brochure.
1:50	Bradshaw comes in again and they go over another dozen details regarding the presentation to the potential customer.
1:55	Jerry Thomas comes in. He is a subordinate of Richardson and has scheduled some key performance appraisals this afternoon in Richardson's office with him present. They briefly talk about how they will handle each.
2:00	Fred Jacobs (a subordinate of Thomas's) comes in. Jerry runs the meeting; he goes over Fred's bonus for the year and the reason for it. Then the three of them talk about Fred's role in the upcoming year. They generally agree and Fred leaves.
2:30	John Kimble comes in. The same format is used again. Richardson asks a lot of questions and praises Kimble at times. The meeting ends on a friendly note with general agreement.
3:00	George Houston comes in. The basic format is repeated.
3:30	When George leaves, they talk briefly about how well they had accomplished what they wanted in the meetings. They talk briefly about some other of Jerry's subordinates.
3:45	Richardson gets a short phone call. His secretary and Bradshaw come in with a list of brief requests.
3:50	He receives a call from Jerry Phillips. Richardson gets his notes from the 11 to 12 meeting on Phillips. They go back and forth on the phone talking about lost business, unhappy subordinates, who did what to whom, what should be done now. It is a long, circular, and sometimes emotional conversation. Near the end Jerry is agreeing with Richardson and thanking him.
4:55	Bradshaw, Wilson, and Holly all step in. Each is following up on different issues that were discussed earlier in the day. Richardson briefly tells them of his conversation with Phillips. Bradshaw and Holly leave.
5:10	Richardson and Wilson have a light conversation on three or four items.
5:20	Jerry Thomas stops in; he describes a new personnel problem and the three of them discuss it. More and more humor finds its way into the conversation. They agree on an action to take.

5:30   Richardson begins to pack up his briefcase. Five people stop by
            briefly, one or two at a time.

5:45 P.M.   He leaves the office.

Appendix B
Positive Critical Incidents Describing
Air Force Officers in the Korean War*

1. A reception center had been set up at an air base in Japan, and new arrivals were required to stay at the center a couple of weeks before being sent on to their overseas outfits. The center was not a pleasant place. The center CO (lieutenant) saw that the enforced idleness of the men being processed at the center was bad for morale and was costing the air force many manhours. He carefully figured out a method whereby personnel coming by ship could go directly to their assigned stations and still have their paper work properly handled. The results were so good that the army adopted the same method. (Problem solving)

2. An air force pilot (captain) landed his plane 400 miles away from home base with a starter so damaged that one engine would not start. The captain wanted to avoid the delay of radioing to the base to send a new starter, which might not have been readily available. He set out to find a replacement part at a nearby marine air station. After considerable persuasion he borrowed a starter, brought it back, and instructed the men how to convert it for his type of plane. It worked fine and the plane was only delayed 1 1/2 hours on its mission to Korea. (Problem solving)

3. An electronics officer (captain) was sent to Korea with some airmen to install some radar equipment at a new radar station. When he arrived at his destination, his equipment was not there. Another officer had been in Korea 2 weeks waiting for equipment, but the captain did not feel justified sitting around with his men. He went to look for his equipment at the port where it should have been shipped. After 2 days, he found the radar equipment, but it had been damaged in transit. He put his men to work repairing the damage and installed the equipment, thereby preventing a serious delay in the use of a vital radar station. (Problem Solving)

4. The colonel was shortly going to take over the command of a fighter wing whose primary function was to protect cargo planes on combat missions. The fighter wing had a poor record, with an average of one cargo plane being lost on every mission. The losses could have been due to the failure of the cargo crews, or to the inefficiency of the fighter protection. The colonel was anxious to find out for himself, and he got permission from one of the cargo squadrons to fly several missions as an observer. He attended their briefings, flew with the cargo crews, and his observations were the basis for improvements in procedures when he assumed command of the fighter

---

* These are shortened versions of selected incidents from Van Fleet and Yukl (1986b).

wing. Fighter protection was improved and plane losses were drastically reduced. (Problem solving, planning-organizing, monitoring)

5. A combat squadron was shipped overseas and arrived when conditions were very crowded on the base. The squadron arrived before the CO, who was delayed. A pilot (captain) in the squadron realized that without leadership, the operation could turn into a complete mess. He got people organized as they arrived, made arrangements for them to have billets, and told them where they would be fed. Before 24 hours elapsed he had the entire squadron set and ready to fly missions. The entire incident involved more than 200 airmen and 60 officers. It was carried off with such smoothness that the commanding general presented the squadron with a commendation with special reference to the captain's contributions. (Problem solving, planning-organizing)

6. The CO (colonel) of an air base in southern Japan was assigned the task of setting up a forward base in Korea. He had to do this extra work without any additional personnel. He selected key people from every department and rearranged assignments so that there would be continuity of personnel and the best qualified persons in charge of each section. Then he used these selected persons and available equipment and supplies to establish the forward base. It was only because of his efficient utilization of people and material that he was able to do this while keeping the old base operating at 100 percent efficiency. (Planning-organizing)

7. The squadron was living under very primitive conditions in unheated tents. The squadron commander (major) made several attempts to get stoves, but none were available through supply channels. It was taking 2 to 3 months to get even regular supplies. The major obtained the clothing sizes for his men and turned in a requisition for winter clothing in the middle of July. The clothing arrived before the cold weather set in. Some of the other commanders did not think to order winter clothing until fall, and their men nearly froze. (Planning-organizing)

8. The CO (major) of an air base unit in Korea was ordered to move his 500 men to an airstrip that had recently been recaptured from the enemy. The move would require a 17-hour trip through territory with guerrillas capable of ambushing the entire unit. Before the move, the major saw to it that everything was extremely well organized and everyone knew their jobs and what to do in case of an ambush. He was careful not to tell the men that the unit preceding them had been fired upon by guerillas. The men had complete confidence in the major and the move occurred as scheduled with no problems. (Planning-organizing, clarifying)

9. A reconnaissance flight unit was being reactivated. The unit had no housing or equipment, and new personnel were arriving all the time. The new CO (captain) organized his personnel and insisted that they do things right rather than in the slipshod manner of their former outfit. He planned which buildings would be needed first, and saw to it that they were constructed right away. Less important construction was put off until there was more time for it. Each evening, the captain worked on a list of the equipment that would be needed when the unit started operations. Once he decided what was needed, he

sought to obtain it as quickly as possible. Wing headquarters was very impressed with how smoothly the incoming personnel were integrated into the unit and how soon it was ready to operate. The captain's men, who had initially objected to his strict insistence on efficiency, were greatly impressed with how much they were able to accomplish under their leader's direction. (Planning-organizing, clarifying)

10. The lieutenant colonel's predecessor had left the supply squadron in very bad shape. Equipment was scattered all over the base and was poorly marked for identification and inventory purposes. Many of the 125 airmen in the squadron were working at jobs for which they had insufficient skills and low interest. When the lieutenant colonel assumed command, he immediately set about learning to know each airman and his capabilities personally. He used this information to reorganize the squadron, placing men where the best use could be made of their skills and experience. Within 4 months the personnel had been reassigned to their new positions, and they willingly worked long, hard hours to bring the outfit into top condition. The next air inspection gave the squadron an excellent rating, the highest it had received in more than two years. (Planning-organizing).

11. Squadron W had a lackadaisical attitude and insubordination among its airmen. The squadron CO (captain) set up a squadron leader chart, delegated authority to certain noncommissioned officers, and listed the airmen that each NCO would supervise. In that way there was no duplication of orders, and each man knew who to turn to for orders and assistance. The NCO's were held responsible for the activities of their men, and within limits, their decisions were enforced without question. The delinquency rate fell off drastically and efficiency improved. The squadron received the highest efficiency rating in the wing, and other CO's came to see how the Captain was getting top production from the men with such little effort. (Planning-organizing, clarifying, delegating)

12. When the lieutenant colonel assumed command of a cargo squadron in southern Japan, things were in bad shape. None of the sections knew what the others were doing. There was duplication of effort, bitterness, and misunderstanding between section heads. Airmen were having to take orders from more than one officer. The lieutenant colonel immediately instituted daily staff meetings with his section heads and some key NCO's to discuss the methods to carry out the mission of the squadron. Disagreements were worked out, deadlines were set, and assignments were made when all concerned were present. Duties were outlined in detail so that the work would be carried out by those most qualified to do it. Within a few months, the improved organization and coordination led to much improved efficiency. The members knew what was expected of them, and believed they were an essential part of a well-run organization. (Planning-organizing, clarifying, managing conflict and team building)

13. The briefing of pilots had been neglected to the point where it had become a matter of going through the motions rather than being a period for help and information giving. The executive officer and the operations officer, both of whom were advocates of the sketchy briefing technique, felt that the pilots themselves were capable but just did not care. The CO (colonel) be-

lieved that the men were doing poorly on the missions because in many cases they did not know what to expect and what to do in the event things did not go exactly right. To test his point of view, the colonel insisted on longer, more thorough briefings. He insisted that the men be told every important detail of the mission, every possibility so far as weather was concerned, and alternative plans to follow in case of some confusion or mixup on the mission. The group's efficiency increased greatly soon after this new briefing policy was instituted, and the unit maintained its excellence during the roughest part of the war. (Informing, clarifying)

14. The wing commander (colonel) of a fighter outfit had more than 1800 men and officers. Living conditions were poor. The officers complained that they did not have china in their mess hall. This made the colonel angry, since the airmen did not even have chairs to sit on, and they really disliked having to stand while eating. The colonel was trying his best to get better equipment and facilities. In the meantime, he ate all his meals with the enlisted men, using tin trays and washing his own tray as they did. This made the inconvenience more bearable to the airmen, because they felt that if the Old Man could stand it, so could they. (Motivating, supporting)

15. When the major assumed command of his combat cargo squadron, they were short of supplies, personnel, and replacements. There was not much the major could do about these things, so he decided that the 250 men in the outfit would need such a high esprit de corps that they could not be overcome by these problems. He learned every man's name, what his job was, and something about the person's background. He was seen around with them, talking to them at work or off duty, getting to know each one on a warm, friendly basis. The major let each man know that he had a vital function to contribute to the squadron. Through his personal interest and friendliness he was able to hold the outfit together with a minimum of unrest and gripes. (Motivating, supporting, networking)

16. The colonel was one of the first men to leave Japan, voluntarily at the outbreak of the war, to establish a bomb wing headquarters in Korea. It was a difficult job, with long hours and shortages of supplies and personnel. In addition, his unit was asked to make low-level bombing missions that were extremely dangerous. The crews he had were not qualified enough to suit the colonel, so he led them himself on several of these missions until he was sure they were capable of carrying out the missions properly. He inspired the entire wing by showing that he was a fearless and capable leader. (Clarifying, motivating)

17. The base unit commander (colonel) was given the assignment of establishing a forward base very close to enemy territory. At the time it was doubtful whether the base could be secured and made habitable. Instead of sending anyone in his place, the colonel took a crew chief and went to survey the situation first-hand. His behavior served as an inspiration to the men who had to follow him to the new base. The new base was successfully established, and it was done faster and more efficiently than expected. Higher command held this act up as an example to other base units given similar missions to accomplish. (Monitoring, motivating)

18. Group headquarters had been putting pressure on the squadron CO (major) because of poor mission results. Reports had come through official channels that the men were not flying low enough in their strafing and bomb runs. The major realized that this might be true, but he also knew that his men were working day and night and flying under a lot of stress. He gathered his men together and told them that he had received some poor reports from higher up. He said that he would not condemn anyone for a poor strike report or try to tell them what they had to do. Instead, he said that he trusted each man and believed they would all do the very best job they knew how to do under the circumstances. The entire operation of the squadron became appreciably more effective, because the pilots were put to the challenge to do their best without being forced. (Motivating)

19. The CO (lieutenant colonel) of a cargo squadron in Japan was assigned the job of resupplying a marine group and evacuating their wounded from Korea. There were only five planes available, and a minimum number of crews. The lieutenant colonel could see that to accomplish the mission, he would have to fly several missions himself. He ended up flying as many missions as the rest of his crews. He worked hard for 18 to 20 hours a day, doing the things that his subordinates were doing and helping out wherever he was needed. The mission was successful and the CO's behavior engendered a feeling of respect for him by all of the squadron personnel. (Motivating)

20. The Colonel became aware that his new lieutenant colonel, the CO of a maintenance squadron, was making changes that upset the organization and caused productivity to drop. He gave the lieutenant colonel a stern lecture on his poor handling of the situation without pulling any punches. Then the colonel called a meeting of the squadron and told the officers and men that they had a big job ahead of them, to keep planes running that are needed to deliver supplies and cargo all over the combat zone. He told them that he was standing by their CO and asked the men to cooperate. The CO began changing his behavior, the men began cooperating, and the squadron became an efficient, hard-working outfit. (Clarifying, motivating, problem solving)

21. The operations officer (captain) of a photo reconnaissance squadron realized that his outfit was not adequately prepared for the type of missions it was going to fly in combat, and he felt it was important to train the men to carry out these missions properly. In order to do this in the most efficient way, he assigned instructors to check the men out on each aspect of the operation. A checklist prepared by the captain indicated exactly what each man must be able to do before he would be considered ready for combat. A man had to be checked out on each item before he was cleared for combat flying. This procedure increased the efficiency of the squadron 100 percent, and it soon became known as a number one outfit. (Clarifying, monitoring)

22. The lieutenant colonel was the CO of a base maintenance squadron. Several airmen returning from the combat had recently been promoted, and some others who had been with the outfit the longest were still without the ranks they deserved. A sergeant who had worked for him for a long time deserved a promotion but was unable to get it because the high NCO ranks were

filled. The lieutenant colonel was so determined to reward the sergeant for his efficient devotion to duty that he made a special effort to get him promoted. He had to go to division headquarters and put up a fight with his superiors in order to get approval for the promotion. (Recognizing/rewarding, supporting)

23. The lieutenant colonel was in charge of an outfit that loaded cargo planes for missions to Korea. He was informed by the pilot of a cargo plane that the sergeant who supervised the loading of his plane made a serious mistake. A load of rockets slipped about four feet when his plane took off, which could have been responsible for the loss of the plane and its crew. The lieutenant colonel called in the sergeant, and instead of bawling him out or threatening his stripes, he explained how serious the mistake was and how important it is to load the planes properly. Then he proceeded to show the sergeant methods for checking and double checking so that every time a plane was loaded, he could be sure that it was done properly. The sergeant was concerned about his mistake and left with a sincere desire to do better. (Clarifying, supporting)

24. The colonel was appointed CO of a new fighter interceptor wing in Korea. Immediately after receiving this appointment he went around to all units in his wing and visited the officers during briefings. He gave them the benefit of his experience by allowing them to ask questions and clear up points of misunderstanding. He told the men he would back them up when they were right, and he said he would be very glad to fly with anyone who had any trouble. The men were impressed that the colonel had enough interest in them to come around to visit and offer his services personally. They respected him and enjoyed working for him. (Networking, supporting)

25. The CO (captain) of a maintenance squadron was known as a hard taskmaster among his men. He expected them to do excellent work with no excuses or slacking off. One week the captain noticed that Sgt. Rhodes was not working up to his usual good standards. When he investigated to discover what was wrong, he learned that Rhode's mother had just undergone a serious operation, leaving his younger sister alone at home to fend for herself. The captain felt that Rhodes could be spared long enough to go home and straighten out his family difficulties. He went to the wing commander to plead for the necessary permission for Rhodes to get an emergency leave. The captain's behavior was reflected in the improved morale of the airmen, who felt that if any of them had a difficult problem, the captain would help them. (Supporting)

26. Living conditions were very poor for the bomber squadron when the lieutenant colonel assumed command. The pressure was on, and the men were discouraged and tired. The lieutenant colonel did what little he could about physical conditions and then set about to improve morale by giving the men something to hold on to when they thought of themselves and their squadron. He developed a slogan ("have faith") for the squadron and had it stenciled on all their gear. It gave each man a feeling that he was part of a special outfit. He had the men put up signs that were a takeoff on civilian signs. For example, a large sign, "Coopers Garage," was put up for the maintenance

chief's crew. This approach gave a boost to the morale of the men, and they became more concerned about doing a good job. The result was that they did more work and better work than other squadrons. (Motivating, team building and conflict management)

27. The CO (lieutenant colonel) of a squadron learned that interracial trouble had arisen among airmen in his squadron, and he was determined to stop it before it got out of hand. He called together the 200 officers and airmen in his outfit and gave them an inspiring speech about democracy and discrimination. He pointed out that they were over there to preserve democracy and democratic principles, and discrimination among themselves was no way to attain this purpose. He put the challenge directly up to the men and had the two racial groups appoint representatives that could hold meetings to iron out any difficulties that might arise in the future. Not only did this help defuse the conflict, but working conditions and squadron morale were improved also. (Conflict management and team building, motivating)

28. The poor bombing record of Wing X became a point of serious disagreement between the pilots and bombardiers. The pilots felt that the bombardiers didn't know their jobs, and the bombardiers didn't think the pilots were flying properly when making the bomb runs. This feud was at a full pitch when the new CO (colonel) of the bomber wing assumed command. He immediately called a meeting of all the crews in the outfit and gave a speech explaining that bombardiers, because of their training, know how to drop bombs and how the planes should be flown during the bomb runs. He illustrated his point by showing movies of bomb drops and the important role the bombardier and pilot both played in executing the mission. He called for cooperation and team work, pointing out the times during a mission when one man should be "in charge" while the other should be helping him perform his duties. The result was that succeeding missions became much more effective. (Conflict management and team building, clarifying)

Appendix C
Example of an LPC Scale

Instructions:

People differ in the ways they think about those with whom they work. On the scale below are pairs of words which are opposite in meaning. You are asked to describe someone with whom you have worked by placing an "X" in one of the eight spaces on the line between the two words. Each space represents how well the adjective fits the person you are describing, as in the following example:

Very neat : ____ : ____ : ____ : ____ : ____ : ____ : ____ : ____ : Not neat

	8	7	6	5	4	3	2	1
	Very neat	Quite neat	Some-what neat	Slight-ly neat	Slight-ly untidy	Some-what untidy	Quite untidy	Very untidy

Now, think of the person with whom you can work least well. The person may be someone you work with now or someone you knew in the past. The person does not have to be the person you like least well, but should be the person with whom you had the most difficulty in getting a job done. Describe this person as he or she appears to you.

Pleasant	: ____ : ____ : ____ : ____ | ____ : ____ : ____ : ____ :	Unpleasant
Friendly	: ____ : ____ : ____ : ____ | ____ : ____ : ____ : ____ :	Unfriendly
Rejecting	: ____ : ____ : ____ : ____ | ____ : ____ : ____ : ____ :	Accepting
Helpful	: ____ : ____ : ____ : ____ | ____ : ____ : ____ : ____ :	Frustrating
Unenthusiastic	: ____ : ____ : ____ : ____ | ____ : ____ : ____ : ____ :	Enthusiastic
Tense	: ____ : ____ : ____ : ____ | ____ : ____ : ____ : ____ :	Relaxed
Distant	: ____ : ____ : ____ : ____ | ____ : ____ : ____ : ____ :	Close
Cold	: ____ : ____ : ____ : ____ | ____ : ____ : ____ : ____ :	Warm
Cooperative	: ____ : ____ : ____ : ____ | ____ : ____ : ____ : ____ :	Uncooperative
Supportive	: ____ : ____ : ____ : ____ | ____ : ____ : ____ : ____ :	Hostile
Boring	: ____ : ____ : ____ : ____ | ____ : ____ : ____ : ____ :	Interesting
Quarrelsome	: ____ : ____ : ____ : ____ | ____ : ____ : ____ : ____ :	Harmonious
Self-assured	: ____ : ____ : ____ : ____ | ____ : ____ : ____ : ____ :	Hesitant
Efficient	: ____ : ____ : ____ : ____ | ____ : ____ : ____ : ____ :	Inefficient
Gloomy	: ____ : ____ : ____ : ____ | ____ : ____ : ____ : ____ :	Cheerful
Open	: ____ : ____ : ____ : ____ | ____ : ____ : ____ : ____ :	Guarded

Source: Adapted from F. E. Fiedler, *A Theory of Leadership Effectiveness*. New York: McGraw-Hill. 1967.

INDEX